WILD FLOWERS
OF THE MEDITERRANEAN

EYEWITNESS ◉ HANDBOOKS

WILD FLOWERS

OF THE MEDITERRANEAN

DAVID BURNIE

Photography by
DEREK HALL

Editorial Consultant
FRANCIS ROSE

DORLING KINDERSLEY

London • New York • Stuttgart

A DORLING KINDERSLEY BOOK

Important Notice
Care has been taken in the preparation of this
book not to harm wild plants. Threatened
species have been photographed either by
using cultivated specimens or by using
techniques that leave wild plants intact.

Project Editor Damien Moore
Project Art Editors Ann Thompson,
Pauline Bayne
Series Editor Jonathan Metcalf
Series Art Editor Peter Cross
Production Controller Caroline Webber

First published in Great Britain in 1995
by Dorling Kindersley Limited,
9 Henrietta Street, London WC2E 8PS

Copyright © 1995
Dorling Kindersley Limited, London
Text copyright © 1995 David Burnie

All rights reserved. No part of this publication
may be reproduced, stored in a retrieval
system, or transmitted in any form or by any
means, electronic, mechanical, photocopying,
recording or otherwise, without the prior
written permission of the copyright owners.

A CIP catalogue record for this book is
available from the British Library

ISBN 0-7513-1029-8 hardcover
ISBN 0-7513-1028-X flexibound

Computer page make-up by Mark Bracey,
Adam Moore, and Damien Moore
Text film output by
The Right Type, Great Britain
Reproduced by Colourscan, Singapore
Printed and bound by
Kyodo Printing Co., Singapore

CONTENTS

INTRODUCTION • 6
The Mediterranean Region 6
How This Book Works 9
Plant Life Cycles 10
Plant Profile 12
Growth Habits 14
Leaf Types 15
Flower Types 16
Fruits and Seeds 18
Habitats 20
Observing Wild Flowers 24
Identification Key 25

CONIFERS • 34
Cypress Family 34
Joint Pine Family 35

DICOTYLEDONS • 36
Oak Family 36
Mulberry Family 36
Nettle Family 37
Sandalwood Family 38
Birthwort Family 39
Rafflesia Family 41
Dock Family 42
Fat Hen Family 43
Amaranth Family 44
Four O'clock Family 45
Pokeweed Family 46
Mesembryanthemum Family 47
Purslane Family 47
Pink Family 48
Buttercup Family 54

Peony Family *62*
Barberry Family *63*
Poppy Family *64*
Caper Family *69*
Cress Family *70*
Mignonette Family *78*
Stonecrop Family *79*
Pittosporum Family *80*
Rose Family *81*
Pea Family *83*
Wood Sorrel Family *120*
Geranium Family *121*
Caltrop Family *123*
Flax Family *124*
Spurge Family *126*
Citrus Family *132*
Spurge Olive Family *132*
Mahogany Family *133*
Milkwort Family *133*
Cashew Family *134*
Balsam Family *135*
Box Family *136*
Buckthorn Family *136*
Mallow Family *137*
Daphne Family *143*
Hypericum Family *145*
Rock-rose Family *146*
Tamarisk Family *152*
Sea Heath Family *152*
Gourd Family *153*
Cactus Family *154*
Loosestrife Family *154*
Myrtle Family *155*
Pomegranate Family *156*
Willowherb Family *156*
Carrot Family *157*
Heather Family *165*
Primrose Family *168*
Thrift Family *171*

Storax Family *172*
Olive Family *173*
Gentian Family *174*
Periwinkle Family *175*
Milkweed Family *176*
Bedstraw Family *177*
Bindweed Family *178*
Borage Family *181*
Vervain Family *189*
Mint Family *190*
Potato Family *203*
Figwort Family *206*
Globularia Family *216*
Acanthus Family *217*
Broomrape Family *218*
Plantain Family *219*
Honeysuckle Family *221*
Valerian Family *223*
Teasel Family *225*
Bellflower Family *225*
Daisy Family *228*

❋

MONOCOTYLEDONS • 255
Posidonia Family *255*
Lily Family *256*
Agave Family *273*
Daffodil Family *273*
Yam Family *277*
Iris Family *278*
Grass Family *283*
Arum Family *288*
Orchid Family *290*

❋

Glossary *308*
Index *309*
Acknowledgments *320*

THE MEDITERRANEAN REGION

The Mediterranean region has an exceptionally rich flora, with over 10,000 species of flowering plant. Most of these are native to the region, but a significant number have been introduced from places as far afield as southern Africa and North America. This book covers herbaceous plants, shrubs, and a number of small trees that are typical of Mediterranean vegetation.

THE MEDITERRANEAN is a region of marked seasonal contrasts. Winters are mild and moist, and only rarely bring frost, whereas summers are warm, with very little rainfall. The summer drought may last for over three months, and has far-reaching effects on plant life. Most plants grow in the cooler months, and contribute to a great burst of flowering in spring. In high summer, the majority of plants are either dormant or dead. The landscape turns dry and dusty, and relatively few wild flowers can be seen.

THE YEARLY CYCLE ▷
Athens has a typical Mediterranean climate, with hot dry summers and mild moist winters.

▽ THE MEDITERRANEAN REGION
The range of olive cultivation provides a rough indication of the extent of the Mediterranean region.

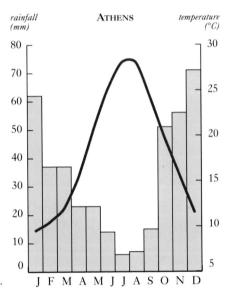

rainfall (mm) — ATHENS — temperature (°C)

J F M A M J J A S O N D

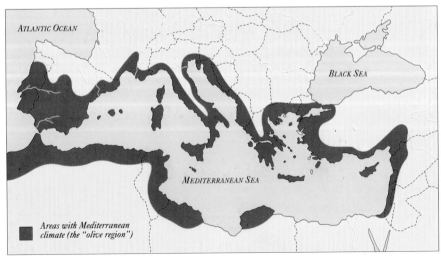

ATLANTIC OCEAN

BLACK SEA

MEDITERRANEAN SEA

◼ Areas with Mediterranean climate (the "olive region")

HISTORY OF A LANDSCAPE

Over 5,000 years ago, much of the Mediterranean region was covered by coniferous and broadleaved forest. Pines and oaks grew close to the sea's edge, and even small islands were well wooded. However, an expanding human population gradually transformed this landscape. Trees were cut down for timber or for charcoal, and herds of browsing goats prevented young saplings growing up to take their place. The result, many centuries later, is a region where natural plant cover is confined to inaccessible places, such as cliffs. Everywhere else, the flora is influenced to some degree by humans. Some plants have thrived in these man-made conditions; others have become much more restricted.

△ WOODED SHORES
*This view of the Turkish coast-
line gives an indication of what
much of the Mediterranean
shoreline once looked like.*

◁ SHAPED BY FIRE
*In parts of the region, summer
fires prevent forests from regenerating. This Corsican hillside is
still scarred 5 years after a fire.*

▽ SEASONAL SPLENDOUR
*A carpet of flowers decorates a
field in Corfu. Flowers like these
have benefited from man-made
changes to the landscape.*

MEDITERRANEAN FLOWERS TODAY

For the wild-flower enthusiast, the changes to the Mediterranean landscape have not all been negative. Many of the region's most interesting flowers can be seen in maquis and garigue (p.22), two kinds of habitat that have been brought about entirely by human activity. Olive groves, and other cultivated ground (p.23), also attract much botanical interest. This is particularly so where the land has not been treated with herbicides – organic farming is still common in this region compared to more intensively farmed parts of Europe. Finally, even roadsides have much to offer. Verge cutting, which helps prevent fire, produces ideal conditions for many orchids. In some parts of the region, this creates a springtime spectacle not to be missed.

PLANT NAMES

Plants are identified by a two-part scientific name, or binomial. The first part of the name identifies a genus, which is a group that usually contains several similar species; the second part identifies a single species within that genus. Scientific names are as unique as fingerprints. Each one applies to just one species, although unrelated species often share the same second name, e.g. *Medicago arborea* and *Lavatera arborea*. The binomial system was devised by the 18th-century Swedish botanist Linnaeus, who travelled widely in the Mediterranean region and described many of its plants.

THE PLANT KINGDOM

The Plant Kingdom is composed of organisms that live by harnessing energy from sunlight, a process called photo-synthesis. With over 250,000 species, flowering plants (or angiosperms) make up the largest group of plants. They are classified into 2 major groups: the mono-cotyledons and dicotyledons (p.10). With the exception of 4 species, all the plants in this book are angiosperms. Those exceptions are the conifers and their allies – the gymnosperms (p.34).

A FAMILY TREE

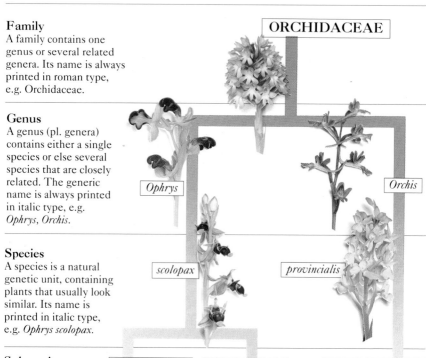

Family
A family contains one genus or several related genera. Its name is always printed in roman type, e.g. Orchidaceae.

ORCHIDACEAE

Genus
A genus (pl. genera) contains either a single species or else several species that are closely related. The generic name is always printed in italic type, e.g. *Ophrys, Orchis*.

Ophrys

Orchis

Species
A species is a natural genetic unit, containing plants that usually look similar. Its name is printed in italic type, e.g. *Ophrys scolopax*.

scolopax

provincialis

Subspecies
A subspecies is a recognized variant of a species. Its name is printed in roman and italic type, e.g. subsp. *apiformis*.

subsp. *heldreichii*

subsp. *apiformis*

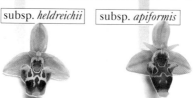

Variety
Variety (var.) and forma (f.) are minor divisions of a species, printed in roman and italic type.

HOW THIS BOOK WORKS

THE PLANTS in this book are arranged in three groups: firstly the Conifers and their Allies, followed by the Dicotyledons and the Monocotyledons (see p.10). The groups are further divided into families, each one introduced by a family heading. The species follow the order set out by the major botanical reference work *Flora Europaea*. Each entry is introduced by the plant's common name, or with the scientific name if no widely used common name exists. Most Mediterranean plants have common names in their countries of origin, but they do not necessarily have a common name in other countries.

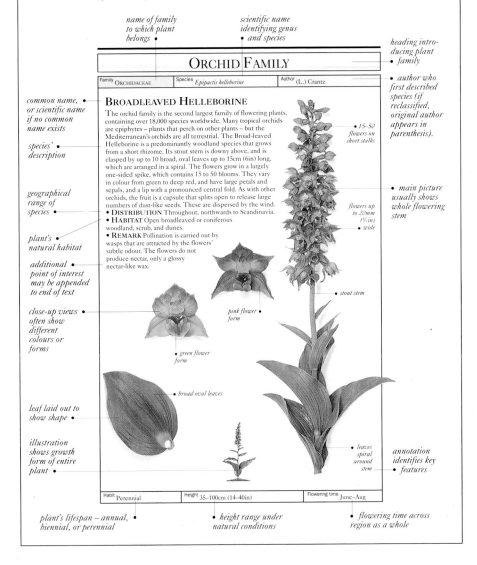

name of family to which plant belongs •

scientific name identifying genus and species

• heading introducing plant family

• author who first described species (if reclassified, original author appears in parentheses).

ORCHID FAMILY

| Family ORCHIDACEAE | Species *Epipactis helleborine* | Author (L.) Crantz |

BROADLEAVED HELLEBORINE

The orchid family is the second largest family of flowering plants, containing over 18,000 species worldwide. Many tropical orchids are epiphytes – plants that perch on other plants – but the Mediterranean's orchids are all terrestrial. The Broad-leaved Helleborine is a predominantly woodland species that grows from a short rhizome. Its stout stem is downy above, and is clasped by up to 10 broad, oval leaves up to 15cm (6in) long, which are arranged in a spiral. The flowers grow in a largely one-sided spike, which contains 15 to 50 blooms. They vary in colour from green to deep red, and have large petals and sepals, and a lip with a pronounced central fold. As with other orchids, the fruit is a capsule that splits open to release large numbers of dust-like seeds. These are dispersed by the wind.
• **DISTRIBUTION** Throughout, northwards to Scandinavia.
• **HABITAT** Open broadleaved or coniferous woodland, scrub, and dunes.
• **REMARK** Pollination is carried out by wasps that are attracted by the flowers' subtle odour. The flowers do not produce nectar, only a glossy nectar-like wax.

common name, or scientific name if no common name exists

species' description

geographical range of species •

plant's natural habitat

additional • point of interest may be appended to end of text

close-up views • often show different colours or forms

leaf laid out to show shape •

illustration shows growth form of entire plant •

• 15–50 flowers on short stalks

• main picture usually shows whole flowering stem

flowers up to 20mm (¾in) • wide

pink flower • form

• green flower form

• stout stem

• broad oval leaves

• leaves spiral around stem

annotation identifies key • features

| Habit Perennial | Height 35–100cm (14–40in) | Flowering time June–Aug |

plant's lifespan – annual, • biennial, or perennial

• height range under natural conditions

• flowering time across region as a whole

PLANT LIFE CYCLES

THE LIFE CYCLE of a typical flowering plant is split into several phases, which are illustrated here. The cycle usually involves sexual reproduction, in which male and female cells are brought together by pollination to form seeds. Each seed contains a tiny rudimentary plant, or embryo, and after germination this plant develops, flowers, and itself sets seed. Many flowering plants can also multiply by asexual reproduction, which does not involve pollination. The parent develops specialized parts, such as runners or bulbils, which eventually develop into new plants.

SEED DISPERSAL

In general, a young plant's chances of survival are increased if it takes root some distance from its parent plant. Plants have evolved many different ways of ensuring that their seeds are dispersed as widely as possible. Some of the principal methods of seed dispersal are outlined on page 19.

GERMINATION

Most seeds remain dormant until germination is triggered by specific external conditions. In some plants – such as the Pot Marigold shown here – the seed-leaves appear above ground soon after germination. In others, the seed-leaves stay below ground level, and supply stored food to the growing plant.

paired seed-leaves

YOUNG SEEDLING

fruit breaks away from plant

SEEDS DISPERSED

cluster of single-seeded fruit (achenes)

FLOWERS AND FRUIT

developing fruit

MONOCOTS AND DICOTS

A monocotyledon (or monocot) is a flowering plant that has a single seed-leaf (cotyledon). A dicotyledon (or dicot) has two seed-leaves. All flowering plants are divided into these two main categories (see also pp.15–17).

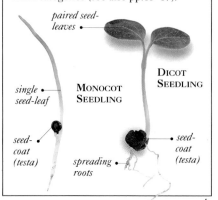

paired seed-leaves •

DICOT SEEDLING

single • seed-leaf

MONOCOT SEEDLING

seed-coat (testa) •

spreading • roots

• seed-coat (testa)

SEED FORMATION

Once a plant has flowered, its energies are channelled into the production of seeds. Seeds are contained within fruits (pp.18–19), with a single fruit encasing one seed, or many. Generally, as seed numbers increase, their size decreases.

rapidly growing
true leaves •

YOUNG
PLANT

• root system with
large surface area
absorbs water
and minerals
from soil

flower-head •
containing many
small flowers
(florets)

MATURE
PLANT

oldest leaves •
begin to die
back

mature root •
system anchors
plant in soil

GROWTH AND DEVELOPMENT

Plants use the energy of sunlight to make
food from two simple substances – water and
carbon dioxide. This process is called photo-
synthesis, and it generally takes place in a
plant's leaves. The early stages of a plant's
life cycle are dominated by the need to
manufacture food. The plant's true leaves
grow rapidly to intercept sufficient sunlight,
and its roots fan out to absorb water from the
soil. As well as taking in water, the roots also
absorb a range of dissolved minerals that are
essential for growth.

PLANT LIFESPANS

Plant lifespans vary from a few months
to a few years. Annual plants, such as the
Common Poppy (*Papaver rhoeas*, p.65),
complete their life cycle in a single growing season. In some annuals this growing
season runs from spring to summer; in
others – called winter annuals – it runs
from autumn to spring. Biennials, such as
Verbascum sinuatum (p.206), generally live
for two growing seasons. During its first
year a biennial plant builds up stores of
food, and in the second year it flowers
and dies. Perennial species live for
more than two years. In a herbaceous
perennial, e.g. Giant Fennel (*Ferula
communis*, p.162), the stems die back after
each growing season, and this limits
their size. In woody perennials,
which include all shrubs and trees,
the stems persist and grow longer
with each passing year.

FLOWERING

Some plants flower just once in their lives,
and then die. Others remain alive after
flowering, and may flower many more
times before their lives come to an end.
This difference is not simply a measure of
how long a plant lives. Whereas the majority
of perennial plants flower every year, some
flower just once – the Century Plant (*Agave
americana*, p.273) being a particularly spectacular example. Flowering itself is often
triggered by changes in day length.

PLANT PROFILE

FLOWERING PLANTS are organized into two distinct parts – a shoot system, which is mainly above ground, and a root system, which is normally below ground. The shoot consists of the stems, with their attached buds, leaves, and flowers. In woody plants, the stems are reinforced by a substance called lignin, which gives the plant rigidity. The roots anchor the plant, and microscopic hairs absorb water and dissolved minerals. Many Mediterranean plants have modified stems that store food for the summer drought.

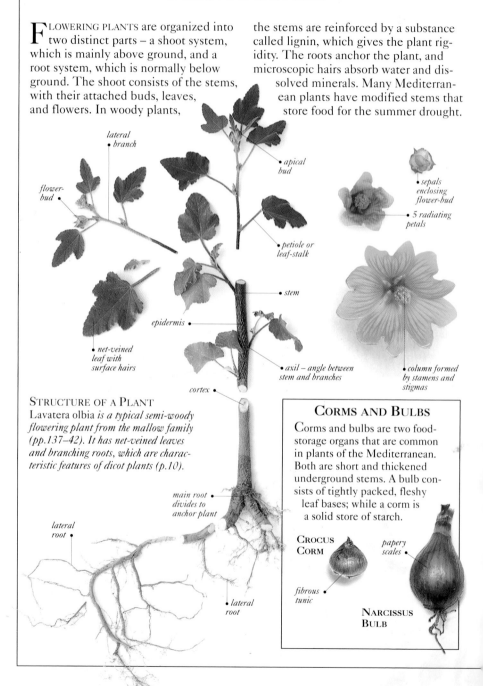

lateral branch

apical bud

flower-bud

sepals enclosing flower-bud

5 radiating petals

petiole or leaf-stalk

stem

epidermis

net-veined leaf with surface hairs

axil – angle between stem and branches

column formed by stamens and stigmas

cortex

STRUCTURE OF A PLANT
Lavatera olbia *is a typical semi-woody flowering plant from the mallow family (pp.137–42). It has net-veined leaves and branching roots, which are characteristic features of dicot plants (p.10).*

main root divides to anchor plant

lateral root

lateral root

CORMS AND BULBS
Corms and bulbs are two food-storage organs that are common in plants of the Mediterranean. Both are short and thickened underground stems. A bulb consists of tightly packed, fleshy leaf bases; while a corm is a solid store of starch.

CROCUS CORM

papery scales

fibrous tunic

NARCISSUS BULB

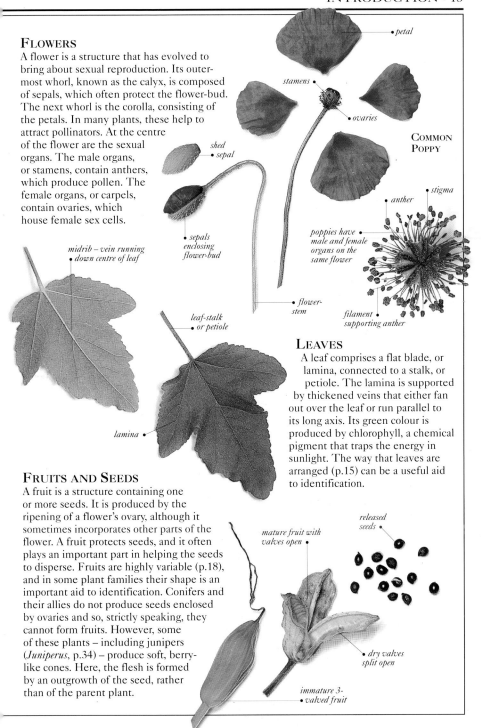

FLOWERS

A flower is a structure that has evolved to bring about sexual reproduction. Its outer-most whorl, known as the calyx, is composed of sepals, which often protect the flower-bud. The next whorl is the corolla, consisting of the petals. In many plants, these help to attract pollinators. At the centre of the flower are the sexual organs. The male organs, or stamens, contain anthers, which produce pollen. The female organs, or carpels, contain ovaries, which house female sex cells.

petal •

stamens •

• ovaries

COMMON POPPY

shed • sepal

• stigma

• anther

poppies have • male and female organs on the same flower

• sepals enclosing flower-bud

filament • supporting anther

midrib – vein running • down centre of leaf

• flower-stem

leaf-stalk • or petiole

LEAVES

A leaf comprises a flat blade, or lamina, connected to a stalk, or petiole. The lamina is supported by thickened veins that either fan out over the leaf or run parallel to its long axis. Its green colour is produced by chlorophyll, a chemical pigment that traps the energy in sunlight. The way that leaves are arranged (p.15) can be a useful aid to identification.

lamina •

FRUITS AND SEEDS

A fruit is a structure containing one or more seeds. It is produced by the ripening of a flower's ovary, although it sometimes incorporates other parts of the flower. A fruit protects seeds, and it often plays an important part in helping the seeds to disperse. Fruits are highly variable (p.18), and in some plant families their shape is an important aid to identification. Conifers and their allies do not produce seeds enclosed by ovaries and so, strictly speaking, they cannot form fruits. However, some of these plants – including junipers (*Juniperus*, p.34) – produce soft, berry-like cones. Here, the flesh is formed by an outgrowth of the seed, rather than of the parent plant.

released seeds •

mature fruit with valves open •

• dry valves split open

immature 3-• valved fruit

GROWTH HABITS

GROWTH HABIT is a term that embraces both a plant's overall form, and the nature of its life cycle (see p.11). This page shows a range of forms commonly seen in Mediterranean plants. When identifying wild plants, remember that growth form is a highly variable feature, and that it is much affected by local conditions, such as shade, wind, and competition from neighbouring plants. Annual plants tend to have green pliable stems, and are often found on disturbed ground. Perennials often have woody stems, and generally reach greater sizes.

STEMLESS
Leaves and flower-stalks arise separately at or close to ground level; the true stem is often below ground.

TUFTED
Stems radiate to form tuft; no central stem or trunk visible.

SPREADING
Stems extend laterally and then ascend some distance from the point where the roots attach.

TRAILING
Stems lax, lying on flat ground or hanging down over slopes.

CLIMBING
Stems supported by nearby plants or other objects.

PROSTRATE
Stems lying flat on the ground, ascending either only slightly or not at all.

ERECT
Stems vertical and well clear of ground, not relying on external support.

SHRUB
Small or medium-sized woody plant with several stems.

TREE
Large woody plant with trunk, branching well above ground.

LEAF TYPES

THE ARRANGEMENT, size, and shape of the leaves are key features in plant identification, particularly when flowers are not present. With a few exceptions, the way that the leaves are arranged is consistent over the whole of a plant. By contrast, leaf size and shape vary greatly according to a leaf's position on a stem. Leaf surface features, i.e. hairs, veins, etc., may also help identification.

LEAF ARRANGEMENT

Instead of arising at random, leaves are arranged in regular patterns on a stem. Plants with opposite leaves have two leaves per node, whereas plants with alternate leaves produce just one. Whorled leaves grow in a ring of three or more that circles the stem.

OPPOSITE **ALTERNATE** **WHORLED**

SIMPLE LEAVES

Simple leaves occur in many shapes, but are not divided into deep lobes or leaflets: the leaf-blade forms a single surface. The leaf margins may be entire (smooth), have small lobes or teeth, and may be flat or undulating.

linear

lanceolate and entire *spathulate and entire* *orbicular and entire* *sagittate*

elliptic with serrate margins *cordate and toothed* *deltoid and crenate*

DISSECTED AND COMPOUND LEAVES

A dissected leaf is one that has deeply cut teeth or lobes. A compound leaf is composed of separate leaflets. The leaflets may themselves be divided.

deeply toothed

pinnately lobed *palmately lobed* *trifoliate*

palmate compound

pinnate with terminal tendrils

bipinnate

MONOCOT LEAVES

Monocot leaves are typically linear, with parallel veins running along the leaf's axis. They usually lack teeth, and may be either flat or channelled. However, although this rule of thumb holds in general, there are several exceptions – two of which are shown here (far right).

typical monocot leaf *cordate monocot leaf* *sagittate monocot leaf*

FLOWER TYPES

OVER MILLIONS OF YEARS, flowers have evolved in a tremendous variety of forms. Insect-pollinated flowers tend to be brightly coloured and scented, and are often shaped to accommodate a particular species of insect. By contrast, wind-pollinated flowers are usually small and drab. Some plants bear their flowers singly, but many others produce flowers in clusters known as inflorescences.

INFLORESCENCE TYPES

SOLITARY FLOWER
This is a flower that grows singly. A plant that bears solitary flowers may have many separate blooms.

SPIKE
A spike is a long inflorescence that is composed of stalkless flowers attached to a common stem.

RACEME
A raceme bears stalked flowers that are borne around a common stem; stalks may or may not be of similar lengths.

CYME
This is a branched inflorescence with each branch ending in a flower; the branches are sometimes symmetrical.

UMBEL
The flowers in an umbel are stalked, and form an umbrella-like shape at the top of a stem.

CORYMB
A corymb is a flat-topped inflorescence formed by flowers or capitula on stalks of diverse lengths.

PANICLE
A panicle is an inflorescence with stalked flowers on repeatedly branching stems.

CAPITULUM
A flower-like capitulum is formed by tightly packed stalkless florets.

FLOWER FORMS

REGULAR FLOWERS

In a regular or "actinomorphic" flower, the flower parts
are arranged about a central point, so the flower has
several axes of symmetry. Regular flow-
ers are characteristic of a number of
important dicot families in the Mediterranean, including the pink family (p.48),
the rock-rose family (p.146), the mallow
family (p.137), and the convolvulus family
(p.178). Most members of the cress family
(p.68) and borage family (p.181) also have
flowers of this type. Plants in the daisy
family (p.228) often appear to have regular
flowers, but each "flower" is actually a
head formed by small florets.

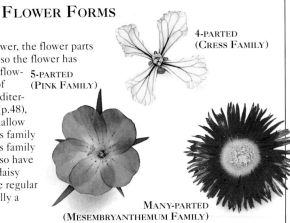

**4-PARTED
(CRESS FAMILY)**

**5-PARTED
(PINK FAMILY)**

**MANY-PARTED
(MESEMBRYANTHEMUM FAMILY)**

IRREGULAR FLOWERS

In an irregular or "zygomorphic" flower, the flower
parts are arranged equally on either side of a
midline, giving the flower just one axis of
symmetry. As in regular flowers, the petals
are often fused. Irregular flowers are found
in many families of dicot plants, including
the pea family (p.83), the mint family (p.190),
and the figwort family (p.206), and they nearly
always indicate pollination by insects. Among
the most fascinating irregular flowers to be found
in the Mediterranean are those belonging to
members of the birthwort family (p.39).

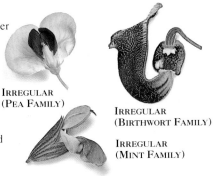

**IRREGULAR
(PEA FAMILY)**

**IRREGULAR
(BIRTHWORT FAMILY)**

**IRREGULAR
(MINT FAMILY)**

MONOCOT FLOWERS

Monocot flowers differ from dicot flowers in
several respects, particularly in the number
of petals (p.25); their sepals and petals –
collectively known as tepals – are often
indistinguishable. Regular monocot
flowers are typical of the lily family
(p.256), but the most remarkable irregular monocot flowers are found in the
orchid family (p.290). Some orchid
flowers have evolved shapes that
imitate female insects. Male insects
are fooled into copulat-
ing with the flowers
and, in doing so, trans-
fer pollen from one
flower to another.

**REGULAR
(IRIS FAMILY)**

REGULAR (IRIS FAMILY)

**IRREGULAR
(ORCHID FAMILY)**

**REGULAR
(LILY FAMILY)**

FRUITS AND SEEDS

I N EVERYDAY PARLANCE, a fruit is a succulent and edible part of a plant. In
botany, the word "fruit" has a far more
precise meaning, and refers to a mature
ovary and the seeds that it contains.

When ripe, some fruits are succulent,
but many others are papery or woody,
and are relatively dry. "Dehiscent" fruits
break open in order to release their seeds;
"indehiscent" fruits are shed intact.

ACHENE
An achene is the simplest type of indehiscent
fruit. It consists of a single seed,
enclosed by a dry fruit wall.
Many achenes have
extensions (feathery
parachutes, hooks,
etc.) that aid
dispersal of
the seed.

• hooked achenes

LOMENTUM
A lomentum (pl. lomenta) is a
dry pod-like fruit that breaks up
into sections, each containing
a single seed. The fruit often
snaps at narrow constrictions,
and each seed usually stays
enclosed within its portion
of the fruit wall. This kind
of fruit is formed by some
members of the pea
and cress families.

• cluster of lomenta

SILICULA AND SILIQUA
A silicula is a dry fruit with a central
partition that splits open when ripe.
It is at least as broad as it is long.
A siliqua is similar, but is usually
much longer than
broad. Many mem-
bers of the cress
family form fruits
of this kind.

• siliqua

• silicula

CAPSULE
A capsule is a dry fruit that develops from
one or more carpels, or seed-forming compartments. When ripe, it may split open in a
variety of ways to release its seeds. Capsules
are formed by plants in many different
families, including the poppy family.

POD
A pod or legume is a form of
dry fruit typical of the pea
family. It develops from a
single carpel, or seed-forming
compartment, and when ripe
splits open along two lines.
Pods can be coiled,
knobbly, or inflated.

*straight
• pod*

*• suture
along which
pod splits*

coiled pod •

inflated pod •

FOLLICLE
A follicle is a dry fruit that develops
from a single carpel. When ripe, it
splits open along one
line. Follicles are
typical of plants in
the periwinkle
family, and are
also formed by
many plants in
the buttercup
family.

*• woody follicles
releasing seeds*

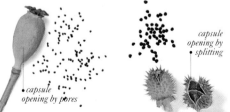

*capsule
opening by
• splitting*

*• capsule
opening by pores*

NUT

A nut is a dry, one-seeded indehiscent fruit with a woody fruit wall. Nuts are formed by many trees; small nuts (known as nutlets) are formed by a range of plants.

nut and cupule

SCHIZOCARP

A schizocarp is a dry fruit that breaks up when ripe to form single-seeded units called mericarps. Plants in the carrot family form schizocarps with two mericarps that are arranged back-to-back.

mericarp

schizocarp

BERRIES

A berry is a soft, succulent fruit that usually contains many seeds. The fruit's flesh aids seed dispersal by attracting animals. When an animal eats the fruit, seeds pass through its body unharmed. Berries are formed by many plants, including members of the gourd and heather families. A drupe is similar, but contains one or more seeds surrounded by a hard wall, which forms a stone. An olive is a typical drupe.

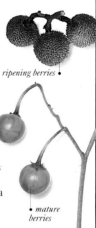

ripening berries

mature berries

SEED DISPERSAL

MECHANICAL DISPERSAL

In mechanical dispersal, tension builds up in a ripening fruit. When the seeds are ripe, this stored energy is suddenly released and the fruit explodes or splits, throwing the seeds away from the parent plant. The Squirting Cucumber (*Ecballium elaterium*, p.153) bears fruit that eject seeds by bursting as they fall.

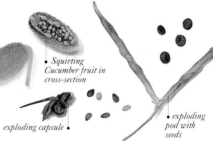

Squirting Cucumber fruit in cross-section

exploding capsule

exploding pod with seeds

ANIMAL DISPERSAL

Animal dispersal occurs in many different ways. Some plants have hooked fruit that attaches to fur. Other plants produce seeds that are coated with sweet substances, and are dispersed by insects. Succulent fruits are eaten by animals, and their seeds are often dispersed in the animal's droppings.

barbed fruit

nutlets with hooks

WIND AND WATER DISPERSAL

Wind dispersal is common in plants that grow in open places, as do many members of the daisy family. Such plants often form fruits with feathery hairs or papery scales. Once the fruit is mature, the wind carries it away. Water dispersal is common in a number of shoreline plants. Their fruits are usually buoyant, and can tolerate salty water.

fruit with feathery hairs

seeds dispersed by wind

HABITATS

THROUGH THE PROCESS of evolution, all plants have become adapted to particular conditions. For example, some need alkaline soil, but others grow only in acid soil. Some can tolerate salty spray and drying winds; others need shade and ample moisture. Different habitats have different conditions and so develop their own plant "communities". The following four pages look at a range of habitats found in the Mediterranean region, and some of the plants that they sustain.

ON THE BEACH
Sea Daffodils flower near a busy beach, where their graceful flowers are all too often picked.

SALT MARSHES

Compared to rocky or sandy shores, salt marshes have a restricted range of flowering plants. However, those that can tolerate the saline conditions often grow in abundance. The glassworts (*Salicornia*, p.43), with their curious fleshy stems, usually grow closest to the water's edge; the higher ground is the preserve of plants such as the Sea Aster (*Aster tripolium*, p.228). Further inland, flat, drained areas are good places to see the Giant Reed (*Arundo donax*, p.287) – a towering grass often planted as a windbreak.

SEA ASTER

SALT MARSH IN SPRING
Swathes of glasswort flank a brackish pool. In late summer, glasswort often turns bright red.

SANDY AND ROCKY SHORES

Coastal sand and rock form two different habitats: one constantly changing; the other extremely stable. The Mediterranean has a small tidal range and, as a result, a variety of plants are able to live on coastal sand close to the water. These include the Sea Rocket (*Cakile maritima*, p.77) and Sea Medick (*Medicago marina*, p.103). The formidably armed Sea Holly (*Eryngium maritimum*, p.157) is widespread, as is Sea Bindweed (*Calystegia soldanella*, p.179), a trailing plant with leathery leaves and handsome funnel-shaped flowers. However, in terms of sheer beauty, nothing can rival Sea Daffodil (*Pancratium maritimum*, p.277). On coastal rocks, a range of woody or woody-based plants can often be found. Sea Heath (*Frankenia laevis*, p.152) often grows on salt-caked ledges. Further away from the sea, plants that are less salt-tolerant appear. On relatively sheltered coasts, these can include Tree Spurge (*Euphorbia dendroides*, p.129) and Tree Mallow (*Lavatera arborea*, p.138).

LADY
ORCHID

PINEWOODS ▷
The umbrella-shaped
Stone Pine, Pinus
pinea, *forms open*
woods in the west of the
region. It bears edible seeds.
Open pinewoods are home
to many orchids, such as
the Lady Orchid (left).

▽ EARLY START
Flowering cyclamens add a
splash of colour to broad-
leaved woodland in March.

CONIFEROUS WOODLAND

In Mediterranean coniferous woodland, the
trees are usually widely spaced, allowing a
variety of plants to spring up on the woodland floor. Shrubby plants that can be found
here often include rock-roses (*Cistus*, p.146),
as well as many members of the pea family
(Leguminosae, p.83). Mediterranean pinewoods are surprisingly good places for spot-
ting orchids, partly because they tend to stand
out against the needle-covered ground. Lady
Orchid (*Orchis purpurea*, p.295) is common
in open pinewoods, as are some of the bee
orchids (*Ophrys*, p.302). One species to look
out for in particular is the strange Violet Bird's
Nest Orchid (*Limodorum abortivum*, p.291),
an impressive wand-like plant up to 80cm
(32in) high that lacks green leaves.

BROADLEAVED WOODLAND

At low altitude, Mediterranean broadleaved
woodland consists mainly of evergreen trees,
such as Holm Oak (*Quercus ilex*). Beneath the
open canopy, a rich shrub layer often develops. The exact mixture of plants depends
on the soil type, but it typically includes Box
(*Buxus sempervirens*, p.136) and Myrtle (*Myrtus
communis*, p.155). In shady woods, Butcher's
Broom (*Ruscus aculeatus*, p.272) is common,
and scrubby woodland margins often contain
Smilax aspersa (p.272). Above about 500m
(1,650ft), deciduous trees become more common. Here, hellebores (*Helleborus*, p.54) may
be seen, and spring brings a flush of colour as
cyclamens (*Cyclamen*, p.168) flower.

HELLEBORUS
LIVIDUS

MAQUIS

Maquis and garigue (below) are characteristic forms of Mediterranean vegetation. Both are produced by deforestation, followed by cutting, grazing, or burning – all of which stop forests regenerating. In maquis, the dominant plants are evergreen shrubs or shrubby trees. These grow up to 5m (16½ft) tall, forming dense thickets that cover hillsides. Common species include the Strawberry Tree (*Arbutus unedo*, p.167). and Myrtle (*Myrtus communis*, p.155). From a distance, maquis often invites exploration, but the presence of well-armed plants such as the Thorny Broom (*Calicotome spinosa*, p.86) is usually enough to deter even the most ardent flower-lover.

MYRTLE

COASTAL MAQUIS
Dark evergreen leaves contrast with the bright yellow flowers of Thorny Broom.

ROCKY GROUND AND GARIGUE

Garigue is open rocky ground dominated by dwarf shrubs generally less than 50cm (20in) high. Brown and parched in summer, it is transformed by the autumn and winter rains, and by spring becomes a botanist's paradise, filled with flowering bulbs, irises, and a profusion of orchids. Garigue is often browsed by goats, but many of its perennial plants have special defences. Thymes (*Thymus*, p.198) and rock-roses (*Cistus*, p.146) contain unpalatable oils; and many of the shrubs have spiny stems. Garigue is usually easier to explore than maquis. It is at its best in spring, but it is worth visiting in autumn, when many late-flowering bulbs come into their own.

LEUZEA CONIFERA

GARIGUE IN FLOWER
Two colour forms of Iris lutescens grow in colonies on a limestone hillside.

GRASSY GROUND AND WAYSIDES

Throughout the Mediterranean, grassy places and waysides contain much of interest for the wild-flower enthusiast, particularly in spring. Grape hyacinths (*Muscari*, p.266) and garlics (*Allium*, p.268) are common throughout, together with a vast range of herbaceous members of the pea family (Leguminosae, p.83). In many grassy places, orchids grow in abundance. Species of particular interest include the Giant Orchid (*Barlia robertiana*, p.299) and the tongue orchids (*Serapias*, p.300). Disturbed and waste ground have their own flora, including mulleins (*Verbascum*, p.206) and Cocklebur (*Xanthium strumarium*, p.233).

CULTIVATED GROUND

Agriculture has a long history in the Mediterranean. However, the rocky ground is often unsuitable for intensive farming, and, as a result, wild flowers have fared better here than in many parts of northern Europe. In spring, olive groves are often ablaze with colour, as swathes of poppies (*Papaver*, p.64) and anemones (*Anemone*, p.56) flower. Ground that is occasionally ploughed provides a habitat for gladioli (*Gladiolus*, p.282) and the tenacious Bermuda Buttercup (*Oxalis pes-caprae*, p.120). Arable fields may contain a wide range of attractive, if troublesome, weeds.

SPRING SPECTACULAR
Wild flowers on a grassy roadside in Crete. Spring comes early to this southerly island, with most lowland flowers blooming in the short period between March and May. At higher altitudes, flowers appear later.

GLADIOLUS
ILLYRICUS

OLIVE GROVES
Poppies flowering in a Greek olive grove. Scenes like this are still common around the Mediterranean, and are a reminder of what can be destroyed by the indiscriminate and often unnecessary use of herbicides.

OBSERVING WILD FLOWERS

FOR THE WILD-FLOWER enthusiast, discovering new plants is always an exciting experience, and part of the enjoyment is derived from recording those discoveries. Use a notebook to summarize details such as location, flower structure, and size, and a camera to capture an image of the plant in its natural habitat. Pressed leaves and flowers may help to identify "difficult" species. Care should always be taken to remove only small parts of a plant.

macro lenses catch fine details

SNAPPING STEMS
Rock Storksbills in windy conditions. A fast shutter speed prevents blurring.

35mm SLR camera

hand lens; this one magnifies by x10

BOTANIST'S EQUIPMENT

A hand lens is essential for investigating the fine structure of flowers or leaves. The lens illustrated is light and folds up when not in use. Paper envelopes are best for storing fruits and seeds. Unlike plastic bags, they are porous, and less likely to promote rotting. A 35mm SLR camera is ideal for most plant photography. A tripod may be needed for obtaining sharp close-up pictures.

notebook may be used as temporary press

notebook and pen

small paper envelopes, ideal for storing seeds

PLANT CONSERVATION

Visitors to the region can encourage conservation by taking care not to harm plants, or to break laws established for their protection. Some Mediterranean plants, e.g. the wild Madonna Lily (right), have international protection under the Convention on International Trade in Endangered Species of Wild Flora and Fauna (CITES), making it illegal to transport certain species from one country to another without a special permit. Many plants are covered by national legislation: in France, for example, about 200 Mediterranean species are protected.

IDENTIFICATION KEY

THE KEY ON PAGES 25–33 is designed to help you identify any Mediterranean flower featured in the book. To use it, you will need to be familiar with principal parts of a flower (see p.13 and p.308). First decide whether a plant is a "dicot" or a "monocot" (see below). A process of further elimination leads you to lists, which direct you to the plant entry pages in the main part of the book.

DICOTYLEDON OR MONOCOTYLEDON?

DICOTYLEDONS

Dicots have two features that are often easy to spot: their leaf-veins often form a net, and their flower-parts are usually arranged in fours or fives, although some have flowers with more parts than this.

Most dicots have broad or dissected leaves, but some have quite narrow leaves. Unlike most monocots, dicots often have woody stems. Nearly all Mediterranean shrubs are dicots.
see below

MONOCOTYLEDONS

A typical monocot has parallel leaf-veins, and its leaves are narrow and linear. Its flower parts are usually divided into three, or multiples of three; petals and sepals are often identical. Many monocots grow from corms and bulbs, and branch either rarely or not at all. In the Mediterranean, few monocots are woody, but some have broad leaves with netted veins that are more typical of dicots.
see pp.32–33

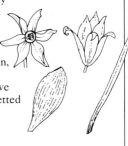

DICOTYLEDONS

FLOWERS SPURRED

FLOWERS NOT SPURRED

Consolida **55**
Fumaria **68**
Impatiens **135**
Misopates **211**
Linaria **212**
Cymbalaria **213**
Kickxia **213**
Centranthus **223**

AGGREGATED FLOWERS

see pp.26–27

PETALS FREE

see pp.28–29

PETALS FUSED OR PARTLY FUSED

see pp.30–31

AGGREGATED

FLOWERS TINY

IN SPIKES,

PANICLES,

OR CATKINS

FLOWERS TINY, IN ROUNDED CLUSTERS

FLOWERS IN UMBELS

STAMENS FREE

Detail

WOODY	HERBACEOUS	WOODY	HERBACEOUS	PLANTS WITHOUT LATEX	PLANTS WITH LATEX

Ficus **36**   Eucalyptus **155**
Acacia **84**
Buxus **136**

Eryngium **157**
Globularia **216**
Scabiosa **224–25**

Quercus **36**
Halimione **43**
Ceratonia **83**
Cotinus **134**
Pistacia **134–35**
Rhamnus **136**
Thymelea **144**
Tamarix **152**
Olea **173**
Phyllirea **173**

Urtica **37**
Parietaria **38**
Polygonum **42**
Rumex **42**
Salicornia **43**
Amaranthus **44**
Salsola **44**
Phytolacca **46**
Plantago **219–20**

Urtica pilulifera **37**
Paronychia **48**
Sarcopterium **82**
Eryngium **157**
Lagoecia **158**
Plantago afra **220**
Xanthium **233**

Euphorbia **127–31**

Echinophora **158**
Scandix **159**
Smyrnium **159**
Crithmum **160**
Foeniculum **160**
Bupleurum **161**
Ferula **162**   Thapsia **164**
Ferulago **163**   Torilis **164**
Tordylium **163**   Daucus **165**

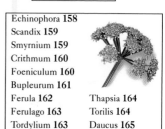

AGGREGATED

FLOWERS IN DISTINCT HEADS

FLOWERS IN FLATTENED CLUSTERS

STAMENS UNITED

Detail

Sedum **80**
Sambucus **221**
Viburnum **221**
Iberis **75**   Achillea **235**
Cardaria **76**   Senecio cineraria **238**

THISTLE-LIKE	CORNFLOWER-LIKE	DAISY-LIKE	DANDELION-LIKE	RAYLESS

Staehelina **241**
Galactites **244**
Leuzea **246**
Centaurea **247–48**
Crupina **248**

Atractylis **240**	Silybum **246**
Carlina **240**	Carduncellus **249**
Echinops **241**	Carthamus **249**
Carduus **242**	Scolymus **250**
Notobasis **242**	
Ptilostemon **243**	
Onopordon **244–45**	
Cynara **245**	

Aster **228**
Bellis **228**
Dittrichia **231**
Inula **231**
Asteriscus **232**
Pallensis **232**
Anthemis **234**
Chamaemelum **235**
Anacyclus **236**
Chrysanthemum **237**
Senecio **238**
Calendula **239**

Catananche **251**
Cichorium **251**
Hyoseris **252**
Urospermum **252**
Tragopogon **253**
Andryala **254**
Crepis **254**
Lactuca **254**

Helichrysum **229**
Phagnalon **230**
Santolina **233**
Anthemis rigida **234**
Otanthus **236**
Cotula **238**

PETALS FREE

PETALS 3

PETALS 4

APPARENTLY NO SEPALS

SEPALS 2

SEPALS 4

APPARENTLY NO SEPALS

STAMENS 2

STAMENS 6

STAMENS 8 OR MORE

PEAFLOWERS

Osyris **38**
Cneorum **132**

Papaver **64–65**
Glaucium **66**
Hypecoum **67**

Cress family
70–77

Anemone
coronaria **56**
Helleborus **54**
Nigella **55**

Clematis **58–59**

Veronica **214**

Capparis **69**
Ruta **132**
Oenothera **156**

Pea family
83–119

PETALS FREE

PETALS 5

PETALS 6 OR MORE

SEPALS PRESENT

SEPALS JOINED AT LEAST HALFWAY

NON-PEAFLOWERS

SEPALS FREE, OR ALMOST FREE

NO EPICALYX, SEPALS VERY UNEQUAL

NO EPICALYX, SEPALS EQUAL

EPICALYX PRESENT

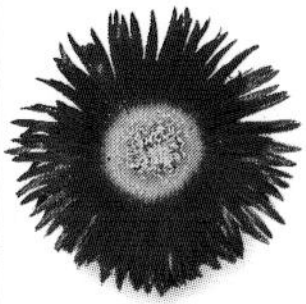

Carprobrotus **47**
Anemone **56–58**
Adonis **59**
Ranunculus ficaria **61**
Paeonia **62–63**
Leontice **63**
Reseda **78–79**
Sedum **80**
Lythrum **154**
Opuntia **154**
Punica **156**

Rock-rose family **146–51**

Mallow family **137–42**

Agrostemma **49**
Silene **49–50**
Saponaria **51**
Vaccaria **51**
Petrorhagia **52**
Dianthus **53**
Punica **156**

Spergularia **48**
Pittosporum **60**
Ranunculus asiaticus **60**
Ranunculus gramineus **61**
Reseda alba **78**
Paeonia **80**
Sedum **80**
Rosa **81–82**

Oxalis **120**
Geranium **121**
Erodium **121–23**
Tribulus **123**
Linum **124–25**
Ruta **132**
Melia **133**
Hypericum **145**

Frankenia **152**
Myrtus **155**
Sambucus **221**

PETALS FUSED OR PARTLY FUSED

FLOWERS 1–2 LIPPED

COROLLA 1-LIPPED

COROLLA 2-LIPPED

PETALS CUPPED, JOINED ONLY AT BASE

FRUIT A BERRY

FRUIT A SMALL DRUPE

FRUIT 4 NUTLETS

FRUIT A CAPSULE

Portulaca **47**
Styrax **172**

Lonicera **222**

Prasium **192**
Scutellaria **192**
Phlomis **193–94**
Lamium **195**
Ballota **195**
Prunella **196**
Stachys **196**
Clinopodium **197**
Origanum **197**
Satureja **197**
Thymus **198**
Rosmarinus **199**
Lavandula **199–200**
Salvia **201–02**

Fumaria **68**
Scrophularia **208–09**
Antirrhinum **210**
Misopates **211**
Linaria **212**
Cymbalaria **213**
Kickxia **213**
Parentucellia **214**
Bellardia **215**
Lathraea **216**
Orobanche **218**

Polygala **133**
Ajuga **190**
Teucrium **190–91**
Acanthus **217**

Vitex **189**

PETALS FUSED OR PARTLY FUSED

FLOWERS NOT LIPPED

FLOWERS TRUMPET- OR FUNNEL- SHAPED

FLOWERS WITH FLAT PETAL LIMBS

FLOWERS TUBULAR OR BELL-SHAPED

COROLLA WITHOUT A TUBE

COROLLA WITH A TUBE

Coris **170**
Anagalis **170**
Borago **187**
Solanum **204**
Verbascum **206–07**
Cyclamen **168–69**
Gomphocarpus **176**
Petromarula **227**

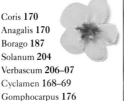

Cytinus **41**
Aristolochia **39–41**
Umbilicus **79**
Bryonia **153**
Ecballium **153**
Calluna **166**
Erica **166**
Arbutus **167**
Cuscuta **178**
Onosma **182**
Cerinthe **183**
Echium **184–85**
Symphytum **185**
Hyoscyamus **203**
Nicotiana **205**
Campanula **225–56**
Legousia **226–27**

Daphne **143–44**   Rubia **178**
Limonium **171–72**   Heliotropium **181**
Blackstonia **174**   Lithodora **182–83**
Centaurium **174**   Alkanna **183**
Nerium **175**   Anchusa **186–87**
Vinca **175–76**   Cynoglossum **188**
Cruciata **177**   Verbena **189**
Vincetoxicum **177**   Mandragora **204**   Centranthus **223**
                                                                                 Valeriana **224**

Bougainvillea **45**
Mirabilis **45**
Calystegia **179**
Convolvulus **179–80**
Datura **205**

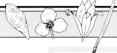

MONOCOTYLEDONS

**LEAVES HEART-
OR ARROW-SHAPED,
OR DISSECTED**

FLOWERS CONSPICUOUS

**FLOWERS IN PANICLES
ON STEM TO
7M (23FT) TALL**

**FLOWERS WITHOUT
LIP OR SPUR**

STAMENS 3

Agave **273**

**OVARY
BELOW TEPALS,
TEPALS FREE**

**OVARY UNDERGROUND,
TEPALS ATTACHED
BENEATH**

Smilax **272**
Tamus **277**
Arum family **288–89**

Iris family **278–82**

Daffodil family
273–77

Colchicum **259**

MONOCOTYLEDONS

LEAVES OVAL TO LINEAR

FLOWERS SMALL
AND INCONSPICUOUS

FLOWERS WITH
LIP OR SPUR

FLOWERS
SOLITARY OR
IN SMALL
CLUSTERS

FLOWERS
IN DENSE
HEADS

STAMENS 6

OVARY ABOVE
TEPALS, TEPALS
JOINED

OVARY ABOVE
TEPALS, TEPALS
FREE

Orchid family
290–307

Posidonia 255
Grass family 283–87

Muscari 266–67

Asphodelus 256–57
Asphodeline 258
Aphyllanthes 258
Gagea 259–60
Tulipa 260–62
Fritillaria 263
Lilium 263   Urginea 265
Ornithogalum 264–65 Scilla 266
                    Allium 268–70

Asparagus 271
Ruscus 272

CONIFERS
AND THEIR ALLIES

CYPRESS FAMILY

Family CUPRESSACEAE	Species *Juniperus oxycedrus*	Author L.

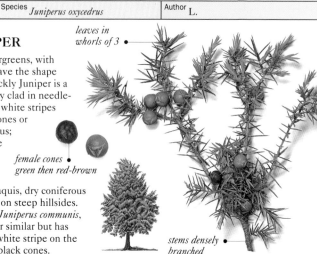

PRICKLY JUNIPER

leaves in whorls of 3

Junipers are aromatic evergreens, with female cones that often have the shape and texture of a berry. Prickly Juniper is a shrub or small tree densely clad in needle-like leaves, each having 2 white stripes on its upper surface. Its cones or "flowers" are inconspicuous; male and female cones are borne on separate plants.
• **DISTRIBUTION** Throughout the region.
• **HABITAT** Garigue, maquis, dry coniferous woods; frequently thrives on steep hillsides.
• **RELATED SPECIES** *Juniperus communis*, Common Juniper, is rather similar but has leaves with only a single white stripe on the upper surfaces, and blue-black cones.

female cones green then red-brown

stems densely branched

Habit Perennial	Height Up to 10m (33ft)	Flowering time Feb–May

Family CUPRESSACEAE	Species *Juniperus phoenicea*	Author L.

PHOENICIAN JUNIPER

cones turn brown when ripe

Phoenician Juniper is a dense, much-branched, evergreen bush or tree with pale brown and flaking bark. Young plants have spreading needle-like leaves, up to 15mm (⅗in) long, but adult plants, like the one shown here, have tiny flat scales. The cones of both sexes are found on the same plant. The female cones are round and berry-like. Initially they are greenish, but they become mid-brown when they ripen in their second year.
• **DISTRIBUTION** Throughout.
• **HABITAT** Rocky exposed hillsides, often close to the coast.

berry-like female cones

scales press tightly against stem

pale brown, flaky bark

Habit Perennial	Height Up to 8m (26ft)	Flowering time Feb–Apr

JOINT PINE FAMILY

Family EPHEDRACEAE	Species *Ephedra fragilis*	Author Desf.

JOINT PINE

The joint pine family contains shrubby, brush-like plants that live mainly in arid places. Like conifers, they do not have true flowers, and their seeds do not develop inside an ovary. This species is a sprawling or mound-like shrub with flexible grooved stems. In the subspecies *fragilis*, which grows in the west of the region, the stems snap easily at their nodes. The "flowers" are minute and stalkless, with male and female flowers growing on separate plants. Female flowers produce red, berry-like fruit.
• **DISTRIBUTION** Throughout.
• **HABITAT** Rocky and scrubby ground.

stems straggle or climb •

small, scale-like leaves •

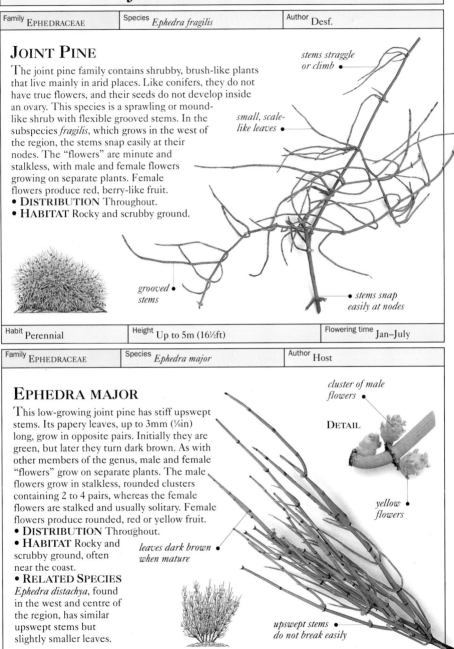

grooved stems •

stems snap easily at nodes •

Habit Perennial	Height Up to 5m (16½ft)	Flowering time Jan–July

Family EPHEDRACEAE	Species *Ephedra major*	Author Host

EPHEDRA MAJOR

This low-growing joint pine has stiff upswept stems. Its papery leaves, up to 3mm (⅛in) long, grow in opposite pairs. Initially they are green, but later they turn dark brown. As with other members of the genus, male and female "flowers" grow on separate plants. The male flowers grow in stalkless, rounded clusters containing 2 to 4 pairs, whereas the female flowers are stalked and usually solitary. Female flowers produce rounded, red or yellow fruit.
• **DISTRIBUTION** Throughout.
• **HABITAT** Rocky and scrubby ground, often near the coast.
• **RELATED SPECIES** *Ephedra distachya*, found in the west and centre of the region, has similar upswept stems but slightly smaller leaves.

cluster of male flowers •

DETAIL

yellow flowers •

leaves dark brown when mature •

upswept stems do not break easily •

Habit Perennial	Height Up to 2m (6½ft)	Flowering time Apr–July

DICOTYLEDONS

OAK FAMILY

Family FAGACEAE	Species *Quercus coccifera*	Author L.

KERMES OAK

A thicket-forming shrub or small tree, the Kermes Oak has grèyish bark, which was once used as a source of tannin. The oval, spiny edged leaves, 15–40mm (⅗–1⅗in) long, are tough and hairless. The male flowers grow in slender catkins, and the female flowers produce prickly cupped acorns that take 2 years to ripen.
• **DISTRIBUTION** Throughout the Mediterranean region, except Corsica and most of Italy.
• **HABITAT** Garigue, maquis, open woodland.

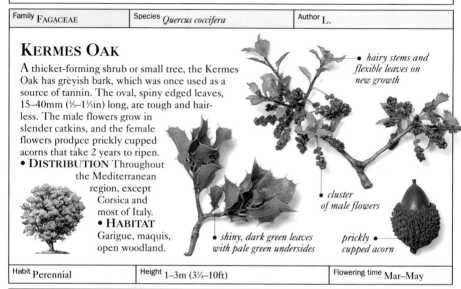

hairy stems and flexible leaves on new growth

cluster of male flowers

shiny, dark green leaves with pale green undersides

prickly cupped acorn

Habit Perennial	Height 1–3m (3¼–10ft)	Flowering time Mar–May

MULBERRY FAMILY

Family MORACEAE	Species *Ficus carica*	Author L.

FIG

The Fig is a deciduous tree or shrub with smooth grey bark, thick, blunt branches, and milky sap. Its alternate leaves, up to 20cm (8in) long, vary in shape from broadly elliptic to palmate, with 3 to 7 lobes and slightly serrated margins. Flowers are hidden inside green, fruit-like growths; those with female flowers develop into edible figs, 50–80mm (2–3⅕in) long.
• **DISTRIBUTION** Throughout the region.
• **HABITAT** Rocky places, fields, gardens.
• **REMARK** In the wild, figs are pollinated by a small species of wasp.

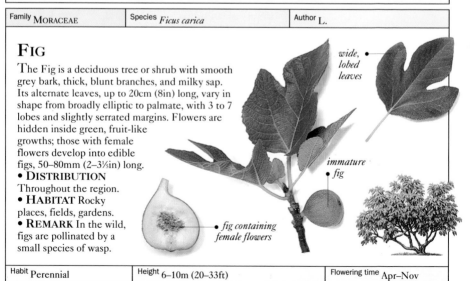

wide, lobed leaves

immature fig

fig containing female flowers

Habit Perennial	Height 6–10m (20–33ft)	Flowering time Apr–Nov

NETTLE FAMILY

Family URTICACEAE	Species *Urtica pilulifera*	Author L.

ROMAN NETTLE

This tall, distinctive nettle is covered with stinging hairs. Its leaves, 20–60mm (⅘–2⅖in) long, are arranged in opposite pairs, and are borne on long stalks with 4 stipules at each node. They are oval or heart-shaped, and have deeply toothed or lobed margins. Male and female flowers are separate, and arise from the leaf-axils. The female flowers hang on long stalks and form spherical heads, about 10mm (⅖in) in diameter. The male flowers are tiny, and grow in branching spikes. The fruit is a small achene.

- **DISTRIBUTION** Throughout the Mediterranean.
- **HABITAT** Damp waste ground rich in nutrients; also rubbish dumps.
- **REMARK** This species was once cultivated for its oily seeds.

female flowers armed with stinging hairs

spike of male flowers

male and female flowers arise from same leaf-axil

leaf bases rounded or heart-shaped

Habit Annual	Height 30–100cm (12–40in)	Flowering time Feb–Oct

Family URTICACEAE	Species *Urtica dubia*	Author Forskål

URTICA DUBIA

Sparingly covered with stinging hairs, this tall nettle has opposite, oval leaves up to 10cm (4in) long, with sharply serrated margins. The leaf-stalks are almost as long as the leaves. Male and female flowers are separate. Male flowers are grouped in straggling racemes that are longer than the leaf-stalks, while the female racemes, attached below the males, are shorter than the leaf-stalks.

- **DISTRIBUTION** Throughout the region.
- **HABITAT** Damp waste ground.
- **RELATED SPECIES** The annual nettle *Urtica urens* is similar, but has shorter racemes with both male and female flowers.

pointed tips to leaves

flowers arise from leaf-axils

leaves rounded or heart-shaped at base

leaf-axils contain 2 small stipules

Habit Annual	Height 15–80cm (6–32in)	Flowering time All year round

Family URTICACEAE	Species *Parietaria diffusa*	Author Mert. & Koch

PELLITORY-OF-THE-WALL

The stems of this widespread plant spread along the ground before growing upwards to form an erect clump. Each stem is covered with short hairs, and often has a reddish tinge. The leaves, up to 50mm (2in) long, are arranged alternately. They are elliptic and stalked, and are fringed with short hairs. The upper surface of the leaves is shiny, although this is frequently obscured by roadside dust. The flowers are inconspicuous, and grow in stalkless, globular clusters attached at the leaf-axils. The black achenes are enclosed by the segments of the flowers.

• **DISTRIBUTION** Throughout.
• **HABITAT** Foot of walls, damp, shady places.
• **RELATED SPECIES** *Parietaria officinalis*, Parietaria, is similar, but is generally un-branched. It is erect, and may grow up to 1m (40in) in height. It has larger leaves, up to 12cm (4¾in) long, and is densely hairy. It is found throughout the Mediterranean region, except the far west.

flower clusters attached at leaf-axils

clusters of flowers along erect portion of stem

leaves fringed with short hairs

elliptic leaves ending in a blunt point

Habit Perennial	Height Up to 40cm (16in)	Flowering time Apr–Oct

SANDALWOOD FAMILY

Family SANTALACEAE	Species *Osyris alba*	Author L.

OSYRIS ALBA

This brush-like, branching shrub has slender, stiff, slightly ribbed stems. The linear to lance-shaped leaves, about 20mm (⅞in) long, have pointed tips, and are alternate. Male and female flowers are borne on separate plants, and both are small, green, and incon-spicuous. Male flowers grow in lateral clusters; female flowers grow singly at the ends of short stalks. The fruit is a red, fleshy berry, 5–7mm (⅕–²⁄₅in) across.

• **DISTRIBUTION** Throughout.
• **HABITAT** Dry rocky places, maquis, forests.
• **REMARK** *Osyris alba* is a hemiparasite, deriving some of its nutrients from other plants.

tips of stems often leafless

DETAIL

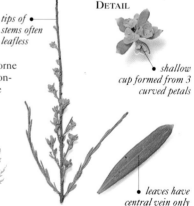

shallow cup formed from 3 curved petals

leaves have central vein only

Habit Perennial	Height 40–120cm (16–48in)	Flowering time Feb–Aug

BIRTHWORT FAMILY

Family ARISTOLOCHIACEAE	Species *Aristolochia pistolochia*	Author L.

ARISTOLOCHIA PISTOLOCHIA

Like all its relatives, this slightly hairy, zigzagging plant is instantly recognizable by its intriguing tubular flowers. Its alternate leaves, borne on short stems, are arrow-shaped and finely toothed. The erect flowers, up to 50mm (2in) long, have purplish throats, dark brown mouths, and inflated chambers at their bases. They produce spherical or pear-shaped fruit, 20–30mm (⅘–1⅛in) across.
• **DISTRIBUTION** W. Mediterranean including N. Africa, eastwards to Corsica and Sardinia.
• **HABITAT** Dry, rocky places.

dark brown mouth of flower

flower-tube almost straight

flowers borne in leaf-axils

leaves bright green above, grey-green below

Habit Perennial	Height 20–80cm (8–32in)	Flowering time Mar–July

Family ARISTOLOCHIACEAE	Species *Aristolochia cretica*	Author Lam.

ARISTOLOCHIA CRETICA

This erect and leathery plant, which branches at its base, has reddish brown, hairy stems, and kidney-shaped, alternate leaves that are at least as broad as their length of up to 60mm (2⅜in). The flowers, 5–12cm (2–4¾in) long, are shaped like miniature saxophones, with hairy throats that lure pollinating insects. Each elongated fruit is 30–60mm (1⅕–2⅖in) across.
• **DISTRIBUTION** Crete and Karpathos.
• **HABITAT** Rocky ground, base of terrace walls.

red veins on undersides of leaves

flower sliced open, showing hair-lined tube

reddish brown stems

finely notched edges to leaves

Habit Perennial	Height 30–60cm (12–24in)	Flowering time Apr–May

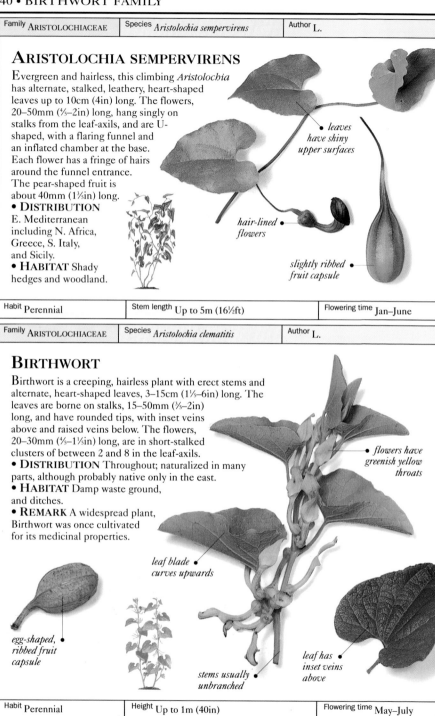

Family ARISTOLOCHIACEAE	Species *Aristolochia sempervirens*	Author L.

ARISTOLOCHIA SEMPERVIRENS

Evergreen and hairless, this climbing *Aristolochia* has alternate, stalked, leathery, heart-shaped leaves up to 10cm (4in) long. The flowers, 20–50mm (⅘–2in) long, hang singly on stalks from the leaf-axils, and are U-shaped, with a flaring funnel and an inflated chamber at the base. Each flower has a fringe of hairs around the funnel entrance. The pear-shaped fruit is about 40mm (1⅗in) long.

• **DISTRIBUTION** E. Mediterranean including N. Africa, Greece, S. Italy, and Sicily.

• **HABITAT** Shady hedges and woodland.

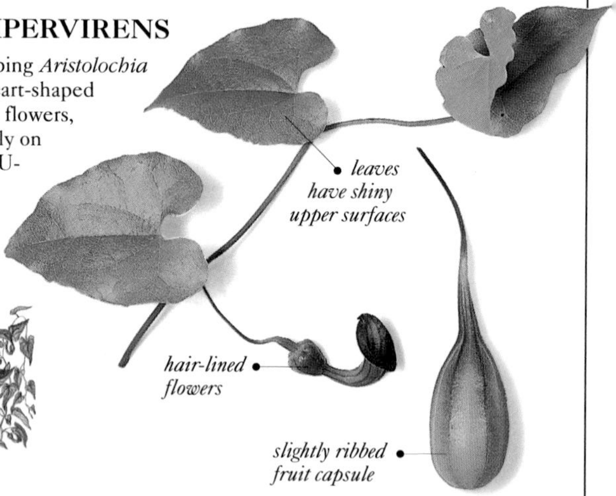
leaves have shiny upper surfaces
hair-lined flowers
slightly ribbed fruit capsule

Habit Perennial	Stem length Up to 5m (16½ft)	Flowering time Jan–June

Family ARISTOLOCHIACEAE	Species *Aristolochia clematitis*	Author L.

BIRTHWORT

Birthwort is a creeping, hairless plant with erect stems and alternate, heart-shaped leaves, 3–15cm (1⅕–6in) long. The leaves are borne on stalks, 15–50mm (⅗–2in) long, and have rounded tips, with inset veins above and raised veins below. The flowers, 20–30mm (⅘–1⅕in) long, are in short-stalked clusters of between 2 and 8 in the leaf-axils.

• **DISTRIBUTION** Throughout; naturalized in many parts, although probably native only in the east.

• **HABITAT** Damp waste ground, and ditches.

• **REMARK** A widespread plant, Birthwort was once cultivated for its medicinal properties.

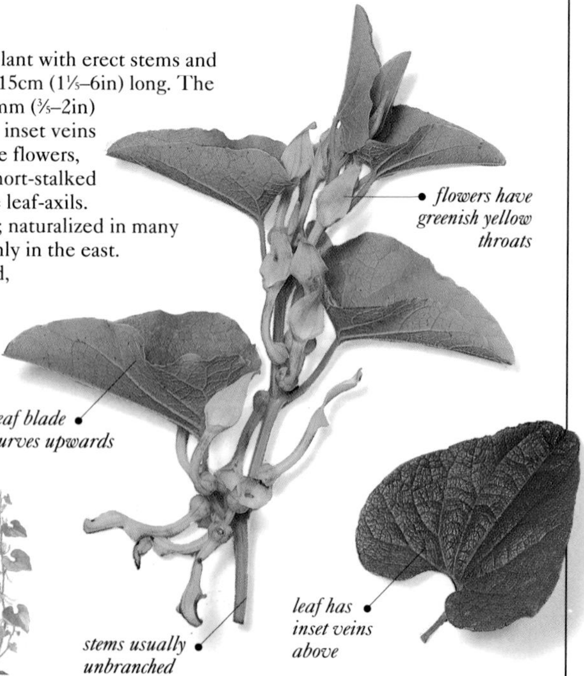
flowers have greenish yellow throats
leaf blade curves upwards
stems usually unbranched
leaf has inset veins above

egg-shaped, ribbed fruit capsule

Habit Perennial	Height Up to 1m (40in)	Flowering time May–July

Family ARISTOLOCHIACEAE	Species *Aristolochia rotunda*	Author L.

ROUND-LEAVED BIRTHWORT

An erect or spreading plant, Round-leaved Birthwort
has several simple or branched, almost hairless
stems growing from an underground tuber. The
leaves, 20–90mm (⅘–3⅗in) long, are stalkless
and clasp the stem with their enlarged basal
lobes. The veins on the upper surfaces of the
leaves are inset; underneath they are raised.
The flowers, 20–50mm (⅘–2in)
long, are erect with a prominent
dark brown flap and a greenish
yellow outer tube. The spherical fruit
is 10–20mm (⅖–⅘in) in diameter.
• **DISTRIBUTION** Throughout,
except N.W. Africa.
• **HABITAT** Damp shady
places, hedges, ditches,
field edges, woods.

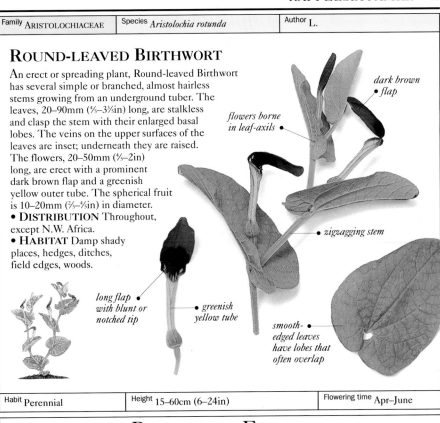

dark brown flap

flowers borne in leaf-axils

zigzagging stem

long flap with blunt or notched tip

greenish yellow tube

smooth-edged leaves have lobes that often overlap

Habit Perennial	Height 15–60cm (6–24in)	Flowering time Apr–June

RAFFLESIA FAMILY

Family RAFFLESIACEAE	Species *Cytinus hypocistis*	Author L.

CYTINUS HYPOCISTIS

This low-growing plant has no green leaves, and
parasitizes rock-roses (see pp.146–49). Despite its
small size, its bright colours make it easy to
spot underneath the host plant. Its
fleshy clusters of 5 to 10 flowers,
12mm (½in) across, are initially
covered with brilliant red-tipped
scales, but these open to reveal the
yellow flowers within. The central
flowers are male, the peripheral ones
female, and all have 4 petals with
serrated edges. The fruit is a berry.
• **DISTRIBUTION** Throughout.
• **HABITAT** Maquis and garigue
beneath rock-rose plants.

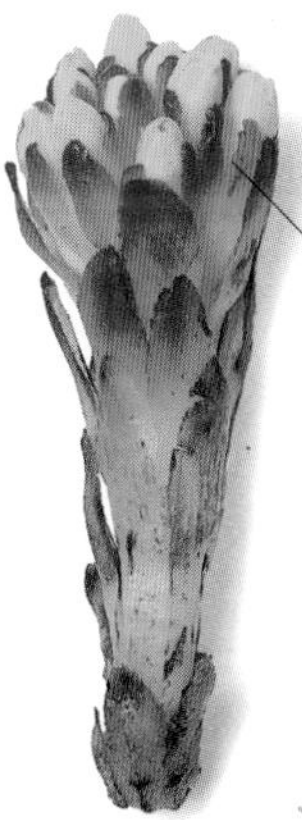

flower cluster borne just above ground level

cluster of male flowers surrounded by female flowers

Habit Perennial	Height 30–70mm (1⅕–2⅘in)	Flowering time Apr–June

DOCK FAMILY

Family POLYGONACEAE	Species *Polygonum maritimum*	Author L.

SEA KNOTGRASS

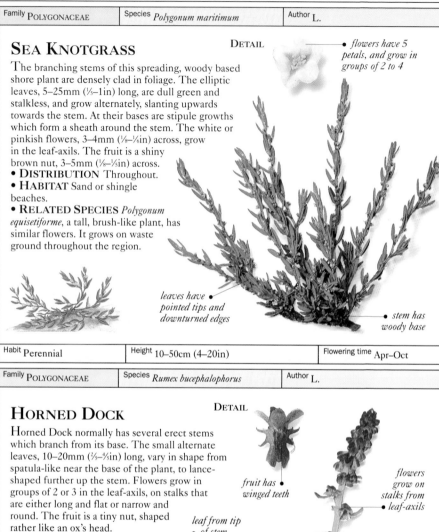

DETAIL

• *flowers have 5 petals, and grow in groups of 2 to 4*

The branching stems of this spreading, woody based shore plant are densely clad in foliage. The elliptic leaves, 5–25mm (⅕–1in) long, are dull green and stalkless, and grow alternately, slanting upwards towards the stem. At their bases are stipule growths which form a sheath around the stem. The white or pinkish flowers, 3–4mm (⅛–⅙in) across, grow in the leaf-axils. The fruit is a shiny brown nut, 3–5mm (⅛–⅕in) across.
• **DISTRIBUTION** Throughout.
• **HABITAT** Sand or shingle beaches.
• **RELATED SPECIES** *Polygonum equisetiforme*, a tall, brush-like plant, has similar flowers. It grows on waste ground throughout the region.

leaves have pointed tips and downturned edges

stem has woody base

Habit Perennial	Height 10–50cm (4–20in)	Flowering time Apr–Oct

Family POLYGONACEAE	Species *Rumex bucephalophorus*	Author L.

HORNED DOCK

DETAIL

Horned Dock normally has several erect stems which branch from its base. The small alternate leaves, 10–20mm (⅖–⅘in) long, vary in shape from spatula-like near the base of the plant, to lance-shaped further up the stem. Flowers grow in groups of 2 or 3 in the leaf-axils, on stalks that are either long and flat or narrow and round. The fruit is a tiny nut, shaped rather like an ox's head.
• **DISTRIBUTION** Throughout.
• **HABITAT** Cultivated ground, rocky and sandy places, often near the sea.
• **REMARK** Horned Dock is a highly variable species. Some plants have only a single stem.

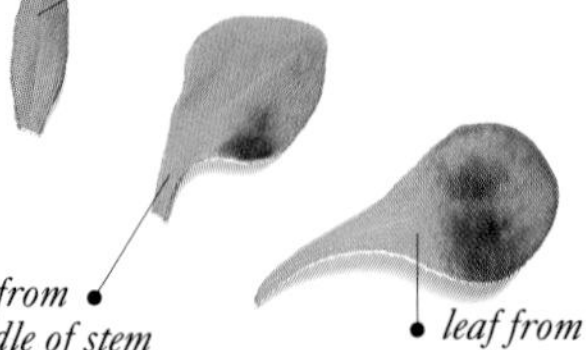

fruit has winged teeth

flowers grow on stalks from leaf-axils

leaf from tip of stem

leaf from middle of stem

leaf from base of stem

Habit Generally annual	Height 10–40cm (4–16in)	Flowering time Mar–Sept

FAT HEN FAMILY

Family CHENOPODIACEAE	Species *Halimione portulacoides*	Author (L.) Aellen

SEA PURSLANE

Ascending or prostrate, Sea Purslane is a small shrub with lax stems, fleshy foliage, and a woody base. Its leaves are arranged mainly in opposite pairs, and range from elliptic to lance-shaped, reaching about 40mm (1⅜in) long, with entire margins. They have a mealy surface, which gives the plant a grey or silvery appearance. The tiny yellowish flowers are formed in long-stalked clusters from the leaf-axils. The male flowers are composed of 4 or 5 segments, whereas the female flowers have just 2 bracts.
• **DISTRIBUTION** Throughout.
• **HABITAT** Salt marshes, beaches, coastal hinterland.

• *clusters of flowers in bud*

• *stem has silvery coloration*

• *leaves are thick and fleshy*

• *leaf margins entire*

Habit Perennial	Height 20–80cm (8–32in)	Flowering time July–Oct

Family CHENOPODIACEAE	Species *Salicornia europaea*	Author L.

GLASSWORT

Glasswort is a fleshy, hairless plant with jointed, succulent stems and opposite, scale-like leaves that lie flat on the stems. The plant is brilliant green in spring, but acquires a red tint towards flowering time in late summer. The flowers, which are borne in the leaf-axils, are extremely small, and are green with yellow anthers. The seeds are up to 1.5mm (¹⁄₁₆in) long, with a membrane-like coat.
• **DISTRIBUTION** Throughout.
• **HABITAT** Salt marshes, at or close to standing water.
• **REMARK** Glasswort frequently grows in swathes, with the individual plants crowded together to form a brightly coloured carpet over wet, salty ground. There are several similar species, which can be distinguished only with some difficulty. All of them have a high salt content, and they were at one time burned to provide soda used in the glass-making process.

• *flowers are borne where leaves meet stem*

upswept branches •

• *branches point upwards*

fleshy, jointed stem •

Habit Annual	Height 10–40cm (4–16in)	Flowering time Aug–Sept

Family CHENOPODIACEAE	Species *Salsola kali*	Author L.

PRICKLY SALTWORT

A variable plant, Prickly Saltwort has spreading, ascending, or erect branches and a straggling appearance. Its stems are green or yellowish, and may or may not have hairs. The fleshy leaves, 10–40mm (⅖–1⅗in) long, are roughly cylindrical with spined tips, the lowest being arranged alternately. The flowers are tiny and inconspicuous, located in groups of one to 3 in the leaf-axils, and are surrounded by spine-tipped scales which are larger and more evident than the flowers themselves. The fruit is winged.
• **DISTRIBUTION** Throughout.
• **HABITAT** Loose beach sand and waste ground; also sometimes inland.
• **RELATED SPECIES** There are many similar species in the region. The widespread *Salsola soda* has soft-tipped leaves. *S. aegea*, from Greece and Crete, reaches only 30cm (12in).

spine-tipped leaves have broad bases

branches grow upwards or horizontally

stem ribbed and sometimes hairy

Habit Annual	Height 10–100cm (4–40in)	Flowering time July–Oct

AMARANTH FAMILY

Family AMARANTHACEAE	Species *Amaranthus cruentus*	Author L.

AMARANTHUS CRUENTUS

This branched plant is generally sparsely haired, although more densely haired at the stem tops. Its alternate, stalked leaves, 5–12cm (2–4¾in) long, are broadly elliptic. The minute flowers grow in dense spikes arising from the leaf-axils and the top of the stem, and they are surrounded by soft scales (bracteoles) which give the spikes a brush-like texture. The tiny fruit is dry and membranous.
• **DISTRIBUTION** Throughout.
• **HABITAT** Waste ground.
• **REMARK** A native of tropical America, this is one of several *Amaranthus* species that have become naturalized in the Mediterranean region. Almost all of them have inconspicuous yellow or green flowers.

dense inflorescence

tiny flowers surrounded by protruding bracteoles

leaves elliptic or oval with a long stalk

lower stem almost hairless

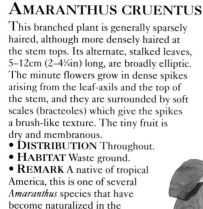

Habit Annual	Height 15–100cm (6–40in)	Flowering time June–Sept

FOUR O'CLOCK FAMILY

Family NYCTAGINACEAE	Species *Bougainvillea glabra*	Author Choisy

BOUGAINVILLEA

The most striking feature of Bougainvillea is its numerous brightly coloured bracts, which are often mistaken for petals. A tall, climbing, woody plant, it has spiny stems that are normally hairless. The leaves, up to 60mm (2⅜in) long, are alternate and short-stalked. The bracts range in colour from pink to dark purple, and are arranged in clusters of 3. Each cluster encloses 3 small, tubular flowers, 14–24mm (½–1in) long, which have cream-coloured mouths.
• **DISTRIBUTION** Throughout.
• **HABITAT** Gardens, walls.
• **REMARK** This species is a native of Brazil.

small, tubular flowers

each bract clasps a single flower

leaf has glossy upper surface

broadly elliptic evergreen leaves taper to a point

Habit Perennial	Height Up to 10m (33ft)	Flowering time All year round

Family NYCTAGINACEAE	Species *Mirabilis jalapa*	Author L.

FOUR O'CLOCK PLANT

The Four O'clock Plant is so named because its flowers usually open in the late afternoon. Generally hairless and much-branched, it has opposite, short-stalked, and broadly elliptic leaves, up to 15cm (6in) long. The flowers, which can be red, yellow, or white, have a 5-pointed, fused calyx and projecting stamens. The flower-tube is up to 30mm (1⅛in) long. The black fruit, 10mm (⅜in) long, is lemon-shaped.
• **DISTRIBUTION** Throughout the region, but most common in west.
• **HABITAT** Cultivated land, and gardens.
• **REMARK** This species is a frequent escape from cultivation; it is native to tropical America.

flowers in clusters at stem tips

tapering leaves

trumpet-shaped flowers

petals roll inwards after flowering

Habit Perennial	Height 50–100cm (20–40in)	Flowering time June–Oct

POKEWEED FAMILY

Family PHYTOLACCACEAE	Species *Phytolacca americana*	Author L.

AMERICAN POKEWEED

Often seen on roadsides and rubbish tips, this vigorous herbaceous plant has erect and slightly fleshy, hairless stems which frequently fork. The hairless, alternate leaves, 10–25cm (4–10in) long, are stalked and elliptic with untoothed margins. Slight swellings are often apparent where the leaf-stalks join the stems. The flowers grow in dense racemes up to 15cm (6in) long, and are pinkish white with 5 segments. The ribbed, berry-like fruit, about 10mm (⅜in) in diameter, is purplish black and pumpkin-shaped. As the fruit forms, the fruiting stalks bend over until they hang downwards.
• **DISTRIBUTION** Throughout.
• **HABITAT** Waste ground, rubbish tips, waysides, gardens.
• **REMARK** A native of N. America, this plant was once grown for a dye made from its fruit, which was used for colouring wine. However, all parts of the plant, including the fruit, are poisonous.

fruiting stalk eventually bends under weight of fruit

alternate leaves

pinkish white flowers grow in dense racemes

large leaves with untoothed margins

fruiting stalk with green unripe fruit

fleshy green stems

Habit Perennial	Height 1–2.5m (3¼–8ft)	Flowering time June–Oct

MESEMBRYANTHEMUM FAMILY

Family AIZOACEAE	Species *Carpobrotus edulis*	Author L.

HOTTENTOT FIG

This fleshy, creeping plant has woody-based stems, which often form extensive mats on roadsides and on coasts. The tapering, waxy leaves, 8–12cm (3⅕–4¾in) long, are triangular in cross-section. They are arranged in opposite pairs and have slightly serrated edges. The spectacular flowers, 60–90mm (2⅖–3⅗in) across, are borne singly, with a circular fringe of numerous, overlapping, linear petals of bright purple, yellow, or orange surrounding the yellow stamens. The fleshy fruit is edible.

- **DISTRIBUTION** Throughout.
- **HABITAT** Coastal areas.

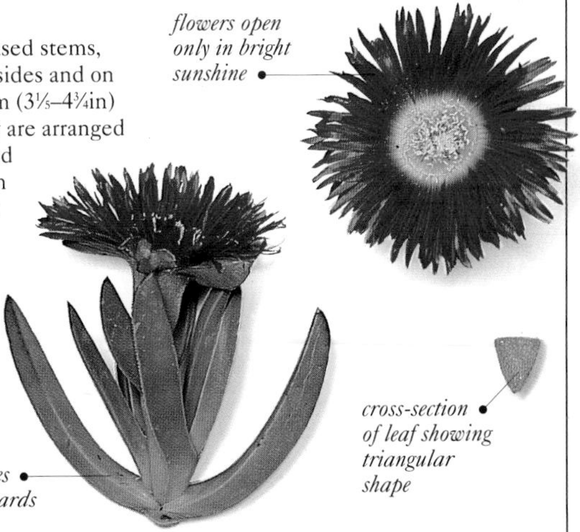
flowers open only in bright sunshine
fleshy leaves curve upwards
cross-section of leaf showing triangular shape

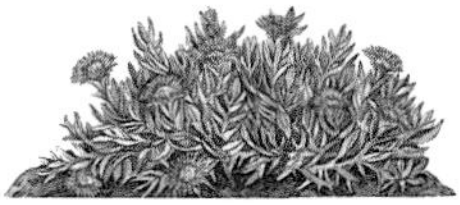

Habit Perennial	Stem length Up to 2m (6½ft)	Flowering time Mar–July

PURSLANE FAMILY

Family PORTULACACEAE	Species *Portulaca oleracea*	Author L.

PURSLANE

With its fleshy stems and glossy leaves, this spreading plant is a common sight on disturbed ground throughout the Mediterranean region. Its hairless, branching stems usually hug the ground. The leaves are spoon-shaped, and are clustered at the stem tips. The flowers, 5mm (⅕in) across, are borne either singly or in groups of 2 or 3, in the forks of the stems.

- **DISTRIBUTION** Throughout.
- **HABITAT** Waste ground and gardens.
- **REMARK** The subspecies *sativa*, cultivated Purslane, is often grown as a salad vegetable. It is an erect plant and is generally much more robust.

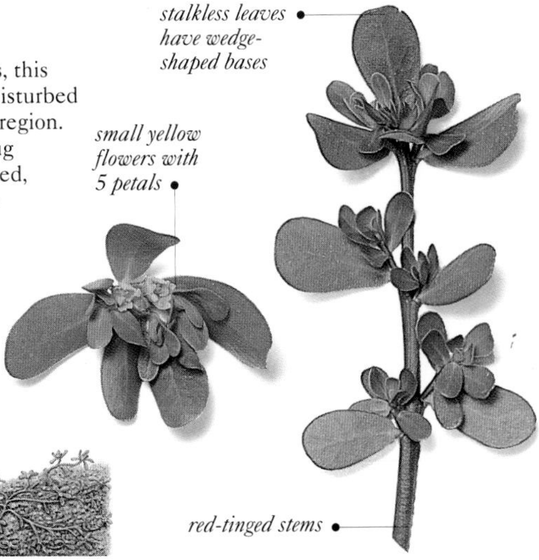
stalkless leaves have wedge-shaped bases
small yellow flowers with 5 petals
red-tinged stems

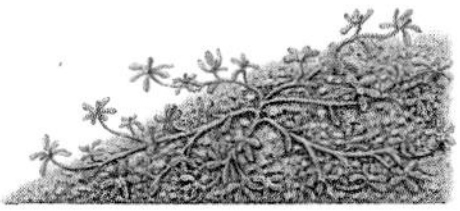

Habit Annual	Stem length Up to 50cm (20in)	Flowering time June–Aug

PINK FAMILY

Family CARYOPHYLLACEAE	Species *Paronychia argentea*	Author Lam.

PARONYCHIA ARGENTEA

A much-branched and mat-forming plant, *Paronychia argentea* has opposite, stalkless, lance-shaped leaves, 4–10mm (⅙–⅖in) long, with pointed tips. The petal-less flowers form at the leaf-axils in clusters that are about 10mm (⅖in) across, and are surrounded by distinctive, silvery, translucent bracts. Each flower has 5 sepals, and each sepal is tipped with a reddish brown bristly point. The fruit is a single-seeded nut.

- **DISTRIBUTION** Throughout.
- **HABITAT** Dry sandy places, including beaches and edges of coastal tracks.
- **RELATED SPECIES** Several similar species are found in mountains bordering the region. *P. capitata*, with longer bracts and narrow, greyish green leaves, is widespread.

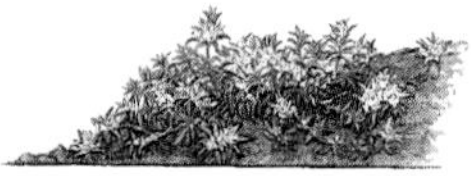

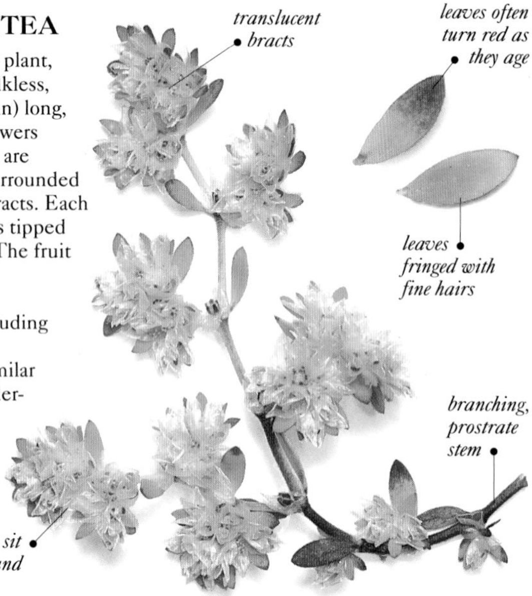
translucent bracts
leaves often turn red as they age
leaves fringed with fine hairs
branching, prostrate stem
flowers sit on ground

Habit Perennial	Stem length Up to 20cm (8in)	Flowering time Apr–June

Family CARYOPHYLLACEAE	Species *Spergularia marina*	Author (L.) Griseb.

LESSER SEA-SPURREY

This short, slender-stemmed plant has opposite, linear, fleshy, pointed leaves and short stipules. The flowers, 5–8mm (⅕–⅓in) across, are borne singly on branching stems. Their petals are largely pink with white near the base, or are sometimes entirely white, and they close rapidly if conditions become dull. The seed capsules are normally wider than the sepals, and contain winged or unwinged seeds, or a mixture of the two.

- **DISTRIBUTION** Throughout.
- **HABITAT** Salt marshes, and stony verges near to the sea.
- **RELATED SPECIES** Similar species include *Spergularia bocconii*, a sticky plant that is common in the west.

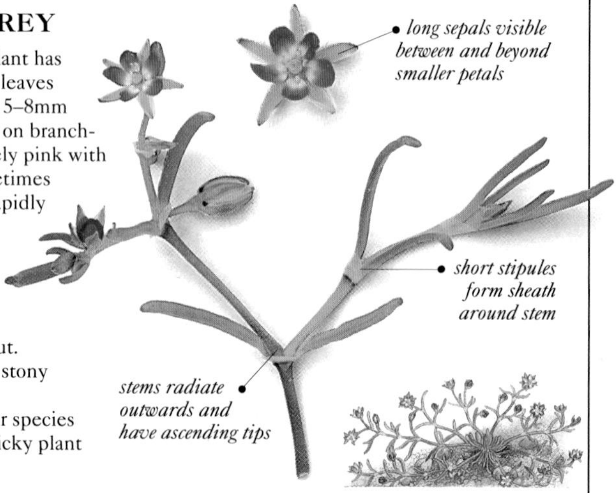
long sepals visible between and beyond smaller petals
short stipules form sheath around stem
stems radiate outwards and have ascending tips

Habit Annual/biennial	Height 70mm (2⅘in)	Flowering time Apr–Aug

Family CARYOPHYLLACEAE	Species *Agrostemma githago*	Author L.

CORNCOCKLE

A native of the eastern Mediterranean,
Corncockle was once a widespread weed. It is a
tall plant, covered in long, soft, greyish hairs, and
its stalkless, opposite leaves are linear or narrowly
lance-shaped, and almost meet around the stems.
The flowers, 30–70mm (1⅕–2⅖in) across, are
pinkish purple and have 5 notched, wedge-
shaped petals. The bases of the sepals
unite to form an urn-shaped tube, and
their narrow tips spread outwards beyond
the petals. The fruit is a capsule containing
rounded seeds, over 3mm (⅛in) in diameter,
which are poisonous.
• **DISTRIBUTION** Throughout.
• **HABITAT** Cornfields,
cultivated land.
• **RELATED SPECIES** A
smaller, more slender, and
less hairy species, *Agrostemma
gracilis*, is found only in Greece
and Asia Minor. Its sepals do
not extend beyond the petals.
Its calyx-tube, which is narrower than that of *A. githago*,
is the same length or longer
than the sepal teeth.

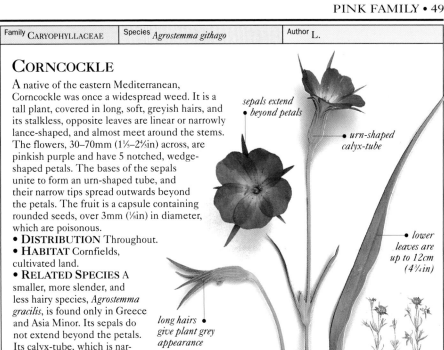

*sepals extend
• beyond petals*

*• urn-shaped
calyx-tube*

*• lower
leaves are
up to 12cm
(4¼in)*

*long hairs •
give plant grey
appearance*

Habit Annual	Height 30–100cm (12–40in)	Flowering time Apr–June

Family CARYOPHYLLACEAE	Species *Silene sericea*	Author All.·

SILENE SERICEA

This low-growing, softly hairy plant has
ascending, branching stems. The leaves are
opposite. They are spatula-shaped at the
base of the stems, and lance-shaped
and curved at the top. Flowers
are borne singly or, rarely, in
clusters of 2 or 3, and have
narrow tubular calyces with 10
distinct stripes. The petals are
pale pink with 2 deep lobes.
The seeds are kidney-shaped.
• **DISTRIBUTION** Italy,
Corsica, Sardinia.
• **HABITAT** Coastal sand.
• **RELATED SPECIES**
Silene colorata, found in the E.
Mediterranean, is similar but
has flowers borne in clusters.

*calyx has stripes
• and pointed teeth*

*petals •
curved
up with
deep
notch*

*pale pink
• flowers*

*lower
leaves up
to 20mm
(⅘in) long •*

Habit Annual	Height Up to 50cm (20in)	Flowering time Mar–June

Family CARYOPHYLLACEAE	Species *Silene gallica*	Author L.

SMALL-FLOWERED CATCHFLY

Like many catchflies, this erect plant is covered in short, sticky hairs. The leaves, 20mm (⅘in) long, are opposite and stalkless. Its flowers may be white or pink, and arise in the leaf-axils. The base of the petals is enclosed by a bulbous calyx with long hairs, prominent veins, and teeth. The fruit is a capsule containing dark brown seeds.
• **DISTRIBUTION** Throughout the region.
• **HABITAT** Cultivated ground, waysides.
• **REMARK** Catchflies are so named because their sticky hairs frequently trap flies and other small insects.

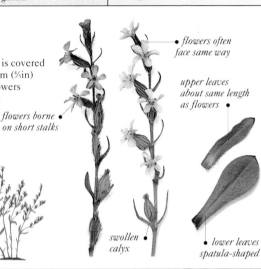

• *flowers often face same way*

upper leaves about same length as flowers •

flowers borne on short stalks

swollen calyx •

• *lower leaves spatula-shaped*

Habit Annual	Height 15–45cm (6–18in)	Flowering time Mar–June

Family CARYOPHYLLACEAE	Species *Silene vulgaris*	Author (Moench) Garcke

BLADDER CAMPION

A highly variable plant, Bladder Campion is generally hairless and woody based, with erect, branching stems and opposite, linear to ovate leaves about 60mm (2⅖in) long. The lower leaves are stalked, whereas the upper ones clasp the stems. The flowers, borne in stalked clusters, have deeply lobed white petals. The distinctively swollen, bladder-like calyces remain after the petals have withered, and form a partial or complete envelope around the seed capsule.
• **DISTRIBUTION** Throughout the region.
• **HABITAT** Cultivated and fallow land, roadsides; on dry or chalky soils.
• **RELATED SPECIES** *Silene alba*, White Campion, is similar but has calyces that are only slightly inflated. It is also found throughout.

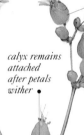

flowers borne in cymes •

calyx remains attached after petals wither •

DETAIL

bladder-like calyx, enclosing base of petals, has 5 teeth

stalkless leaves from upper part of stem •

stem woody towards base •

thread-like, protruding stigmas

Habit Perennial	Height Up to 60cm (24in)	Flowering time Apr–Aug

| Family CARYOPHYLLACEAE | Species *Saponaria officinalis* | Author L. |

SOAPWORT

Soapwort spreads vigorously by underground runners, and has erect and normally hairless stems. Its ovate to lance-shaped leaves, 40–70mm (1⅗–2⅖in) long, are predominantly stalkless, and have pointed tips and 3 parallel veins. The flowers, which are 40mm (1⅗in) in diameter, have an intense fragrance and are borne in dense, oppositely arranged clusters, with a terminal cluster at the tip of the stem. They have pink petals, without notches. The fruit is a cylindrical capsule, which splits to release the seeds.
• **DISTRIBUTION** Throughout.
• **HABITAT** Damp waysides.
• **RELATED SPECIES** *Saponaria calabrica*, found from Italy eastwards, is a smaller, more delicate plant with rounded petals and a sticky texture.

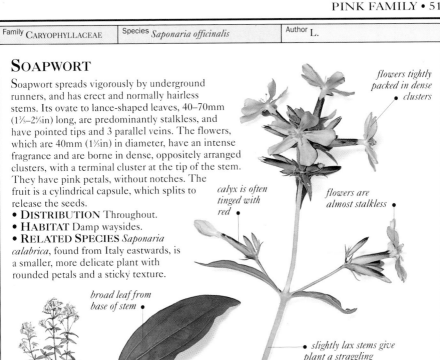

flowers tightly packed in dense clusters

calyx is often tinged with red

flowers are almost stalkless

broad leaf from base of stem

slightly lax stems give plant a straggling appearance

| Habit Perennial | Height 30–90cm (12–36in) | Flowering time Apr–July |

| Family CARYOPHYLLACEAE | Species *Vaccaria pyramidata* | Author Medicus |

COW BASIL

An erect, branched, hairless plant, Cow Basil has a distinctive grey-blue bloom and winged calyces. Its opposite leaves, up to 50mm (2in) long, are ovate with pointed tips, and have a waxy texture. The upper leaves clasp the stem. The pink flowers are borne singly on long stalks in many-branched clusters, and their petals may be notched or entire. Their calyces are swollen, with 5 flattened wings and a constricted throat, producing a distinctive urn-shaped outline. The seeds are borne in an egg-shaped capsule.
• **DISTRIBUTION** Throughout.
• **HABITAT** Cultivated land.
• **REMARK** Cow Basil is a widespread field weed.

pointed teeth at apex of calyx

broad, clasping leaves from middle part of stem

petals may be slightly notched

slender stem

| Habit Annual | Height 30–60cm (12–24in) | Flowering time May–June |

Family CARYOPHYLLACEAE	Species *Petrorhagia glumacea*	Author (Chaub. & Bory) Ball & Heywood

PETRORHAGIA GLUMACEA

An erect plant with slender, sparingly branched stems, *Petrorhagia glumacea* has paired, linear leaves which are arranged in opposite pairs and which sheathe the stems. The flowers are about 20mm (⅘in) across, and are borne in compact heads of between 2 and 5, which are surrounded by distinctive brown, dry, papery bracts. The 5 petals are veined. They are bright purple, wedge-shaped, and often have ragged edges. The calyces are tubular, 15mm (⅗in) long, and have 5 extremely short teeth. The seeds form in a 4-toothed capsule.
• **DISTRIBUTION** Balkans, Crete.
• **HABITAT** Rocks, grassy ground, and track edges.
• **REMARK** This variable species is sometimes divided into 2 subspecies, one of which, subsp. *obcordata*, has petals that are entire rather than ragged.

dry, papery bracts enclose a cluster of up to 5 flowers

petals often have irregularly cut outer margins

leaves and stem hairless

undersides of petals pale-coloured

Habit Annual	Height Up to 50cm (20in)	Flowering time May–June

Family CARYOPHYLLACEAE	Species *Petrorhagia velutina*	Author (Gussone) Ball & Heywood

PETRORHAGIA VELUTINA

A delicate, almost grass-like plant, *Petrorhagia velutina* normally branches only at its base. The middle part of the stem is covered with short, sticky hairs, and the slender, paired stem-leaves meet to form a sheath that is at least twice as long as it is wide. The flowers, less than 10mm (⅖in) across, are borne in the same manner as those of *P. glumacea* (above) but differ in having bracts with pointed tips, and pink, twin-lobed, veined petals. The fruit is a 4-toothed capsule.
• **DISTRIBUTION** Throughout.
• **HABITAT** Rocky or grassy ground.
• **RELATED SPECIES** *P. prolifera* is similar, but its leaf-sheaths are about as long as they are wide, and there are more flowers in each head.

flowers appear singly

pointed tips to outer bracts

deeply notched petals

grass-like basal leaves grow in a rosette at ground level

Habit Annual	Height 10–50cm (4–20in)	Flowering time Mar–May

Family CARYOPHYLLACEAE	Species *Dianthus carthusianorum*	Author L.

CARTHUSIAN PINK

This variable, hairless pink has a tuft of grass-like leaves at its base. Where the stem-leaves meet, they form a sheath that is much longer than the diameter of the stem. The flowers grow in clusters and have cylindrical calyces, constricting slightly at the tip. As in all *Dianthus* species, the calyx is surrounded by a set of opposing bracts, which in this case are about half as long as the calyx. The veined flowers, which are 20–30mm (⅘–1⅛in) in diameter, are deep pink with 5 distinctive toothed petals.
• **DISTRIBUTION** Throughout the Mediterranean region, except Greece; also widespread throughout W. and C. Europe.
• **HABITAT** Dry, grassy places, open woodland.

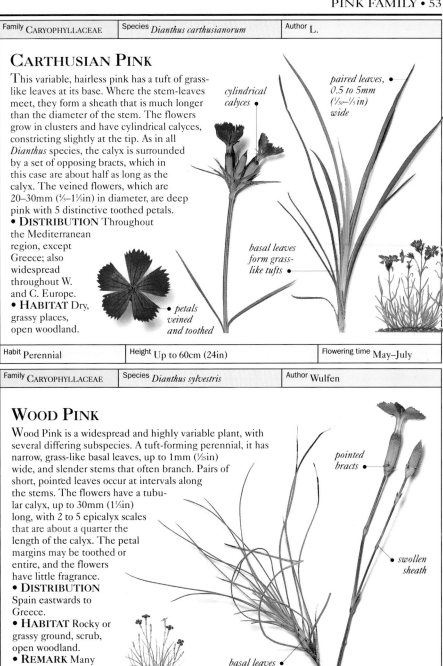

cylindrical calyces •

paired leaves, •
0.5 to 5mm
(¹/₅₀–⅕in)
wide

basal leaves
form grass-
like tufts •

• *petals*
veined
and toothed

Habit Perennial	Height Up to 60cm (24in)	Flowering time May–July

Family CARYOPHYLLACEAE	Species *Dianthus sylvestris*	Author Wulfen

WOOD PINK

Wood Pink is a widespread and highly variable plant, with several differing subspecies. A tuft-forming perennial, it has narrow, grass-like basal leaves, up to 1mm (¹/₂₅in) wide, and slender stems that often branch. Pairs of short, pointed leaves occur at intervals along the stems. The flowers have a tubular calyx, up to 30mm (1⅛in) long, with 2 to 5 epicalyx scales that are about a quarter the length of the calyx. The petal margins may be toothed or entire, and the flowers have little fragrance.
• **DISTRIBUTION** Spain eastwards to Greece.
• **HABITAT** Rocky or grassy ground, scrub, open woodland.
• **REMARK** Many other *Dianthus* species are found in the region.

pointed
bracts •

• *swollen*
sheath

basal leaves •
in compact tufts

• *woody rootstock*

Habit Perennial	Height 10–60cm (4–24in)	Flowering time May–July

BUTTERCUP FAMILY

Family RANUNCULACEAE	Species *Helleborus lividus*	Author Aiton

HELLEBORUS LIVIDUS

This robust, poisonous plant has palmate, compound leaves, which sheathe the stems and persist through the winter. In the subspecies *corsicus*, the leaf margins have spiny teeth; in subspecies *lividus*, the teeth are small or absent. Each flower, 30–60mm (1⅕–2⅜in) across, has 5 sepals, and lance-shaped bracts. The seeds form in clusters of 3 to 4 follicles with beak-like tips.
• **DISTRIBUTION** Subsp. *corsicus*: Corsica and Sardinia; subsp. *lividus*: Balearic Islands.
• **HABITAT** Woodland and shady sites.

• clusters of flowers facing same way

leaves divided into 3 segments •

stalked, • leathery leaves

SUBSP. CORSICUS

Habit Perennial	Height 20–80cm (8–32in)	Flowering time Nov–Apr

Family RANUNCULACEAE	Species *Helleborus foetidus*	Author L.

STINKING HELLEBORE

Stinking Hellebore gets its name from the distinctive foul smell exuded when it is crushed. It is similar to *Helleborus lividus* (above), except that its leaves are divided into between 7 and 11 narrow, linear segments. The flowers, 10–30mm (⅖–1⅕in) across, are smaller, and the sepals often develop characteristic reddish purple margins. It usually has 3 follicles.
• **DISTRIBUTION** W. Mediterranean, eastwards as far as Italy.
• **HABITAT** Dry, rocky woods.
• **RELATED SPECIES** The similar species *H. cyclophyllus*, found in the E. Mediterranean, has broader leaflets.

drooping, bell-shaped • flowers

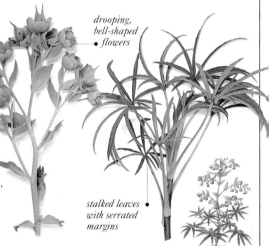

stalked leaves with serrated margins

Habit Perennial	Height 20–80cm (8–32in)	Flowering time Jan–Apr

Family RANUNCULACEAE	Species *Nigella damascena*	Author L.

LOVE-IN-A-MIST

An attractive plant that is often cultivated, Love-in-a-Mist has striking pale blue or white flowers, 40–50mm (1⅗–2in) across, which are borne singly. The leaves are alternate, and much-divided into narrow, thread-like segments. The flowers have a ring of bracts similar to the leaves, and numerous prominent stamens. After flowering, the joined carpels inflate to form a dry, spherical fruit up to 30mm (1⅛in) across.
• **DISTRIBUTION** Throughout the region.
• **HABITAT** Olive groves, fields, and stony, fallow land.
• **RELATED SPECIES** *Nigella arvensis*, a similar, widespread species, has smaller flowers without spreading bracts.

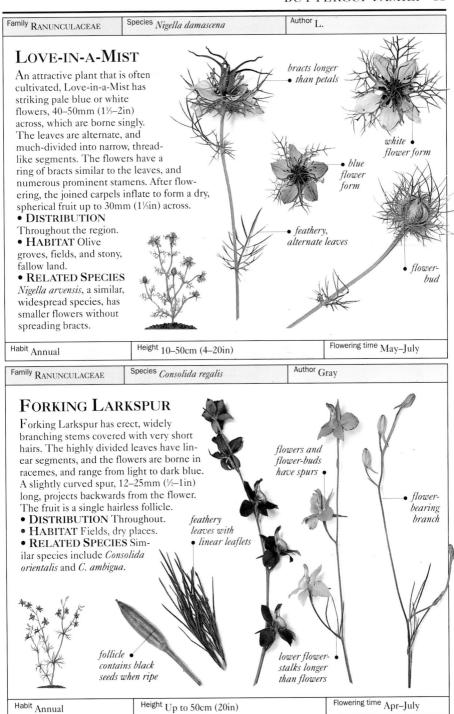

bracts longer than petals

white flower form

blue flower form

feathery, alternate leaves

flower-bud

Habit Annual	Height 10–50cm (4–20in)	Flowering time May–July

Family RANUNCULACEAE	Species *Consolida regalis*	Author Gray

FORKING LARKSPUR

Forking Larkspur has erect, widely branching stems covered with very short hairs. The highly divided leaves have linear segments, and the flowers are borne in racemes, and range from light to dark blue. A slightly curved spur, 12–25mm (½–1in) long, projects backwards from the flower. The fruit is a single hairless follicle.
• **DISTRIBUTION** Throughout.
• **HABITAT** Fields, dry places.
• **RELATED SPECIES** Similar species include *Consolida orientalis* and *C. ambigua*.

flowers and flower-buds have spurs

flower-bearing branch

feathery leaves with linear leaflets

follicle contains black seeds when ripe

lower flower-stalks longer than flowers

Habit Annual	Height Up to 50cm (20in)	Flowering time Apr–July

Family RANUNCULACEAE	Species *Anemone coronaria*	Author L.

CROWN ANEMONE

Small but exceptionally showy, Crown Anemone is one of the highlights of early spring in the Mediterranean region. Its stems are covered with short, white hairs. The basal leaves are stalked, and divided into 3 lobed segments, which are triangular in outline; leaves higher up the stem are deeply cut into narrow divisions. The conspicuous flowers, 35–65mm (1⅖–2⅗in) in diameter, are borne singly. They may be red, violet, blue, or white, with one colour usually being predominant in a particular area. They have 5 to 8 overlapping, oval, petal-like sepals, dark blue anthers, and a ruff of leafy bracts beneath. The flowers open wide in bright sunshine, closing up at dusk and in dull weather. The woolly achenes are borne in spreading heads.

• **DISTRIBUTION** Throughout.
• **HABITAT** Pastures, olive groves.
• **REMARK** Frequently cultivated for its beautiful flowers; garden varieties are often double-petalled.

cup-shaped sepals fold inwards in dull conditions

number of sepals varies from 5 to 8

silky hairs on underside of sepals

ruff of divided bracts

stems covered with short, white hairs

basal leaves with 3 finely divided, lobed segments

numerous stamens with dark blue anthers

Habit Perennial	Height 15–45cm (6–18in)	Flowering time Jan–Apr

Family RANUNCULACEAE	Species *Anemone pavonina*	Author L.

ANEMONE PAVONINA

This striking plant is similar to *Anemone coronaria* (opposite) but has 7 to 12 slender sepals. The basal leaves are variable, but often have lobed leaflets instead of being deeply divided. The ruff of bracts is situated some distance down the stem from the flower, and the bracts are lance-shaped, rather than finely divided. The flowers are red, pink, or purple, and often have a white central ring. As with other anemones, the fruit is an achene.
• **DISTRIBUTION** S.W. France to Turkey.
• **HABITAT** Cultivated land, pastures.

cup-shaped flower composed of numerous sepals

3-lobed leaves, variably subdivided

ruff of undivided bracts distant from flower

leaf stems arise from ground level

flowers often have pale inner ring

Habit Perennial	Height 15–40cm (6–16in)	Flowering time Feb–Apr

Family RANUNCULACEAE	Species *Anemone heldreichii*	Author Boiss.

ANEMONE HELDREICHII

An erect plant, this species is similar in structure to *Anemone pavonina* (above), but it is smaller and less robust, and has flowers with 12 to 19 very slender sepals. The leaves have 3 broad, heart-shaped lobes. The flower stem has a ruff of lance-shaped bracts situated some distance below the flower.
• **DISTRIBUTION** Crete, Karpathos, Ionian Islands.
• **HABITAT** Hillsides and grassy or rocky fields.
• **REMARK** This species is considered by some botanical authorities to be a variety of *A. hortensis* (see p.58).

sepals overlap only slightly

pale sepals with pink undersides

flower stems densely hairy

leaves in 3 lobes with division extending to stem

Habit Perennial	Height 15–30cm (6–12in)	Flowering time Feb–Apr

Family RANUNCULACEAE	Species *Anemone hortensis*	Author L.

ANEMONE HORTENSIS

Frequently cultivated in gardens, this delicate anemone has stems surrounded by a rosette of divided leaves. Each stem carries a whorl of narrow bracts, some distance below the flower. The flowers have 12 to 19 sepals, usually pale purple, with a span of up to 50mm (2in). As with other anemones, the flowers are borne singly. The fruit is a woolly achene.
• **DISTRIBUTION** W. and C. Mediterranean, excluding Spain.
• **HABITAT** Fields, olive groves, vineyards, gardens.
• **REMARK** The naming of anemones has often changed. *Anemone pavonina* (see p.57) was once considered to be a form of this species, and *A. heldreichii* (see p.57) frequently still is.

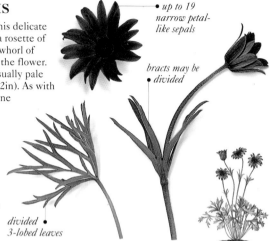

• *up to 19 narrow petal-like sepals*

bracts may be divided

divided 3-lobed leaves

Habit Perennial	Height 15–45cm (6–18in)	Flowering time Feb–Apr

Family RANUNCULACEAE	Species *Clematis flammula*	Author L.

FRAGRANT CLEMATIS

Fragrant Clematis is a deciduous, woody climber which supports itself by its leaf-stalks. These are sensitive to contact, and they wrap themselves around anything near by. The plant's young stems are green and slightly ribbed, developing a fibrous bark as they mature. The leaves, borne in opposite pairs, are doubly divided, with leaflets about 10mm (⅜in) long. The flowers grow in loose clusters, and are white and highly fragrant, with 4 or 5 petal-like lobes and a conspicuous tuft of stamens. Each flower is up to 30mm (1⅛in) across, and its "petals" are downy on the outside surface, but hairless inside. The flattened achenes have a feathery plume.
• **DISTRIBUTION** Throughout the region.
• **HABITAT** Maquis, hedges, frequently straggling over old walls.

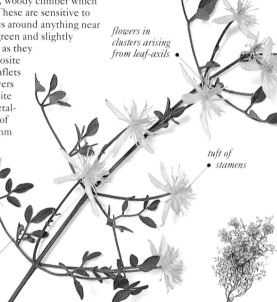

flowers in clusters arising from leaf-axils

tuft of stamens

leaves in opposite pairs

Habit Perennial	Height Up to 5m (16½ft)	Flowering time May–Aug

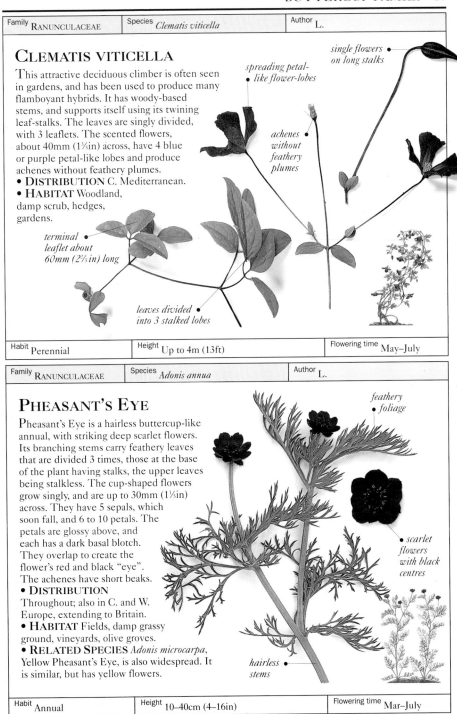

Family RANUNCULACEAE	Species *Clematis viticella*	Author L.

CLEMATIS VITICELLA

This attractive deciduous climber is often seen in gardens, and has been used to produce many flamboyant hybrids. It has woody-based stems, and supports itself using its twining leaf-stalks. The leaves are singly divided, with 3 leaflets. The scented flowers, about 40mm (1⅝in) across, have 4 blue or purple petal-like lobes and produce achenes without feathery plumes.
• **DISTRIBUTION** C. Mediterranean.
• **HABITAT** Woodland, damp scrub, hedges, gardens.

spreading petal-like flower-lobes

single flowers on long stalks

achenes without feathery plumes

terminal leaflet about 60mm (2⅖in) long

leaves divided into 3 stalked lobes

Habit Perennial	Height Up to 4m (13ft)	Flowering time May–July

Family RANUNCULACEAE	Species *Adonis annua*	Author L.

PHEASANT'S EYE

Pheasant's Eye is a hairless buttercup-like annual, with striking deep scarlet flowers. Its branching stems carry feathery leaves that are divided 3 times, those at the base of the plant having stalks, the upper leaves being stalkless. The cup-shaped flowers grow singly, and are up to 30mm (1⅛in) across. They have 5 sepals, which soon fall, and 6 to 10 petals. The petals are glossy above, and each has a dark basal blotch. They overlap to create the flower's red and black "eye". The achenes have short beaks.
• **DISTRIBUTION** Throughout; also in C. and W. Europe, extending to Britain.
• **HABITAT** Fields, damp grassy ground, vineyards, olive groves.
• **RELATED SPECIES** *Adonis microcarpa*, Yellow Pheasant's Eye, is also widespread. It is similar, but has yellow flowers.

feathery foliage

scarlet flowers with black centres

hairless stems

Habit Annual	Height 10–40cm (4–16in)	Flowering time Mar–July

Family RANUNCULACEAE	Species *Ranunculus asiaticus*	Author L.

TURBAN BUTTERCUP

An erect plant with downy stems, Turban Buttercup is frequently confused with *Anemone coronaria*, Crown Anemone, (see p.56). The most obvious distinguishing features of this species are its ring of 5 elliptic, concave sepals beneath the cup-shaped flowers, and its less divided leaves. The highly variable lower leaves grow directly from the roots on long stalks, and are either undivided or divided into 3 groups of wedge-like segments. The stem-leaves are virtually stalkless and have narrower, linear segments. The attractive flowers may be red, white, yellow, or purple, and are 30–50mm (1⅕–2in) in diameter. The fruit is an egg-shaped achene, 2–3mm (¹⁄₁₂–⅛in) long, with a hooked spur.

• **DISTRIBUTION** E. Mediterranean, from Crete to Turkey, the Levant and N. Africa.

• **HABITAT** Rocky, grassy, cultivated land.

• **REMARK** The species normally occurs locally in just one of its colour forms. The red form is common on Rhodes, and occurs with the white form on Crete. The yellow form can be seen in N.E. Crete, and elsewhere in the range.

DETAIL

• *ring of sepals turned down beneath flower*

• *angled petals form deep cup*

• *stems covered with fine hairs, giving grey-green*

• *each stem bears between 1 and 5 flowers*

• *cylindrical fruiting head of achenes with hooked spurs*

• *narrowly divided leaves hug stem*

• *basal leaves very variable, with lobes either entire or cut*

Habit Perennial	Height 10–30cm (4–12in)	Flowering time Feb–May

Family RANUNCULACEAE	Species *Ranunculus ficaria*	Author L.

LESSER CELANDINE

Lesser Celandine is a hairless plant, with a fleshy texture and glossy leaves. The subspecies *ficariiformis*, shown here, is prevalent in many parts of the Mediterranean region, and is robust with a stout, hollow stem. The heart-shaped leaves, up to 50mm (2in) across, have long stalks sheathing the stem. The leaf edges are lobed and the tips are blunt. The shining yellow flowers are borne singly, and are up to 50mm (2in) across. They have 8 to 12 petals, which are twice as long as the 3 sepals. The fruit is an oval achene with a short beak. In subspecies *ficariiformis*, it is hairy.
• **DISTRIBUTION** Throughout the region; also found northwards throughout Europe, including the British Isles and Scandinavia.
• **HABITAT** Damp, shady places, riverbanks.

flowers have 8–12 elliptic petals

upper surface of leaf glossy; lower surface dull light green

numerous stamens with yellow anthers

Habit Perennial	Height 5–30cm (2–12in)	Flowering time Feb–Apr

Family RANUNCULACEAE	Species *Ranunculus gramineus*	Author L.

RANUNCULUS GRAMINEUS

This slender buttercup has long, linear leaves resembling blades of grass. Most of the leaves arise at the base of the plant, but shorter leaves are also borne on the forked stems. The flowers are about 20mm (⅘in) across, and are either solitary or in small groups. The base of the flower is cupped by narrow, dull yellow sepals that are about half as long as the petals. The fruit, 3mm (⅛in) long, is flattened and keeled, with a short spur.
• **DISTRIBUTION** W. Mediterranean eastwards to Italy and Sardinia.
• **HABITAT** Dry rocky hillsides, garigue.
• **RELATED SPECIES** A large number of *Ranunculus* species grow in the region. *R. bullatus*, a widespread species with a rosette of oval leaves, flowers during autumn and winter.

flowers carried on long stalks

spherical flower-bud

numerous long stamens

small, sparse stem-leaves

parallel-veined basal leaves form a grass-like rosette

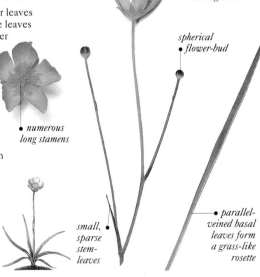

Habit Perennial	Height 20–50cm (8–20in)	Flowering time Apr–July

PEONY FAMILY

Family PAEONIACEAE	Species *Paeonia mascula*	Author (L.) Miller

PAEONIA MASCULA

Peonies are mound-forming herbaceous perennials, with large leaves and flamboyant flowers. Of the dozen or so species found in the Mediterranean, *Paeonia mascula* is one of the more widespread. It grows from swollen underground stems, and its leaves are twice divided into 9 to 16 broad leaflets. The leaves are dark green and hairless above, and hairless or hairy beneath. The flowers are up to 14cm (5½in) across, with spreading red petals, yellow anthers, and 5 sepals. The numerous stamens surround a cluster of 3 to 5 downy follicles, which split open when ripe to release large blackish seeds.

• **DISTRIBUTION** C. Mediterranean, including Algeria; also in parts of C. Europe, and naturalized on Steepholm, an island in the Bristol Channel.

• **HABITAT** Grassy and bushy places, meadows; frequently cultivated.

• **REMARK** Peonies have a long history of medicinal use, although in Europe they are now grown only for ornament. Many species have suffered from over-collection.

flowers borne singly on leafy stems

3–5 prominent follicles in centre of flower

ripening follicles

up to 16 leaflets

dark green leaves hairless above

stems hairy or hairless

Habit Perennial	Height Up to 90cm (36in)	Flowering time May–June

Family PAEONIACEAE	Species *Paeonia officinalis*	Author L.

COMMON PEONY

Often shorter than *Paeonia mascula* (opposite), this species has 17 to 30 narrower leaflets, which are themselves sometimes partly divided. The leaves are green and hairless above, and hairy beneath. The red flowers, up to 12cm (4¾in) across, have spreading rather than cupped petals. Each flower has a cluster of red-stalked stamens surrounding 2 or 3 hairy follicles. The follicles contain several large seeds, and split when ripe.
• **DISTRIBUTION** W. and C. Mediterranean.
• **HABITAT** Grassy scrub, meadows; frequently cultivated as a single- and double-flowered form.
• **RELATED SPECIES** Most Mediterranean peonies have reddish flowers, but in 2 eastern species the flowers are white. These are *P. rhodia*, found only on Rhodes, and *P. clusii*, found only on Crete and Karpathos.

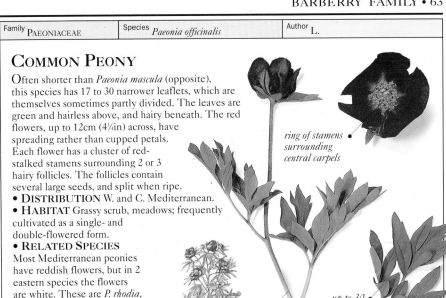

ring of stamens surrounding central carpels

stems bear single flowers

up to 30 leaflets

Habit Perennial	Height Up to 50cm (20in)	Flowering time May–June

BARBERRY FAMILY

Family BERBERIDACEAE	Species *Leontice leontopetalum*	Author L.

LEONTICE

This curious-looking plant, with its pyramid-shaped flower-heads, grows from a tuber and has hairless, bluish green stems and leaves. The leaves, up to about 15cm (6in) across, are divided into threes, either 2 or 3 times. The flowers, up to 15mm (⅗in) across, produce oval, bladder-like fruit.
• **DISTRIBUTION** N. Africa, Greece, Turkey.
• **HABITAT** Olive groves, fields, particularly those that are regularly ploughed.
• **RELATED SPECIES** *Bongardia chrysopogon* has open clusters of fewer flowers.

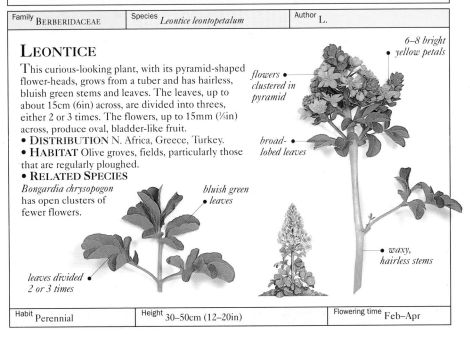

6–8 bright yellow petals

flowers clustered in pyramid

broad-lobed leaves

bluish green leaves

leaves divided 2 or 3 times

waxy, hairless stems

Habit Perennial	Height 30–50cm (12–20in)	Flowering time Feb–Apr

POPPY FAMILY

Family PAPAVERACEAE	Species *Papaver somniferum*	Author L.

OPIUM POPPY

Cultivated in the region since ancient times, the Opium Poppy is a hairless plant with a blue-green hue and a slightly fleshy texture. The leaves are up to 12cm (4¾in) long, the uppermost clasping the stem. The flowers are variable but unmistakable, their broad petals forming a deep bowl up to 90mm (3⅜in) across. The seed capsule is oval or round.
• **DISTRIBUTION** Throughout.
• **HABITAT** Disturbed ground, waysides, fields, vineyards, olive groves, gardens.

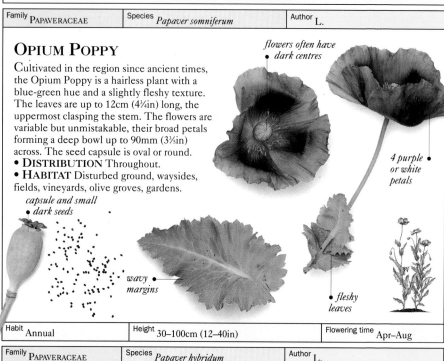

flowers often have dark centres

4 purple or white petals

capsule and small dark seeds

wavy margins

fleshy leaves

Habit Annual	Height 30–100cm (12–40in)	Flowering time Apr–Aug

Family PAPAVERACEAE	Species *Papaver hybridum*	Author L.

ROUGH POPPY

Over a dozen species of red-flowered poppy grow in the region, and of these about 4, including the Rough Poppy, occur throughout. This erect or spreading plant has bristly stems, and its leaves, up to 10cm (4in) long, are once or twice divided. Each flower produces a seed capsule with distinctive pale bristles.
• **DISTRIBUTION** Throughout.
• **HABITAT** Fields, waysides, and waste ground.

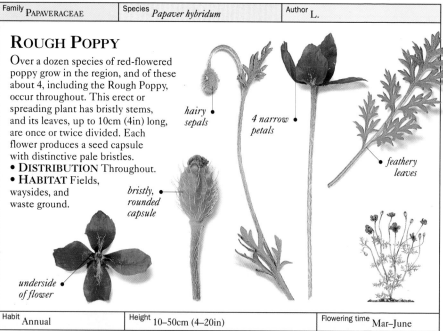

hairy sepals

4 narrow petals

feathery leaves

bristly, rounded capsule

underside of flower

Habit Annual	Height 10–50cm (4–20in)	Flowering time Mar–June

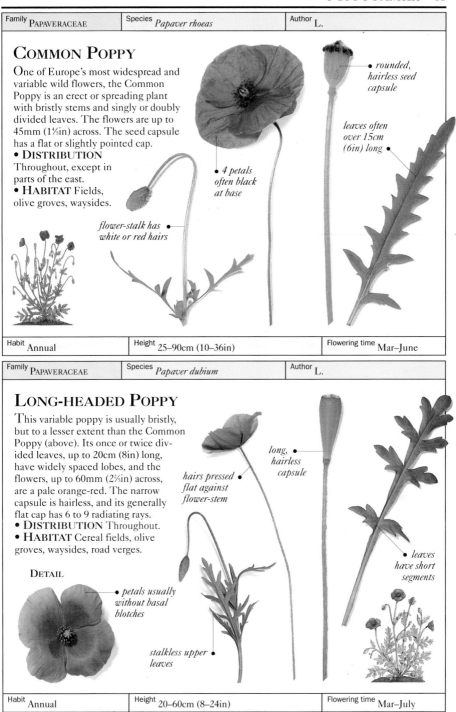

Family PAPAVERACEAE	Species *Papaver rhoeas*	Author L.

COMMON POPPY

One of Europe's most widespread and variable wild flowers, the Common Poppy is an erect or spreading plant with bristly stems and singly or doubly divided leaves. The flowers are up to 45mm (1⅛in) across. The seed capsule has a flat or slightly pointed cap.
• **DISTRIBUTION** Throughout, except in parts of the east.
• **HABITAT** Fields, olive groves, waysides.

• rounded, hairless seed capsule

leaves often over 15cm (6in) long •

• 4 petals often black at base

flower-stalk has • white or red hairs

Habit Annual	Height 25–90cm (10–36in)	Flowering time Mar–June

Family PAPAVERACEAE	Species *Papaver dubium*	Author L.

LONG-HEADED POPPY

This variable poppy is usually bristly, but to a lesser extent than the Common Poppy (above). Its once or twice divided leaves, up to 20cm (8in) long, have widely spaced lobes, and the flowers, up to 60mm (2⅜in) across, are a pale orange-red. The narrow capsule is hairless, and its generally flat cap has 6 to 9 radiating rays.
• **DISTRIBUTION** Throughout.
• **HABITAT** Cereal fields, olive groves, waysides, road verges.

DETAIL

long, • hairless capsule

hairs pressed • flat against flower-stem

• leaves have short segments

• petals usually without basal blotches

stalkless upper • leaves

Habit Annual	Height 20–60cm (8–24in)	Flowering time Mar–July

Family PAPAVERACEAE	Species *Glaucium flavum*	Author Crantz

YELLOW HORNED POPPY

The Yellow Horned Poppy is a widespread coastal plant, with a blue-green hue and a fleshy texture. Its stems are almost hairless, and when broken they exude a thick yellow latex, which is poisonous. The lowest leaves are up to 35cm (14in) long, and are pinnately lobed with wavy margins and sporadic white hairs. They have short stalks, but those higher up are stalkless. The flowers, up to 75mm (3in) across, have 4 yellow petals which overlap to form a cup. The capsule, up to 30cm (12in) long, is often curved.

• **DISTRIBUTION**
Throughout; widespread throughout Europe, including British Isles.

• **HABITAT**
Coastal sand and shingle, disturbed ground near to the sea, rubbish dumps.

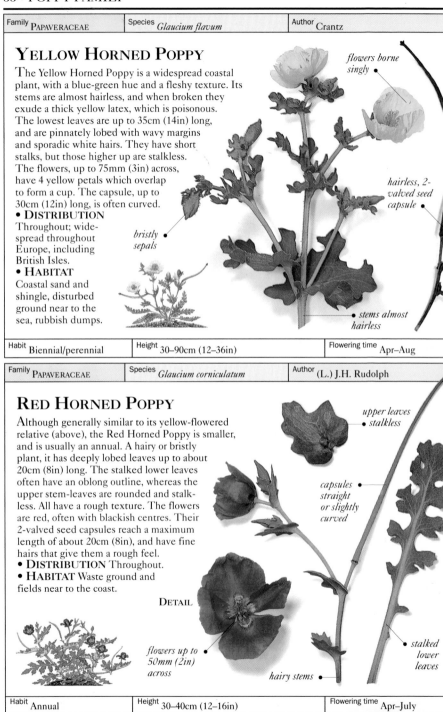

flowers borne singly

hairless, 2-valved seed capsule

bristly sepals

stems almost hairless

Habit Biennial/perennial	Height 30–90cm (12–36in)	Flowering time Apr–Aug

Family PAPAVERACEAE	Species *Glaucium corniculatum*	Author (L.) J.H. Rudolph

RED HORNED POPPY

Although generally similar to its yellow-flowered relative (above), the Red Horned Poppy is smaller, and is usually an annual. A hairy or bristly plant, it has deeply lobed leaves up to about 20cm (8in) long. The stalked lower leaves often have an oblong outline, whereas the upper stem-leaves are rounded and stalkless. All have a rough texture. The flowers are red, often with blackish centres. Their 2-valved seed capsules reach a maximum length of about 20cm (8in), and have fine hairs that give them a rough feel.

• **DISTRIBUTION** Throughout.
• **HABITAT** Waste ground and fields near to the coast.

DETAIL

upper leaves stalkless

capsules straight or slightly curved

flowers up to 50mm (2in) across

hairy stems

stalked lower leaves

Habit Annual	Height 30–40cm (12–16in)	Flowering time Apr–July

Family PAPAVERACEAE	Species *Hypecoum procumbens*	Author L.

HYPECOUM PROCUMBENS

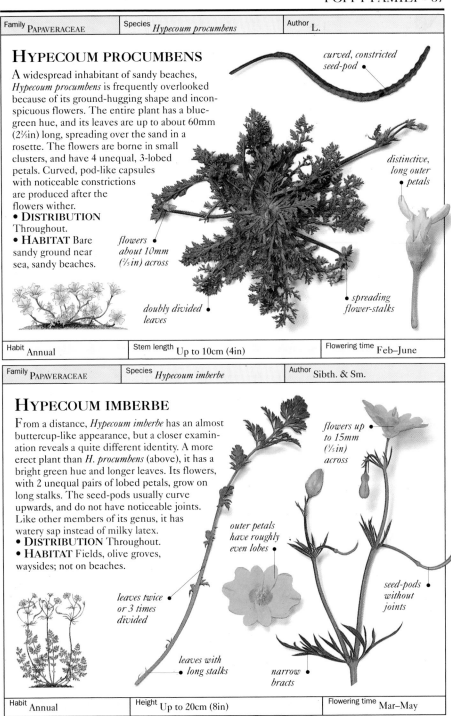

A widespread inhabitant of sandy beaches, *Hypecoum procumbens* is frequently overlooked because of its ground-hugging shape and inconspicuous flowers. The entire plant has a blue-green hue, and its leaves are up to about 60mm (2⅜in) long, spreading over the sand in a rosette. The flowers are borne in small clusters, and have 4 unequal, 3-lobed petals. Curved, pod-like capsules with noticeable constrictions are produced after the flowers wither.
• **DISTRIBUTION** Throughout.
• **HABITAT** Bare sandy ground near sea, sandy beaches.

curved, constricted seed-pod

distinctive, long outer petals

flowers about 10mm (⅖in) across

doubly divided leaves

spreading flower-stalks

Habit Annual	Stem length Up to 10cm (4in)	Flowering time Feb–June

Family PAPAVERACEAE	Species *Hypecoum imberbe*	Author Sibth. & Sm.

HYPECOUM IMBERBE

From a distance, *Hypecoum imberbe* has an almost buttercup-like appearance, but a closer examination reveals a quite different identity. A more erect plant than *H. procumbens* (above), it has a bright green hue and longer leaves. Its flowers, with 2 unequal pairs of lobed petals, grow on long stalks. The seed-pods usually curve upwards, and do not have noticeable joints. Like other members of its genus, it has watery sap instead of milky latex.
• **DISTRIBUTION** Throughout.
• **HABITAT** Fields, olive groves, waysides; not on beaches.

flowers up to 15mm (⅗in) across

outer petals have roughly even lobes

leaves twice or 3 times divided

leaves with long stalks

narrow bracts

seed-pods without joints

Habit Annual	Height Up to 20cm (8in)	Flowering time Mar–May

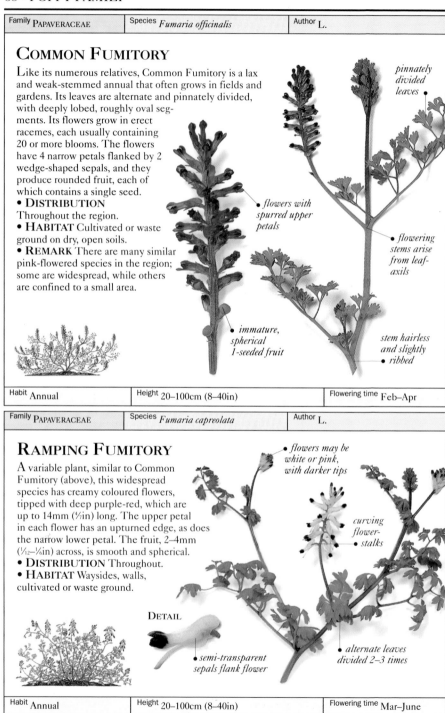

Family PAPAVERACEAE	Species *Fumaria officinalis*	Author L.

COMMON FUMITORY

Like its numerous relatives, Common Fumitory is a lax
and weak-stemmed annual that often grows in fields and
gardens. Its leaves are alternate and pinnately divided,
with deeply lobed, roughly oval seg-
ments. Its flowers grow in erect
racemes, each usually containing
20 or more blooms. The flowers
have 4 narrow petals flanked by 2
wedge-shaped sepals, and they
produce rounded fruit, each of
which contains a single seed.
• **DISTRIBUTION**
Throughout the region.
• **HABITAT** Cultivated or waste
ground on dry, open soils.
• **REMARK** There are many similar
pink-flowered species in the region;
some are widespread, while others
are confined to a small area.

pinnately divided leaves

flowers with spurred upper petals

flowering stems arise from leaf-axils

immature, spherical 1-seeded fruit

stem hairless and slightly ribbed

Habit Annual	Height 20–100cm (8–40in)	Flowering time Feb–Apr

Family PAPAVERACEAE	Species *Fumaria capreolata*	Author L.

RAMPING FUMITORY

A variable plant, similar to Common
Fumitory (above), this widespread
species has creamy coloured flowers,
tipped with deep purple-red, which are
up to 14mm (⅗in) long. The upper petal
in each flower has an upturned edge, as does
the narrow lower petal. The fruit, 2–4mm
(¹⁄₁₂–⅛in) across, is smooth and spherical.
• **DISTRIBUTION** Throughout.
• **HABITAT** Waysides, walls,
cultivated or waste ground.

flowers may be white or pink, with darker tips

curving flower-stalks

DETAIL

semi-transparent sepals flank flower

alternate leaves divided 2–3 times

Habit Annual	Height 20–100cm (8–40in)	Flowering time Mar–June

CAPER FAMILY

Family CAPPARIDACEAE	Species *Capparis spinosa*	Author L.

CAPER

Sprawling and hairless, this lax-stemmed shrub is generally but not consistently spiny, and has very conspicuous flowers which often rest on the ground. Its leathery, paddle-shaped leaves, up to 50mm (2in) long, are arranged alternately, and are carried on short stalks. The flowers grow on longer stalks from the leaf-axils, and tend to bloom one at a time as the stem that carries them grows. Each flower, 50–70mm (2–2⅗in) in diameter, has 4 curled white petals and 4 purplish green sepals. The flower's most eyecatching feature is its profusion of pink or purple stamens, which are up to twice as long as the petals. The fruit is a green berry, up to 50mm (2in) long, with pink flesh and many seeds.
• **DISTRIBUTION** Throughout.
• **HABITAT** Rocky places and walls, often near the sea.
• **REMARK** Often cultivated. Culinary capers are prepared by pickling the flower-buds.
• **RELATED SPECIES** A similar species, *Capparis ovata*, has sharp-tipped, slightly hairy, oblong to elliptical leaves. It has smaller flowers and is widespread in drier areas.

flower-buds arise from leaf-axils

stem may be spiny or spineless

stems lie on ground or trail over rocks

dense cluster of stamens

protruding style

flower-buds slightly flattened

leaves have heart-shaped base and rounded tips

Habit Perennial	Height 30–100cm (12–40in)	Flowering time May–Sept

CRESS FAMILY

Family CRUCIFERAE	Species *Isatis tinctoria*	Author L.

WOAD

Woad is a robust plant with tall, slender flowering stems. The basal leaves are oval with long stalks whereas the alternate stem-leaves have an arrow-head shape, with the stalkless notch of the arrowhead clasping the stem. The yellow flowers are about 4mm (⅛in) across, and, as with all members of the cress family, have 4 petals. They grow in dense, branched clusters, and are frequently present at the same time as the conspicuous, oar-shaped, hanging fruit.
• **DISTRIBUTION** Throughout.
• **HABITAT** Dry, rocky places.
• **REMARK** Woad was once cultivated as a source of blue dye.

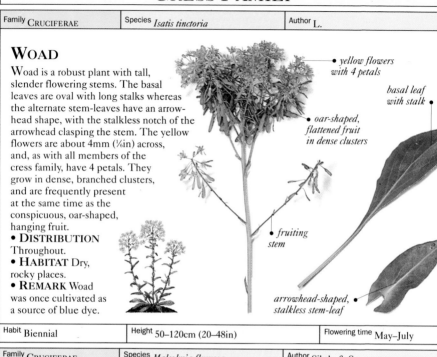

yellow flowers with 4 petals

basal leaf with stalk

oar-shaped, flattened fruit in dense clusters

fruiting stem

arrowhead-shaped, stalkless stem-leaf

Habit Biennial	Height 50–120cm (20–48in)	Flowering time May–July

Family CRUCIFERAE	Species *Malcolmia flexuosa*	Author Sibth. & Sm.

MALCOLMIA FLEXUOSA

This rather straggling plant branches at its base, and is covered throughout with sparse, short, white hairs. The fleshy leaves are elliptic to egg-shaped; the margins may be toothed or untoothed. The pinkish purple flowers are 12–25mm (½–1in) in diameter, and are borne singly at the top of branched stems. Each flower has 4 sepals, 2 of which have distinctive W-shaped bases. The seeds develop in a cylindrical capsule (siliqua), which is between 35 and 80mm (1⅖–3⅛in) long and up to 3mm (⅛in) in diameter.
• **DISTRIBUTION** Aegean region.
• **HABITAT** Coastal cliffs and sandy seashores.
• **RELATED SPECIES** *Malcomia maritima*, Virginia Stock, which is also found in the Aegean region, has narrower siliquas.

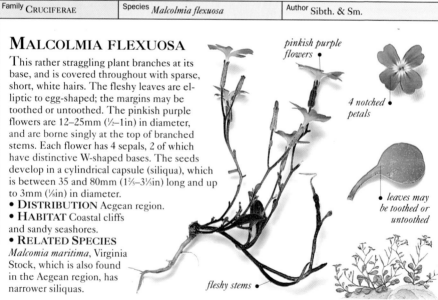

pinkish purple flowers

4 notched petals

leaves may be toothed or untoothed

fleshy stems

Habit Annual	Height 10–35cm (4–14in)	Flowering time Feb–May

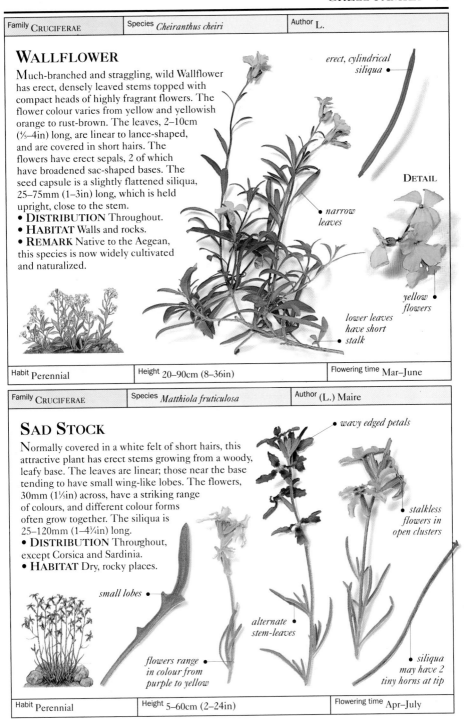

| Family CRUCIFERAE | Species *Cheiranthus cheiri* | Author L. |

WALLFLOWER

Much-branched and straggling, wild Wallflower has erect, densely leaved stems topped with compact heads of highly fragrant flowers. The flower colour varies from yellow and yellowish orange to rust-brown. The leaves, 2–10cm (⅘–4in) long, are linear to lance-shaped, and are covered in short hairs. The flowers have erect sepals, 2 of which have broadened sac-shaped bases. The seed capsule is a slightly flattened siliqua, 25–75mm (1–3in) long, which is held upright, close to the stem.
• **DISTRIBUTION** Throughout.
• **HABITAT** Walls and rocks.
• **REMARK** Native to the Aegean, this species is now widely cultivated and naturalized.

erect, cylindrical siliqua •

DETAIL

• *narrow leaves*

yellow • *flowers*

lower leaves have short • *stalk*

| Habit Perennial | Height 20–90cm (8–36in) | Flowering time Mar–June |

| Family CRUCIFERAE | Species *Matthiola fruticulosa* | Author (L.) Maire |

SAD STOCK

Normally covered in a white felt of short hairs, this attractive plant has erect stems growing from a woody, leafy base. The leaves are linear; those near the base tending to have small wing-like lobes. The flowers, 30mm (1⅛in) across, have a striking range of colours, and different colour forms often grow together. The siliqua is 25–120mm (1–4¾in) long.
• **DISTRIBUTION** Throughout, except Corsica and Sardinia.
• **HABITAT** Dry, rocky places.

wavy edged petals •

• *stalkless flowers in open clusters*

small lobes •

alternate • *stem-leaves*

flowers range • *in colour from purple to yellow*

• *siliqua may have 2 tiny horns at tip*

| Habit Perennial | Height 5–60cm (2–24in) | Flowering time Apr–July |

Family CRUCIFERAE	Species *Matthiola tricuspidata*	Author (L.) R.Br.

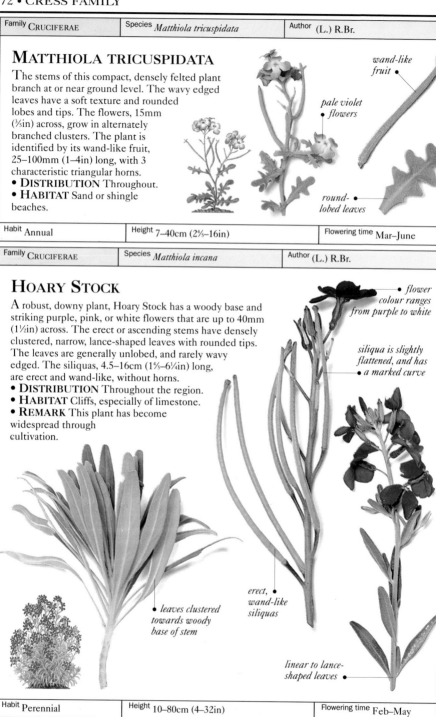

MATTHIOLA TRICUSPIDATA

The stems of this compact, densely felted plant branch at or near ground level. The wavy edged leaves have a soft texture and rounded lobes and tips. The flowers, 15mm (⅗in) across, grow in alternately branched clusters. The plant is identified by its wand-like fruit, 25–100mm (1–4in) long, with 3 characteristic triangular horns.
• **DISTRIBUTION** Throughout.
• **HABITAT** Sand or shingle beaches.

wand-like fruit

pale violet flowers

round-lobed leaves

Habit Annual	Height 7–40cm (2⅗–16in)	Flowering time Mar–June

Family CRUCIFERAE	Species *Matthiola incana*	Author (L.) R.Br.

HOARY STOCK

A robust, downy plant, Hoary Stock has a woody base and striking purple, pink, or white flowers that are up to 40mm (1½in) across. The erect or ascending stems have densely clustered, narrow, lance-shaped leaves with rounded tips. The leaves are generally unlobed, and rarely wavy edged. The siliquas, 4.5–16cm (1⅗–6¼in) long, are erect and wand-like, without horns.
• **DISTRIBUTION** Throughout the region.
• **HABITAT** Cliffs, especially of limestone.
• **REMARK** This plant has become widespread through cultivation.

flower colour ranges from purple to white

siliqua is slightly flattened, and has a marked curve

leaves clustered towards woody base of stem

erect, wand-like siliquas

linear to lance-shaped leaves

Habit Perennial	Height 10–80cm (4–32in)	Flowering time Feb–May

Family CRUCIFERAE	Species *Arabis verna*	Author (L.) R.Br.

ARABIS VERNA

A delicate, sparsely hairy plant, *Arabis verna* has slender, little-branching stems surrounded by a rosette of leaves at the base. The leaves all have coarsely toothed edges. The basal leaves are oval, and taper to an untoothed stalk, whereas the stem-leaves are spoon-shaped to heart-shaped, and clasp the stem. The flowers, 5–8mm (1/5–1/3in) long, are borne in branched clusters of up to 10. The petals are purple, and have yellow or white bases (claws), and the sepals are hairy. The wand-like siliqua, 45–60mm (1 4/5–2 2/5in) long, is erect or spreading.

• **DISTRIBUTION** Throughout.
• **HABITAT** Grassy or rocky places, roadside gravel; often at altitude.
• **RELATED SPECIES** One of many similar species in the region is *Arabis recta*, which has white flowers.

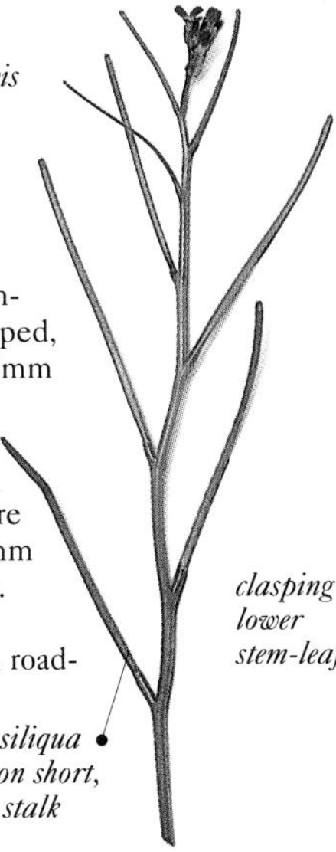
erect siliqua held on short, thick stalk

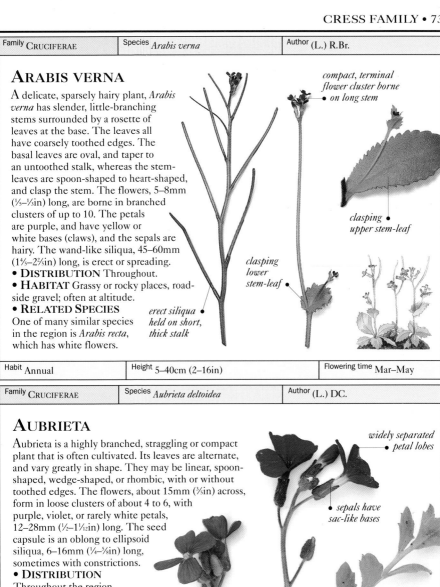

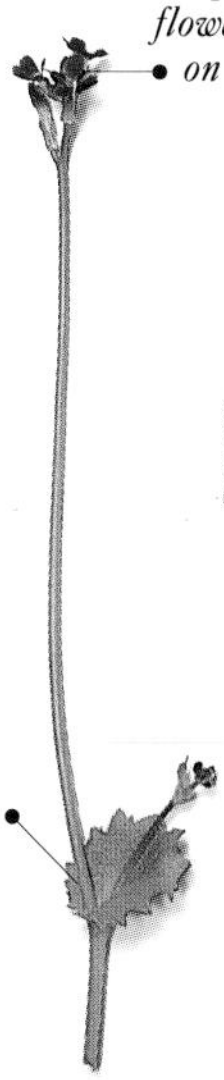
compact, terminal flower cluster borne on long stem
clasping lower stem-leaf

clasping upper stem-leaf

Habit Annual	Height 5–40cm (2–16in)	Flowering time Mar–May

Family CRUCIFERAE	Species *Aubrieta deltoidea*	Author (L.) DC.

AUBRIETA

Aubrieta is a highly branched, straggling or compact plant that is often cultivated. Its leaves are alternate, and vary greatly in shape. They may be linear, spoon-shaped, wedge-shaped, or rhombic, with or without toothed edges. The flowers, about 15mm (3/5in) across, form in loose clusters of about 4 to 6, with purple, violet, or rarely white petals, 12–28mm (1/2–1 1/12in) long. The seed capsule is an oblong to ellipsoid siliqua, 6–16mm (1/4–5/8in) long, sometimes with constrictions.

• **DISTRIBUTION** Throughout the region.
• **HABITAT** Rock crevices and walls.

widely separated petal lobes
sepals have sac-like bases

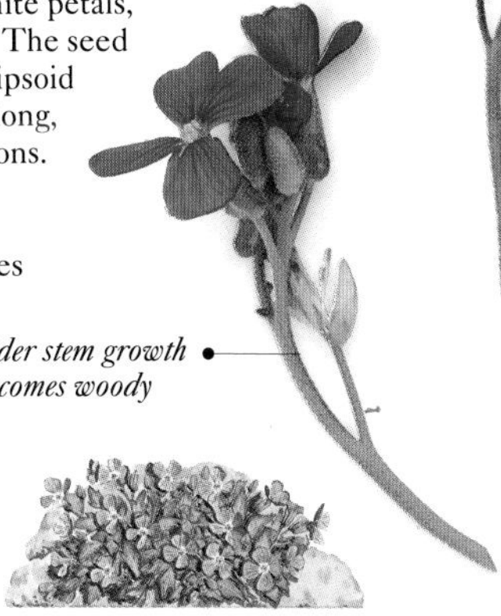
older stem growth becomes woody

young stems densely hairy

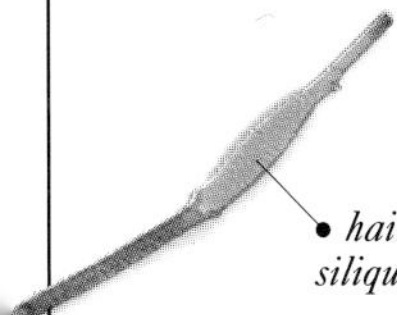
hairy siliqua

Habit Perennial	Height 5–20cm (2–8in)	Flowering time Apr–June

| Family CRUCIFERAE | Species *Lunaria annua* | Author L. |

HONESTY

Tall and robust, Honesty has bristly stems, and striking heads of numerous purple or, rarely, white flowers. The leaves, 3–15cm (1⅕–6in) long, are triangular, oval, or lance-shaped, with jagged teeth. The seeds are contained in an unmistakable, flat, translucent, coin-shaped silicula, up to 60mm (2⅖in) in diameter.
• **DISTRIBUTION** Throughout the Mediterranean region.
• **HABITAT** Woods, thickets, and waysides.

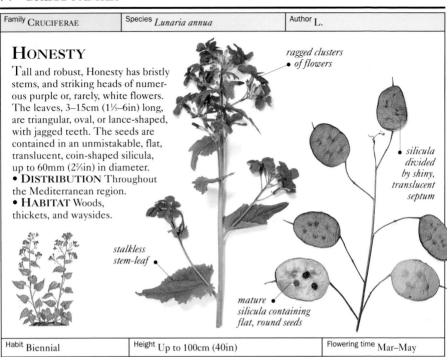

ragged clusters of flowers

silicula divided by shiny, translucent septum

stalkless stem-leaf

mature silicula containing flat, round seeds

| Habit Biennial | Height Up to 100cm (40in) | Flowering time Mar–May |

| Family CRUCIFERAE | Species *Alyssum saxatile* | Author L. |

GOLDEN ALYSSUM

Golden Alyssum is a woody based and hairy plant, with a dense basal rosette of grey-green leaves, and slender, erect stems topped with domed heads of small yellow flowers. The basal leaves are either undivided or have pinnate lobes; the stem-leaves are alternate, with finely toothed edges. The flowers have notched or 2-lobed petals. The hairless silicula, 4–9mm (⅙–⅜in) across, is disc-shaped:
• **DISTRIBUTION** From Italy eastwards.
• **HABITAT** Rocky ground.
• **REMARK** *Alyssum saxatile* is a variable species that is often cultivated as an ornamental garden plant.

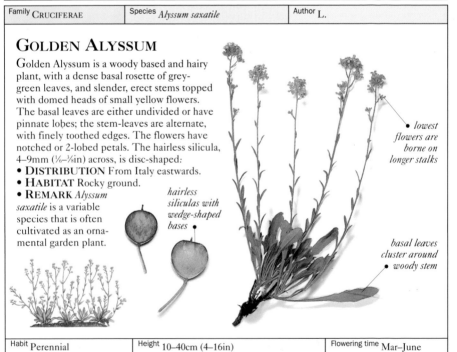

lowest flowers are borne on longer stalks

hairless siliculas with wedge-shaped bases

basal leaves cluster around woody stem

| Habit Perennial | Height 10–40cm (4–16in) | Flowering time Mar–June |

Family CRUCIFERAE	Species *Lobularia maritima*	Author (L.) Desvaux

SWEET ALISON

A highly branched, spreading plant, Sweet Alison is often cultivated. Its leaves, about 30mm (1⅛in) long, are lance-shaped and are usually coated with short, flattened, white hairs, although to a variable degree. The ascending or erect stems are topped with dense clusters of small, white or slightly pink flowers, about 5mm (⅛in) across. The silicula, which is up to 3.5mm (⅛in) long is roughly egg-shaped and slightly hairy.
• **DISTRIBUTION** Throughout.
• **HABITAT** Dry, rocky or sandy places.

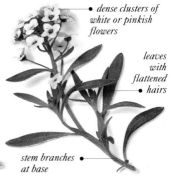

• dense clusters of white or pinkish flowers

leaves with flattened hairs

stem branches at base

Habit Perennial	Height 10–40cm (4–16in)	Flowering time Apr–Sept

Family CRUCIFERAE	Species *Clypeola jonthlaspi*	Author L.

DISC CRESS

An inconspicuous, downy plant, Disc Cress is more notable for its fruit than its flowers. The stems bear alternate, elliptic, and sharply pointed leaves. The tiny yellow flowers form in branched clusters. The disc-shaped fruit, 2–5mm (½–⅕in) across, is winged.
• **DISTRIBUTION** Throughout the region.
• **HABITAT** Sandy or rocky ground.

• raceme elongates as fruit forms

leaves densely • clustered on stem

• mature fruit hangs downwards

Habit Annual	Height Up to 20cm (8in)	Flowering time Mar–May

Family CRUCIFERAE	Species *Iberis amara*	Author L.

CANDYTUFT

Candytuft has erect, ribbed, hairy stems branching to form flat-topped or slightly domed corymbs of white or purplish flowers. The leaves, about 30mm (1⅛in) long, are alternate, linear to spoon-shaped, and often have toothed edges. Some lower leaves may be slightly lobed. The fruit, 3–5mm (⅛–⅕in) across, is disc-shaped with triangular lobes.
• **DISTRIBUTION** Spain, Italy, France.
• **HABITAT** Fields and dry, rocky hillsides on limestone.

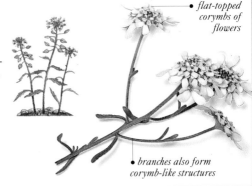

• flat-topped corymbs of flowers

• branches also form corymb-like structures

Habit Annual	Height 10–40cm (4–16in)	Flowering time Apr–Aug

Family CRUCIFERAE	Species *Biscutella didyma*	Author L.

BISCUTELLA DIDYMA

This widespread plant has erect, slender, branching stems. The elliptic basal leaves, up to 80mm (3⅕in) long, often form a rosette; the stem-leaves are smaller, alternate, and stalkless. The flowers are borne in racemes, which elongate as the plant produces its characteristic fruit. The fruit is shaped like 2 joined discs.

• **DISTRIBUTION** C. and E. Mediterranean, from Corsica and Italy.

• **HABITAT** Dry, waste, or rocky ground, garigue.

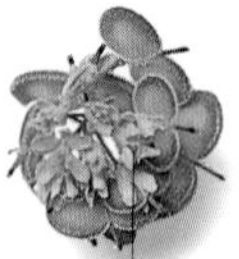
small yellow flowers

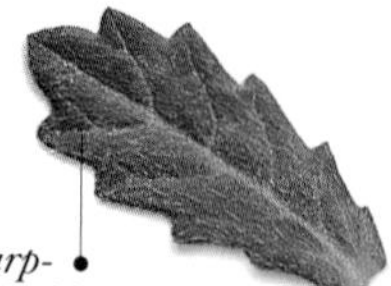
sharp-toothed leaves

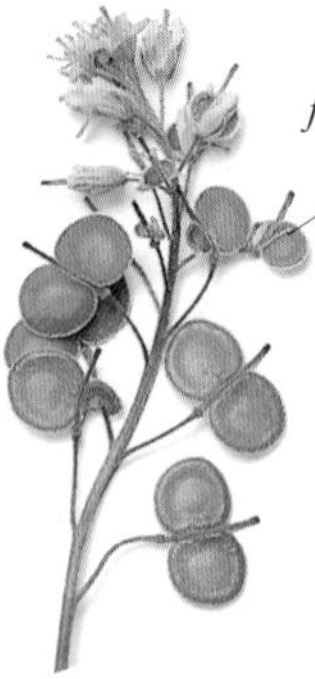
spectacle-like fruit with hairy margins

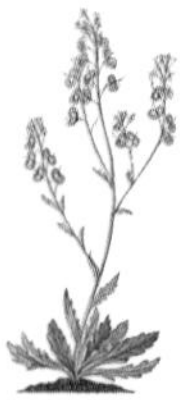

Habit Annual	Height 10–40cm (4–16in)	Flowering time Jan–May

Family CRUCIFERAE	Species *Cardaria draba*	Author (L.) Desvaux

HOARY CRESS

A stout plant with ridged stems, Hoary Cress often forms large roadside clumps. The leaves are broadly oval or lance-shaped, with pointed tips and irregularly toothed edges. The lower leaves are stalked, whereas the stem-leaves are clasping, with downward pointing lobes. The tiny white flowers, with petals about 4mm (⅙in) long, have a cabbage-like smell, and form in dense heads. The fruit, 3–5mm (⅛–⅕in) across, is swollen and heart-shaped.

• **DISTRIBUTION** Throughout.

• **HABITAT** Waste ground, roadsides.

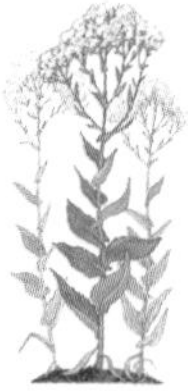

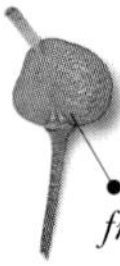
swollen fruit

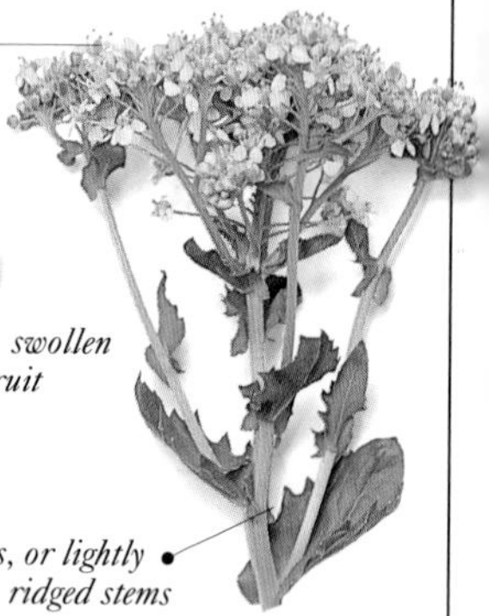
dense, flat-topped flower-heads
hairless, or lightly haired, ridged stems

Habit Perennial	Height 15–90cm (6–36in)	Flowering time Feb–June

Family CRUCIFERAE	Species *Eruca vesicaria*	Author (L.) Cavanilles

ROCKET

Leafy and rather lax, Rocket has branching, hairy stems. Its deeply lobed leaves, 2–15cm (⅘–6in) long, are sometimes pinnately divided. The terminal lobe is much larger than the 2 to 5 narrower lateral lobes. The flowers are borne in long racemes, and form erect, ellipsoid fruit, 12–25mm (½–1in) long.

• **DISTRIBUTION** Throughout the region.

• **HABITAT** Coastal waysides, waste or cultivated ground.

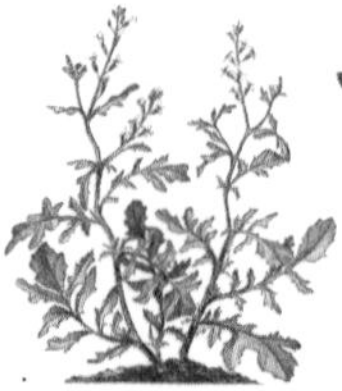

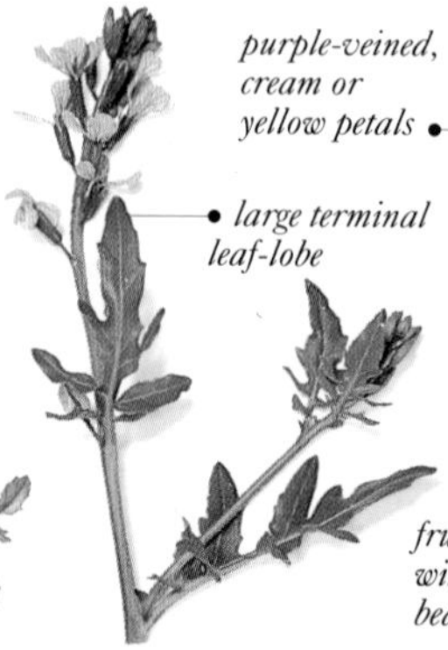
large terminal leaf-lobe

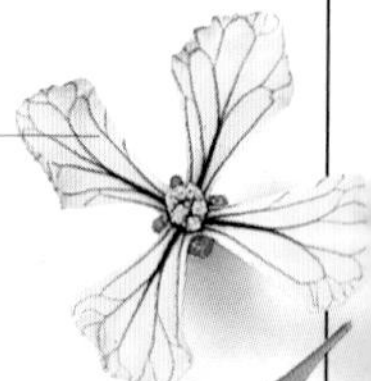
purple-veined, cream or yellow petals

DETAIL

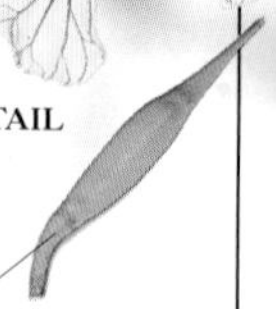
fruit with sharp beak

Habit Annual	Height 20–100cm (8–40in)	Flowering time Feb–June

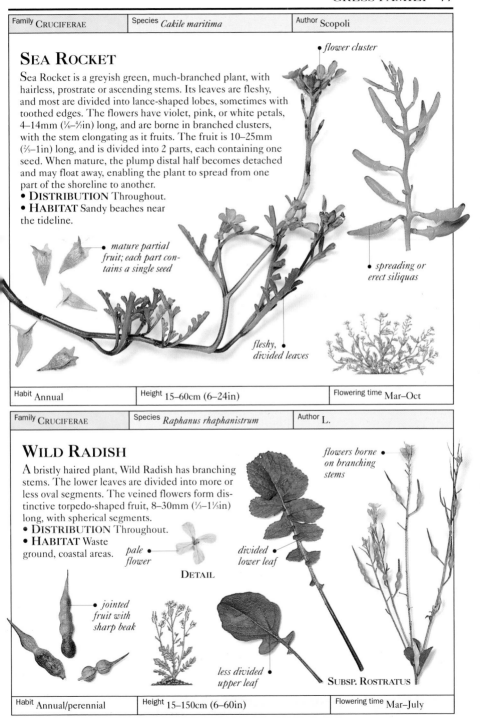

Family	Species	Author
CRUCIFERAE	*Cakile maritima*	Scopoli

SEA ROCKET

Sea Rocket is a greyish green, much-branched plant, with hairless, prostrate or ascending stems. Its leaves are fleshy, and most are divided into lance-shaped lobes, sometimes with toothed edges. The flowers have violet, pink, or white petals, 4–14mm (1/6–4/7in) long, and are borne in branched clusters, with the stem elongating as it fruits. The fruit is 10–25mm (2/5–1in) long, and is divided into 2 parts, each containing one seed. When mature, the plump distal half becomes detached and may float away, enabling the plant to spread from one part of the shoreline to another.

- **DISTRIBUTION** Throughout.
- **HABITAT** Sandy beaches near the tideline.

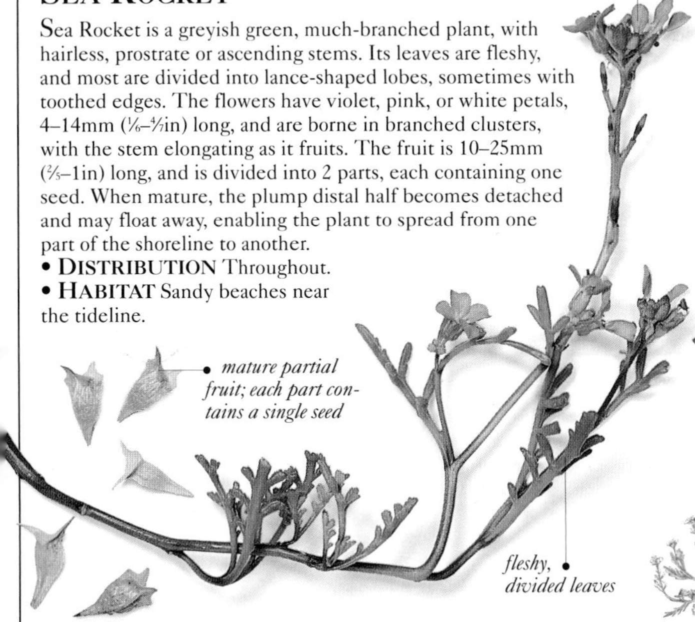
flower cluster
fleshy, divided leaves

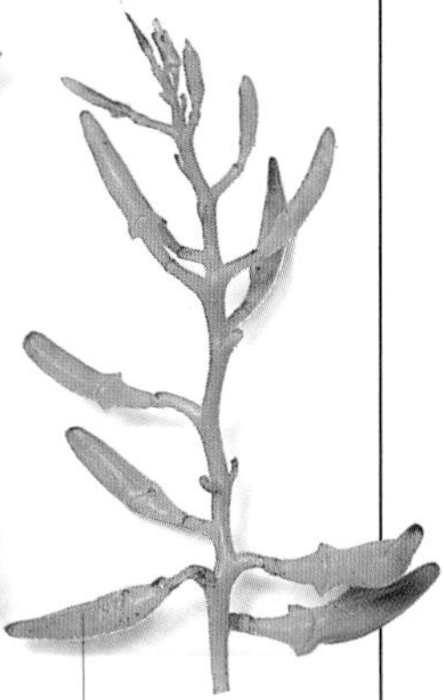
spreading or erect siliquas
mature partial fruit; each part contains a single seed

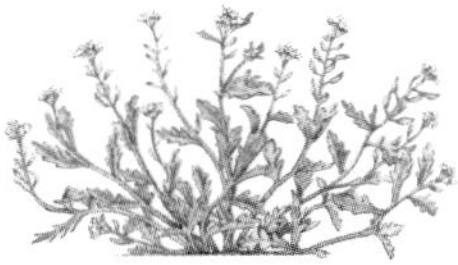

Habit	Height	Flowering time
Annual	15–60cm (6–24in)	Mar–Oct

Family	Species	Author
CRUCIFERAE	*Raphanus rhaphanistrum*	L.

WILD RADISH

A bristly haired plant, Wild Radish has branching stems. The lower leaves are divided into more or less oval segments. The veined flowers form distinctive torpedo-shaped fruit, 8–30mm (1/3–1 1/5in) long, with spherical segments.

- **DISTRIBUTION** Throughout.
- **HABITAT** Waste ground, coastal areas.

pale flower

DETAIL

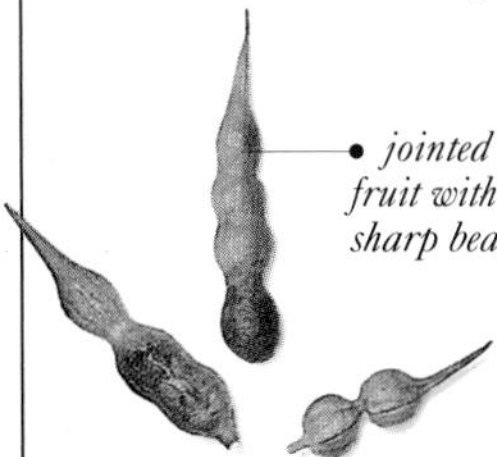
jointed fruit with sharp beak

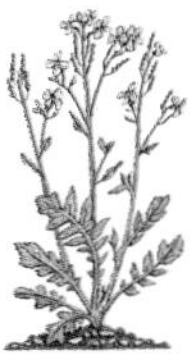

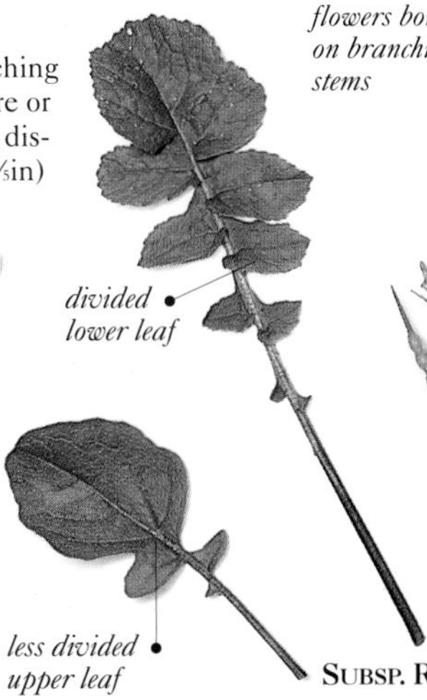
divided lower leaf
less divided upper leaf

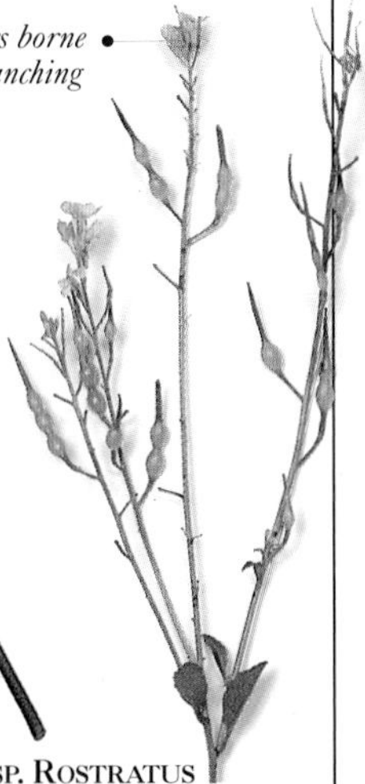
flowers borne on branching stems

SUBSP. ROSTRATUS

Habit	Height	Flowering time
Annual/perennial	15–150cm (6–60in)	Mar–July

MIGNONETTE FAMILY

Family RESEDACEAE	Species *Reseda alba*	Author L.

WHITE MIGNONETTE

White Mignonette has dense foliage, and tall, ridged, stems that branch above. The alternate leaves are dark shiny green and much divided, with 5 to 15 pairs of wavy lobes. The dull white flowers, up to 6mm (¼in) long, grow in dense racemes, and have 5 or 6 lobed, cream-coloured petals. There are about 20 prominent stamens, which persist after the petals wither. The fruit is a capsule, up to 15mm (⅜in) across.

• **DISTRIBUTION**
W. and C. Mediterranean region, eastwards to Crete.

• **HABITAT**
Disturbed ground, waste ground, and waysides.

• *flowers borne on stalks up to 8mm (⅓in) long*

dull white flowers

lance-shaped lobes

stem branches some distance above ground

Habit Annual/perennial	Height 30–80cm (12–32in)	Flowering time Mar–Sept

Family RESEDACEAE	Species *Reseda lutea*	Author L.

WILD MIGNONETTE

Similar in structure to White Mignonette (above), this species is less robust, with greenish yellow flowers. The stems tend to branch at some distance above the ground. The leaves, 5–15cm (2–6in) long, are much divided, with 1 to 4 pairs of long, narrow, lance-shaped lobes, which often have secondary lobes attached. The leaf edges are slightly rough and crinkly. The seed capsules, 7–12mm (⅖–½in) long, are roughly ellipsoid. They are normally held erect, and are divided into 3 parts.

• **DISTRIBUTION**
Throughout the region.

• **HABITAT** Disturbed ground, fields; on dry or chalky soils.

• **REMARK** Wild Mignonette is native to S. and W. Europe but, as with White Mignonette, it is now widely naturalized in more northern latitudes.

narrow leaf-lobes, often sub-divided •

fruit generally held erect •

• *stem branches some distance above ground*

Habit Annual/perennial	Height 20–60cm (8–24in)	Flowering time Mar–July

Family RESEDACEAE	Species *Reseda media*	Author Lag.

RESEDA MEDIA

This inconspicuous mignonette has erect or ascending stems, which branch at the base and are covered with short hairs. The leaves are alternate, long, and narrow, with up to 4 pairs of small side lobes. The white upper petals have beard-like tufts. The fruit is a capsule, which hangs downwards.
• **DISTRIBUTION** Spain.
• **HABITAT** Disturbed or waste ground.

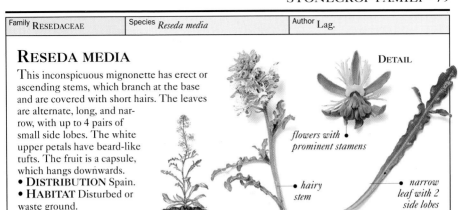

DETAIL

flowers with prominent stamens

hairy stem

narrow leaf with 2 side lobes

Habit Annual/biennial	Height 10–50cm (4–20in)	Flowering time Apr–Sept

STONECROP FAMILY

Family CRASSULACEAE	Species *Umbilicus rupestris*	Author (Salis.) Dandy

NAVELWORT

Fleshy and hairless, Navelwort has distinctive circular basal leaves with central stalks. The stem is often single, although the plant sometimes branches from the base. The basal leaves are concave above, having a depression where the stalk meets the leaf, and are roughly round, with wavy edges. The stem-leaves become progressively smaller, more kidney-shaped, and then linear. The flowers, 7–10mm (⅜–⅜in) long, are tubular, and range in colour from pale green, to yellow or pinkish.
• **DISTRIBUTION** Throughout.
• **HABITAT** Shady crevices in rocks and walls.
• **REMARK** A similar, widespread species, *Umbilicus horizontalis*, has a more leafy stem, and smaller, stalkless flowers.

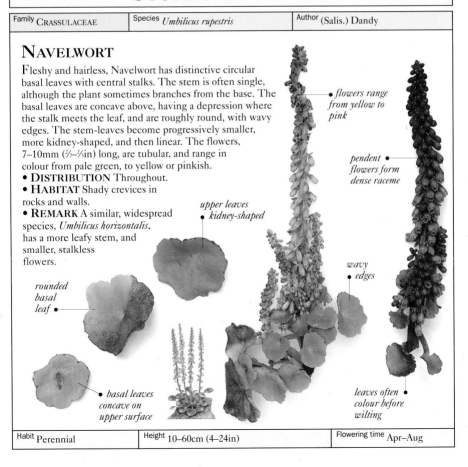

flowers range from yellow to pink

pendent flowers form dense raceme

upper leaves kidney-shaped

wavy edges

rounded basal leaf

basal leaves concave on upper surface

leaves often colour before wilting

Habit Perennial	Height 10–60cm (4–24in)	Flowering time Apr–Aug

Family CRASSULACEAE	Species *Sedum sediforme*	Author (Jacquin) Pau

SEDUM SEDIFORME

Fleshy and hairless with a woody base, this widespread stonecrop has erect stems closely covered with spirally arranged, overlapping leaves. The thick, waxy leaves, 10–20mm (⅖–⅘in) long, are lance-shaped with a pointed tip. The flower-buds are arranged in a rounded cluster, which gradually unfurls to form a group of flower-bearing branches that slope upwards, and then curve down towards their tips. The flowers have 5 to 8 greenish yellow petals, and are about 15mm (⅗in) across. The leaves tend to fall from the stems as the flowers bloom. The fruit is a group of upright follicles containing vey small seeds.

• **DISTRIBUTION** Throughout.
• **HABITAT** Rocky ground.
• **REMARK** There are many other species of *Sedum* in the Mediterranean region. Most are found on dry, rocky ground.

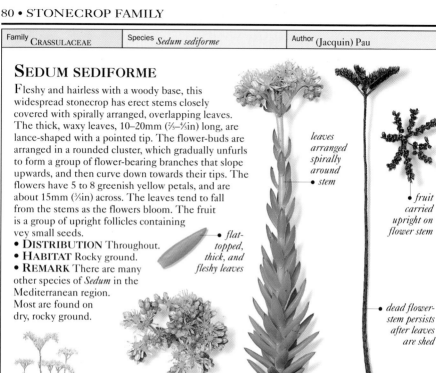

leaves arranged spirally around stem

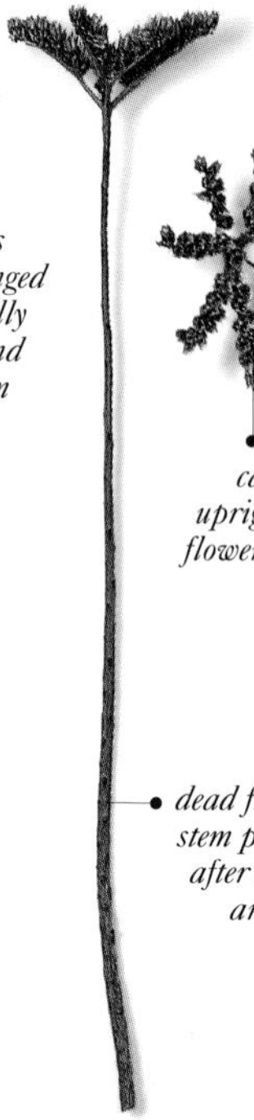
dead flower-stem persists after leaves are shed

fruit carried upright on flower stem

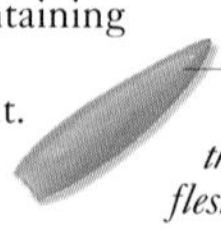
flat-topped, thick, and fleshy leaves

flowers have 5–8 petals

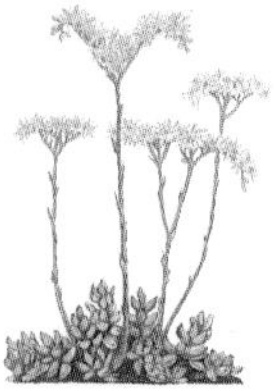

Habit Perennial	Height 15–60cm (6–24in)	Flowering time May–Aug

PITTOSPORUM FAMILY

Family PITTOSPORACEAE	Species *Pittosporum tobira*	Author (Thunberg) W. T. Aiton

JAPANESE PITTOSPORUM

This shrub or small tree has rosette-like clusters of leaves, 5–8cm (2–3⅕in) long, growing at the tips of the branches. The scented flowers, about 2cm (⅘in) across, grow in umbel-like groups and have rounded white petals which turn yellowish. The fruit is leathery and brown when ripe.

• **DISTRIBUTION** Throughout.
• **HABITAT** Gardens, parks.
• **REMARK** A native of Japan and China, often grown for ornament.

curved margins
5-petalled flowers
hairless, leathery, oval leaves
upper surface of leaf shiny

Habit Perennial	Height 2–10m (6½–33ft)	Flowering time Mar–Aug

ROSE FAMILY

Family ROSACEAE	Species *Rosa canina*	Author L.

DOG ROSE

A deciduous shrub with straggling stems, the Dog Rose has alternate leaves divided into 5 to 7 broadly elliptic leaflets. The flowers, about 70mm (2⅓in) across, have pink or white petals. The fruit is an ellipsoid hip, which turns red when ripe.
• **DISTRIBUTION** Throughout, except in the extreme east; also north to British Isles.
• **HABITAT** Hedges, woods, scrub.

leafy, pinnately lobed sepals

pink or white flowers borne in clusters of 2 to 5

hairless leaves lack sticky glands

Habit Perennial	Height Up to 3m (10ft)	Flowering time Mar–May

Family ROSACEAE	Species *Rosa nitidula*	Author Besser

ROSA NITIDULA

A close relative of the Dog Rose (above), *Rosa nitidula* often has doubly-toothed leaflets, with conspicuous glands on their margins, and undersides that give the plant a sticky texture. As with the Dog Rose, the flowers may be pink or white, and are up to 70mm (2⅓in) in diameter when fully open. They produce hips that often have a bristly or glandular surface.
• **DISTRIBUTION** Throughout; also north to Great Britain and Scandinavia.
• **HABITAT** Hedges, thickets.

flowers pink or white, in clusters

sepals glandular, and often pinnately divided

toothed margins

wing-like stipules with glands on margins

curved spines

flower-stalk with glandular projections

Habit Perennial	Height 1–2m (3¼–6½ft)	Flowering time Apr–Aug

Family ROSACEAE	Species *Rosa sempervirens*	Author L.

ROSA SEMPERVIRENS

A widespread wild rose, this evergreen species
has long, sparsely spined, clambering stems.
The glossy leaves have 3 to 7 roughly egg-shaped,
leathery leaflets, with serrated edges and pointed tips.
The flowers are borne in branched clusters of 3 to 7
blooms. Each flower, about 50mm (2in) across, has
white petals and sharply pointed, ovate sepals
covered with tiny stalked glands. The
fruit, about 10mm (⅜in) long, is a
smooth, red, ovoid hip.
• **DISTRIBUTION** Throughout.
• **HABITAT** Hedges, open woods,
scrub; often near the coast.
• **REMARK** The most widespread wild
rose of the region, often found at sea level.

*columnar style
projects above
stamens*

*flower-stalks
sparsely
glandular*

*smooth
and glossy
upper surfaces*

Habit Perennial	Height 1–5m (3¼–16½ft)	Flowering time Mar–July

Family ROSACEAE	Species *Sarcopterium spinosum*	Author (L.) Spach

THORNY BURNET

A dense, spiny, and domed shrub,
Thorny Burnet sheds its leaves early
in summer. Its new growth is covered
in short hairs, whereas the
older branches are stiff,
brown, and hairless. The
leaves, 10mm (⅜in) long, are divided
into 9 to 15 leaflets with downturned,
serrated edges. The tiny flowers grow
in densely packed heads, with the male
flowers towards the base. The fruit is
red and slightly fleshy.
• **DISTRIBUTION** E. Mediterranean, from Sardinia and Italy.
• **HABITAT** Dry areas, garigue.

*small flowers and
leaves protected
by spines*

*feathery
stigmas
of female
flowers*

*honeycomb
of spines formed
by forked side-
branches*

woody stem

Habit Perennial	Height 30–60cm (12–24in)	Flowering time Mar–May

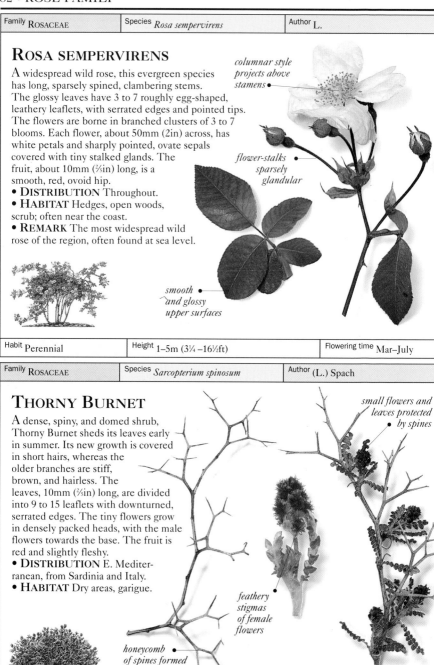

PEA FAMILY

Family LEGUMINOSAE	Species *Cercis siliquastrum*	Author L.

JUDAS TREE

The pretty pink flowers of this deciduous tree grow directly from the trunk and branches, and often appear before the leaves. The smooth, heart- or kidney-shaped leaves, 7–12cm (2⅘– 4¾in) long, are shiny when young, but become dull on maturity. The flowers, 20mm (⅘in) long, consist of 3 upper petals and 2 larger lower ones. The fruit is a flattened pod, 6–10cm (2⅖–4in) long, which is smooth and brown when ripe, containing several small seeds.
• **DISTRIBUTION** Throughout the region.
• **HABITAT** Rocky hills, maquis, woods, gardens.
• **REMARK** A native of the E. Mediterranean, the Judas Tree is widely cultivated for its ornamental value, as well as for its hard, finely veined wood.

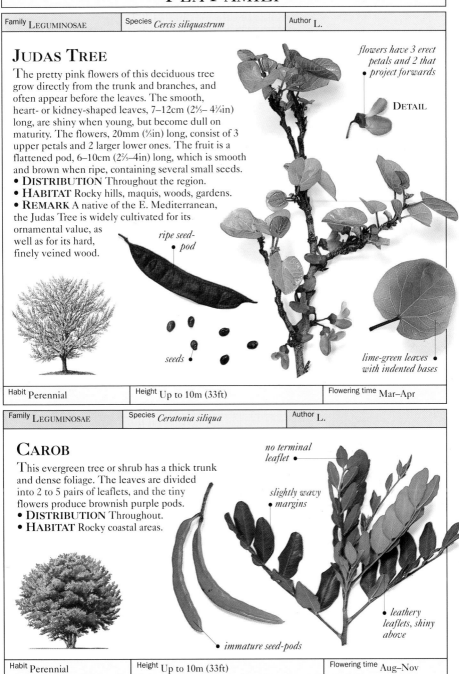

flowers have 3 erect petals and 2 that • project forwards

DETAIL

ripe seed-• pod

seeds •

lime-green leaves • with indented bases

Habit Perennial	Height Up to 10m (33ft)	Flowering time Mar–Apr

Family LEGUMINOSAE	Species *Ceratonia siliqua*	Author L.

CAROB

This evergreen tree or shrub has a thick trunk and dense foliage. The leaves are divided into 2 to 5 pairs of leaflets, and the tiny flowers produce brownish purple pods.
• **DISTRIBUTION** Throughout.
• **HABITAT** Rocky coastal areas.

no terminal leaflet •

slightly wavy • margins

• leathery leaflets, shiny above

immature seed-pods

Habit Perennial	Height Up to 10m (33ft)	Flowering time Aug–Nov

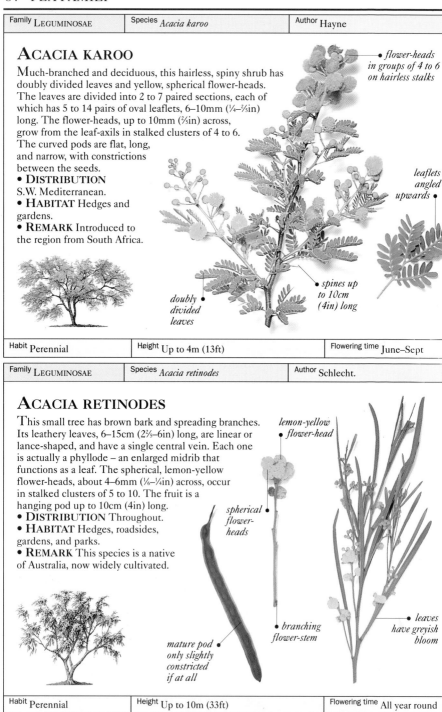

Family LEGUMINOSAE	Species *Acacia karoo*	Author Hayne

ACACIA KAROO

Much-branched and deciduous, this hairless, spiny shrub has doubly divided leaves and yellow, spherical flower-heads. The leaves are divided into 2 to 7 paired sections, each of which has 5 to 14 pairs of oval leaflets, 6–10mm (¼–⅖in) long. The flower-heads, up to 10mm (⅖in) across, grow from the leaf-axils in stalked clusters of 4 to 6. The curved pods are flat, long, and narrow, with constrictions between the seeds.
• **DISTRIBUTION** S.W. Mediterranean.
• **HABITAT** Hedges and gardens.
• **REMARK** Introduced to the region from South Africa.

flower-heads in groups of 4 to 6 on hairless stalks

leaflets angled upwards

doubly divided leaves

spines up to 10cm (4in) long

Habit Perennial	Height Up to 4m (13ft)	Flowering time June–Sept

Family LEGUMINOSAE	Species *Acacia retinodes*	Author Schlecht.

ACACIA RETINODES

This small tree has brown bark and spreading branches. Its leathery leaves, 6–15cm (2⅖–6in) long, are linear or lance-shaped, and have a single central vein. Each one is actually a phyllode – an enlarged midrib that functions as a leaf. The spherical, lemon-yellow flower-heads, about 4–6mm (⅙–¼in) across, occur in stalked clusters of 5 to 10. The fruit is a hanging pod up to 10cm (4in) long.
• **DISTRIBUTION** Throughout.
• **HABITAT** Hedges, roadsides, gardens, and parks.
• **REMARK** This species is a native of Australia, now widely cultivated.

lemon-yellow flower-head

spherical flower-heads

leaves have greyish bloom

mature pod only slightly constricted if at all

branching flower-stem

Habit Perennial	Height Up to 10m (33ft)	Flowering time All year round

Family LEGUMINOSAE	Species *Anagyris foetida*	Author L.

ANAGYRIS FOETIDA

This deciduous shrub has an unpleasant smell when bruised or broken. Its leaves are stalked, and divided into 3 stalkless, elliptic leaflets, 30–70mm (1⅕–2⅘in) long, with hairless upper surfaces and finely haired undersides. The greenish yellow flowers grow in small, hanging clusters. The upper petal is marked with black and is much shorter than the other 4. The pod, 10–20cm (4–8in) long, contains seeds that turn violet or yellow when ripe.
• **DISTRIBUTION** Throughout.
• **HABITAT** Roadsides, dry fields on limestone.

trifoliate
leaves

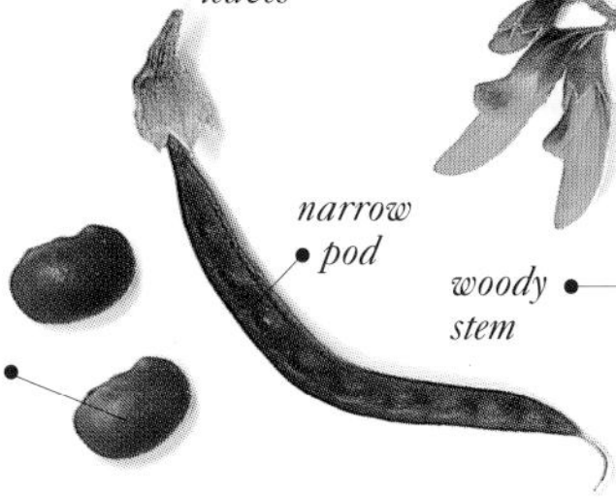
narrow
pod
ripe seed

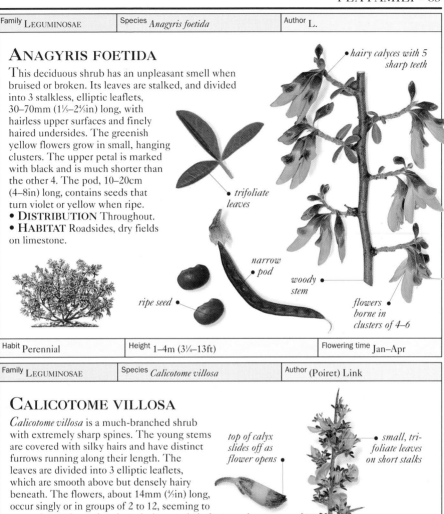

hairy calyces with 5
sharp teeth
woody
stem
flowers
borne in
clusters of 4–6

Habit Perennial	Height 1–4m (3¼–13ft)	Flowering time Jan–Apr

Family LEGUMINOSAE	Species *Calicotome villosa*	Author (Poiret) Link

CALICOTOME VILLOSA

Calicotome villosa is a much-branched shrub with extremely sharp spines. The young stems are covered with silky hairs and have distinct furrows running along their length. The leaves are divided into 3 elliptic leaflets, which are smooth above but densely hairy beneath. The flowers, about 14mm (⁴⁄₇in) long, occur singly or in groups of 2 to 12, seeming to cover almost the entire plant. A characteristic feature of this genus is the calyx, part of which splits off like a hat when the flower opens. The pod, 25–40mm (1–1⅗in) long, is densely covered with long, silky hairs.
• **DISTRIBUTION** Throughout, but more common in the east.
• **HABITAT** Dry, rocky hillsides.

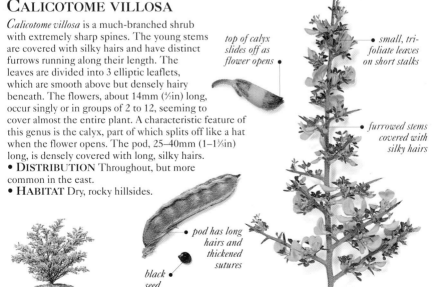

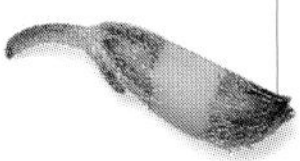
top of calyx
slides off as
flower opens

pod has long
hairs and
thickened
sutures
black
seed

small, tri-
foliate leaves
on short stalks
furrowed stems
covered with
silky hairs

Habit Perennial	Height Up to 3m (10ft)	Flowering time Feb–June

Family LEGUMINOSAE	Species *Calicotome spinosa*	Author (L.) Link

THORNY BROOM

Thorny Broom is a much-branched shrub with springy stems and long, stiff spines that can inflict painful wounds. The stems, leaves, and bright yellow flowers are much like those of *Calicotome villosa* (see p.85), although considerably less hairy. The flowers, 12–18mm (½–5/7in) long, are usually borne singly, although sometimes they may be in small clusters. The tip of the calyx breaks away as the flower-bud opens. The seed-pod, about 30mm (1⅕in) long, is either hairless or sparsely haired. Unlike the pod of *C. villosa*, it does not have a prominent suture.

- **DISTRIBUTION** W. Mediterranean.
- **HABITAT** Dry, rocky ground, maquis.

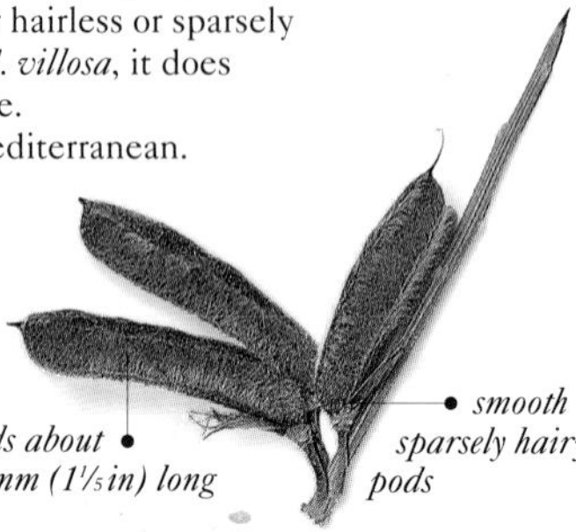
pods about 30mm (1⅕in) long
smooth or sparsely hairy pods

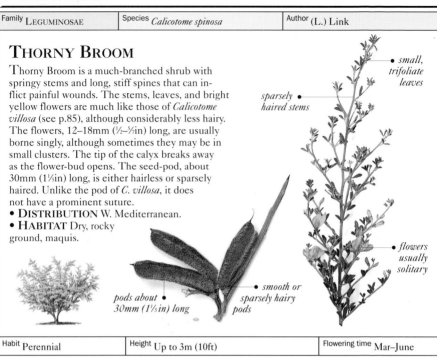

small, trifoliate leaves
sparsely haired stems
flowers usually solitary

Habit Perennial	Height Up to 3m (10ft)	Flowering time Mar–June

Family LEGUMINOSAE	Species *Cytisus villosus*	Author Pourret

CYTISUS VILLOSUS

Spineless and much-branched, this shrub has long and supple stems that are 5-angled and hairy when young. The leaves are hairless above, finely haired beneath, and are divided into 3 elliptic leaflets, 15–30mm (⅗–1⅕in) long. The yellow flowers grow singly or in groups of 2 or 3. The upper petal is sharply folded back, and has red-brown streaks at its base. The pod, 20–45mm (⅘–1⅘in) long, is slightly curved.

- **DISTRIBUTION** Throughout.
- **HABITAT** Woods and maquis; less common on limestone.
- **REMARK** There are many other *Cytisus* species (brooms) in the region, often at altitude.

pod becomes hairless when ripe

flowers in leaf-axils at stem tips

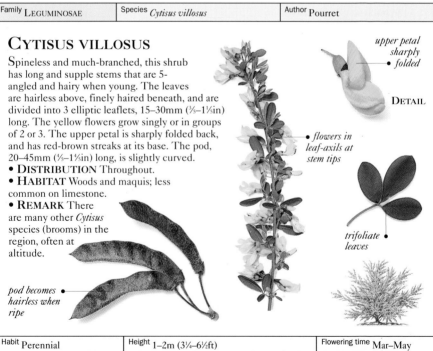

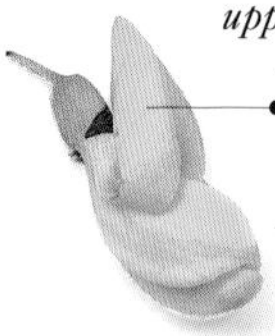
upper petal sharply folded
DETAIL

trifoliate leaves

Habit Perennial	Height 1–2m (3¼–6½ft)	Flowering time Mar–May

| Family LEGUMINOSAE | Species *Genista scorpius* | Author (L.) DC. |

GENISTA SCORPIUS

Like many members of its genus, this densely branched, spiny shrub, has undivided leaves. The leaves of this species, only about 3–12mm (⅛–½in) long, are inconspicuous, with smooth and glossy upper surfaces, and slightly hairy undersides. The bright yellow flowers are borne either directly on the spines, or on short stalks attached to them. The pods, 15–40mm (⅗–1⅗in) long, are hairless.

• **DISTRIBUTION** France and Spain.
• **HABITAT** Garigue, maquis.
• **REMARK** There are many other *Genista* species, especially in the west. All have yellow flowers with a 2-lipped calyx. *G. cinerea* is a spineless example.

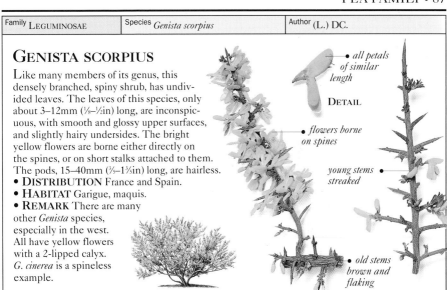

all petals
of similar
length

DETAIL

flowers borne
on spines

young stems
streaked

old stems
brown and
flaking

| Habit Perennial | Height 20–60cm (8–24in) | Flowering time Mar–June |

| Family LEGUMINOSAE | Species *Spartium junceum* | Author L. |

SPANISH BROOM

Spanish Broom is a spineless shrub with supple, smooth stems and large, extremely fragrant flowers. The small, sparse leaves, 10–30mm (⅖–1⅕in) long, are lance-shaped. They are almost stalkless, and are smooth above but covered with flattened silky hairs beneath. The flowers, up to 25mm (1in) across, have an orb-shaped, erect standard petal, and wings that often spread widely. The flattened pods, containing 10 to 18 seeds, become brown and hairless.

• **DISTRIBUTION** Throughout.
• **HABITAT** Maquis, garigue, waysides; mainly on calcareous ground.

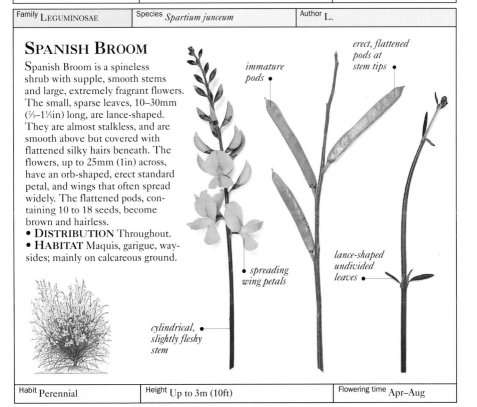

erect, flattened
pods at
stem tips

immature
pods

spreading
wing petals

lance-shaped
undivided
leaves

cylindrical,
slightly fleshy
stem

| Habit Perennial | Height Up to 3m (10ft) | Flowering time Apr–Aug |

Family LEGUMINOSAE	Species *Ulex parviflorus*	Author Pourret

ULEX PARVIFLORUS

Like all gorses, this shrub is densely
branched, and is armed with spines,
which are modified stems and leaves.
On very young plants, the leaves are
divided into 3 parts; on adult plants, the
leaves are undivided, with sharp tips. The
yellow flowers, up to 12mm (½in) long,
grow in the axils of the spines. Each has a
characteristic 2-lipped calyx that is longer
than the wing petals but slightly shorter
than the standard and keel. The fruit is a
hairy pod, 10–15mm (⅖–⅗in) long, brown or
black when ripe, and containing one to 3 seeds.
• **DISTRIBUTION**
Spain, France, Bal-
earic Islands, N.W.
Africa.
• **HABITAT** Open
rocky places, esp-
ecially on acid soils.

leaves and
stems covered
with short hairs

flowers attached
at the axils of
• spines

DETAIL

2-lipped •
calyx with with
flattened hairs

Habit Perennial	Height Up to 150cm (60in)	Flowering time Apr–May

Family LEGUMINOSAE	Species *Adenocarpus telonensis*	Author (Loisel.) DC.

ADENOCARPUS TELONENSIS

This straggly shrub has spineless stems and alternate
branches that are sparingly covered with small
leaves. Each leaf is 3–8mm (⅛–⅓in) long, and is
divided into 3 elliptic leaflets, which are hairless
on top and slightly hairy beneath. The yellow,
short-stalked flowers grow in clusters of 2
to 7, and have an upright standard petal
about 15mm (⅗in) long. The calyces
are hairy, with tubular bases, and have
2 divided lips. The fruit is a pod, which
is densely covered with silky hairs and
characteristic sticky protrusions.
• **DISTRIBUTION** Spain, France.
• **HABITAT** Maquis.
• **RELATED SPECIES** *Adenocarpus
complicatus* is a similar but taller species,
with flowers in racemes.

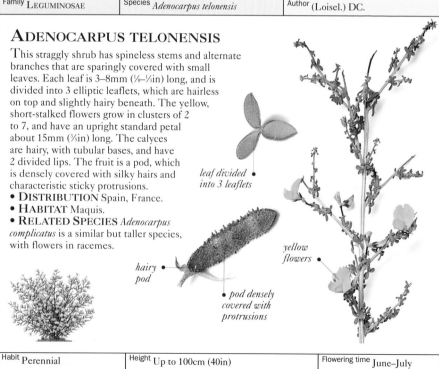

leaf divided •
into 3 leaflets

hairy •
pod

• pod densely
covered with
protrusions

yellow
flowers •

Habit Perennial	Height Up to 100cm (40in)	Flowering time June–July

Family LEGUMINOSAE	Species *Lupinus albus*	Author L.

WHITE LUPIN

Lupins are distinctive members of the pea
family, with leaves that are divided into
a fan of elliptic leaflets. The White
Lupin has upright, branching stems
covered in short hairs, and its largest
leaflets are about 50mm (2in) long and
15mm (⅗in) broad. The white or blue flowers
grow in short racemes, and are about 15mm (⅗in)
long, with hairy, 2-lipped calyces up to 8mm (⅓in)
long. The fruit is a hairy pod, which is 6–10cm
(2⅖–4in) long, containing 2 to 4
yellow seeds.
• **DISTRIBUTION**
S. Balkans, Aegean.
• **HABITAT** Acid soils,
cultivated ground.
• **REMARK** This
species is widely
naturalized throughout
the Mediterranean.

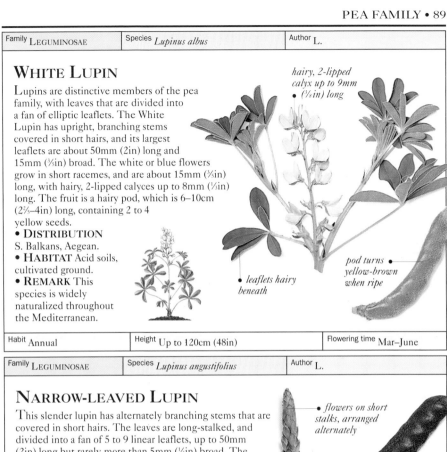

*hairy, 2-lipped
calyx up to 9mm
(⅜in) long*

*pod turns
yellow-brown
when ripe*

*leaflets hairy
beneath*

Habit Annual	Height Up to 120cm (48in)	Flowering time Mar–June

Family LEGUMINOSAE	Species *Lupinus angustifolius*	Author L.

NARROW-LEAVED LUPIN

This slender lupin has alternately branching stems that are
covered in short hairs. The leaves are long-stalked, and
divided into a fan of 5 to 9 linear leaflets, up to 50mm
(2in) long but rarely more than 5mm (⅕in) broad. The
flowers are pale blue, up to 12mm (½in) long, and are
borne alternately, forming a flower-head that can reach
a length of 20cm (8in). The calyces are hairy, with 2 lips.
The upper lip is divided into 2, and is half the size
of the lower, which has 3 irregular teeth. The seed-
pod is hairy, and contains 4 to 6 smooth seeds.
• **DISTRIBUTION** Throughout.
• **HABITAT** Maquis, garigue, and
fields; common on
sandy soils.

*flowers on short
stalks, arranged
alternately*

*pod turns
yellow, brown, or
black when ripe*

*narrow
stipules at
base of leaf-
stalks*

*leaves hairless
on top, hairy
below*

Habit Annual	Height 20–80cm (8–32in)	Flowering time Mar–July

Family LEGUMINOSAE	Species *Lupinus varius*	Author L.

LUPINUS VARIUS

A dense covering of long hairs gives this attractive lupin a silk-like texture. The hairs clothe the erect and sparingly branched stems, the leaf-stalks, and both sides of the leaves. Each leaf is divided into between 9 and 11 leaflets, which are broadly lance-shaped with slightly extended, sharp tips. The flowers, up to 17mm (⅔in) long, are arranged in irregular whorls in a compact head. They are predominantly blue, with a white, yellow, or pale purple blotch on the standard. The lower lip of the calyx is scarcely toothed. The pod, up to 50mm (2in) long, contains 3 to 4 flattened seeds and turns brown when ripe. It, too, is covered with soft hairs.
• **DISTRIBUTION** Throughout.
• **HABITAT** Dry, sandy ground; typically on acid soil.

pod covered with soft hairs •

compact • flower-heads

leaves have • 9–11 leaflets

dense covering • of long hairs

Habit Annual	Height 20–50cm (8–20in)	Flowering time Mar–June

Family LEGUMINOSAE	Species *Lupinus micranthus*	Author Guss.

LUPINUS MICRANTHUS

Similar in many ways to *Lupinus varius* (above), this plant has erect or ascending stems covered in grey or brown hairs. Each leaf has 5 to 7 egg- or wedge-shaped leaflets, up to 70mm (2⅘in) long. The flowers reach a length of 14mm (½in). The ripe pods are reddish brown.
• **DISTRIBUTION** Throughout the region.
• **HABITAT** Maquis, waysides; prefers dry, acid soils.

• leaves with 5–7 leaflets

white blotch at centre of • standard

small, narrow • stipules at base of leaf-stalks

Habit Annual	Height 10–40cm (4–16in)	Flowering time Feb–June

Family LEGUMINOSAE	Species *Colutea arborescens*	Author L.

BLADDER SENNA

With its curiously inflated pods, Bladder Senna is one of the most distinctive Mediterranean members of the pea family. An erect, spineless shrub, it has much-branched stems that are green and downy when young. The older, woody growth is covered in bark, which peels in strips. Its leaves are divided into 7 to 13 leaflets, which are elliptic and often have a notch at their tips. The flowers are up to 20mm (⅜in) long, and they grow in stalked clusters of 3 to 8. The bladder-like pods, up to 70mm (2⅜in) long, have papery walls and contain numerous smooth, kidney-shaped seeds. The pods inflate and turn reddish brown when ripe.

• **DISTRIBUTION** Throughout.
• **HABITAT** Limestone hills, woods, garigue, gardens.

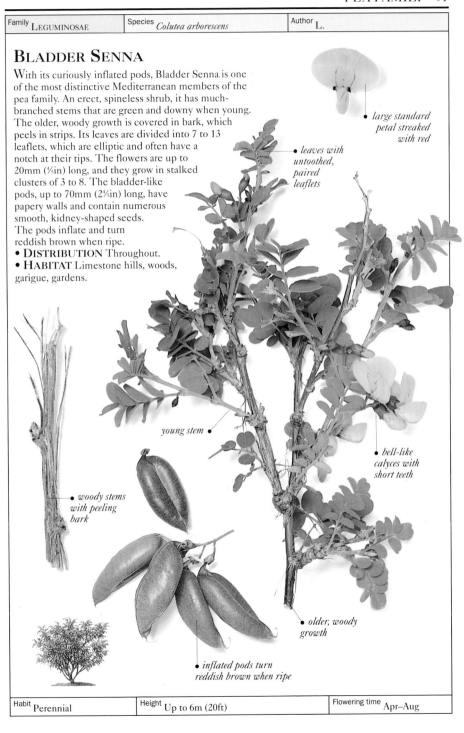

large standard petal streaked with red

leaves with untoothed, paired leaflets

young stem

bell-like calyces with short teeth

woody stems with peeling bark

older, woody growth

inflated pods turn reddish brown when ripe

Habit Perennial	Height Up to 6m (20ft)	Flowering time Apr–Aug

| Family LEGUMINOSAE | Species *Astragalus hamosus* | Author L. |

ASTRAGALUS HAMOSUS

This inconspicuous plant is a typical small milk-vetch, belonging to an important genus that includes dozens of species throughout the region. Its lax stems are covered in short hairs, as are the undersides of its leaves. Each leaf is up to 15cm (6in) long, and is divided into 17 to 25 oval leaflets. The pale yellow flowers grow in stalked clusters of 5 to 14. The characteristic curved pod is almost hairless, and is up to 50mm (2in) long.

• **DISTRIBUTION**
Throughout the region.

• **HABITAT** Fields, waysides, rocky ground near the sea.

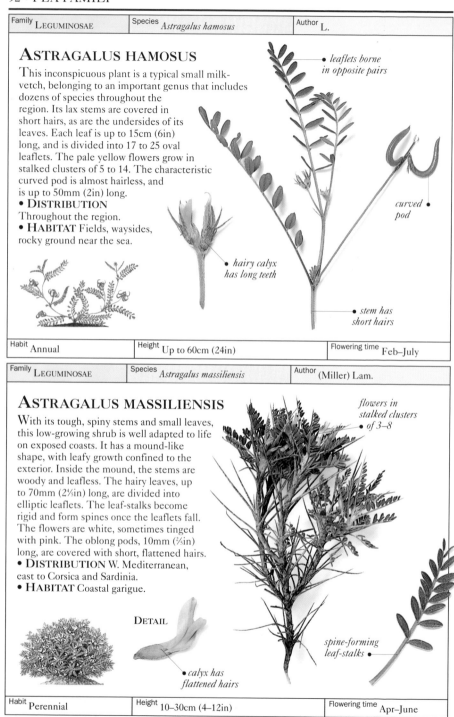

• *leaflets borne in opposite pairs*

• *curved pod*

• *hairy calyx has long teeth*

• *stem has short hairs*

| Habit Annual | Height Up to 60cm (24in) | Flowering time Feb–July |

| Family LEGUMINOSAE | Species *Astragalus massiliensis* | Author (Miller) Lam. |

ASTRAGALUS MASSILIENSIS

With its tough, spiny stems and small leaves, this low-growing shrub is well adapted to life on exposed coasts. It has a mound-like shape, with leafy growth confined to the exterior. Inside the mound, the stems are woody and leafless. The hairy leaves, up to 70mm (2⅗in) long, are divided into elliptic leaflets. The leaf-stalks become rigid and form spines once the leaflets fall. The flowers are white, sometimes tinged with pink. The oblong pods, 10mm (⅜in) long, are covered with short, flattened hairs.

• **DISTRIBUTION** W. Mediterranean, east to Corsica and Sardinia.

• **HABITAT** Coastal garigue.

DETAIL

flowers in stalked clusters of 3–8

spine-forming leaf-stalks •

• *calyx has flattened hairs*

| Habit Perennial | Height 10–30cm (4–12in) | Flowering time Apr–June |

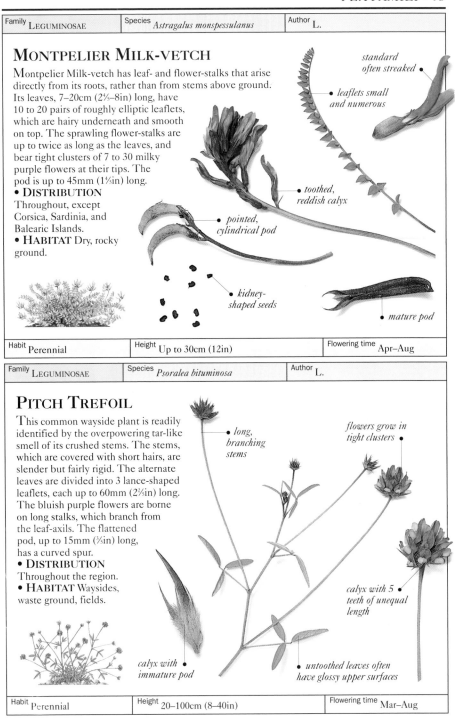

Family LEGUMINOSAE	Species *Astragalus monspessulanus*	Author L.

MONTPELIER MILK-VETCH

Montpelier Milk-vetch has leaf- and flower-stalks that arise directly from its roots, rather than from stems above ground. Its leaves, 7–20cm (2⅘–8in) long, have 10 to 20 pairs of roughly elliptic leaflets, which are hairy underneath and smooth on top. The sprawling flower-stalks are up to twice as long as the leaves, and bear tight clusters of 7 to 30 milky purple flowers at their tips. The pod is up to 45mm (1⅛in) long.

• **DISTRIBUTION** Throughout, except Corsica, Sardinia, and Balearic Islands.
• **HABITAT** Dry, rocky ground.

standard often streaked •

• leaflets small and numerous

• toothed, reddish calyx

• pointed, cylindrical pod

• kidney-shaped seeds

• mature pod

Habit Perennial	Height Up to 30cm (12in)	Flowering time Apr–Aug

Family LEGUMINOSAE	Species *Psoralea bituminosa*	Author L.

PITCH TREFOIL

This common wayside plant is readily identified by the overpowering tar-like smell of its crushed stems. The stems, which are covered with short hairs, are slender but fairly rigid. The alternate leaves are divided into 3 lance-shaped leaflets, each up to 60mm (2⅜in) long. The bluish purple flowers are borne on long stalks, which branch from the leaf-axils. The flattened pod, up to 15mm (⅗in) long, has a curved spur.

• **DISTRIBUTION** Throughout the region.
• **HABITAT** Waysides, waste ground, fields.

• long, branching stems

flowers grow in tight clusters •

calyx with 5 • teeth of unequal length

calyx with • immature pod

• untoothed leaves often have glossy upper surfaces

Habit Perennial	Height 20–100cm (8–40in)	Flowering time Mar–Aug

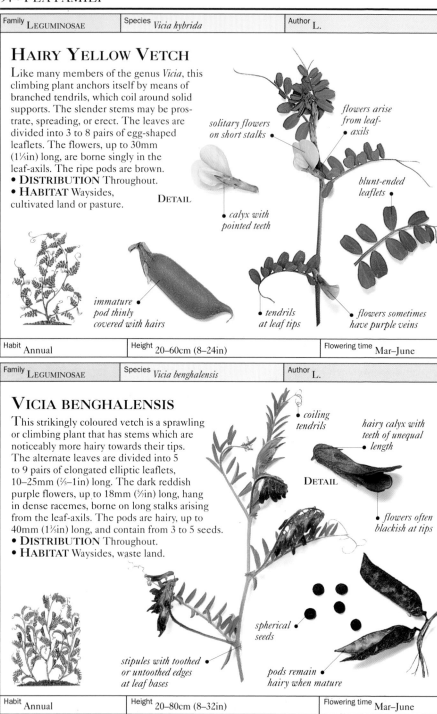

Family LEGUMINOSAE	Species *Vicia hybrida*	Author L.

HAIRY YELLOW VETCH

Like many members of the genus *Vicia*, this climbing plant anchors itself by means of branched tendrils, which coil around solid supports. The slender stems may be prostrate, spreading, or erect. The leaves are divided into 3 to 8 pairs of egg-shaped leaflets. The flowers, up to 30mm (1⅛in) long, are borne singly in the leaf-axils. The ripe pods are brown.
• **DISTRIBUTION** Throughout.
• **HABITAT** Waysides, cultivated land or pasture.

solitary flowers on short stalks •

flowers arise from leaf-axils •

DETAIL

blunt-ended leaflets •

• calyx with pointed teeth

immature • pod thinly covered with hairs

• tendrils at leaf tips

flowers sometimes have purple veins

Habit Annual	Height 20–60cm (8–24in)	Flowering time Mar–June

Family LEGUMINOSAE	Species *Vicia benghalensis*	Author L.

VICIA BENGHALENSIS

This strikingly coloured vetch is a sprawling or climbing plant that has stems which are noticeably more hairy towards their tips. The alternate leaves are divided into 5 to 9 pairs of elongated elliptic leaflets, 10–25mm (⅖–1in) long. The dark reddish purple flowers, up to 18mm (⅝in) long, hang in dense racemes, borne on long stalks arising from the leaf-axils. The pods are hairy, up to 40mm (1⅝in) long, and contain from 3 to 5 seeds.
• **DISTRIBUTION** Throughout.
• **HABITAT** Waysides, waste land.

• coiling tendrils

hairy calyx with teeth of unequal • length

DETAIL

• flowers often blackish at tips

spherical • seeds

stipules with toothed • or untoothed edges at leaf bases

pods remain • hairy when mature

Habit Annual	Height 20–80cm (8–32in)	Flowering time Mar–June

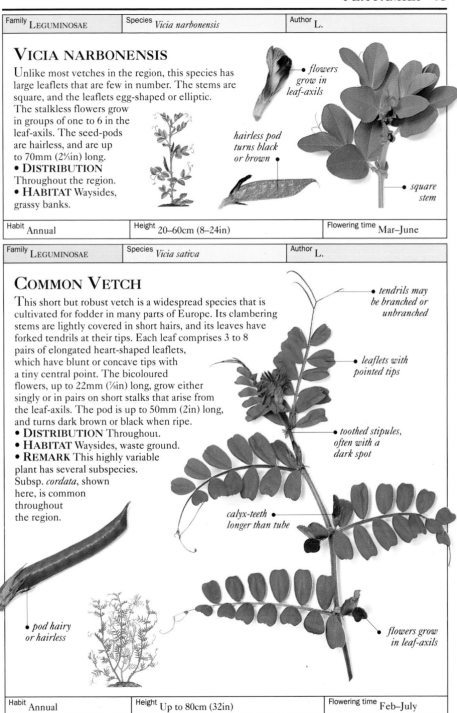

| Family LEGUMINOSAE | Species *Vicia narbonensis* | Author L. |

VICIA NARBONENSIS

Unlike most vetches in the region, this species has large leaflets that are few in number. The stems are square, and the leaflets egg-shaped or elliptic. The stalkless flowers grow in groups of one to 6 in the leaf-axils. The seed-pods are hairless, and are up to 70mm (2⅗in) long.
• **DISTRIBUTION** Throughout the region.
• **HABITAT** Waysides, grassy banks.

flowers grow in leaf-axils

hairless pod turns black or brown

square stem

| Habit Annual | Height 20–60cm (8–24in) | Flowering time Mar–June |

| Family LEGUMINOSAE | Species *Vicia sativa* | Author L. |

COMMON VETCH

This short but robust vetch is a widespread species that is cultivated for fodder in many parts of Europe. Its clambering stems are lightly covered in short hairs, and its leaves have forked tendrils at their tips. Each leaf comprises 3 to 8 pairs of elongated heart-shaped leaflets, which have blunt or concave tips with a tiny central point. The bicoloured flowers, up to 22mm (⅞in) long, grow either singly or in pairs on short stalks that arise from the leaf-axils. The pod is up to 50mm (2in) long, and turns dark brown or black when ripe.
• **DISTRIBUTION** Throughout.
• **HABITAT** Waysides, waste ground.
• **REMARK** This highly variable plant has several subspecies. Subsp. *cordata*, shown here, is common throughout the region.

tendrils may be branched or unbranched

leaflets with pointed tips

toothed stipules, often with a dark spot

calyx-teeth longer than tube

pod hairy or hairless

flowers grow in leaf-axils

| Habit Annual | Height Up to 80cm (32in) | Flowering time Feb–July |

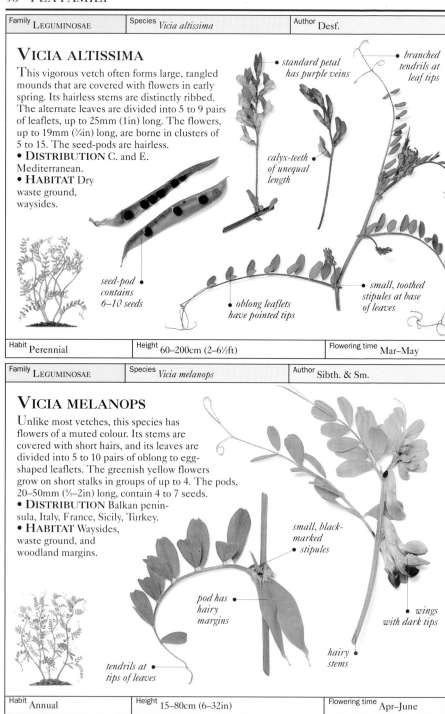

Family LEGUMINOSAE	Species *Vicia altissima*	Author Desf.

VICIA ALTISSIMA

This vigorous vetch often forms large, tangled mounds that are covered with flowers in early spring. Its hairless stems are distinctly ribbed. The alternate leaves are divided into 5 to 9 pairs of leaflets, up to 25mm (1in) long. The flowers, up to 19mm (¾in) long, are borne in clusters of 5 to 15. The seed-pods are hairless.
• **DISTRIBUTION** C. and E. Mediterranean.
• **HABITAT** Dry waste ground, waysides.

standard petal has purple veins

branched tendrils at leaf tips

calyx-teeth of unequal length

seed-pod contains 6–10 seeds

oblong leaflets have pointed tips

small, toothed stipules at base of leaves

Habit Perennial	Height 60–200cm (2–6½ft)	Flowering time Mar–May

Family LEGUMINOSAE	Species *Vicia melanops*	Author Sibth. & Sm.

VICIA MELANOPS

Unlike most vetches, this species has flowers of a muted colour. Its stems are covered with short hairs, and its leaves are divided into 5 to 10 pairs of oblong to egg-shaped leaflets. The greenish yellow flowers grow on short stalks in groups of up to 4. The pods, 20–50mm (⅘–2in) long, contain 4 to 7 seeds.
• **DISTRIBUTION** Balkan peninsula, Italy, France, Sicily, Turkey.
• **HABITAT** Waysides, waste ground, and woodland margins.

small, black-marked stipules

pod has hairy margins

wings with dark tips

hairy stems

tendrils at tips of leaves

Habit Annual	Height 15–80cm (6–32in)	Flowering time Apr–June

| Family LEGUMINOSAE | Species *Lathyrus annuus* | Author L. |

ANNUAL YELLOW VETCHLING

calyx teeth of equal length

This delicate climbing plant has winged stems, a feature that helps to distinguish most *Lathyrus* species from those in the genus *Vicia* (see pp.94–96). Its stems are hairless, and become winged towards their tips. The leaves consist of a V-shaped pair of blade-like leaflets, 5–15cm (2–6in) long, with a central much-branched tendril, and tiny blade-like stipules at the base. The flowers, up to 18mm (⅔in) long, are borne on long stalks, and grow in groups of up to 3. The hairless pods may reach 80mm (3⅓in) long, and turn brown when ripe.
• **DISTRIBUTION** Throughout.
• **HABITAT** Hedges, waste or cultivated ground.

flowers often have orange veins

branched tendril

pod contains 7 or 8 seeds

leaves with parallel ribs

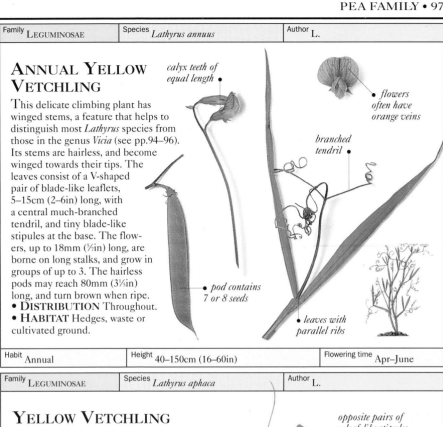

| Habit Annual | Height 40–150cm (16–60in) | Flowering time Apr–June |

| Family LEGUMINOSAE | Species *Lathyrus aphaca* | Author L. |

YELLOW VETCHLING

Yellow Vetchling is notable for its unusual "leaves", which are actually not leaves at all, but highly enlarged stipules. The hairless stems are slender and quadrangular, and do not have wings. The stipules are arranged in opposite pairs, and are up to 50mm (2in) long. They clasp the stem like 2 hands, and between them are the true leaves, which have become reduced to form tendrils. The yellow flowers, up to 18mm (⅔in) long, are borne singly on long stalks from the leaf-axils, and have calyx-teeth that are 3 times as long as the flower-tube. The hairless seed-pods, up to 35mm (1⅜in) long, turn brown when ripe, and contain 6 to 8 seeds.
• **DISTRIBUTION** Throughout the region.
• **HABITAT** Waysides, cultivated land, and pine forests.

opposite pairs of leaf-like stipules

yellow flowers

calyx-teeth up to 3 times as long as tube

tendrils arise between stipules

pod turns brown when ripe

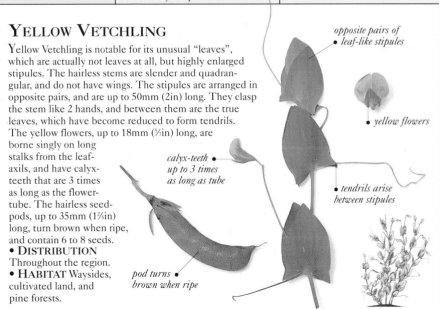

| Habit Annual | Height 30–100cm (12–40in) | Flowering time Feb–June |

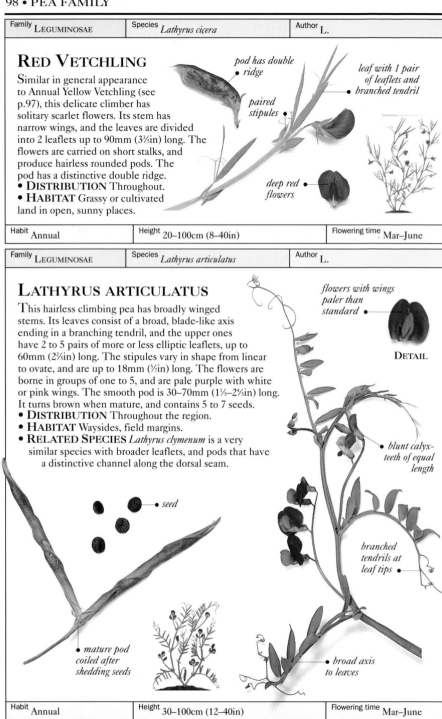

Family LEGUMINOSAE	Species *Lathyrus cicera*	Author L.

RED VETCHLING

Similar in general appearance
to Annual Yellow Vetchling (see
p.97), this delicate climber has
solitary scarlet flowers. Its stem has
narrow wings, and the leaves are divided
into 2 leaflets up to 90mm (3⅜in) long. The
flowers are carried on short stalks, and
produce hairless rounded pods. The
pod has a distinctive double ridge.
• **DISTRIBUTION** Throughout.
• **HABITAT** Grassy or cultivated
land in open, sunny places.

*pod has double
ridge*

*paired
stipules*

*leaf with 1 pair
of leaflets and
branched tendril*

*deep red
flowers*

Habit Annual	Height 20–100cm (8–40in)	Flowering time Mar–June

Family LEGUMINOSAE	Species *Lathyrus articulatus*	Author L.

LATHYRUS ARTICULATUS

This hairless climbing pea has broadly winged
stems. Its leaves consist of a broad, blade-like axis
ending in a branching tendril, and the upper ones
have 2 to 5 pairs of more or less elliptic leaflets, up to
60mm (2⅜in) long. The stipules vary in shape from linear
to ovate, and are up to 18mm (⅝in) long. The flowers are
borne in groups of one to 5, and are pale purple with white
or pink wings. The smooth pod is 30–70mm (1⅕–2⅗in) long.
It turns brown when mature, and contains 5 to 7 seeds.
• **DISTRIBUTION** Throughout the region.
• **HABITAT** Waysides, field margins.
• **RELATED SPECIES** *Lathyrus clymenum* is a very
  similar species with broader leaflets, and pods that have
  a distinctive channel along the dorsal seam.

*flowers with wings
paler than
standard*

DETAIL

*blunt calyx-
teeth of equal
length*

seed

*branched
tendrils at
leaf tips*

*mature pod
coiled after
shedding seeds*

*broad axis
to leaves*

Habit Annual	Height 30–100cm (12–40in)	Flowering time Mar–June

Family LEGUMINOSAE	Species *Lathyrus latifolius*	Author L.

BROAD-LEAVED EVERLASTING PEA

The flowers of this vigorous climber make conspicuous patches of colour in high summer. Its stems are hairless or slightly hairy, and have very broad wings. The leaves have a winged axis and 2 lance-shaped leaflets up to 15cm (6in) long, and they terminate in branched tendrils. The long flower-stalks bear up to 15 purplish pink flowers, 20–30mm (⅘–1⅕in) long, and they form brown pods that contain 10 to 15 seeds.

• **DISTRIBUTION** Throughout the region.

• **HABITAT** Hedges, waysides.

• **RELATED SPECIES** *Lathyrus sylvestris*, is similar, but has narrower leaflets and stipules, and shorter pods.

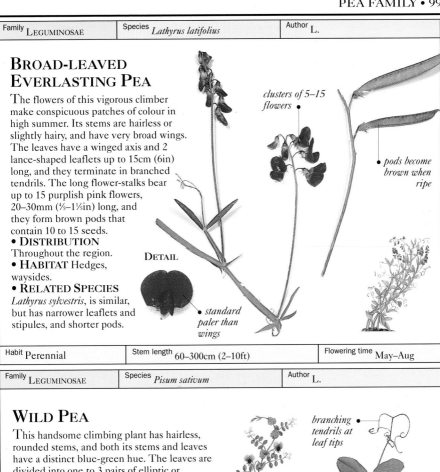

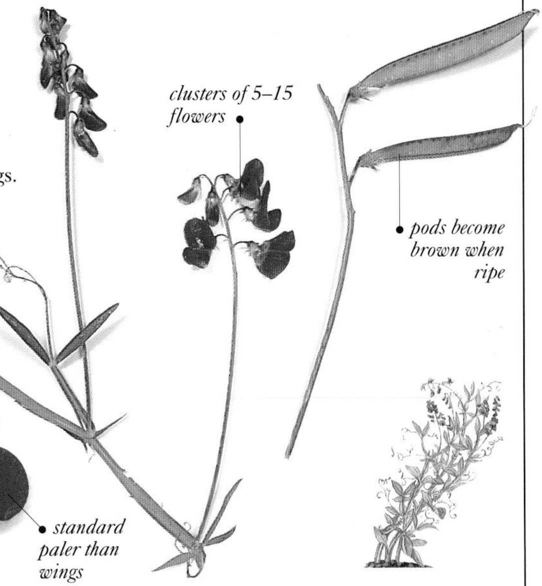
clusters of 5–15 flowers
pods become brown when ripe
standard paler than wings

DETAIL

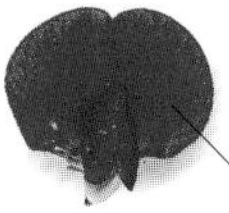

Habit Perennial	Stem length 60–300cm (2–10ft)	Flowering time May–Aug

Family LEGUMINOSAE	Species *Pisum sativum*	Author L.

WILD PEA

This handsome climbing plant has hairless, rounded stems, and both its stems and leaves have a distinct blue-green hue. The leaves are divided into one to 3 pairs of elliptic or rounded leaflets up to 70mm (2⅘in) long, and terminate in branched tendrils. At the base of the leaf-stalks are pairs of heart-shaped stipules with toothed margins, which clasp the stem. The flowers are either solitary or in clusters of up to 3. They have deep pink standards, and deep purple wings. The seed-pods turn yellow or brown when ripe, and are 3–12cm (1⅕– 4¾in) long with inset veins, and contain up to 10 seeds.

• **DISTRIBUTION** Throughout the region.

• **HABITAT** Thickets, woods, field edges.

• **REMARK** Wild Pea has a long history of cultivation.

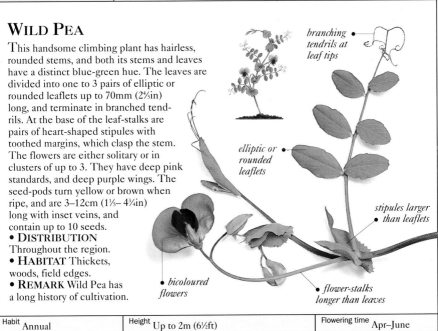

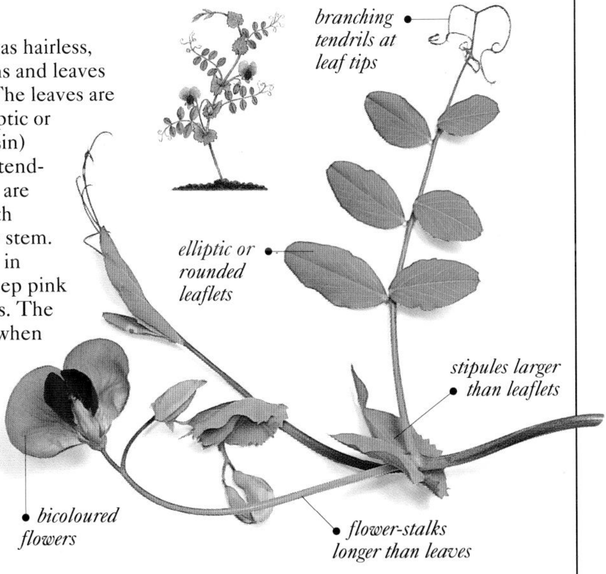
branching tendrils at leaf tips
elliptic or rounded leaflets
stipules larger than leaflets
bicoloured flowers
flower-stalks longer than leaves

Habit Annual	Height Up to 2m (6½ft)	Flowering time Apr–June

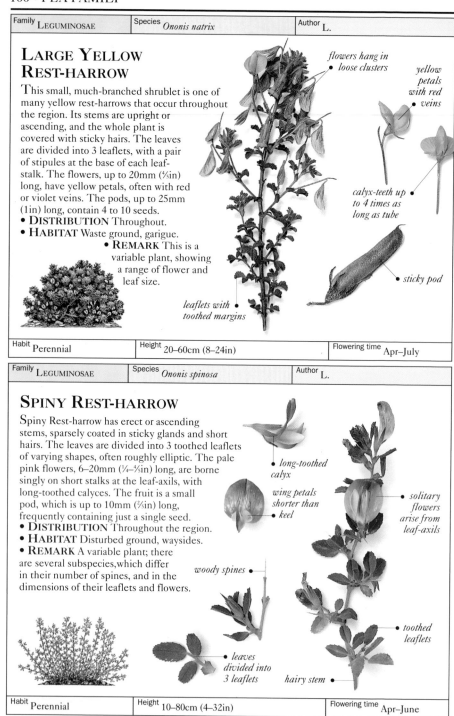

Family LEGUMINOSAE	Species *Ononis natrix*	Author L.

LARGE YELLOW REST-HARROW

This small, much-branched shrublet is one of many yellow rest-harrows that occur throughout the region. Its stems are upright or ascending, and the whole plant is covered with sticky hairs. The leaves are divided into 3 leaflets, with a pair of stipules at the base of each leaf-stalk. The flowers, up to 20mm (⅘in) long, have yellow petals, often with red or violet veins. The pods, up to 25mm (1in) long, contain 4 to 10 seeds.
• **DISTRIBUTION** Throughout.
• **HABITAT** Waste ground, garigue.
 • **REMARK** This is a variable plant, showing a range of flower and leaf size.

flowers hang in
• loose clusters

yellow
petals
with red
• veins

calyx-teeth up •
to 4 times as
long as tube

• sticky pod

leaflets with •
toothed margins

Habit Perennial	Height 20–60cm (8–24in)	Flowering time Apr–July

Family LEGUMINOSAE	Species *Ononis spinosa*	Author L.

SPINY REST-HARROW

Spiny Rest-harrow has erect or ascending stems, sparsely coated in sticky glands and short hairs. The leaves are divided into 3 toothed leaflets of varying shapes, often roughly elliptic. The pale pink flowers, 6–20mm (¼–⅘in) long, are borne singly on short stalks at the leaf-axils, with long-toothed calyces. The fruit is a small pod, which is up to 10mm (⅜in) long, frequently containing just a single seed.
• **DISTRIBUTION** Throughout the region.
• **HABITAT** Disturbed ground, waysides.
• **REMARK** A variable plant; there are several subspecies,which differ in their number of spines, and in the dimensions of their leaflets and flowers.

• long-toothed
calyx

wing petals
shorter than
• keel

• solitary
flowers
arise from
leaf-axils

woody spines •

• toothed
leaflets

• leaves
divided into
3 leaflets

hairy stem •

Habit Perennial	Height 10–80cm (4–32in)	Flowering time Apr–June

Family LEGUMINOSAE	Species *Melilotus alba*	Author Medicus

WHITE MELILOT

Sometimes grown as a fodder crop known as Bokhara Clover, this is the most common white-flowered melilot in the Mediterranean region. Its stems are slender and hairless, with frequent branches. The alternately arranged, stalked leaves are divided into 3 oval leaflets with serrated edges, each up to 30mm (1⅛in) long. The flowering stems bear long loose clusters of small white blooms, which are generally about 4mm (⅛in) long. The fruit is a small pod which contains a single seed. When it is fully matured, it turns greyish brown in colour.

• **DISTRIBUTION** Throughout the region.
• **HABITAT** Open uncultivated ground and waysides.
• **REMARK**
Like other melilots, White Melilot contains a chemical called coumarin, which is strongly redolent of newly mown hay.

flower-head up to 75mm (3in) long

small white flowers

pointed stipules at base of leaves

leaflets with toothed margins

Habit Annual/biennial	Height 30–150cm (12–60in)	Flowering time May–Aug

Family LEGUMINOSAE	Species *Melilotus indica*	Author (L.) All.

SMALL MELILOT

Although smaller than the White Melilot (above), this common plant is very similar in form, with slightly ribbed, branching stems. The leaves are divided into 3 leaflets, up to 20mm (⅘in) long, and the upper leaves tend to have narrower leaflets than the lower ones. The tiny yellow flowers, from 2–3mm (1/12–⅛in) long, are borne in dense racemes that are up to 30mm (1⅛in) long. The hairless pods are roughly spherical, and up to 3mm (⅛in) in diameter. They are olive green when ripe.

• **DISTRIBUTION** Throughout.
• **HABITAT** Waste ground; damp, sandy soil.

dense raceme containing 10 or more tiny flowers

leaves divided into 3 toothed leaflets

needle-like stipules

pods with network of veins

Habit Annual	Height 15–50cm (6–20in)	Flowering time Apr–June

Family LEGUMINOSAE	Species *Melilotus neapolitana*	Author Ten.

MELILOTUS NEAPOLITANA

A plant of waysides and open spaces, this plant shares many of the characteristics of the Small Melilot (see p.101). It has short, erect stems which are hairy towards their tips, and wedge-shaped leaflets. The stipules are lance-shaped and without teeth. The flowers are borne in short racemes which reach a length of about 10mm (⅜in). The fruit, 3mm (⅛in) long, has a distinct conical beak, and ripens to a yellowish brown.
• **DISTRIBUTION** Throughout.
• **HABITAT** Open ground, cultivated land.

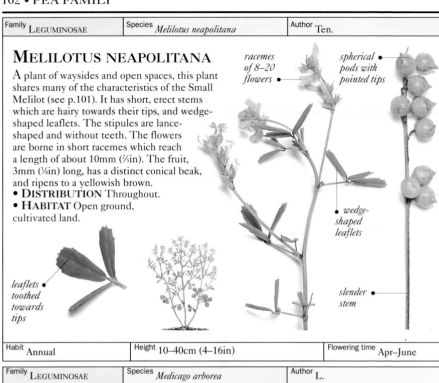

racemes of 8–20 flowers

spherical pods with pointed tips

wedge-shaped leaflets

leaflets toothed towards tips

slender stem

Habit Annual	Height 10–40cm (4–16in)	Flowering time Apr–June

Family LEGUMINOSAE	Species *Medicago arborea*	Author L.

TREE MEDICK

This attractive, leafy shrub is widely cultivated, and is frequently seen on roadsides in many parts of the region. Its young stems are green and softly hairy, as are the undersides of its leaves. The leaves are stalked, and each one is divided into 3 wedge- or heart-shaped leaflets, about 10mm (⅜in) long. The leaflets are often folded upwards, exposing their lower surfaces. The stalked, orange-yellow flowers are up to 15mm (⅝in) long, and are borne in branched heads of 4 to 8 at the stem tips. As with other medicks, the fruit is a pod that coils up tightly as it grows.
• **DISTRIBUTION** Throughout.
• **HABITAT** Dry, rocky places, roadsides, gardens.
• **REMARK** Originally a native of the E. Mediterranean, now widespread through cultivation.

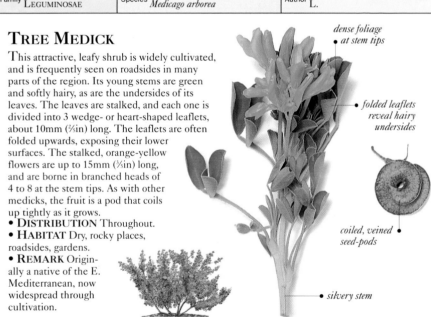

dense foliage at stem tips

folded leaflets reveal hairy undersides

coiled, veined seed-pods

silvery stem

Habit Perennial	Height 1–4m (3¼–13ft)	Flowering time Feb–Aug

Family LEGUMINOSAE	Species *Medicago marina*	Author L.

SEA MEDICK

A creeping plant with dense foliage, Sea Medick is a very widespread inhabitant of sandy shores. The entire plant is covered in dense, woolly hair. The leaves are alternate and stalked, and the stipules are conspicuous, with clearly pointed tips. The flowers are borne in heads of 5 to 12 yellow-orange blooms, about 6mm (¼in) long. The coiled pods often have small spines along their margins.
• **DISTRIBUTION** Throughout the region.
• **HABITAT** Coastal sand and dunes.

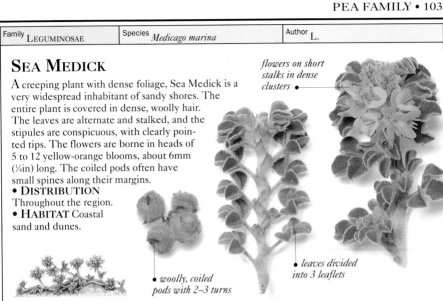

flowers on short stalks in dense clusters •

• leaves divided into 3 leaflets

• woolly, coiled pods with 2–3 turns

Habit Perennial	Stem length 10–50cm (4–20in)	Flowering time Mar–Aug

Family LEGUMINOSAE	Species *Medicago orbicularis*	Author (L.) Bartal.

LARGE DISC MEDICK

This sprawling medick is one of several annual species that leave their large, spiral pods scattered over open ground. A prostrate plant, its stems are either hairless or sparsely hairy. The leaves are divided into 3 leaflets, up to 15mm (⅝in) long, which are oval or wedge-shaped, with toothed margins towards their tips. The stipules are deeply toothed. The flowers are no more than 4mm (⅛in) long, and are either solitary or in clusters of up to 5. The pod is up to 20mm (⅝in) across.
• **DISTRIBUTION** Throughout.
• **HABITAT** Cultivated or stony ground.
• **RELATED SPECIES** *Medicago scutellata* (see p.104), has bowl-shaped pods. *M. rugosa*, found in the C. and E. Mediterranean, has snail-like pods.

mature pods • with 4–6 turns

small • flowers on short stems

pods may have glandular hairs • when young

• trifoliate toothed leaves

• sparsely hairy stem

Habit Annual	Stem length 20–90cm (8–36in)	Flowering time Apr–June

Family LEGUMINOSAE	Species *Medicago scutellata*	Author (L.) Miller

MEDICAGO SCUTELLATA

A plant similar in form to *Medicago orbicularis*, Large Disc Medick (see p.103), this species differs chiefly in the shape of its pods. The stem, the undersides of the leaflets, and the seed-pods are covered in sticky glandular hairs. The leaflets are elliptical or wedge-shaped, and the margin distant from the stalk is toothed. The stipules are broadly lance-shaped and also toothed. The flowers, which are up to 7mm (⅜in) long, grow in groups of up to 3. The coiled pods, which can reach a diameter of 18mm (⅝in), form a bowl-shaped spiral with a thickened outer edge.
• **DISTRIBUTION**
Throughout.
• **HABITAT**
Cultivated, dry,
or stony land.

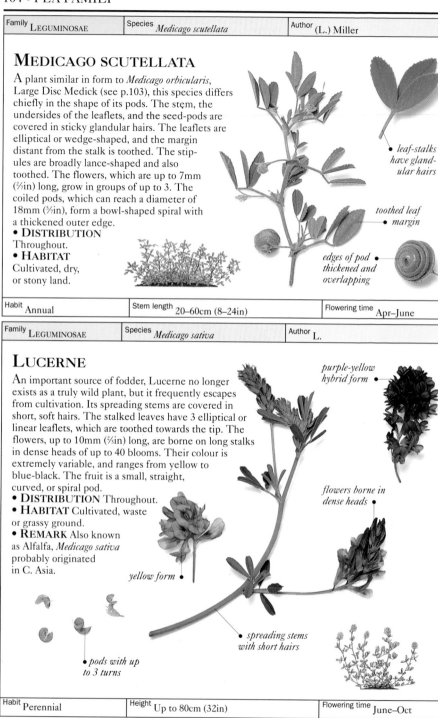

leaf-stalks have glandular hairs

toothed leaf margin

edges of pod thickened and overlapping

Habit Annual	Stem length 20–60cm (8–24in)	Flowering time Apr–June

Family LEGUMINOSAE	Species *Medicago sativa*	Author L.

LUCERNE

An important source of fodder, Lucerne no longer exists as a truly wild plant, but it frequently escapes from cultivation. Its spreading stems are covered in short, soft hairs. The stalked leaves have 3 elliptical or linear leaflets, which are toothed towards the tip. The flowers, up to 10mm (⅜in) long, are borne on long stalks in dense heads of up to 40 blooms. Their colour is extremely variable, and ranges from yellow to blue-black. The fruit is a small, straight, curved, or spiral pod.
• **DISTRIBUTION** Throughout.
• **HABITAT** Cultivated, waste
or grassy ground.
• **REMARK** Also known
as Alfalfa, *Medicago sativa*
probably originated
in C. Asia.

purple-yellow hybrid form

flowers borne in dense heads

yellow form

spreading stems with short hairs

pods with up to 3 turns

Habit Perennial	Height Up to 80cm (32in)	Flowering time June–Oct

Family LEGUMINOSAE	Species *Trifolium angustifolium*	Author L.

NARROW-LEAVED CRIMSON CLOVER

This distinctive plant is one of a large number of clovers in the region (the island of Crete alone, for example, has over 30 species). It is covered with flattened hairs, and its upright stems branch at the base, before spreading and ascending. The stalked leaves are divided into 3 narrow, pointed, leaflets, 20–80mm (⅘–3⅕in) long. They have winged, lance-shaped stipules at their bases. The pink flowers have hairy, long-toothed calyces, which give the dense, conical flower-heads, up to 80mm (3⅕in) tall, a brush-like appearance. Each flower produces a small pod, which is enveloped by the calyx.
• **DISTRIBUTION** Throughout the Mediterranean region. 
• **HABITAT** Dry, waste or cultivated land; usually on acid soils.

brush-like flower-head

pink flowers

grass-like leaflets

slender, erect stem

Habit Annual	Height 10–50cm (4–20in)	Flowering time Apr–July

Family LEGUMINOSAE	Species *Trifolium stellatum*	Author L.

STAR CLOVER

Small but conspicuous, Star Clover has upright stems branching at the base and coated with soft, spreading hairs. The leaves are stalked, and divided into 3 heart-shaped leaflets with slightly toothed tips. The stipules are broad, toothed, and shaped like cockle shells, with green margins and prominent veins. The flowers are pink or, more rarely, purple or yellow, and are borne in heads up to 25mm (1in) wide, which become spherical as they mature and fruit. The star-like calyces have long, pointed teeth.
• **DISTRIBUTION** Throughout.
• **HABITAT** Waysides, fields, open garigue.

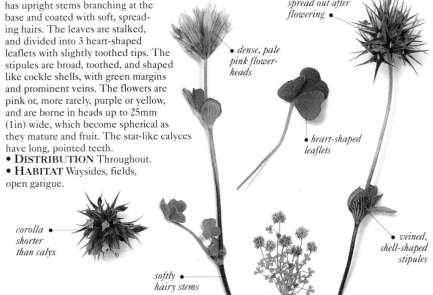

star-shaped calyces spread out after flowering

dense, pale pink flower-heads

heart-shaped leaflets

corolla shorter than calyx

softly hairy stems

veined, shell-shaped stipules

Habit Annual	Height 8–30cm (3⅕–12in)	Flowering time Mar–July

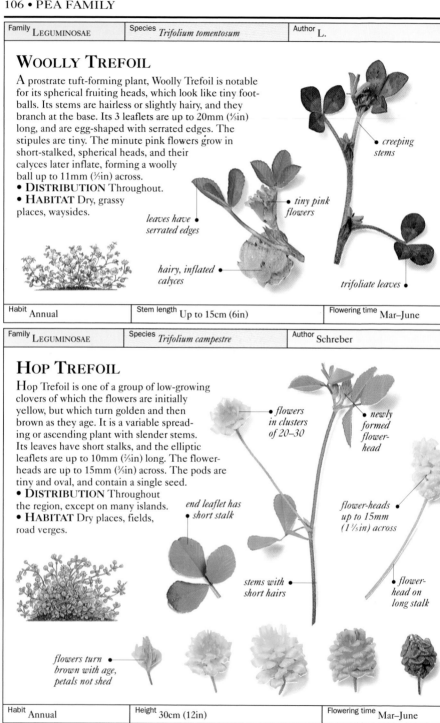

Family LEGUMINOSAE	Species *Trifolium tomentosum*	Author L.

WOOLLY TREFOIL

A prostrate tuft-forming plant, Woolly Trefoil is notable for its spherical fruiting heads, which look like tiny footballs. Its stems are hairless or slightly hairy, and they branch at the base. Its 3 leaflets are up to 20mm (⅘in) long, and are egg-shaped with serrated edges. The stipules are tiny. The minute pink flowers grow in short-stalked, spherical heads, and their calyces later inflate, forming a woolly ball up to 11mm (½in) across.
• **DISTRIBUTION** Throughout.
• **HABITAT** Dry, grassy places, waysides.

creeping stems

tiny pink flowers

leaves have serrated edges

hairy, inflated calyces

trifoliate leaves

Habit Annual	Stem length Up to 15cm (6in)	Flowering time Mar–June

Family LEGUMINOSAE	Species *Trifolium campestre*	Author Schreber

HOP TREFOIL

Hop Trefoil is one of a group of low-growing clovers of which the flowers are initially yellow, but which turn golden and then brown as they age. It is a variable spreading or ascending plant with slender stems. Its leaves have short stalks, and the elliptic leaflets are up to 10mm (⅜in) long. The flowerheads are up to 15mm (⅝in) across. The pods are tiny and oval, and contain a single seed.
• **DISTRIBUTION** Throughout the region, except on many islands.
• **HABITAT** Dry places, fields, road verges.

flowers in clusters of 20–30

newly formed flower-head

end leaflet has short stalk

flower-heads up to 15mm (1⅓in) across

stems with short hairs

flower-head on long stalk

flowers turn brown with age, petals not shed

Habit Annual	Height 30cm (12in)	Flowering time Mar–June

| Family LEGUMINOSAE | Species *Dorycnium hirsutum* | Author (L.) Ser. |

DORYCNIUM HIRSUTUM

This spreading herbaceous plant or small shrub has erect stems that are often woody at the base and hairy at the tips. The leaves have 5 oblong, pointed leaflets, up to 25mm (1in) long. Two of the leaflets flank the stem, which makes them look much like stipules. The white or pink flowers are up to 20mm (⅘in) long, with dark-tipped keels. The fruit is a cylindrical pod, up to 12mm (½in) long. As the pods ripen, they become glossy red, and look like small berries when seen from a distance. They turn brown when mature.
• **DISTRIBUTION** Throughout.
• **HABITAT** Dry, stony or sandy places, maquis, garigue.

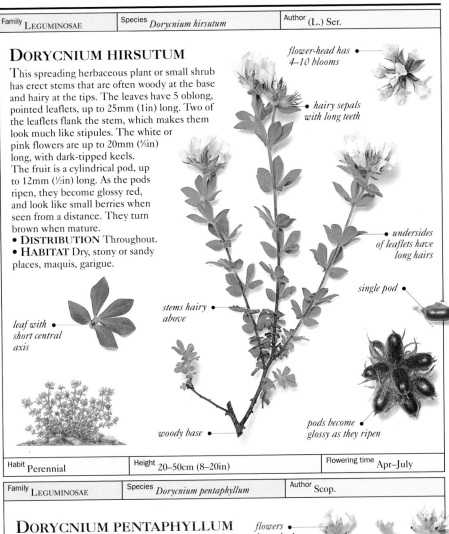

flower-head has 4–10 blooms

hairy sepals with long teeth

undersides of leaflets have long hairs

single pod

stems hairy above

leaf with short central axis

pods become glossy as they ripen

woody base

| Habit Perennial | Height 20–50cm (8–20in) | Flowering time Apr–July |

| Family LEGUMINOSAE | Species *Dorycnium pentaphyllum* | Author Scop. |

DORYCNIUM PENTAPHYLLUM

Similar in form to *Dorycnium hirsutum* (above), this variable herbaceous plant or small shrub is less hairy, and its leaves lack any stalk or central axis. The leaflets are much narrower, and the flowers are up to 6mm (¼in) long. The pods are oval or almost spherical, up to 5mm (⅕in) in diameter, and brown when ripe.
• **DISTRIBUTION** Throughout.
• **HABITAT** Dry, rocky places, maquis, garigue.

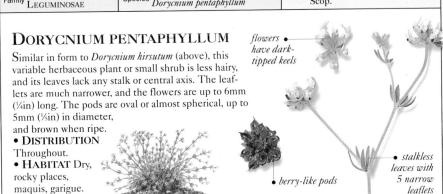

flowers have dark-tipped keels

stalkless leaves with 5 narrow leaflets

berry-like pods

| Habit Perennial | Height 10–80cm (4–32in) | Flowering time Apr–July |

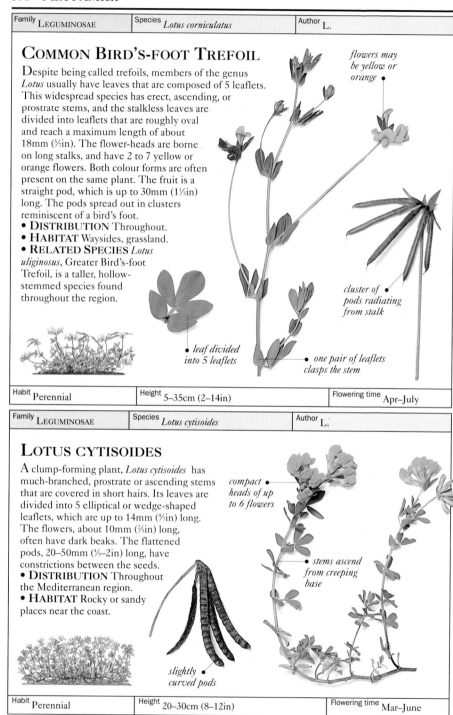

Family LEGUMINOSAE	Species *Lotus corniculatus*	Author L.

COMMON BIRD'S-FOOT TREFOIL

Despite being called trefoils, members of the genus *Lotus* usually have leaves that are composed of 5 leaflets. This widespread species has erect, ascending, or prostrate stems, and the stalkless leaves are divided into leaflets that are roughly oval and reach a maximum length of about 18mm (⅔in). The flower-heads are borne on long stalks, and have 2 to 7 yellow or orange flowers. Both colour forms are often present on the same plant. The fruit is a straight pod, which is up to 30mm (1⅛in) long. The pods spread out in clusters reminiscent of a bird's foot.

• **DISTRIBUTION** Throughout.
• **HABITAT** Waysides, grassland.
• **RELATED SPECIES** *Lotus uliginosus*, Greater Bird's-foot Trefoil, is a taller, hollow-stemmed species found throughout the region.

flowers may be yellow or orange

cluster of pods radiating from stalk

• leaf divided into 5 leaflets

one pair of leaflets clasps the stem

Habit Perennial	Height 5–35cm (2–14in)	Flowering time Apr–July

Family LEGUMINOSAE	Species *Lotus cytisoides*	Author L.

LOTUS CYTISOIDES

A clump-forming plant, *Lotus cytisoides* has much-branched, prostrate or ascending stems that are covered in short hairs. Its leaves are divided into 5 elliptical or wedge-shaped leaflets, which are up to 14mm (⅗in) long. The flowers, about 10mm (⅜in) long, often have dark beaks. The flattened pods, 20–50mm (⅘–2in) long, have constrictions between the seeds.

• **DISTRIBUTION** Throughout the Mediterranean region.
• **HABITAT** Rocky or sandy places near the coast.

compact heads of up to 6 flowers

stems ascend from creeping base

slightly curved pods

Habit Perennial	Height 20–30cm (8–12in)	Flowering time Mar–June

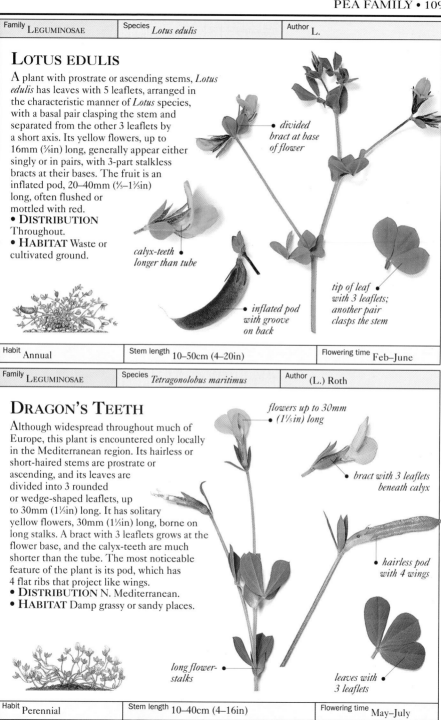

Family LEGUMINOSAE	Species *Lotus edulis*	Author L.

LOTUS EDULIS

A plant with prostrate or ascending stems, *Lotus edulis* has leaves with 5 leaflets, arranged in the characteristic manner of *Lotus* species, with a basal pair clasping the stem and separated from the other 3 leaflets by a short axis. Its yellow flowers, up to 16mm (⅝in) long, generally appear either singly or in pairs, with 3-part stalkless bracts at their bases. The fruit is an inflated pod, 20–40mm (⅘–1⅗in) long, often flushed or mottled with red.
• **DISTRIBUTION** Throughout.
• **HABITAT** Waste or cultivated ground.

divided bract at base of flower

calyx-teeth longer than tube

tip of leaf with 3 leaflets; another pair clasps the stem

inflated pod with groove on back

Habit Annual	Stem length 10–50cm (4–20in)	Flowering time Feb–June

Family LEGUMINOSAE	Species *Tetragonolobus maritimus*	Author (L.) Roth

DRAGON'S TEETH

Although widespread throughout much of Europe, this plant is encountered only locally in the Mediterranean region. Its hairless or short-haired stems are prostrate or ascending, and its leaves are divided into 3 rounded or wedge-shaped leaflets, up to 30mm (1⅕in) long. It has solitary yellow flowers, 30mm (1⅕in) long, borne on long stalks. A bract with 3 leaflets grows at the flower base, and the calyx-teeth are much shorter than the tube. The most noticeable feature of the plant is its pod, which has 4 flat ribs that project like wings.
• **DISTRIBUTION** N. Mediterranean.
• **HABITAT** Damp grassy or sandy places.

flowers up to 30mm (1⅕in) long

bract with 3 leaflets beneath calyx

hairless pod with 4 wings

long flower-stalks

leaves with 3 leaflets

Habit Perennial	Stem length 10–40cm (4–16in)	Flowering time May–July

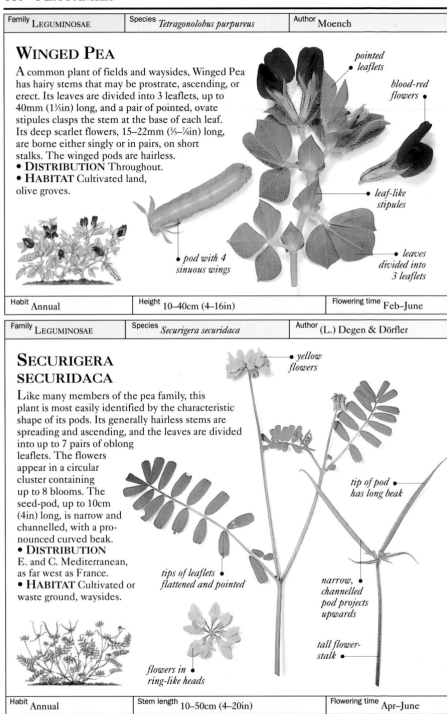

Family LEGUMINOSAE	Species *Tetragonolobus purpureus*	Author Moench

WINGED PEA

A common plant of fields and waysides, Winged Pea has hairy stems that may be prostrate, ascending, or erect. Its leaves are divided into 3 leaflets, up to 40mm (1⅜in) long, and a pair of pointed, ovate stipules clasps the stem at the base of each leaf. Its deep scarlet flowers, 15–22mm (⅗–⅞in) long, are borne either singly or in pairs, on short stalks. The winged pods are hairless.
• **DISTRIBUTION** Throughout.
• **HABITAT** Cultivated land, olive groves.

pointed leaflets

blood-red flowers

leaf-like stipules

leaves divided into 3 leaflets

pod with 4 sinuous wings

Habit Annual	Height 10–40cm (4–16in)	Flowering time Feb–June

Family LEGUMINOSAE	Species *Securigera securidaca*	Author (L.) Degen & Dörfler

SECURIGERA SECURIDACA

Like many members of the pea family, this plant is most easily identified by the characteristic shape of its pods. Its generally hairless stems are spreading and ascending, and the leaves are divided into up to 7 pairs of oblong leaflets. The flowers appear in a circular cluster containing up to 8 blooms. The seed-pod, up to 10cm (4in) long, is narrow and channelled, with a pronounced curved beak.
• **DISTRIBUTION** E. and C. Mediterranean, as far west as France.
• **HABITAT** Cultivated or waste ground, waysides.

yellow flowers

tip of pod has long beak

tips of leaflets flattened and pointed

narrow, channelled pod projects upwards

tall flower-stalk

flowers in ring-like heads

Habit Annual	Stem length 10–50cm (4–20in)	Flowering time Apr–June

Family	Species	Author
LEGUMINOSAE	*Anthyllis tetraphylla*	L.

BLADDER VETCH

Bladder Vetch gets its name from the shape of its calyces, which swell up like balloons after its flowers have withered. Its stems are either prostrate or ascending. The leaves have up to 5 leaflets, the terminal one being elliptic and much larger than the others. The pale yellow flowers appear in clusters of up to 7 in the leaf-axils. The calyces inflate until they reach a diameter of about 12mm (½in), and develop a reddish tinge. The pods generally contain 2 seeds.
• **DISTRIBUTION** Throughout the region.
• **HABITAT** Garigue, cultivated or waste ground.

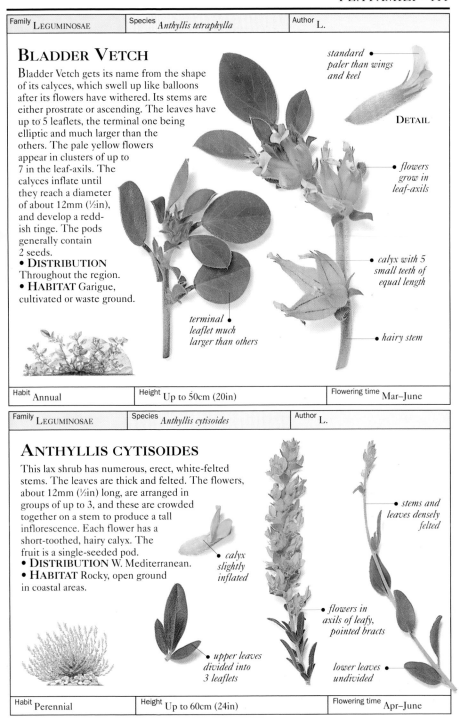

standard • *paler than wings and keel*

DETAIL

flowers grow in leaf-axils

calyx with 5 small teeth of equal length

terminal leaflet much larger than others

hairy stem

Habit	Height	Flowering time
Annual	Up to 50cm (20in)	Mar–June

Family	Species	Author
LEGUMINOSAE	*Anthyllis cytisoides*	L.

ANTHYLLIS CYTISOIDES

This lax shrub has numerous, erect, white-felted stems. The leaves are thick and felted. The flowers, about 12mm (½in) long, are arranged in groups of up to 3, and these are crowded together on a stem to produce a tall inflorescence. Each flower has a short-toothed, hairy calyx. The fruit is a single-seeded pod.
• **DISTRIBUTION** W. Mediterranean.
• **HABITAT** Rocky, open ground in coastal areas.

stems and leaves densely felted

calyx slightly inflated

flowers in axils of leafy, pointed bracts

upper leaves divided into 3 leaflets

lower leaves undivided

Habit	Height	Flowering time
Perennial	Up to 60cm (24in)	Apr–June

Family LEGUMINOSAE	Species *Anthyllis hermanniae*	Author L.

ANTHYLLIS HERMANNIAE

A much-branched shrub, *Anthyllis hermanniae* has white-felted young stems which develop flexible spines when they mature. The small leaves are covered with silky hairs, especially beneath, and are either simple or divided into 3 leaflets, which are often folded upwards. The yellow flowers grow in groups of up to 3 in the leaf-axils, and are spread out along the flowering stems to form open racemes. The calyx is about half the length of the corolla, and the teeth of the sepals are shorter than the tube. The fruit is a pointed, single-seeded pod.
• DISTRIBUTION
Throughout, except Spain and France.
• HABITAT Garigue, open places near coasts.

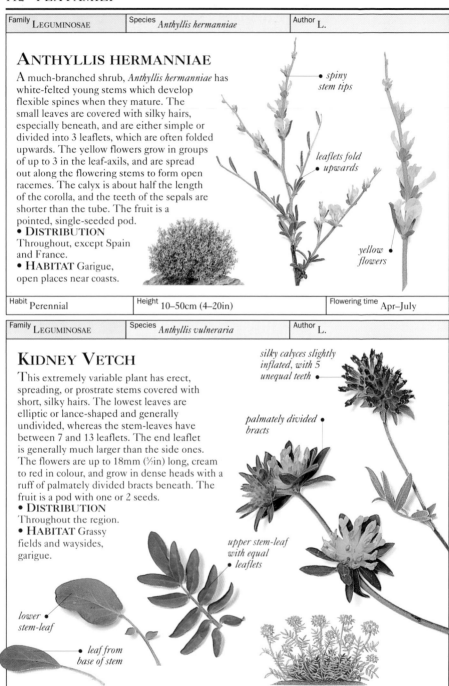

spiny stem tips

leaflets fold upwards

yellow flowers

Habit Perennial	Height 10–50cm (4–20in)	Flowering time Apr–July

Family LEGUMINOSAE	Species *Anthyllis vulneraria*	Author L.

KIDNEY VETCH

This extremely variable plant has erect, spreading, or prostrate stems covered with short, silky hairs. The lowest leaves are elliptic or lance-shaped and generally undivided, whereas the stem-leaves have between 7 and 13 leaflets. The end leaflet is generally much larger than the side ones. The flowers are up to 18mm (⅝in) long, cream to red in colour, and grow in dense heads with a ruff of palmately divided bracts beneath. The fruit is a pod with one or 2 seeds.
• DISTRIBUTION
Throughout the region.
• HABITAT Grassy fields and waysides, garigue.

silky calyces slightly inflated, with 5 unequal teeth

palmately divided bracts

upper stem-leaf with equal leaflets

lower stem-leaf

leaf from base of stem

Habit Annual/perennial	Height Up to 40cm (16in)	Flowering time Mar–July

Family LEGUMINOSAE	Species *Ornithopus compressus*	Author L.

ORNITHOPUS COMPRESSUS

A prostrate or ascending plant, *Ornithopus compressus* has downy stems that branch from the base. Its leaves are divided into between 7 and 18 pairs of densely arrayed elliptic to oval leaflets with pointed tips. The yellow flowers, up to 8mm (⅓in) long, grow in heads of 3 to 5, with a leafy, pinnately divided bract beneath. The curved pods, 20–50mm (⅘–2in) long, have little or no constriction between the segments.
• **DISTRIBUTION** Throughout.
• **HABITAT** Dry, sandy ground, fields, open woods.
• **RELATED SPECIES** *Ornithopus pinnatus*, Orange Bird's-foot, is a similar but less hairy species with fewer leaflets, and orange-yellow flowers without bracts.

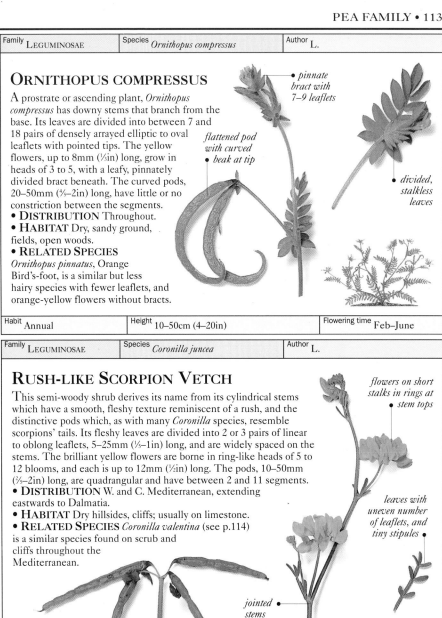

pinnate bract with 7–9 leaflets

flattened pod with curved beak at tip

divided, stalkless leaves

Habit Annual	Height 10–50cm (4–20in)	Flowering time Feb–June

Family LEGUMINOSAE	Species *Coronilla juncea*	Author L.

RUSH-LIKE SCORPION VETCH

This semi-woody shrub derives its name from its cylindrical stems which have a smooth, fleshy texture reminiscent of a rush, and the distinctive pods which, as with many *Coronilla* species, resemble scorpions' tails. Its fleshy leaves are divided into 2 or 3 pairs of linear to oblong leaflets, 5–25mm (⅕–1in) long, and are widely spaced on the stems. The brilliant yellow flowers are borne in ring-like heads of 5 to 12 blooms, and each is up to 12mm (½in) long. The pods, 10–50mm (⅖–2in) long, are quadrangular and have between 2 and 11 segments.
• **DISTRIBUTION** W. and C. Mediterranean, extending eastwards to Dalmatia.
• **HABITAT** Dry hillsides, cliffs; usually on limestone.
• **RELATED SPECIES** *Coronilla valentina* (see p.114) is a similar species found on scrub and cliffs throughout the Mediterranean.

flowers on short stalks in rings at stem tops

leaves with uneven number of leaflets, and tiny stipules

jointed stems

hanging, jointed pods

pods have up to 11 segments

Habit Perennial	Height 20–100cm (8–40in)	Flowering time Mar–June

Family LEGUMINOSAE	Species *Coronilla scorpioides*	Author (L.) Koch

ANNUAL SCORPION VETCH

This sprawling, hairless plant has a characteristic blue-green colour, and slightly waxy texture. The leaves are stalkless and fleshy: the lower being simple, and the upper ones divided into 3 rounded leaflets. The end leaflet, up to 40mm (1⅝in) long, is by far the largest. The flowers are borne in stalked, ring-like heads of 2 to 5 blooms, at the tops of short stems. The calyx is much shorter than the corolla, with blunt teeth. The fruit is a curved, constricted pod, up to 60mm (2⅜in) long.
• **DISTRIBUTION**
Throughout the region.
• **HABITAT** Cultivated or waste ground, dry open places, often as a weed.

flowers up to 8mm (⅓in) long

stalkless leaves with very broad leaflets

curved pods with up to 11 segments

Habit Annual	Height 10–40cm (4–16in)	Flowering time Mar–June

Family LEGUMINOSAE	Species *Coronilla valentina*	Author L.

CORONILLA VALENTINA

Sometimes seen in gardens, this decorative shrub has much-branched, hairless stems, and leaves that are divided into 2 to 6 pairs of leaflets, up to 20mm (⅘in) long, with notched or pointed tips. The flowers, 7–12mm (⅜–½in) long, are borne in ring-like heads of 4 to 12 blooms. The pod is up to 50mm (2in) long; when ripe its segments break up into single-seeded units.
• **DISTRIBUTION**
Throughout the region.
• **HABITAT** Scrub, cliffs, stony ground; usually on limestone.
• **RELATED SPECIES**
Coronilla emerus is a slightly taller shrub found in the centre and east of the region.

all leaflets of similar size

cluster of ripe pods

crown-like clusters of flowers

leaflets have pale undersides

Habit Perennial	Height Up to 100cm (40in)	Flowering time Feb–June

Family LEGUMINOSAE	Species *Coronilla varia*	Author L.

CROWN VETCH

This handsome member of the *Coronilla* genus is a widespread plant, sometimes grown for fodder, whose range extends well beyond the Mediterranean region. The hairless stems are spreading to erect, and the alternate leaves are divided into between 7 and 12 pairs of leaflets. The leaflets, up to 20mm (⅘in) long, are oblong to elliptical, often ending in small points. The flowers grow in crown-like heads, which are borne on stalks that are longer than the leaves. There are 10 to 20 flowers per head, each up to 15mm (⅗in) long, usually with white wings and pink or purple standards. The pod is up to 50mm (2in) long at maturity, with a quadrangular cross-section and 3 to 8 segments. Mature pods break easily into single-seeded sections.

• **DISTRIBUTION** Throughout on the mainland but absent from many islands.

• **HABITAT** Fields or waste ground; occasionally found in gardens.

• **RELATED SPECIES** Similar species include *Coronilla globosa*, found on Crete, which has heads of up to 40 white flowers, and *C. cretica* (see p.116).

10–20 flowers per head

flowers arranged in a ring

immature seed-pods

flowers often bicoloured; tip of keel purple

small membranous stipules at base of leaves

leaflets often have small points

leaves divided into 7–12 pairs of leaflets

hairless ribbed stem

Habit Perennial	Height 20–120cm (8–48in)	Flowering time Mar–July

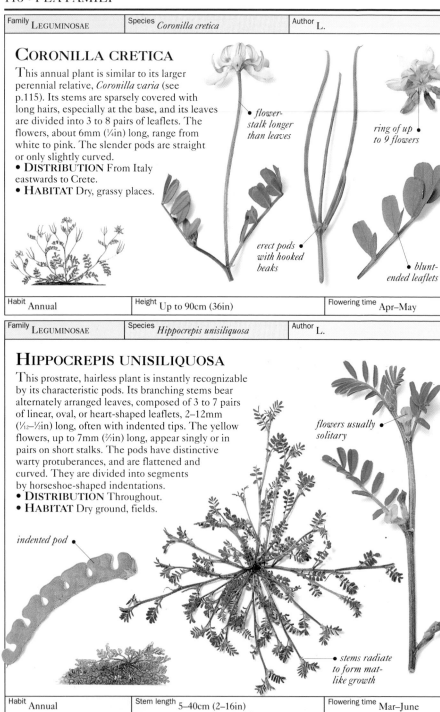

| Family LEGUMINOSAE | Species *Coronilla cretica* | Author L. |

CORONILLA CRETICA

This annual plant is similar to its larger perennial relative, *Coronilla varia* (see p.115). Its stems are sparsely covered with long hairs, especially at the base, and its leaves are divided into 3 to 8 pairs of leaflets. The flowers, about 6mm (¼in) long, range from white to pink. The slender pods are straight or only slightly curved.
• **DISTRIBUTION** From Italy eastwards to Crete.
• **HABITAT** Dry, grassy places.

• flower-stalk longer than leaves

ring of up • to 9 flowers

erect pods • with hooked beaks

• blunt-ended leaflets

| Habit Annual | Height Up to 90cm (36in) | Flowering time Apr–May |

| Family LEGUMINOSAE | Species *Hippocrepis unisiliquosa* | Author L. |

HIPPOCREPIS UNISILIQUOSA

This prostrate, hairless plant is instantly recognizable by its characteristic pods. Its branching stems bear alternately arranged leaves, composed of 3 to 7 pairs of linear, oval, or heart-shaped leaflets, 2–12mm (1/12–½in) long, often with indented tips. The yellow flowers, up to 7mm (⅔in) long, appear singly or in pairs on short stalks. The pods have distinctive warty protuberances, and are flattened and curved. They are divided into segments by horseshoe-shaped indentations.
• **DISTRIBUTION** Throughout.
• **HABITAT** Dry ground, fields.

flowers usually • solitary

indented pod •

• stems radiate to form mat-like growth

| Habit Annual | Stem length 5–40cm (2–16in) | Flowering time Mar–June |

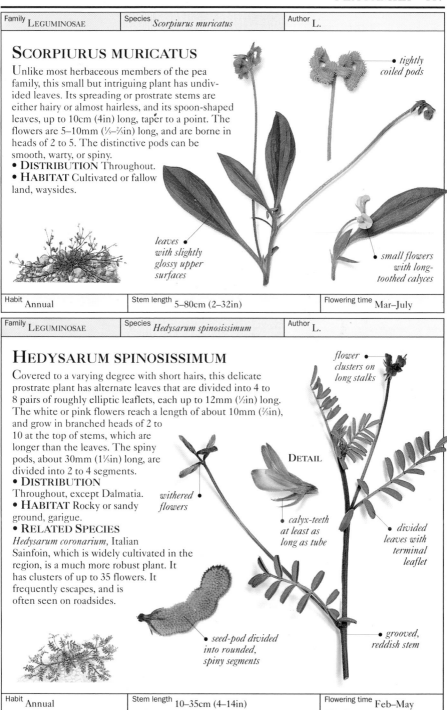

Family LEGUMINOSAE	Species *Scorpiurus muricatus*	Author L.

SCORPIURUS MURICATUS

Unlike most herbaceous members of the pea family, this small but intriguing plant has undivided leaves. Its spreading or prostrate stems are either hairy or almost hairless, and its spoon-shaped leaves, up to 10cm (4in) long, taper to a point. The flowers are 5–10mm (⅕–⅖in) long, and are borne in heads of 2 to 5. The distinctive pods can be smooth, warty, or spiny.
• **DISTRIBUTION** Throughout.
• **HABITAT** Cultivated or fallow land, waysides.

tightly coiled pods

leaves with slightly glossy upper surfaces

small flowers with long-toothed calyces

Habit Annual	Stem length 5–80cm (2–32in)	Flowering time Mar–July

Family LEGUMINOSAE	Species *Hedysarum spinosissimum*	Author L.

HEDYSARUM SPINOSISSIMUM

Covered to a varying degree with short hairs, this delicate prostrate plant has alternate leaves that are divided into 4 to 8 pairs of roughly elliptic leaflets, each up to 12mm (½in) long. The white or pink flowers reach a length of about 10mm (⅖in), and grow in branched heads of 2 to 10 at the top of stems, which are longer than the leaves. The spiny pods, about 30mm (1⅛in) long, are divided into 2 to 4 segments.
• **DISTRIBUTION** Throughout, except Dalmatia.
• **HABITAT** Rocky or sandy ground, garigue.
• **RELATED SPECIES** *Hedysarum coronarium*, Italian Sainfoin, which is widely cultivated in the region, is a much more robust plant. It has clusters of up to 35 flowers. It frequently escapes, and is often seen on roadsides.

flower clusters on long stalks

DETAIL

withered flowers

calyx-teeth at least as long as tube

divided leaves with terminal leaflet

seed-pod divided into rounded, spiny segments

grooved, reddish stem

Habit Annual	Stem length 10–35cm (4–14in)	Flowering time Feb–May

| Family LEGUMINOSAE | Species *Onobrychis aequidentata* | Author (Sibth. & Sm.) D'Urv. |

ONOBRYCHIS AEQUIDENTATA

This slender, erect or spreading plant is covered with short hairs, and has leaves that are divided into 5 to 8 pairs of elliptic to linear leaflets. The flower-stalks are much longer than the leaves, and bear one to 4 pinkish purple flowers, up to 14mm (½in) long. The calyx has narrow, pointed teeth, which are about 4 to 5 times as long as the tube. The disc-shaped, pitted pod is 6–12mm (¼–½in) across.
• **DISTRIBUTION** Throughout the region; rarer in the west.
• **HABITAT** Fields and waysides.
• **RELATED SPECIES** *Onobrychis crista-galli* is similar but has flower-stalks that are no longer than its leaves.

flowers widely spaced

flower-stalks much longer than leaves

toothed pod clasped by pointed calyx

narrow leaflets with terminal point

| Habit Annual | Height Up to 40cm (16in) | Flowering time Mar–July |

| Family LEGUMINOSAE | Species *Onobrychis caput-galli* | Author (L.) Lam. |

COCK'S-COMB SAINFOIN

A prostrate, spreading, or erect plant similar to *Onobrychis aequidentata* (above), Cock's-comb Sainfoin has stems that are slightly hairy or hairless. Its leaves have 4 to 7 pairs of linear to elliptic leaflets, each about 20mm (⅘in) long. The flower-stalks are roughly as long as the leaves, and they carry compact clusters of up to 8 purple flowers, up to 8mm (⅓in) long. The calyx-teeth are from 2 to 4 times as long as the tube. The distinctive pod is 6–10mm (¼–⅜in) across, and has spiny teeth on its sides as well as on its margin.
• **DISTRIBUTION** Throughout, except the Balearic Islands, Corsica, and Sardinia.
• **HABITAT** Fields and waysides.
• **RELATED SPECIES** There are also several perennial species of *Onobrychis* found in the region, including *O. viciifolia* (see opposite). All have rounded, flattened, toothed pods.

DETAIL

flower-stalks no longer than leaves

narrow, pointed calyx-teeth

leaflets of equal size

spiny 1-seeded pods

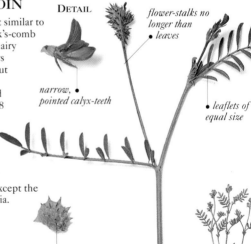

| Habit Annual | Height 10–90cm (4–36in) | Flowering time Mar–July |

Family LEGUMINOSAE	Species *Onobrychis viciifolia*	Author Scop.

SAINFOIN

Sainfoin is a widely cultivated plant common not only in fields but also on roadsides, where it often establishes itself. Its erect stems are covered with short hairs, and its leaves are divided into 6 to 14 pairs of linear to oblong leaflets, up to 35mm (1⅜in) long. The pink flowers are borne in dense racemes, and are about 12mm (½in) long. The pods are plump but slightly flattened, up to 8mm (⅓in) across, with toothed ridges and netted surfaces.
• **DISTRIBUTION** Throughout.
• **HABITAT** Fields, waste ground, roadsides.
• **REMARK**
Probably native
to C. Europe;
there are many
cultivated forms
of this plant with
differing charac-
teristics.

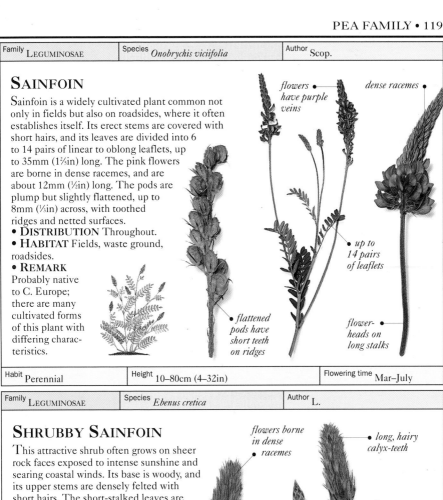

flowers •
have purple
veins

dense racemes •

• up to
14 pairs
of leaflets

• flattened
pods have
short teeth
on ridges

flower- •
heads on
long stalks

Habit Perennial	Height 10–80cm (4–32in)	Flowering time Mar–July

Family LEGUMINOSAE	Species *Ebenus cretica*	Author L.

SHRUBBY SAINFOIN

This attractive shrub often grows on sheer rock faces exposed to intense sunshine and searing coastal winds. Its base is woody, and its upper stems are densely felted with short hairs. The short-stalked leaves are divided into either 3 or 5 leaflets, up to 30mm (1⅛in) long, which are elliptic to oblong and covered with silky hairs. Its pink or purple flowers appear in dense racemes. Their very hairy calyces give the unopened flower-heads a soft silky feel. Small pods form within the calyces, each containing up to 2 seeds.
• **DISTRIBUTION** Crete.
• **HABITAT** Cliffs and rocky hillsides.

flowers borne
in dense
• racemes

• long, hairy
calyx-teeth

• leaf with
3 leaflets

dry membranous
bracts beneath
flowers

hairy upper •
stems

• leaf with
5 leaflets

Habit Perennial	Height Up to 50cm (20in)	Flowering time Apr–May

SORREL FAMILY

Family OXALIDACEAE	Species *Oxalis articulata*	Author Savigny

PINK OXALIS

The sorrel family contains many decorative plants, and several – including this species – have been introduced into the region, later establishing themselves in the wild. Pink Oxalis grows from a swollen rhizome, and forms a leafy mound topped by flowers. Each leaf has 3 heart-shaped leaflets, about 25mm (1in) wide, with minute orange speckles. As with many members of this genus, the leaflets fold down at night. The pink flowers, borne in clusters of up to a dozen, have long stalks and 5 petals, which open only in bright sunshine. After withering, the flowers produce cylindrical seed capsules up to 10mm (⅖in) long, which explode when ripe.
• **DISTRIBUTION** W. Mediterranean; introduced from South America.
• **HABITAT** Waste ground, gardens.

5 petals • overlapping at base

• clusters of flowers on long stalks

• slightly downy, heart-shaped leaflets

Habit Perennial	Height Up to 35cm (14in)	Flowering time Apr–Sept

Family OXALIDACEAE	Species *Oxalis pes-caprae*	Author L.

BERMUDA BUTTERCUP

In spring, large stretches of the Mediterranean hinterland turn brilliant yellow as this beautiful but troublesome weed comes into bloom. The plant grows from bulbous roots, and its leaves form an open mound. Each leaf is divided into 3 heart-shaped leaflets, up to 30mm (1⅛in) wide, and the surface of each leaflet is slightly hairy, often with a number of black specks. The flowers, borne on long stems in clusters of up to 12, have short stalks. They usually have 5 petals, although a double-petalled form, often splashed with red, is common throughout the region. Despite the energy spent on flowering, Mediterranean plants rarely produce seeds. Instead, they spread by forming small bulbils that are all too easily scattered by the plough.
• **DISTRIBUTION** Throughout the region.
• **HABITAT** Olive groves, vineyards; particularly common in damp areas.

double-flowered form with red • tinge

• single-flowered form

3-parted • leaves with black specks

smooth • stem

Habit Perennial	Height 10–50cm (4–20in)	Flowering time Dec–May

GERANIUM FAMILY

Family GERANIACEAE	Species *Geranium tuberosum*	Author L.

TUBEROUS CRANESBILL

As its name indicates, this handsome perennial grows from a tuber. It usually has a single stem, surrounded by leaves arising directly from the ground. The leaves are greyish and, as with other members of this genus, are palmately lobed. The purplish flowers, about 25mm (1in) across, are borne in branching clusters. After flowering, the "crane's bill" – a beak-like fruit – develops, containing 5 seeds, which are catapulted away when the fruit is ripe.

• **DISTRIBUTION** C. and E. Mediterranean.
• **HABITAT** Waysides, fields, rocky ground; often cultivated.

notched petals

purplish flowers

leaves deeply cut into several narrow lobes

Habit Perennial	Height Up to 20cm (8in)	Flowering time Feb–May

Family GERANIACEAE	Species *Erodium petraeum*	Author (Gouan) Willd.

ROCK STORKSBILL

Storksbills can be distinguished from cranesbills (above) by their leaves, which are usually pinnate or pinnately lobed, and also by their fruit, which has a slight spiral twist. This western species is highly variable, but is usually covered with velvety hairs. Its finely divided leaves are carried on stalks up to 80mm (3⅛in) long. The flowers, up to 25mm (1in) across, grow in clusters of up to 5 and have violet, pink, or white petals. The fruit is up to 30mm (1⅛in) long; unlike the cranesbill's, it does not catapult its seeds.

• **DISTRIBUTION** S.W. France, Spain.
• **HABITAT** Exposed rocky ground; usually on limestone.

petals without notches

petals have contrasting veins

fruit has short beak

leaves arising from woody stock

Habit Perennial	Height Up to 20cm (8in)	Flowering time Apr–June

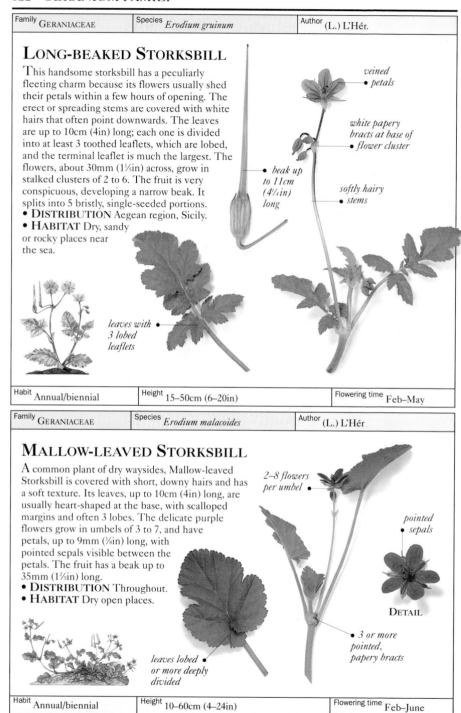

| Family GERANIACEAE | Species *Erodium gruinum* | Author (L.) L'Hér. |

LONG-BEAKED STORKSBILL

This handsome storksbill has a peculiarly
fleeting charm because its flowers usually shed
their petals within a few hours of opening. The
erect or spreading stems are covered with white
hairs that often point downwards. The leaves
are up to 10cm (4in) long; each one is divided
into at least 3 toothed leaflets, which are lobed,
and the terminal leaflet is much the largest. The
flowers, about 30mm (1⅛in) across, grow in
stalked clusters of 2 to 6. The fruit is very
conspicuous, developing a narrow beak. It
splits into 5 bristly, single-seeded portions.
• **DISTRIBUTION** Aegean region, Sicily.
• **HABITAT** Dry, sandy
or rocky places near
the sea.

veined • petals

white papery bracts at base of • flower cluster

beak up to 11cm (4¼in) long

softly hairy • stems

leaves with • 3 lobed leaflets

| Habit Annual/biennial | Height 15–50cm (6–20in) | Flowering time Feb–May |

| Family GERANIACEAE | Species *Erodium malacoides* | Author (L.) L'Hér. |

MALLOW-LEAVED STORKSBILL

A common plant of dry waysides, Mallow-leaved
Storksbill is covered with short, downy hairs and has
a soft texture. Its leaves, up to 10cm (4in) long, are
usually heart-shaped at the base, with scalloped
margins and often 3 lobes. The delicate purple
flowers grow in umbels of 3 to 7, and have
petals, up to 9mm (⅜in) long, with
pointed sepals visible between the
petals. The fruit has a beak up to
35mm (1⅜in) long.
• **DISTRIBUTION** Throughout.
• **HABITAT** Dry open places.

2–8 flowers per umbel •

pointed • sepals

DETAIL

• 3 or more pointed, papery bracts

leaves lobed • or more deeply divided

| Habit Annual/biennial | Height 10–60cm (4–24in) | Flowering time Feb–June |

Family GERANIACEAE	Species *Erodium moschatum*	Author (L.) L'Hér.

MUSK STORKSBILL

In keeping with its name, this erect or spreading plant has a characteristically musky smell, and it is covered with hairs that sometimes give it a sticky texture. The leaves are up to 20cm (8in) long, and are divided into alternate, roughly egg-shaped leaflets with toothed margins. The leaflets are themselves divided, although not generally as far as their midribs. The flowers are borne in stalked clusters of 5 to 12 blooms, and each one forms a beaked fruit up to 45mm (1⅛in) long.

• **DISTRIBUTION** Throughout the region.
• **HABITAT** Fields or waste ground.

cluster of beaked fruit

DETAIL

slender pink petals

flower clusters borne on long, slender stems

stems covered with sticky hairs

Habit Annual/biennial	Height 10–50cm (4–20in)	Flowering time Mar–May

CALTROP FAMILY

Family ZYGOPHYLLACEAE	Species *Tribulus terrestris*	Author L.

SMALL CALTROPS

The Small Caltrops takes its name from the Old English word "calcatrippe" – a metal ball armed with 4 spikes: the spiny fruit is like a miniature version of this weapon. The plant has creeping stems, covered with short white hairs. The leaves are divided into 5 to 8 pairs of roughly elliptic leaflets, and the flowers, about 8mm (⅓in) across, grow in the leaf-axils. The warty fruit, armed with spines, sticks to shoes with great tenacity.

• **DISTRIBUTION** Throughout the region.
• **HABITAT** Dry, open places, waste or sandy ground.
• **REMARK** Also known as Maltese Cross.

leaves without terminal leaflets

opposite leaves often of different sizes

spiny fruit about 10mm (⅖in) across

Habit Annual	Stem length 10–60cm (4–24in)	Flowering time May–Sept

Flax Family

Family LINACEAE	Species *Linum narbonense*	Author L.

Linum narbonense

Like most flaxes, *Linum narbonense* is best seen in sunny conditions, because its sky-blue petals close in dull weather. An erect, hairless plant, it has slender stems densely clad with narrow, stalkless leaves that have either one or 3 main veins. The delicate flowers, borne in branching heads, are 30–40mm (1⅕–1⅗in) across, and have pointed sepals with papery edges. The fruit is a rounded capsule.

• **Distribution** W. and C. Mediterranean.

• **Habitat** Open, rocky or sandy ground.

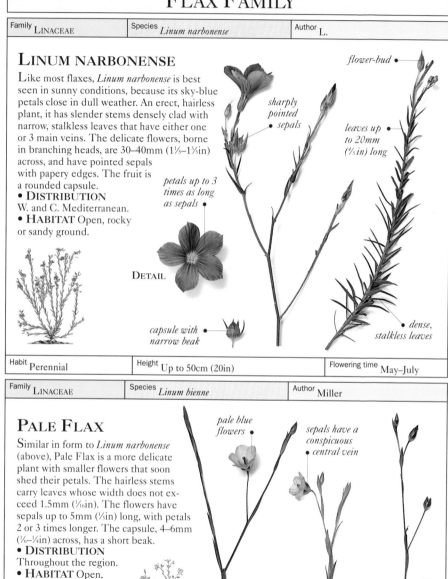

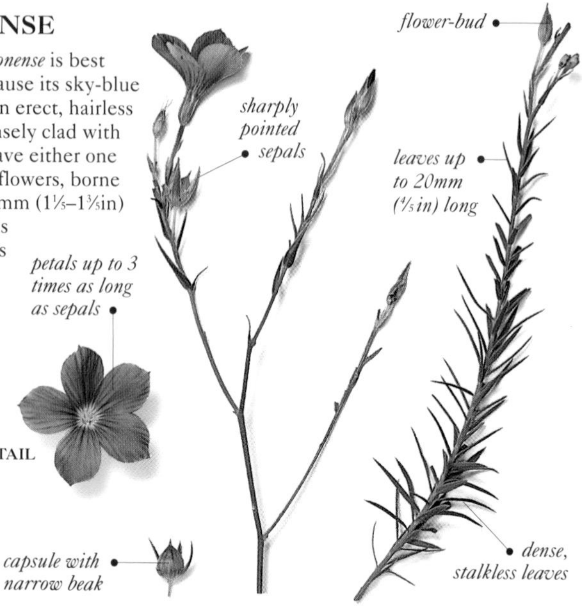
flower-bud
sharply pointed sepals
leaves up to 20mm (⅘in) long
petals up to 3 times as long as sepals
Detail
capsule with narrow beak
dense, stalkless leaves

Habit Perennial	Height Up to 50cm (20in)	Flowering time May–July

Family LINACEAE	Species *Linum bienne*	Author Miller

Pale Flax

Similar in form to *Linum narbonense* (above), Pale Flax is a more delicate plant with smaller flowers that soon shed their petals. The hairless stems carry leaves whose width does not exceed 1.5mm (1⁄16in). The flowers have sepals up to 5mm (⅕in) long, with petals 2 or 3 times longer. The capsule, 4–6mm (⅙–¼in) across, has a short beak.

• **Distribution** Throughout the region.

• **Habitat** Open, rocky or sandy ground.

• **Related Species** L. *usitatissimum*, cultivated Flax, is very similar but more robust.

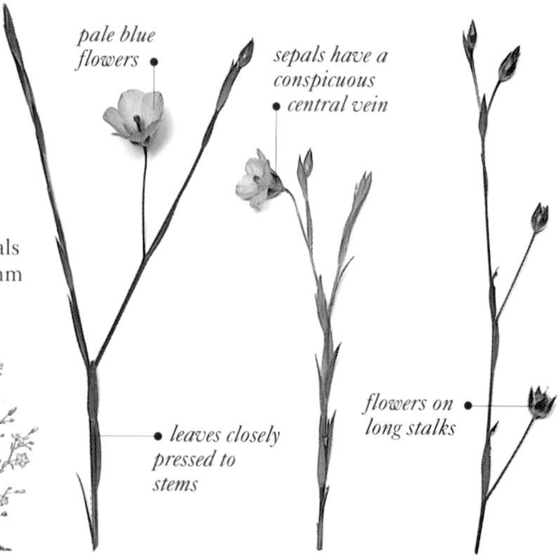
pale blue flowers
sepals have a conspicuous central vein
leaves closely pressed to stems
flowers on long stalks

Habit Biennial/perennial	Height 6–60cm (2⅖–24in)	Flowering time Apr–July

Family LINACEAE	Species *Linum strictum*	Author L.

UPRIGHT YELLOW FLAX

This flax is a common inhabitant of vineyards and other dry places, but its small flowers often make it less than conspicuous. Its stems are erect, branching either near the base or higher up. The leaves are narrow with finely toothed margins that feel distinctly rough. The flowers have yellow petals up to 6mm (¼in) long, and sepals about half this size, with sticky hairs and teeth. The fruit is a capsule, 2mm (¹⁄₁₂in) in diameter, with a minute beak.
• **DISTRIBUTION** Throughout the region.
• **HABITAT** Dry, open places, vineyards.
• **RELATED SPECIES** *Linum trigynum* is similar, but has smooth-edged leaves. It is also found throughout the region.

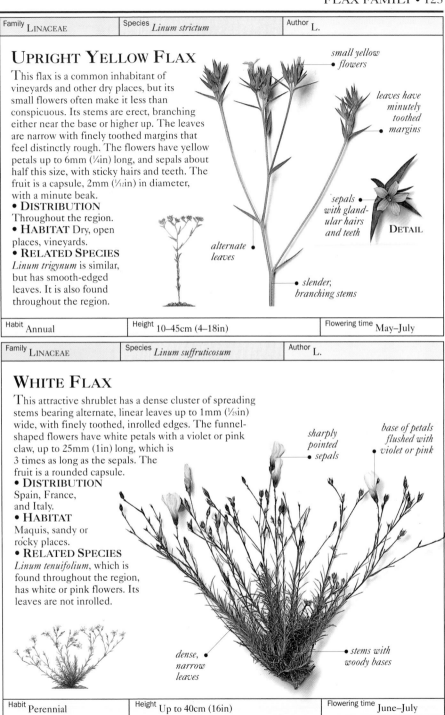

small yellow flowers

leaves have minutely toothed margins

sepals with glandular hairs and teeth

DETAIL

alternate leaves

slender, branching stems

Habit Annual	Height 10–45cm (4–18in)	Flowering time May–July

Family LINACEAE	Species *Linum suffruticosum*	Author L.

WHITE FLAX

This attractive shrublet has a dense cluster of spreading stems bearing alternate, linear leaves up to 1mm (¹⁄₂₅in) wide, with finely toothed, inrolled edges. The funnel-shaped flowers have white petals with a violet or pink claw, up to 25mm (1in) long, which is 3 times as long as the sepals. The fruit is a rounded capsule.
• **DISTRIBUTION** Spain, France, and Italy.
• **HABITAT** Maquis, sandy or rocky places.
• **RELATED SPECIES** *Linum tenuifolium*, which is found throughout the region, has white or pink flowers. Its leaves are not inrolled.

sharply pointed sepals

base of petals flushed with violet or pink

dense, narrow leaves

stems with woody bases

Habit Perennial	Height Up to 40cm (16in)	Flowering time June–July

SPURGE FAMILY

Family EUPHORBIACEAE	Species *Ricinus communis*	Author L.

CASTOR OIL PLANT

This fast-growing shrub has smooth, branching, reddish
stems, and alternately arranged, stalked leaves up to 60cm
(24in) across. The leaves are palmately divided with lance-
shaped lobes; the edges of the leaves are irregularly toothed.
The separate male and female flowers are borne together
in dense, upright, branching heads: the male flowers have
many yellow stamens, and the female flowers have beard-
like globes of red stigmas. The fruit is a smooth or spiky
capsule, 20mm (⅘in) in diameter, containing
3 marbled, reddish brown seeds.
• **DISTRIBUTION** Throughout.
• **HABITAT** Cultivated or waste
ground, dry riverbeds.
• **REMARK** A native of tropical Africa, the
Castor Oil Plant is widely cultivated and naturalized in other parts of the world. Its seeds are the
source of castor oil, but they also contain the protein
ricin, which is a powerful poison.

female flowers with red stigmas

seed capsule may be spiny or smooth

male flower with yellow stamens

side-branch bearing flowers

large glossy leaves

red upper leaf

shiny, bean-like seeds

Habit Annual/perennial	Height Up to 4m (13ft)	Flowering time Feb–Sept

Family EUPHORBIACEAE	Species *Euphorbia characias*	Author L.

LARGE MEDITERRANEAN SPURGE

Of the many spurges in the region, this species is perhaps the most majestic and eye-catching when in flower. Its tall, stout stems form a bulky, rounded clump, and are closely covered with very short hairs, giving the plant a furry texture. As with all members of the genus *Euphorbia*, the stems exude a milky latex when cut. The lower halves of the stems tend to be reddish brown and devoid of leaves, the upper halves green and clothed with dense ranks of stalkless, lance-shaped leaves, up to 13cm (5in) long. The dense flower-heads are composed of cyathia – cup-shaped structures that contain nectar glands, several male flowers, and a single female flower with a hanging ovary. In the subspecies *characias*, shown here, the nectar glands are brownish red, whereas in subspecies *wulfenii*, they are yellow. The fruit is a hairy, berry-like capsule, up to 7mm (⅖in) in diameter, containing 3 seeds.
• **DISTRIBUTION** Throughout; subsp. *characias* in west of region, subsp. *wulfenii* in east.
• **HABITAT** Dry, open ground, maquis.

dense flower-
• heads

flower-bearing
rays in upper
leaf-axils

• young non-
flowering stem
with dense foliage

spirally •
arranged
leaves

• leafless
lower stems
woody at base

• single cyathium with
brown nectar glands
and hanging ovary

Habit Perennial	Height 80–180cm (32–72in)	Flowering time Jan–July

Family EUPHORBIACEAE	Species *Euphorbia helioscopia*	Author L.

SUN SPURGE

This erect, hairless spurge normally has a single, unbranched reddish stem, and alternate, stalkless, spatula-shaped leaves. The tips of the leaves have serrated edges. The flat-topped flowering heads are composed of 5 rays, ringed by 5 large bracts. Each of the main rays divides into 3 smaller rays, which themselves divide twice. The flowers are small and green, with conspicuous ovaries. The seed capsule is up to 3.5mm (⅛in) in diameter.
• **DISTRIBUTION** Throughout.
• **HABITAT** Disturbed or waste ground.
• **REMARK** Sun Spurge is one of a number of fast-growing annual species that colonize disturbed ground. It is found throughout Europe, although it is rarer in the extreme north.

flat-topped clusters of green flowers •

leaves with rounded tips and serrated • edges

reddish stem •

Habit Annual	Height 10–50cm (4–20in)	Flowering time Feb–May

Family EUPHORBIACEAE	Species *Euphorbia acanthothamnos*	Author Heldr. & Sart. ex Boiss.

GREEK SPINY SPURGE

A low-growing, domed shrub, Greek Spiny Spurge develops an impenetrable network of woody, branching stems. Its dense and brilliant green spring foliage grows on new shoots. The leaves are elliptic, up to 20mm (⅘in) long, with blunt or pointed tips. The flower-heads have 3 to 4 forking rays with yellowish leaves, and in the year after flowering, the rays become woody to form sharp-tipped spines. The fruit is a warty, channelled capsule, up to 4mm (⅙in) across, containing 3 smooth, brown seeds.
• **DISTRIBUTION** Aegean region.
• **HABITAT** Open rocky places, garigue.
• **RELATED SPECIES** *Euphorbia spinosa* is similar but has darker leaves, and woody rays without sharp points.

• woody spines

• branching, woody stems

elliptic • leaves

• umbels of 3–4 forking rays of yellowish flowers

Habit Perennial	Height 10–30cm (4–12in)	Flowering time Mar–May

| Family EUPHORBIACEAE | Species *Euphorbia dendroides* | Author L. |

TREE SPURGE

The Tree Spurge is one of several Mediterranean plants that shed their leaves at the end of spring, in preparation for the dry period ahead. A hairless, tall shrub, it has an open appearance, with thick stems that are often grey towards the base, merging to form a short trunk. The stems are topped by clusters of lance-shaped leaves, up to 60mm (2⅜in) long. During winter and early spring, the leaves are brilliant green, but as summer approaches, they turn an autumnal red or brown before falling. The flowers are borne in umbels with between 5 and 8 rays, and are cupped by bright yellow leaves that have a rounded shape. The smooth, grey fruit capsule is about 6mm (¼in) long.
• **DISTRIBUTION** Throughout the region.
• **HABITAT** Cliffs and rocky ground near the sea.
• **REMARK** Like most spurges, this plant contains a milky, fiery-tasting latex that gives it protection from browsing animals.

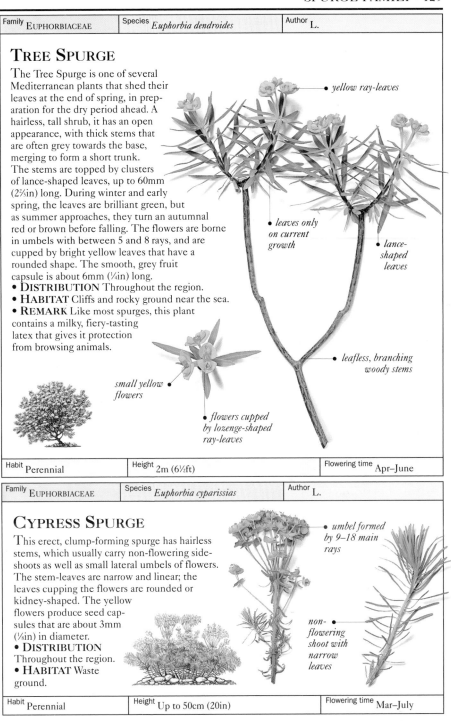

• *yellow ray-leaves*

• *leaves only on current growth*

• *lance-shaped leaves*

• *leafless, branching woody stems*

small yellow flowers •

• *flowers cupped by lozenge-shaped ray-leaves*

| Habit Perennial | Height 2m (6½ft) | Flowering time Apr–June |

| Family EUPHORBIACEAE | Species *Euphorbia cyparissias* | Author L. |

CYPRESS SPURGE

This erect, clump-forming spurge has hairless stems, which usually carry non-flowering side-shoots as well as small lateral umbels of flowers. The stem-leaves are narrow and linear; the leaves cupping the flowers are rounded or kidney-shaped. The yellow flowers produce seed capsules that are about 3mm (⅛in) in diameter.
• **DISTRIBUTION** Throughout the region.
• **HABITAT** Waste ground.

• *umbel formed by 9–18 main rays*

non-flowering shoot with narrow leaves •

| Habit Perennial | Height Up to 50cm (20in) | Flowering time Mar–July |

Family EUPHORBIACEAE	Species *Euphorbia paralias*	Author L.

SEA SPURGE

This widespread inhabitant of sandy beaches has hairless, erect, and slightly fleshy stems, and the whole plant, particularly during early growth, has a blue-green appearance. The stems branch at the base, and carry dense ranks of oblong or elliptic leaves, up to 30mm (1⅛in) long, which project at right-angles. Towards the top of the stem, the leaves become broader and more oval. The umbels have 3 to 6 rays, and are subdivided into 2 up to 3 times. The flowers have notched nectar glands with minute horns, and produce seed capsules that are up to 6mm (¼in) across.

flowers cupped by heart-shaped, pointed leaves

• leaves broader towards stem-top

- **DISTRIBUTION**
Throughout the region.
- **HABITAT** Sandy beaches, dunes, shingle.
- **RELATED SPECIES**
A similar species, *Euphorbia pithyusa*, grows on coastal sand in the W. Mediterranean.

fleshy, closely • packed leaves without visible midribs

Habit Perennial	Height 25–70cm (10–28in)	Flowering time May–Sept

Family EUPHORBIACEAE	Species *Euphorbia rigida*	Author Bieb.

EUPHORBIA RIGIDA

The stems of this robust spurge have a woody base, and are fleshy in texture, with a grey, waxy bloom that is easily marked when touched. The leaves are lance-shaped and pointed, up to 60mm (2⅜in) long, and are densely crowded on the stem. Each flower-head is composed of between 6 and 12 short rays, which are subdivided once or twice, and the flowers are cupped by a pair of rounded bracts which have a terminal point. The most conspicuous features of the flowers are their large, hanging, 3-part ovaries, and their nectar glands, which are bright red. The glands are crescent-shaped, and each tip ends in a tiny yellow lobe. The seed capsule is up to 8mm (⅓in) long.

• umbels of short rays

• rounded bracts

• narrow, pointed leaves

- **DISTRIBUTION**
Scattered localities through-out the region, although more common in the east.
- **HABITAT** Dry, rocky ground; usually on limestone.

Habit Perennial	Height 30–50cm (12–20in)	Flowering time Apr–June

| Family EUPHORBIACEAE | Species *Euphorbia maculata* | Author L. |

EUPHORBIA MACULATA

A native of North America, this small, prostrate spurge is well established as a weed in many parts of the Mediterranean region. Its hairy stems have a reddish tinge, and the closely packed, asymmetrical leaves, which are up to 12mm (½in) long, have a dark central blotch. The flowers grow from the leaf-axils, and are solitary or in small groups. The seed capsule is less than 2mm (½in) in diameter.
• **DISTRIBUTION** W. and C. Mediterranean.
• **HABITAT** Disturbed ground.

paddle-shaped leaves with dark markings

flowers often solitary

| Habit Annual | Stem length Up to 20cm (8in) | Flowering time May–July |

| Family EUPHORBIACEAE | Species *Euphorbia peplis* | Author L. |

PURPLE SPURGE

A widespread inhabitant of sandy shores, Purple Spurge is a prostrate, mat-forming plant with succulent, hairless stems. The stems usually branch in 4 from the point where they join, and they generally have a reddish tinge. The leaves are up to 12mm (½in) long, and are oblong or elliptical, with rounded or notched tips, and distinctly asymmetrical lobes where they meet the short leaf-stalk. The flowers are barely noticeable, and have red nectar glands. The seed capsule is up to 5mm (⅕in) across, with a smooth surface.
• **DISTRIBUTION** Throughout.
• **HABITAT** Sandy shores.
• **RELATED SPECIES**
Euphorbia peplus, Petty Spurge, is a small, erect plant of waste ground, very different from *E. peplis* in form, if not in name.

single flower

inconspicuous flowers

asymmetrical leaves, sometimes sickle-shaped

4 fleshy stems branching from base

| Habit Annual | Stem length 40cm (16in) | Flowering time May–Sept |

RUE FAMILY

Family RUTACEAE	Species *Ruta chalapensis*	Author L.

FRINGED RUE

This erect, hairless plant has a powerful, almost choking odour, which is readily sampled by crushing some of its leaves. The stems are woody at the base but green above, and bear bipinnate leaves, about 20cm (8in) long, with elliptical leaflets. The yellow flowers grow in open clusters at the tips of the stems. They have 4 or 5 petals with fringed margins, and conspicuous oval or lance-shaped sepals with pointed tips. The fruit is a hairless, lobed capsule.
• **DISTRIBUTION** Throughout the region.
• **HABITAT** Dry, rocky places, waysides, garigue.

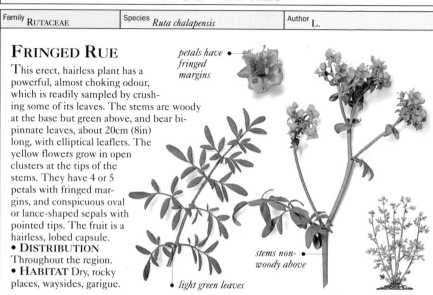

petals have fringed margins

stems non-woody above

light green leaves

Habit Perennial	Height 20–80cm (8–32in)	Flowering time Mar–July

CNEORUM FAMILY

Family CNEORACEAE	Species *Cneorum tricoccon*	Author L.

CNEORUM TRICOCCON

An erect evergreen shrub, *Cneorum tricoccon* has hairless stems and stalk-less linear leaves up to 30mm (1⅛in) long. The leaves are held close to the stems, giving the plant an upswept appearance. The inconspicuous flowers grow sparsely on short stalks arising from the leaf-axils. Each flower has 3 or 4 spreading petals. The fruit has 3 or 4 sections, and turns red, then black, when ripe.
• **DISTRIBUTION** W. Mediterranean as far east as Italy, excluding Corsica.
• **HABITAT** Dry, rocky places.

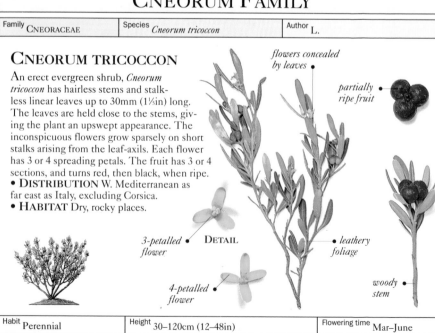

flowers concealed by leaves

partially ripe fruit

3-petalled flower **DETAIL**

4-petalled flower

leathery foliage

woody stem

Habit Perennial	Height 30–120cm (12–48in)	Flowering time Mar–June

MAHOGANY FAMILY

Family MELIACEAE	Species *Melia azederach*	Author L.

INDIAN BEAD TREE

This deciduous shrub or small tree has alternate, bipinnate leaves up to 90cm (36in) long, with hairless elliptical leaflets, up to 50mm (2in) long. Its 5- or 6-petalled flowers grow in loose clusters, and vary in colour from cream to lilac. The poisonous, bead-like fruit turns brown when ripe.
• **DISTRIBUTION** Native to E. Asia; naturalized in the Balkans; widely cultivated elsewhere.
• **HABITAT** Gardens, roadsides.

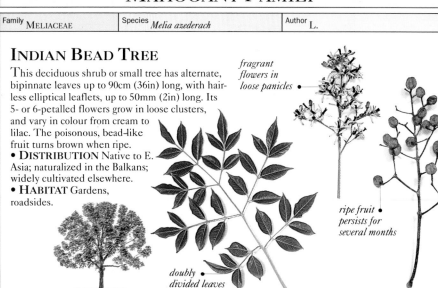

fragrant flowers in loose panicles •

• *ripe fruit persists for several months*

doubly • *divided leaves*

Habit Perennial	Height Up to 15m (50ft)	Flowering time May–June

MILKWORT FAMILY

Family POLYGALACEAE	Species *Polygala nicaeensis*	Author Risso ex Koch

NICEAN MILKWORT

A very variable plant with a woody base, Nicean Milkwort has erect or ascending stems that bear stalkless, linear leaves which are broadest at the base of the plant. The flowers, in clusters of up to 40, may be pink, blue, or white. They have 3 joined petals, one of which is fringed, and these are clasped by 2 flattened sepals, up to 11mm (⅜in) long. The fruit is a small capsule.
• **DISTRIBUTION** Throughout, except some islands including the Balearics, Sardinia, and Crete.
• **HABITAT** Dry, grassy or stony places.
• **REMARK** There are several similar species in the region, many being confined to mountainous areas.

• *flower-heads lengthen during flowering*

• *small linear leaves*

flattened • *sepals*

Habit Perennial	Height 15–40cm (6–16in)	Flowering time Apr–July

CASHEW FAMILY

Family ANACARDIACEAE	Species *Cotinus coggygria*	Author Scop.

SMOKE TREE

This deciduous shrub has supple, hairless stems and a resinous odour. Its leaves are stalked, with round or indented tips. The tiny cream-coloured flowers grow in dense branched clusters, up to 20cm (8in) long. Each cluster contains many infertile branches that develop long purple hairs, which make the whole inflorescence resemble a reddish puff of smoke. The shiny brown fruit is kidney-shaped.
• **DISTRIBUTION** Eastwards from S.E. France.
• **HABITAT** Open woodland in dry, sunny situations.

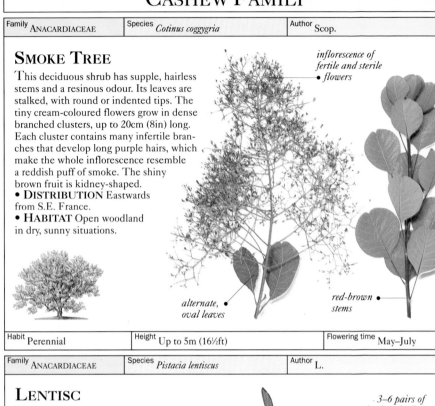

inflorescence of fertile and sterile flowers

alternate, oval leaves

red-brown stems

Habit Perennial	Height Up to 5m (16½ft)	Flowering time May–July

Family ANACARDIACEAE	Species *Pistacia lentiscus*	Author L.

LENTISC

The Lentisc is one of several evergreen Mediterranean trees that manage to look fresh even in the height of summer. Its spreading branches carry pinnate leaves with winged axes. The flowers, about 3mm (⅛in) across, grow in clusters from the leaf-axils. Each plant bears flowers of one sex only. The female flowers are yellowy green; the males are dark red. The fruit is a small berry.
• **DISTRIBUTION** Throughout.
• **HABITAT** Maquis.
• **REMARK** The plant's pungent resin is the source of mastic, which has many culinary and medical uses. It is also commonly known as the Mastic Tree.

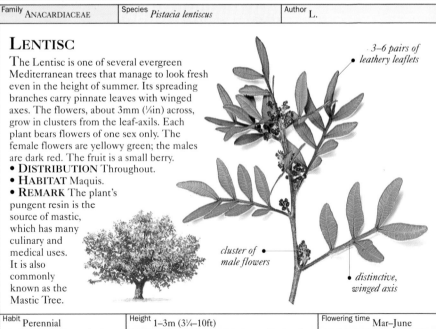

3–6 pairs of leathery leaflets

cluster of male flowers

distinctive, winged axis

Habit Perennial	Height 1–3m (3¼–10ft)	Flowering time Mar–June

| Family ANACARDIACEAE | Species *Pistacia terebinthus* | Author L. |

TURPENTINE TREE

This small deciduous tree or shrub has dark red-brown stems and pinnate leaves, but unlike the Lentisc (see opposite), its leaf axes are not winged. The leathery leaflets are in opposite pairs, and are very aromatic, with a strong resinous smell. Each plant has either male or female flowers, brownish red in colour, which both form in long-branched clusters. The fruit, about 7mm (⅕in) long, turns red and then brown when ripe.
• **DISTRIBUTION** Throughout.
• **HABITAT** Open woods, maquis; especially on limestone.

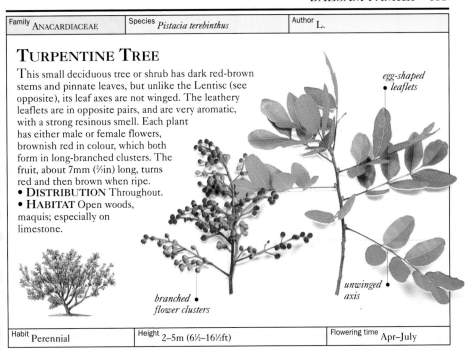

egg-shaped leaflets

unwinged axis

branched flower clusters

| Habit Perennial | Height 2–5m (6½–16½ft) | Flowering time Apr–July |

BALSAM FAMILY

| Family BALSAMINACEAE | Species *Impatiens balfourii* | Author Hooker fil. |

KASHMIR BALSAM

A native of the Himalayas, this attractive plant is locally common where conditions are cool and damp. Its erect stems are hairless and fleshy, and vary in colour from pale green to red. The leaves, up to 13cm (5in) long, have short stalks and serrated edges. The flowers, up to 40mm (1⅗in) long, are borne in small clusters, with each flower hanging from a short stalk. As in other species of *Impatiens*, one sepal is very enlarged and forms a sac with a connected nectar-bearing spur. The seed capsule explodes when ripe.
• **DISTRIBUTION** Naturalized in France and Italy.
• **HABITAT** Woodland margins, usually at altitude.

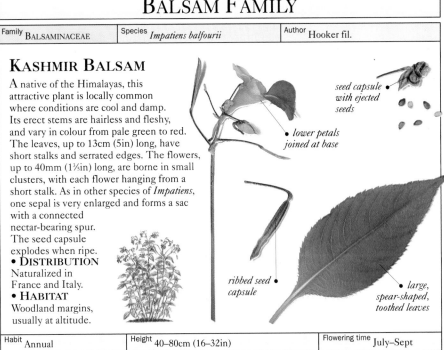

seed capsule with ejected seeds

lower petals joined at base

ribbed seed capsule

large, spear-shaped, toothed leaves

| Habit Annual | Height 40–80cm (16–32in) | Flowering time July–Sept |

BOX FAMILY

Family BUXACEAE	Species *Buxus sempervirens*	Author L.

BOX

A slow-growing evergreen shrub or small tree, Box has a mild but characteristic odour. On young specimens the bark is smooth and brown; on older plants it is cracked and grey. The leaves reach a length of 30mm (1⅓in). The flowers, about 2mm (¹⁄₁₂in) long, grow in clusters in the leaf-axils; each cluster contains a female flower and about 6 male flowers. The fruit is a small brown or grey capsule.
• **DISTRIBUTION** Throughout the region.
• **HABITAT** Dry woodland and hillsides; frequently cultivated for dwarf hedging.

inconspicuous yellow male flowers

leathery leaves: shiny above, duller beneath

immature capsule

top view of seed capsule

Habit Perennial	Height 2–8m (6½–26ft)	Flowering time Mar–Apr

BUCKTHORN FAMILY

Family RHAMNACEAE	Species *Rhamnus alaternus*	Author L.

MEDITERRANEAN BUCKTHORN

This thornless evergreen shrub is a common plant of limestone hillsides throughout the region. Its bark is reddish grey, and its hairless branches carry short-stalked leathery leaves with toothed edges. The leaves are up to 60mm (2⅜in) long; they can be spear- or egg-shaped. Flowers of both sexes grow from the leaf-axils, but on separate plants. The flowers are pale yellow, petal-less, and cup-shaped; the female flowers grow in erect clusters, and the male flowers are pendent. The fruit is spherical, and up to 6mm (¼in) across. As it ripens it turns red, and then black.
• **DISTRIBUTION** Throughout the region.
• **HABITAT** Garigue, maquis, woods.

pale green underside of leaves

leaves with rounded or pointed tips

unripe red fruit

fruit in small clusters

Habit Perennial	Height 1–5m (3¼–16½ft)	Flowering time Feb–Apr

MALLOW FAMILY

Family MALVACEAE	Species *Malva cretica*	Author Cav.

MALVA CRETICA

This delicate member of the mallow family has erect or spreading stems covered with fine hairs. The lower leaves are rounded and slightly toothed, whereas the leaves further up the stem become progressively more divided into deep, toothed lobes. The pink flowers, about 20mm (⅔in) across, are borne singly on long stalks that grow from the leaf-axils. The calyx is bristly with long teeth and, as with many members of the mallow family, it is cupped by a separate whorl known as an epicalyx. In this species, the epicalyx has 3 narrow, unfused segments. The fruit is a doughnut-like ring of flattened, coin-shaped seeds.
• **DISTRIBUTION** From Italy eastwards.
• **HABITAT** Olive groves, pastures, stony ground.

leaf from top of stem

epicalyx • has unfused segments

leaf from middle of stem

leaf from base of stem

• pink flower cupped by calyx and epicalyx

Habit Annual	Height 20–40cm (8–16in)	Flowering time Apr–June

Family MALVACEAE	Species *Malva sylvestris*	Author L.

COMMON MALLOW

A robust plant with erect or sprawling hairy stems, Common Mallow can be seen on verges and waysides throughout the region. Its leaves, about 40mm (1⅗in) long, are rounded or heart-shaped. The flowers grow in clusters from the leaf-axils, and are borne separately on long stalks. Each flower, up to 50mm (2in) across, has petals that do not overlap. The epicalyx has 3 unfused segments. The seeds have netted surfaces.
• **DISTRIBUTION** Throughout the region.
• **HABITAT** Cultivated or fallow land, waysides.
• **RELATED SPECIES** *Lavatera cretica* (see p.139) is similar, but has epicalyx segments that are joined towards the base.

DETAIL

• toothed leaf has lobes that vary in depth

bilobed • petals

many flowers grow from a • single leaf-axil

petals • spiralled in bud

Habit Biennial/perennial	Height 30–120cm (12–48in)	Flowering time Mar–June

Family MALVACEAE	Species *Lavatera arborea*	Author L.

TREE MALLOW

An impressive, robust plant with a woody base, Tree
Mallow looks very much like a perennial, but in fact
rarely survives for more than 2 growing seasons.
The tips of its stems have a downy texture, as do
the leaves – particularly on their undersides. The
leaves vary in shape and size, being up to 20cm (8in)
long with 5 to 7 lobes at the base of the plant, and about
40mm (1⅜in) long with a heart-shaped outline at the stem
tips. The flowers grow in clusters from the leaf-axils, and are
pink with deep purple centres and radiating veins. They are
up to 50mm (2in) across, and have 3 epicalyx segments. The
fruit contains between 6 and 8 flattened seeds.
• **DISTRIBUTION** W. and C. Mediterranean, as
far east as Greece; often cultivated.
• **HABITAT** Sandy and bare ground
near to the sea.

• *clusters of
flowers borne
in leaf-axils*

*fruit surrounded
by dry epicalyx
segments* •

*flattened
seeds* •

• *heart-shaped leaf
from stem tip*

*leaves have
downy texture* •

• *stout stem
with woody
base*

• *lobed leaf from
base of stem*

Habit Biennial	Height 1–3m (3¼–10ft)	Flowering time Apr–June

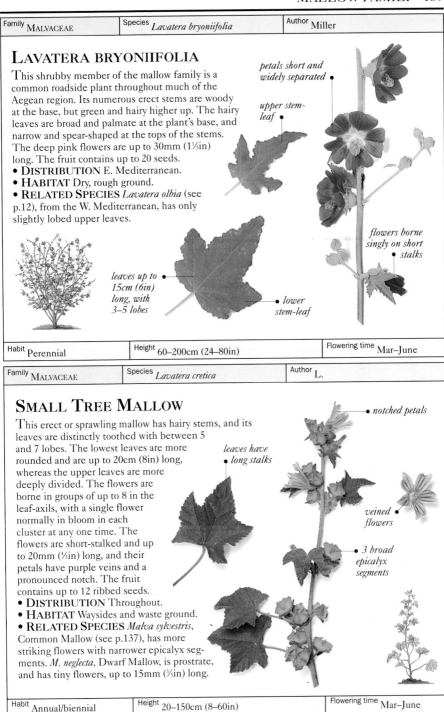

Family MALVACEAE	Species *Lavatera bryoniifolia*	Author Miller

LAVATERA BRYONIIFOLIA

This shrubby member of the mallow family is a
common roadside plant throughout much of the
Aegean region. Its numerous erect stems are woody
at the base, but green and hairy higher up. The hairy
leaves are broad and palmate at the plant's base, and
narrow and spear-shaped at the tops of the stems.
The deep pink flowers are up to 30mm (1⅕in)
long. The fruit contains up to 20 seeds.
• **DISTRIBUTION** E. Mediterranean.
• **HABITAT** Dry, rough ground.
• **RELATED SPECIES** *Lavatera olbia* (see
p.12), from the W. Mediterranean, has only
slightly lobed upper leaves.

petals short and widely separated

upper stem-leaf

flowers borne singly on short stalks

leaves up to 15cm (6in) long, with 3–5 lobes

lower stem-leaf

Habit Perennial	Height 60–200cm (24–80in)	Flowering time Mar–June

Family MALVACEAE	Species *Lavatera cretica*	Author L.

SMALL TREE MALLOW

This erect or sprawling mallow has hairy stems, and its
leaves are distinctly toothed with between 5
and 7 lobes. The lowest leaves are more
rounded and are up to 20cm (8in) long,
whereas the upper leaves are more
deeply divided. The flowers are
borne in groups of up to 8 in the
leaf-axils, with a single flower
normally in bloom in each
cluster at any one time. The
flowers are short-stalked and up
to 20mm (⅘in) long, and their
petals have purple veins and a
pronounced notch. The fruit
contains up to 12 ribbed seeds.
• **DISTRIBUTION** Throughout.
• **HABITAT** Waysides and waste ground.
• **RELATED SPECIES** *Malva sylvestris*,
Common Mallow (see p.137), has more
striking flowers with narrower epicalyx segments. *M. neglecta*, Dwarf Mallow, is prostrate,
and has tiny flowers, up to 15mm (⅗in) long.

notched petals

leaves have long stalks

veined flowers

3 broad epicalyx segments

Habit Annual/biennial	Height 20–150cm (8–60in)	Flowering time Mar–June

Family MALVACEAE	Species *Lavatera maritima*	Author Gouan

SEA MALLOW

Even when not in flower, Sea Mallow is readily identified by its dense covering of short hairs, which often trap dust borne on the coastal wind. An erect or straggling shrub, its stems are bare and woody below, but downy towards their tips. Compared to most shrubby mallows, its leaves are small. They may reach 8cm (3⅛in) but are often much shorter, and are divided into 5 shallow lobes, with short stalks up to 30mm (1⅛in) long. The leaves at the top of the plant are more angular than those at the base. The handsome flowers grow either singly or in pairs, and are up to 40mm (1⅝in) wide, with pale pink petals that are deeply flushed and streaked with red towards their bases. The fruit contains up to 13 seeds, with sharp ridges.
• **DISTRIBUTION** W. Mediterranean, including N.W. Africa, eastwards as far as Italy.
• **HABITAT** Exposed rocky ground near to the sea.
• **REMARK** A relatively uncommon species, Sea Mallow is protected by law in some areas. It is sometimes cultivated.

large pink flowers, flushed and streaked with red •

• conspicuous yellow anthers

• leaves have 5 shallow lobes

angular • upper leaf

• flowers flanked by leaves

woody stem •

Habit Perennial	Height 30–120cm (1–4ft)	Flowering time Feb–May

Family MALVACEAE	Species *Lavatera trimestris*	Author L.

ANNUAL LAVATERA

An erect plant with spreading branches, this vigorous mallow carries its flowers on characteristically long stalks. Its stems are hairy, particularly towards their tips, and the lobed leaves, which reach 60mm (2⅜in) in length, vary in shape, being rounded towards the base of the plant and more deeply divided higher up. The large flowers, up to 70mm (2¾in) wide, are very prominent, with pale pink petals that are streaked with veins of darker pink. The 3 segments of the epicalyx are joined together to form a cup, which enlarges as the fruit forms.
• **DISTRIBUTION** Eastwards to Greece.
• **HABITAT** Fallow land, untended vineyards, gardens.

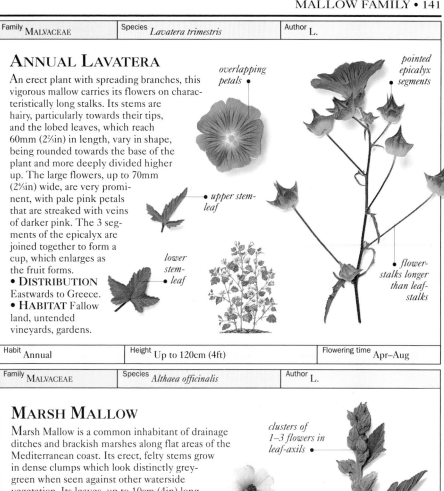

overlapping petals

pointed epicalyx segments

upper stem-leaf

lower stem-leaf

flower-stalks longer than leaf-stalks

Habit Annual	Height Up to 120cm (4ft)	Flowering time Apr–Aug

Family MALVACEAE	Species *Althaea officinalis*	Author L.

MARSH MALLOW

Marsh Mallow is a common inhabitant of drainage ditches and brackish marshes along flat areas of the Mediterranean coast. Its erect, felty stems grow in dense clumps which look distinctly grey-green when seen against other waterside vegetation. Its leaves, up to 10cm (4in) long, have serrated edges and shallow lobes. The flowers grow either singly or in clusters from the leaf-axils, and are very pale pink or almost white, with a darker centre and faint, radiating veins. The petals have 2 rounded lobes, and there are up to 9 narrow epicalyx segments.
• **DISTRIBUTION** Throughout.
• **HABITAT** Damp places near the sea.
• **REMARK** Marsh Mallow roots were once used to make confectionery.

clusters of 1–3 flowers in leaf-axils

pale flowers with slightly bilobed petals

downy stems and leaves

lower stem-leaf

Habit Perennial	Height 60–120cm (2–4ft)	Flowering time June–Sept

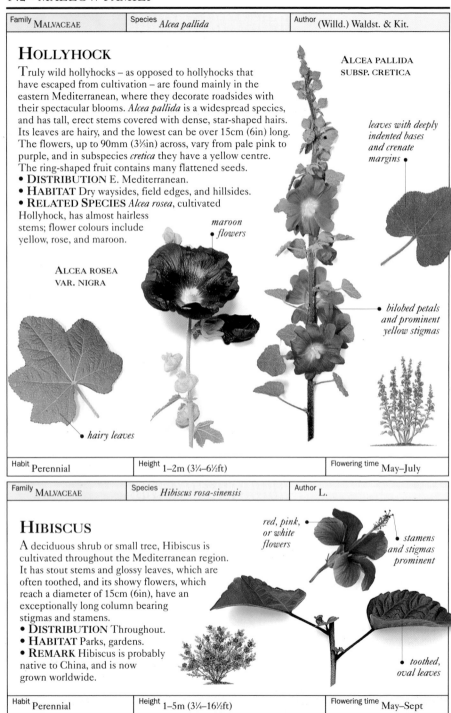

| Family MALVACEAE | Species *Alcea pallida* | Author (Willd.) Waldst. & Kit. |

HOLLYHOCK

Truly wild hollyhocks – as opposed to hollyhocks that have escaped from cultivation – are found mainly in the eastern Mediterranean, where they decorate roadsides with their spectacular blooms. *Alcea pallida* is a widespread species, and has tall, erect stems covered with dense, star-shaped hairs. Its leaves are hairy, and the lowest can be over 15cm (6in) long. The flowers, up to 90mm (3⅜in) across, vary from pale pink to purple, and in subspecies *cretica* they have a yellow centre. The ring-shaped fruit contains many flattened seeds.
• **DISTRIBUTION** E. Mediterranean.
• **HABITAT** Dry waysides, field edges, and hillsides.
• **RELATED SPECIES** *Alcea rosea*, cultivated Hollyhock, has almost hairless stems; flower colours include yellow, rose, and maroon.

ALCEA PALLIDA SUBSP. CRETICA

leaves with deeply indented bases and crenate margins •

maroon • flowers

• bilobed petals and prominent yellow stigmas

ALCEA ROSEA VAR. NIGRA

• hairy leaves

| Habit Perennial | Height 1–2m (3¼–6½ft) | Flowering time May–July |

| Family MALVACEAE | Species *Hibiscus rosa-sinensis* | Author L. |

HIBISCUS

A deciduous shrub or small tree, Hibiscus is cultivated throughout the Mediterranean region. It has stout stems and glossy leaves, which are often toothed, and its showy flowers, which reach a diameter of 15cm (6in), have an exceptionally long column bearing stigmas and stamens.
• **DISTRIBUTION** Throughout.
• **HABITAT** Parks, gardens.
• **REMARK** Hibiscus is probably native to China, and is now grown worldwide.

red, pink, or white flowers

• stamens and stigmas prominent

• toothed, oval leaves

| Habit Perennial | Height 1–5m (3¼–16½ft) | Flowering time May–Sept |

DAPHNE FAMILY

Family THYMELAEACEAE	Species *Daphne gnidium*	Author L.

DAPHNE GNIDIUM

An erect evergreen shrub with dense foliage, *Daphne gnidium* has slender, clumped stems that branch only at the base. The leaves, up to 50mm (2in) long, are smooth and stalkless with pointed tips. They slant upwards, revealing their duller and paler under-sides. The flowers are off-white and lightly scented. They have 4 petals and are about 5mm (⅕in) across. The fleshy fruit is initially green, but later becomes orange or red, and finally black. Like all parts of the plant, it is very poisonous.
• **DISTRIBUTION** Throughout, but less common in the east.
• **HABITAT** Garigue, maquis, woods.

flowers and fruit often present at same time

smooth, stalkless leaves

flower clusters at tips of stems

leaves densely clustered around stem

Habit Perennial	Height 50–200cm (20–80in)	Flowering time Mar–Oct

Family THYMELAEACEAE	Species *Daphne sericea*	Author Vahl

DAPHNE SERICEA

Like many members of the *Daphne* family, this branching evergreen shrub distinguishes itself by an exquisite fragrance when in flower. Its young shoots are hairy, and its leaves are glossy above and hairy below. The leaves are more or less stalkless with pointed or blunted tips. Clusters of pink flowers, up to 14mm (⅗in) long, grow at the tips of the stems, or at the leaf-axils. They have deep throats, and are covered on the outside with silky hairs. The fruit is reddish brown, and the whole plant is poisonous.
• **DISTRIBUTION** E. Mediterranean, as far west as Italy.
• **HABITAT** Maquis, woodlands, rocky places, especially near the coast and usually on calcareous ground.

clustered flowers

young leaves

woody, branching stem

mature leaf

Habit Perennial	Height 50–150cm (20–60in)	Flowering time Feb–June

Family THYMELAEACEAE	Species *Daphne laureola*	Author L.

SPURGE LAUREL

Spurge Laurel is an erect or slightly spreading shrub with infrequently branching stems. The leaves are leathery and glossy above, and are clustered at the tips of the stems. They reach a maximum length of about 13cm (5in), and their widest part is nearer the apex than the middle. The pale yellow-green flowers grow in spreading or hanging clusters from the leaf-axils, and have a mild honey-like fragrance. They are up to 12mm (½in) long, and the petals are joined for much of their length. The fruit is an egg-shaped berry, about 8mm (⅓in) long, which turns black when ripe.
• **DISTRIBUTION** Throughout, especially in the west.
• **HABITAT** Woodland, stony hillsides; usually on calcareous ground.

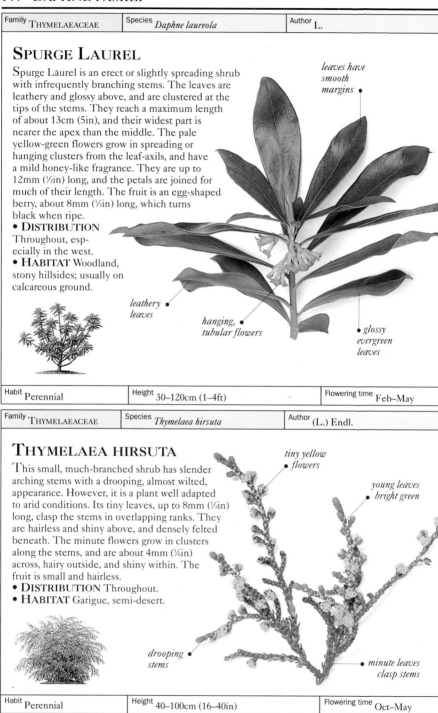

leaves have smooth margins •

leathery • leaves

• hanging, tubular flowers

• glossy evergreen leaves

Habit Perennial	Height 30–120cm (1–4ft)	Flowering time Feb–May

Family THYMELAEACEAE	Species *Thymelaea hirsuta*	Author (L.) Endl.

THYMELAEA HIRSUTA

This small, much-branched shrub has slender arching stems with a drooping, almost wilted, appearance. However, it is a plant well adapted to arid conditions. Its tiny leaves, up to 8mm (⅓in) long, clasp the stems in overlapping ranks. They are hairless and shiny above, and densely felted beneath. The minute flowers grow in clusters along the stems, and are about 4mm (⅙in) across, hairy outside, and shiny within. The fruit is small and hairless.
• **DISTRIBUTION** Throughout.
• **HABITAT** Garigue, semi-desert.

tiny yellow • flowers

young leaves • bright green

drooping • stems

• minute leaves clasp stems

Habit Perennial	Height 40–100cm (16–40in)	Flowering time Oct–May

ST. JOHN'S WORT FAMILY

Family GUTTIFERAE	Species *Hypericum empetrifolium*	Author Willd.

HYPERICUM EMPETRIFOLIUM

The St. John's worts – members of the genus *Hypericum* – are readily identified by their 5-petalled yellow flowers, brush-like stamens, and numerous tiny glands. *Hypericum empetrifolium* is a clump-forming shrub with erect or spreading stems. Its new shoots are densely clad in narrow, hairless leaves, up to 12mm (½in) long. The flowers have glossy yellow petals, which fold back to reveal prominent stamens. The fruit is a small capsule.
• **DISTRIBUTION** Greece, Aegean islands, Turkey.
• **HABITAT** Rocky ground, maquis.

petals up to 12mm (½in) across

young shoot with dense foliage

petals 3–4 times longer than sepals

DETAIL

leaves in groups of 3

small black glands on sepal margins

glossy red-green stem

Habit Perennial	Height Up to 50cm (20in)	Flowering time Mar–July

Family GUTTIFERAE	Species *Hypericum perforatum*	Author L.

PERFORATE ST. JOHN'S WORT

Perforate St. John's Wort is a variable, erect plant with hairless stems that frequently branch. The stems are cylindrical, but have 2 raised ribs. The triangular or wedge-shaped leaves, up to 30mm (1⅛in) long, have rounded edges and a number of trans-lucent dots, which give them a perforated appear-ance. They grow in pairs that clasp the stem. The flowers are borne in flat-tened clusters, and are up to 30mm (1⅛in) across. The petals usually have scattered black glands, and these are even more apparent on the much smaller sepals.
• **DISTRIBUTION** Throughout.
• **HABITAT** Grassy ground, waysides.

petals with scattered black glands

translucent dots "perforate" leaves

sepals with black glands and streaks

ribbed stem

leaves in opposite pairs

Habit Perennial	Height Up to 100cm (40in)	Flowering time Apr–July

ROCK-ROSE FAMILY

Family CISTACEAE	Species *Cistus albidus*	Author L.

GREY-LEAVED CISTUS

The members of the genus *Cistus* include some of the most ornamental of all Mediterranean flowers. All are evergreen shrubs, and many are aromatic. Unlike true roses (see p.81), with which they are sometimes confused, they have undivided leaves arranged in opposite pairs, and do not form hips. The Grey-leaved Cistus is a western species, and is fairly low-growing. Its flat, elliptical leaves, up to 50mm (2in) long, are not aromatic. Both its leaves and stems are covered with a dense greyish white down. The purplish pink flowers, up to 60mm (2⅜in) across, grow in small clusters. As with all *Cistus* species, they have 5 papery petals that are crumpled rather like those of poppies, and 5 unequal sepals. The petals soon fall, leaving the plant surrounded by their withering remains. The fruit is a dry capsule which splits open to release a large number of small seeds.

• **DISTRIBUTION** W. Mediterranean, from N. Africa to Italy.
• **HABITAT** Garigue, maquis.

numerous yellow anthers

densely haired leaves with flat margins

stems densely covered with down

crumpled petals

leaves arranged in opposite pairs

Habit Perennial	Height 50–100cm (20–40in)	Flowering time Apr–June

Family CISTACEAE	Species *Cistus incanus*	Author L.

CISTUS INCANUS

Of all the rock-roses that grow in the Mediterranean region, this species is among the most flamboyant and eye-catching when in flower. An erect or spreading shrub, its stems are covered in small, white hairs. Its oval leaves, which grow in opposite pairs on short stalks, have veins that are inset on their upper sides, and raised on their undersides. The leaf size varies considerably. Subspecies *incanus* has leaves up to 50mm (2in) long with fairly flat margins, whereas subspecies *creticus* has smaller leaves, up to 25mm (1in) long, with margins that undulate strongly. The flowers grow singly or in small clusters, and can reach 60mm (2⅜in) across. They have orange stamens, broad papery petals, and short sepals covered in long, fine, white hairs. The fruit is a hairy capsule containing numerous seeds.

• **DISTRIBUTION** Throughout, but rarer in the west. Subsp. *creticus* is restricted to Greece and the Aegean; subsp. *incanus* is widespread.

• **HABITAT** Garigue, maquis.

• **REMARK** This species is also known as *Cistus creticus* and *C. villosus*.

short-lived petals •

style same length • as stamens

petals appear crumpled •

small leaves with strongly undulating margins •

SUBSP. CRETICUS

large leaves with flat • or slightly undulating margins

prominent veins on underside of leaves •

SUBSP. INCANUS

Habit Perennial	Height 30–100cm (12–40in)	Flowering time Feb–June

Family CISTACEAE	Species *Cistus ladanifer*	Author L.

GUM CISTUS

The Gum Cistus is a tall, pleasantly fragrant shrub with narrow and very sticky leaves. The leaves, up to 80mm (3⅛in) long, are slightly downy beneath, with very short stalks. Their upper surfaces are glossy, but often become dulled by trapped dust. The impressive flowers, up to 10cm (4in) across, grow singly on long stalks. They usually have a ring of 5 purple blotches, although these may be missing, particularly on plants from southern Spain. Each flower produces a 10-chambered seed capsule.

• **DISTRIBUTION** W. Mediterranean.
• **HABITAT** Maquis, garigue, open pine woods, and dry hillsides.
• **REMARK** The gum produced by this species of *Cistus* is used in perfumery.

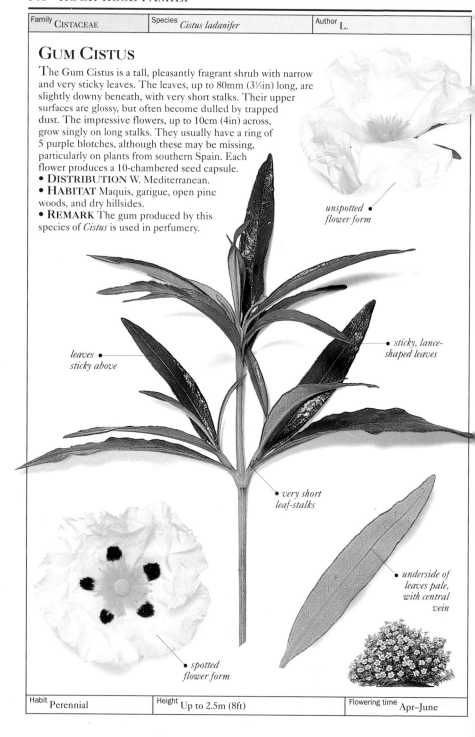

unspotted • flower form

leaves • sticky above

• sticky, lance- shaped leaves

• very short leaf-stalks

• underside of leaves pale, with central vein

• spotted flower form

Habit Perennial	Height Up to 2.5m (8ft)	Flowering time Apr–June

Family CISTACEAE	Species *Cistus monspeliensis*	Author L.

NARROW-LEAVED CISTUS

This strongly aromatic, compact, much-branched, evergreen shrub has sticky, sparsely haired, reddish brown stems and equally sticky foliage. The stalkless leaves, up to 50mm (2in) long, are arranged in opposite pairs, and are broadly linear. At first, the leaves are bright green, but they turn darker and finally brown as the summer progresses. The flowers, up to 30mm (1⅛in) across, grow in stalked clusters of 2 to 8. They have yellow stamens, and 5 broad, wedge-shaped sepals. The fruit is a flattened capsule.
• **DISTRIBUTION** Throughout.
• **HABITAT** Garigue, maquis; usually on acid soils.
• **REMARK** Narrow-leaved Cistus is a characteristic plant of open maquis, and often grows in large colonies. It quickly regenerates after fires.

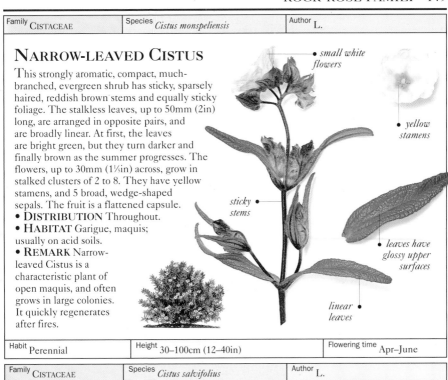

small white flowers

yellow stamens

sticky stems

leaves have glossy upper surfaces

linear leaves

Habit Perennial	Height 30–100cm (12–40in)	Flowering time Apr–June

Family CISTACEAE	Species *Cistus salvifolius*	Author L.

SAGE-LEAVED CISTUS

A bushy, evergreen shrub with little aroma, Sage-leaved Cistus has red-green stems lightly covered with hairs. The pale green leaves, up to 40mm (1⅝in) long, are stalked, and broadly elliptic in shape. They have undulating edges, and are slightly hairy on both sides. The flowers, up to 50mm (2in) across, are borne on long stalks, either singly or in small groups. The seeds develop in a hairy capsule up to 8mm (⅜in) long.
• **DISTRIBUTION** Throughout the region.
• **HABITAT** Garigue and maquis.
• **RELATED SPECIES** *Cistus populifolius* is similar but has leaves with deeper, heart-shaped bases.

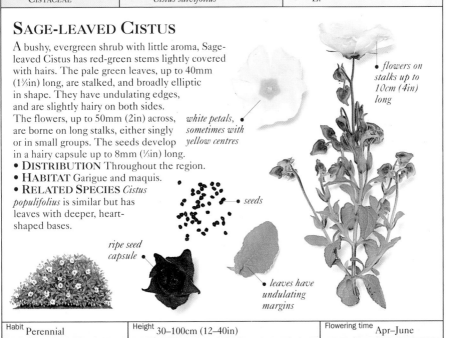

flowers on stalks up to 10cm (4in) long

white petals, sometimes with yellow centres

seeds

ripe seed capsule

leaves have undulating margins

Habit Perennial	Height 30–100cm (12–40in)	Flowering time Apr–June

Family CISTACEAE	Species *Halimium halimifolium*	Author (L.) Willk.

HALIMIUM HALIMIFOLIUM

An erect, bushy shrub with a silvery green appearance, *Halimium halimifolium* often forms large stands on rocky or sandy ground near the coast. Its densely branching stems carry leaves that grow in opposite pairs on short stalks. The leaves, up to 40mm (1⅜in) long, are elliptic to lance-shaped with pointed tips, and are covered with tiny hairs and scales that give the plant its characteristic coloration. The flowers grow in clusters on long stalks. They are about 30mm (1⅛in) across, and have small sepals covered in scales. Some of the flowers have a dark magenta spot at the base of each petal, but others are entirely yellow. The fruit is a capsule with 3 valves.

• **DISTRIBUTION** S. Spain, islands of the W. Mediterranean, Italy.

• **HABITAT** Coastal maquis, garigue, sandy soil including dunes and beaches.

• **RELATED SPECIES** Other spotted members of the rock-rose family include *Cistus ladanifer*, Gum Cistus (see p.148), and *Tuberaria guttata*, Spotted Rock-rose, which is a much smaller, annual plant that grows along waysides and on bare ground throughout the Mediterranean region.

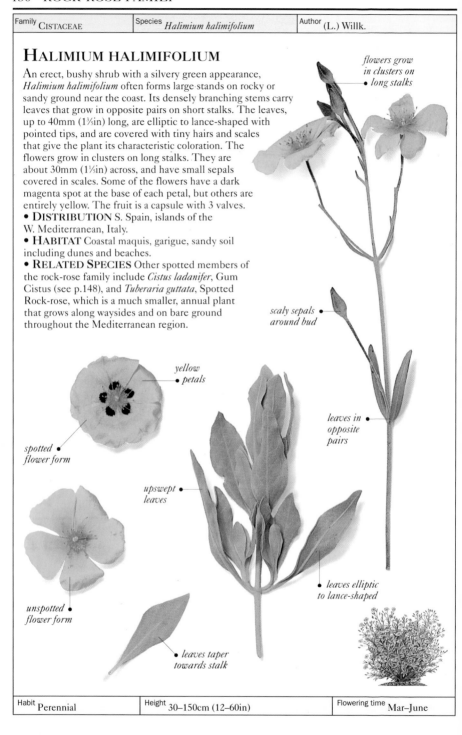

flowers grow
in clusters on
• long stalks

scaly sepals •
around bud

yellow
• petals

spotted •
flower form

upswept •
leaves

leaves in •
opposite
pairs

unspotted •
flower form

• leaves elliptic
to lance-shaped

• leaves taper
towards stalk

Habit Perennial	Height 30–150cm (12–60in)	Flowering time Mar–June

Family CISTACEAE	Species *Helianthemum apenninum*	Author (L.) Miller

WHITE ROCK-ROSE

A shrublet with a branching base and straggling growth, White Rock-rose has stems that are covered with small white hairs when young. The linear leaves, up to 30mm (1⅛in) long, are arranged in opposite pairs. Their margins are rolled under, and they have woolly undersides and small, narrow stipules. The stalked flowers, up to 30mm (1⅛in) in diameter, grow in clusters of 3 to 10, and are white with yellow centres and stamens. As with other members of the rock-rose family, there are 5 sepals – the 2 outer ones being much smaller than the inner 3. The fruit is a capsule, which is about as long as the larger sepals.
• **DISTRIBUTION** Throughout the region.
• **HABITAT** Dry, rocky places.
• **REMARK** This species extends northwards to N. France and S. England. A pink-petalled form occurs in the Balearic Islands.

hairy sepals; 2 sepals very small

white petals with yellow centres

leaves covered with hairs on underside

Habit Perennial	Height Up to 50cm (20in)	Flowering time Mar–June

Family CISTACEAE	Species *Helianthemum lavandulifolium*	Author Miller

HELIANTHEMUM LAVANDULIFOLIUM

There are many species of *Helianthemum* throughout the region, and identifying them can be a challenge. However, *Helianthemum lavandulifolium* poses no such problems, because its flowers are borne in a very characteristic way. This small, erect shrublet is covered with hairs, which give it a grey felty appearance. Its leaves, up to 50mm (2in) long, are narrowly elliptic with pointed tips. The yellow flowers grow in tightly packed, coiled branches, which uncoil as the flowers open. The petals are up to 10mm (⅜in) long, and the sepals are of unequal length. The fruit is a capsule.
• **DISTRIBUTION** Throughout, except for islands in the west, and the extreme east.
• **HABITAT** Garigue, stony fields, open woods.

3–5 flower-bearing stems

old flowers hang from stem

leaves have down-turned edges

leaves with very short stalks and tiny stipules

Habit Perennial	Height 10–50cm (4–20in)	Flowering time Apr–June

TAMARISK FAMILY

Family TAMARICACEAE	Species *Tamarix gallica*	Author L.

TAMARISK

This small, feathery tree or bush has reddish brown bark, and slender, hairless stems. The alternate, blue-green leaves are up to 4mm (⅛in) long, and clasp the stems. The pinkish white flowers are only about 5mm (⅛in) across, but they are arranged in abundant, dense spikes, which give the whole tree a pink coloration. The seeds have short tufts of hair.
• **DISTRIBUTION** Native to the southwest, but widely cultivated.
• **HABITAT** Damp, salty places, gardens.

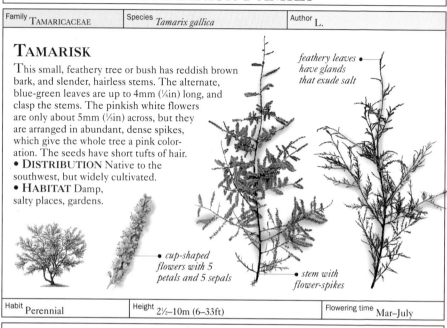

feathery leaves have glands that exude salt

• *cup-shaped flowers with 5 petals and 5 sepals*

stem with flower-spikes

Habit Perennial	Height 2½–10m (6–33ft)	Flowering time Mar–July

SEA HEATH FAMILY

Family FRANKENIACEAE	Species *Frankenia laevis*	Author L.

SEA HEATH

Sea Heath is a prostrate, mat-forming shore plant with a characteristically brittle texture. Its sprawling stems have woody bases, and branch frequently. The stalkless, linear leaves, up to 5mm (⅕in) long, grow in oppositely arranged clusters. They have down-curved edges and are often covered by a whitish crust. The pale pink flowers are cup-shaped, with 5 petals up to 6mm (¼in) long, yellow stamens, and hairy sepals. They grow either singly or in small clusters all along the upper branches. The fruit is a small capsule.
• **DISTRIBUTION** W. Mediterranean, eastwards to Italy.
• **HABITAT** Sand or shingle near the sea.

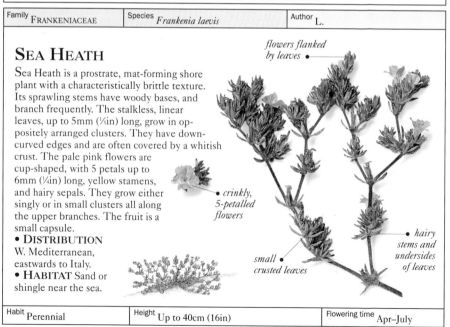

flowers flanked by leaves

• *crinkly, 5-petalled flowers*

small crusted leaves

• *hairy stems and undersides of leaves*

Habit Perennial	Height Up to 40cm (16in)	Flowering time Apr–July

GOURD FAMILY

Family CUCURBITACEAE	Species *Ecballium elaterium*	Author A. Richard

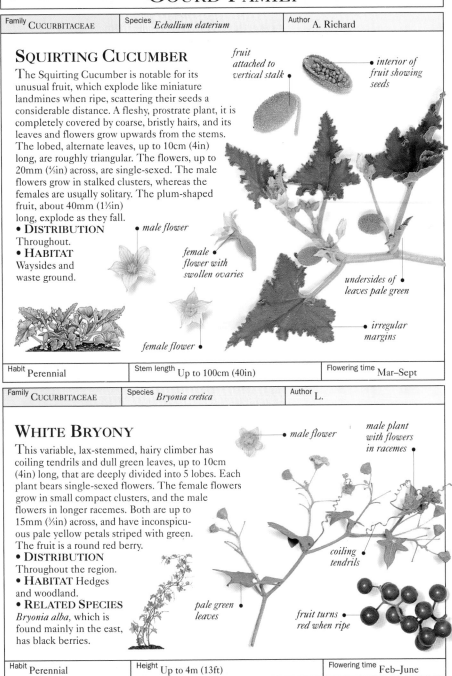

SQUIRTING CUCUMBER

The Squirting Cucumber is notable for its
unusual fruit, which explode like miniature
landmines when ripe, scattering their seeds a
considerable distance. A fleshy, prostrate plant, it is
completely covered by coarse, bristly hairs, and its
leaves and flowers grow upwards from the stems.
The lobed, alternate leaves, up to 10cm (4in)
long, are roughly triangular. The flowers, up to
20mm (⅘in) across, are single-sexed. The male
flowers grow in stalked clusters, whereas the
females are usually solitary. The plum-shaped
fruit, about 40mm (1⅗in)
long, explode as they fall.
• **DISTRIBUTION**
Throughout.
• **HABITAT**
Waysides and
waste ground.

fruit attached to vertical stalk

interior of fruit showing seeds

male flower

female flower with swollen ovaries

undersides of leaves pale green

irregular margins

female flower

Habit Perennial	Stem length Up to 100cm (40in)	Flowering time Mar–Sept

Family CUCURBITACEAE	Species *Bryonia cretica*	Author L.

WHITE BRYONY

This variable, lax-stemmed, hairy climber has
coiling tendrils and dull green leaves, up to 10cm
(4in) long, that are deeply divided into 5 lobes. Each
plant bears single-sexed flowers. The female flowers
grow in small compact clusters, and the male
flowers in longer racemes. Both are up to
15mm (⅗in) across, and have inconspicuous pale yellow petals striped with green.
The fruit is a round red berry.
• **DISTRIBUTION**
Throughout the region.
• **HABITAT** Hedges
and woodland.
• **RELATED SPECIES**
Bryonia alba, which is
found mainly in the east,
has black berries.

male flower

male plant with flowers in racemes

coiling tendrils

pale green leaves

fruit turns red when ripe

Habit Perennial	Height Up to 4m (13ft)	Flowering time Feb–June

CACTUS FAMILY

Family CACTACEAE	Species *Opuntia maxima*	Author Miller

PRICKLY PEAR

Prickly Pears are natives of the Americas. They
have paddle-like stems interrupted by constricted
joints, and minute leaves that soon fall. Many species
bear spines. In *Opuntia maxima*, the stem segments are up
to 40cm (16in) long, with spines in clusters of one to 4. The
bright yellow flowers are up to 10cm (4in) across, and
produce egg-shaped fruit with flat tops.
• **DISTRIBUTION** Naturalized throughout.
• **HABITAT** Dry places, rocky slopes.

fruit up to •
90mm (3⅗in)
long

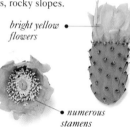

bright yellow •
flowers

spines in •
clusters
of 1–4

• numerous
stamens

Habit Perennial	Height 1–3m (3¼–10ft)	Flowering time Mar–July

LOOSESTRIFE FAMILY

Family LYTHRACEAE	Species *Lythrum junceum*	Author Banks & Solander

LYTHRUM JUNCEUM

An erect, hairless, and clump-forming plant, *Lythrum junceum*
branches at the base, and has square stems that often spread
before growing upwards. The leaves are alternate, stalkless,
and elliptic, and up to 22mm (⅞in) long. They have rounded
bases and a marked central rib, and tend to be broader at
the base of the plant and narrower at the top. The
6-petalled flowers are about 15mm (⅝in) across,
and grow singly, without a stalk, in the leaf-axils.
The fruit is a small capsule.
• **DISTRIBUTION** Throughout.
• **HABITAT** Damp ground,
riversides.
• **REMARK** The flowers have 3
slightly different forms, with a
single form on any one plant.
• **RELATED SPECIES** *Lythrum
acutangulum*, found in Spain and
France, is an annual with much
smaller, pale pink flowers.

• flowers in
leaf-axils

stalkless •
leaves

erect square •
stems, often
crowded in a
clump

Habit Usually perennial	Height 20–70cm (8–28in)	Flowering time Mar–Sept

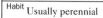

MYRTLE FAMILY

Family MYRTACEAE	Species *Myrtus communis*	Author L.

MYRTLE

Long prized for its delicious fragrance, Myrtle is an erect and densely branched evergreen shrub. Its stalkless leaves, up to 30mm (1⅛in) long, are elliptic with pointed tips. They are glossy above with an in-set central rib, and duller below with tiny glands. The scented flowers grow on long stalks from the leaf-axils. Each flower is about 20mm (⅛in) across, and has 5 white petals and numerous prominent stamens. The fruit is a blue-black berry, up to 10mm (⅜in) long.
• **DISTRIBUTION** Throughout.
• **HABITAT** Damp places, garigue, maquis.
• **REMARK** Myrtle flowers are traditionally worn in bridal wreaths. Its oil is used medicinally and in the production of perfume.

flowers spherical in bud

dark green aromatic leaves •

• opposite, leathery leaves

stamens • as long as or longer than petals

• densely branching stems

Habit Perennial	Height 1–5m (3¼–16½ft)	Flowering time Apr–Aug

Family MYRTACEAE	Species *Eucalyptus camaldulensis*	Author Dehnh.

RED GUM

A native of Australia, Red Gum was introduced into the region in the early 1800s. It is a fast-growing tree with smooth, dull white bark. On young trees the leaves are blue-green, short, and rounded; on older trees they become scythe-shaped with sharp tips, and are up to 22cm (8¾in) long. The flowers are borne at the leaf-axils in stalked umbels of 5 to 10.
• **DISTRIBUTION** Throughout.
• **HABITAT** Gardens, coastal ground.
• **REMARK** Many other *Eucalyptus* species are found in the Mediterranean.

fruit with an indented cross • on cap

long feathery • stamens

• mature fruit up to 8mm (⅓in) across

• leaves in opposite pairs

aromatic stems and leaves •

Habit Perennial	Height Up to 20m (65ft)	Flowering time All year round

POMEGRANATE FAMILY

Family PUNICACEAE	Species *Punica granatum*	Author L.

POMEGRANATE

A spiny, deciduous shrub or tree, the Pomegranate has grey-brown bark. Its leaves are up to 80mm (3⅓in) long, and are hairless and leathery. The striking red flowers are about 40mm (1⅗in) across, and are cupped by a fleshy red calyx. The edible fruit reaches 80mm (3⅓in) across, and contains numerous seeds in a juicy pulp.
- **DISTRIBUTION** Throughout the region.
- **HABITAT** Gardens, hedges, thickets, maquis.
- **REMARK** A native of S.W. Asia, cultivated in the Mediterranean region since ancient times.

opposite, •
oblong to egg-
shaped leaves

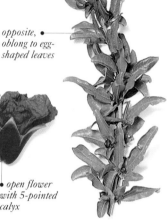

bright red •
flower-bud

• *open flower*
with 5-pointed
calyx

Habit Perennial	Height 2–7m (6½–23ft)	Flowering time May–Sept

WILLOWHERB FAMILY

Family ONAGRACEAE	Species *Oenothera suaveolens*	Author Pers.

OENOTHERA SUAVEOLENS

As with most evening primroses, this plant is at its most attractive just after sunset, when the day's flowers are freshly opened. An erect, robust species, it has hairy stems without spots, and broadly lance-shaped leaves up to 12cm (4¾in) long. The flowers are about 80mm (3⅓in) across. Each flower lasts just a single night, and withers as the following morning progresses. The fruit is a long capsule.
- **DISTRIBUTION** W. and C. Mediterranean.
- **HABITAT** Waste ground, dunes, gardens.
- **RELATED SPECIES** Several similar species are naturalized in the Mediterranean region, all either of North American origin or the result of hybridization. They include *Oenothera erythrosepala*, Large-flowered Evening Primrose, which has leaves with undulating margins, and red-spotted stems.

large, slightly
bilobed
• *petals*

long, pointed
• *flower-bud*

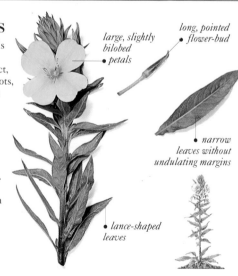

• *narrow*
leaves without
undulating margins

• *lance-shaped*
leaves

Habit Biennial	Height 30–150cm (12–60in)	Flowering time May–July

CARROT FAMILY

Family UMBELLIFERAE	Species *Eryngium maritimum*	Author L.

SEA HOLLY

Most members of the carrot family have flowers in spreading umbrella-like heads, or umbels, and soft or fleshy, pinnately divided leaves. Sea Holly and its relatives depart from this general plan. In this species, the stems are ribbed and stiff, and the entire plant has a characteristic silvery blue bloom. The leaves are hard and spiny, and are stalked and broad at the base, and stalkless and squarer higher up. The tiny blue flowers develop in compact, round heads, up to 30mm (1⅛in) across, and produce small, scaly fruit.
• **DISTRIBUTION** Throughout.
• **HABITAT** Sandy beaches and dunes.

rosette of spiny bracts

ribbed stems

lower leaves with 3–5 lobes, up to 15cm (6in) long

compact flower-heads

Habit Perennial	Height 15–60cm (6–24in)	Flowering time Jun–Sept

Family UMBELLIFERAE	Species *Eryngium campestre*	Author L.

FIELD ERYNGO

Field Eryngo has stout, ribbed stems and leathery leaves that are edged with spines. The blades of the lowest leaves reach up to 20cm (8in) long. The tiny greenish white flowers are arranged in domed clusters up to 15mm (⅗in) across. The fruit has overlapping scales.
• **DISTRIBUTION** Throughout.
• **HABITAT** Fields, dry places.
• **RELATED SPECIES** *Eryngium amethystinum*, Blue Eryngo, which grows in dry places in the east of the region, has spine-tipped leaves that are more narrowly divided.

divided leaf from base of stem

spiny bracts much longer than flower-head

pale flowers in compact head

Habit Perennial	Height 20–70cm (8–28in)	Flowering time May–July

Family UMBELLIFERAE	Species *Lagoecia cuminoides*	Author L.

LAGOECIA CUMINOIDES

An erect and distinctly aromatic plant, *Lagoecia cuminoides* has slender branching stems that rarely grow more than 30cm (12in) high. The leaves are stalkless and feathery, and up to 70mm (2⅜in) long. They are pinnate, and have tiny alternate leaflets, which are sharply lobed and toothed, and which tend to be broader at the base of the plant and narrower at the top. The small white flowers form in ball-shaped umbels, up to 15mm (⅗in) in diameter, which grow from the leaf-axils. The fruit is covered with short hairs.

• **DISTRIBUTION** Throughout the Mediterranean region.
• **HABITAT** Rocky, dry, fallow land.

• *small, spherical flower-heads*

small, pinnately divided leaves •

feathery •
bracts beneath flower-head

Habit Annual	Height 6–30cm (2⅖–12in)	Flowering time Apr–May

Family UMBELLIFERAE	Species *Echinophora spinosa*	Author L.

ECHINOPHORA SPINOSA

This erect or rather straggling shore plant is armed with sharp spines. Its stems are fleshy and slightly hairy, and they branch frequently to give the plant an angular shape. The leaves are alternate, thick, and rigid. They are divided into narrow, spine-tipped leaflets, which are themselves usually subdivided, and they have a central groove on the upper surface. Their bases clasp the stems. The white flowers grow in umbels with between 4 and 8 hairy rays, and these have spiny bracts at the base. The fruit is ridged and oval, with a covering formed by the male flowers.

• **DISTRIBUTION** W. and C. Mediterranean.
• **HABITAT** Sandy beaches.

spiny bracts beneath umbels •

ridged stems •

leaves up to •
15cm (6in)
long

partial umbels with ring of male flowers

Habit Perennial	Height 20–80cm (8–32in)	Flowering time June–Oct

Family UMBELLIFERAE	Species *Scandix pecten-veneris*	Author L.

SHEPHERD'S NEEDLE

This diminutive and variable plant
is usually noticed for its conspicuous
needle-shaped fruit rather than for
its flowers. It is generally erect or
ascending, and its branching stems
are grooved and covered in short
hairs. The leaves are pinnate, up
to 80mm (3⅛in) long, and are subdivided up to 3 times. The flowers
form in umbels with a maximum of
just 3 rays. Each flower is up to 5mm (⅕in)
across, and its outer petals are often slightly
enlarged. The characteristic, hairy "needles"
grow in small clusters and are up to 80mm
(3⅛in) long, although in some forms of the
plant they reach only 15mm (⅝in).
• **DISTRIBUTION** Throughout the region.
• **HABITAT** Cultivated fields, fallow ground.

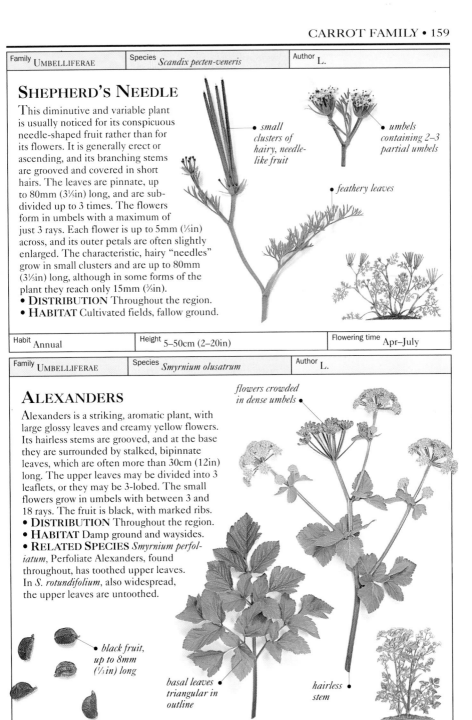

• *small
clusters of
hairy, needle-
like fruit*

• *umbels
containing 2–3
partial umbels*

• *feathery leaves*

Habit Annual	Height 5–50cm (2–20in)	Flowering time Apr–July

Family UMBELLIFERAE	Species *Smyrnium olusatrum*	Author L.

ALEXANDERS

Alexanders is a striking, aromatic plant, with
large glossy leaves and creamy yellow flowers.
Its hairless stems are grooved, and at the base
they are surrounded by stalked, bipinnate
leaves, which are often more than 30cm (12in)
long. The upper leaves may be divided into 3
leaflets, or they may be 3-lobed. The small
flowers grow in umbels with between 3 and
18 rays. The fruit is black, with marked ribs.
• **DISTRIBUTION** Throughout the region.
• **HABITAT** Damp ground and waysides.
• **RELATED SPECIES** *Smyrnium perfoliatum*, Perfoliate Alexanders, found
throughout, has toothed upper leaves.
In *S. rotundifolium*, also widespread,
the upper leaves are untoothed.

*flowers crowded
in dense umbels* •

• *black fruit,
up to 8mm
(⅓in) long*

*basal leaves •
triangular in
outline*

*hairless •
stem*

Habit Biennial	Height 50–150cm (20–60in)	Flowering time Feb–June

Family UMBELLIFERAE	Species *Crithmum maritimum*	Author L.

Rock Samphire

Rock Samphire is one of a small
number of shore plants that can
withstand frequent wetting by salt
spray. It is spreading and has a woody
base, and its hairless, fleshy stems and
leaves have a grey-green hue. The
leaves are alternate and are pinnately
divided either once or twice, each lobe being up
to 50mm (2in) long. The leaves are 4-sided, and
are upswept rather like miniature antlers.
The pale yellow flowers form in
densely packed umbels, up to
80mm (3⅛in) across, that have
between 8 and 36 rays,
and they produce
ribbed, egg-shaped
fruit that is up to
6mm (¼in) long.
• **DISTRIBUTION**
Throughout.
• **HABITAT** Rocks
close to the sea.

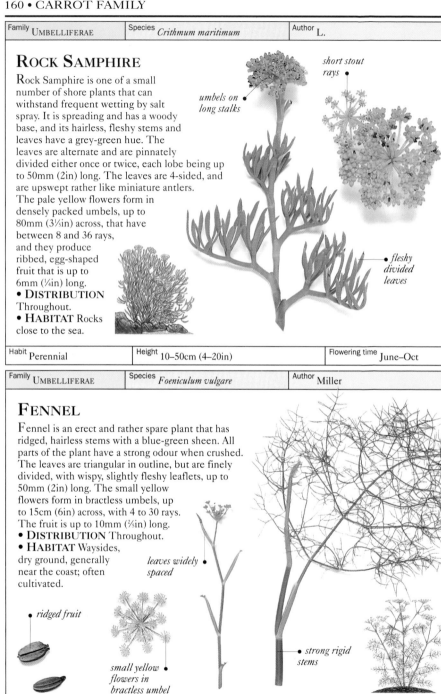

*short stout
rays*

*umbels on
long stalks*

*fleshy
divided
leaves*

Habit Perennial	Height 10–50cm (4–20in)	Flowering time June–Oct

Family UMBELLIFERAE	Species *Foeniculum vulgare*	Author Miller

Fennel

Fennel is an erect and rather spare plant that has
ridged, hairless stems with a blue-green sheen. All
parts of the plant have a strong odour when crushed.
The leaves are triangular in outline, but are finely
divided, with wispy, slightly fleshy leaflets, up to
50mm (2in) long. The small yellow
flowers form in bractless umbels, up
to 15cm (6in) across, with 4 to 30 rays.
The fruit is up to 10mm (⅜in) long.
• **DISTRIBUTION** Throughout.
• **HABITAT** Waysides,
dry ground, generally
near the coast; often
cultivated.

*leaves widely
spaced*

ridged fruit

*small yellow
flowers in
bractless umbel*

*strong rigid
stems*

Habit Biennial/perennial	Height Up to 2.5m (8ft)	Flowering time Apr–Sept

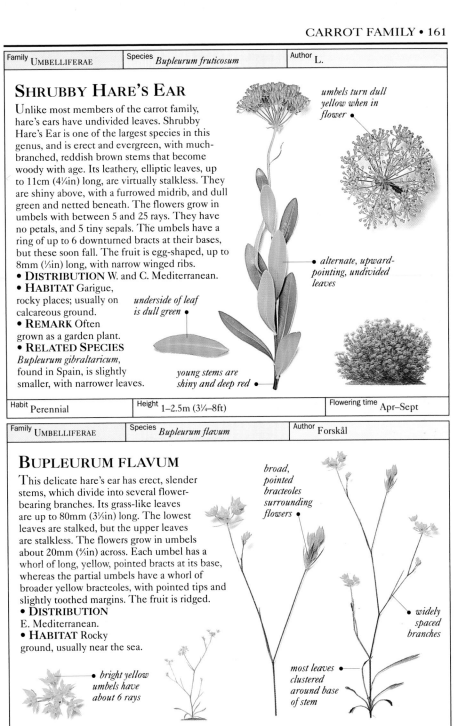

Family UMBELLIFERAE	Species *Bupleurum fruticosum*	Author L.

SHRUBBY HARE'S EAR

Unlike most members of the carrot family, hare's ears have undivided leaves. Shrubby Hare's Ear is one of the largest species in this genus, and is erect and evergreen, with much-branched, reddish brown stems that become woody with age. Its leathery, elliptic leaves, up to 11cm (4¼in) long, are virtually stalkless. They are shiny above, with a furrowed midrib, and dull green and netted beneath. The flowers grow in umbels with between 5 and 25 rays. They have no petals, and 5 tiny sepals. The umbels have a ring of up to 6 downturned bracts at their bases, but these soon fall. The fruit is egg-shaped, up to 8mm (⅓in) long, with narrow winged ribs.

- **DISTRIBUTION** W. and C. Mediterranean.
- **HABITAT** Garigue, rocky places; usually on calcareous ground.
- **REMARK** Often grown as a garden plant.
- **RELATED SPECIES** *Bupleurum gibraltaricum*, found in Spain, is slightly smaller, with narrower leaves.

umbels turn dull yellow when in flower •

• alternate, upward-pointing, undivided leaves

underside of leaf is dull green •

young stems are shiny and deep red •

Habit Perennial	Height 1–2.5m (3¼–8ft)	Flowering time Apr–Sept

Family UMBELLIFERAE	Species *Bupleurum flavum*	Author Forskål

BUPLEURUM FLAVUM

This delicate hare's ear has erect, slender stems, which divide into several flower-bearing branches. Its grass-like leaves are up to 80mm (3⅛in) long. The lowest leaves are stalked, but the upper leaves are stalkless. The flowers grow in umbels about 20mm (⅘in) across. Each umbel has a whorl of long, yellow, pointed bracts at its base, whereas the partial umbels have a whorl of broader yellow bracteoles, with pointed tips and slightly toothed margins. The fruit is ridged.

- **DISTRIBUTION** E. Mediterranean.
- **HABITAT** Rocky ground, usually near the sea.

broad, pointed bracteoles surrounding flowers •

• widely spaced branches

• bright yellow umbels have about 6 rays

most leaves • clustered around base of stem

Habit Annual	Height 20–75cm (8–30in)	Flowering time Apr–June

Family UMBELLIFERAE	Species *Ferula communis*	Author L.

GIANT FENNEL

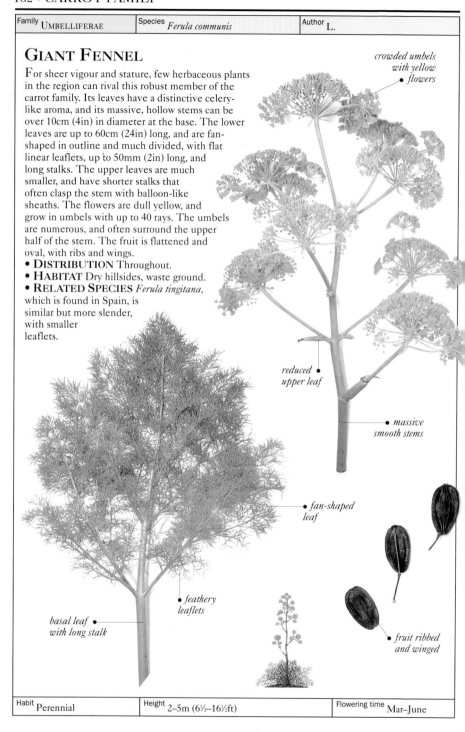

crowded umbels with yellow flowers

For sheer vigour and stature, few herbaceous plants in the region can rival this robust member of the carrot family. Its leaves have a distinctive celery-like aroma, and its massive, hollow stems can be over 10cm (4in) in diameter at the base. The lower leaves are up to 60cm (24in) long, and are fan-shaped in outline and much divided, with flat linear leaflets, up to 50mm (2in) long, and long stalks. The upper leaves are much smaller, and have shorter stalks that often clasp the stem with balloon-like sheaths. The flowers are dull yellow, and grow in umbels with up to 40 rays. The umbels are numerous, and often surround the upper half of the stem. The fruit is flattened and oval, with ribs and wings.

• **DISTRIBUTION** Throughout.

• **HABITAT** Dry hillsides, waste ground.

• **RELATED SPECIES** *Ferula tingitana*, which is found in Spain, is similar but more slender, with smaller leaflets.

reduced upper leaf

massive smooth stems

fan-shaped leaf

feathery leaflets

basal leaf with long stalk

fruit ribbed and winged

Habit Perennial	Height 2–5m (6½–16½ft)	Flowering time Mar–June

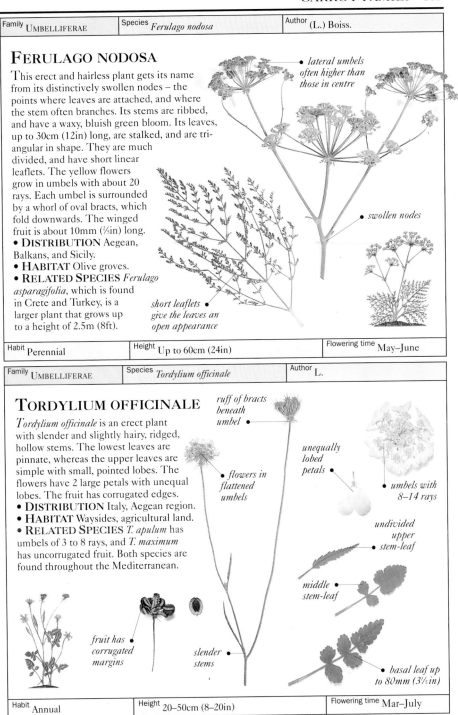

| Family UMBELLIFERAE | Species *Ferulago nodosa* | Author (L.) Boiss. |

FERULAGO NODOSA

This erect and hairless plant gets its name from its distinctively swollen nodes – the points where leaves are attached, and where the stem often branches. Its stems are ribbed, and have a waxy, bluish green bloom. Its leaves, up to 30cm (12in) long, are stalked, and are triangular in shape. They are much divided, and have short linear leaflets. The yellow flowers grow in umbels with about 20 rays. Each umbel is surrounded by a whorl of oval bracts, which fold downwards. The winged fruit is about 10mm (⅖in) long.
• **DISTRIBUTION** Aegean, Balkans, and Sicily.
• **HABITAT** Olive groves.
• **RELATED SPECIES** *Ferulago asparagifolia*, which is found in Crete and Turkey, is a larger plant that grows up to a height of 2.5m (8ft).

lateral umbels often higher than those in centre

swollen nodes

short leaflets give the leaves an open appearance

| Habit Perennial | Height Up to 60cm (24in) | Flowering time May–June |

| Family UMBELLIFERAE | Species *Tordylium officinale* | Author L. |

TORDYLIUM OFFICINALE

Tordylium officinale is an erect plant with slender and slightly hairy, ridged, hollow stems. The lowest leaves are pinnate, whereas the upper leaves are simple with small, pointed lobes. The flowers have 2 large petals with unequal lobes. The fruit has corrugated edges.
• **DISTRIBUTION** Italy, Aegean region.
• **HABITAT** Waysides, agricultural land.
• **RELATED SPECIES** *T. apulum* has umbels of 3 to 8 rays, and *T. maximum* has uncorrugated fruit. Both species are found throughout the Mediterranean.

ruff of bracts beneath umbel

flowers in flattened umbels

unequally lobed petals

umbels with 8–14 rays

undivided upper stem-leaf

middle stem-leaf

fruit has corrugated margins

slender stems

basal leaf up to 80mm (3⅕in)

| Habit Annual | Height 20–50cm (8–20in) | Flowering time Mar–July |

Family UMBELLIFERAE	Species *Thapsia villosa*	Author L.

THAPSIA VILLOSA

This erect plant has hairless, solid stems, which are glossy and finely ridged. The leaves are slightly hairy. The lower leaves, up to 35cm (14in) long, are stalked, with a triangular outline, and are finely divided. Their flat leaflets, which have toothed margins, give them a fern-like appearance. The upper leaves are reduced to papery sheaths that clasp the stems. The umbels usually lack bracts. The largest umbels are about 12cm (4¾in) across, with 9 to 24 rays and small yellow flowers. The elliptical fruit, up to 15mm (⅝in) long, has lateral wings, notched at either end.

• **DISTRIBUTION** Spain, S. France, N.W. Africa.
• **HABITAT** Dry hillsides, often near the coast.
• **RELATED SPECIES** *Thapsia maxima*, which is found in Spain, is more or less hairless. *T. garganica*, which is found eastwards to Crete, has linear leaflets that are often untoothed.

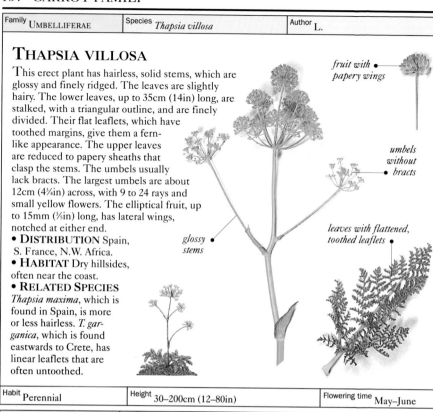

fruit with papery wings

umbels without bracts

glossy stems

leaves with flattened, toothed leaflets

Habit Perennial	Height 30–200cm (12–80in)	Flowering time May–June

Family UMBELLIFERAE	Species *Torilis arvensis*	Author (Hudson) Link

SPREADING HEDGE-PARSLEY

Spreading Hedge-parsley is a highly variable, slightly hairy plant with distinctive spiny fruit. Its stem can be branching or relatively unbranched, and its leaves are usually doubly divided, with toothed margins, the upper leaves often being 3-lobed. The flowers are borne in umbels with 2 to 12 rays. The umbels have at most a single bract, but the partial umbels have numerous bracteoles. The fruit is up to 6mm (¼in) long.

• **DISTRIBUTION** Throughout.
• **HABITAT** Fields, waysides.
• **REMARK** Several subspecies are recognized.

bracts absent, or 1 bract only

spiny, egg-shaped fruit

umbels have 2–12 rays

leaves bipinnate

Habit Annual	Height Up to 100cm (40in)	Flowering time May–Sept

Family UMBELLIFERAE	Species *Daucus carota*	Author L.

WILD CARROT

A highly variable plant, Wild Carrot can be short and compact, or tall and spreading. Its stems are hairy or hairless, and are often ridged. The leaves are twice or thrice pinnate, and have lance-shaped leaflets. At the base of the stem the leaves can be up to 35cm (14in) long, whereas further up they are much shorter. The central flower is often deep purple, all the others being white. After flowering, the umbels become deeply concave, or even close up into a ball, and they produce spiny, furrowed, egg-shaped fruit, up to 4mm (⅛in) long.

• **DISTRIBUTION** Throughout.
• **HABITAT** Coasts, dry ground.

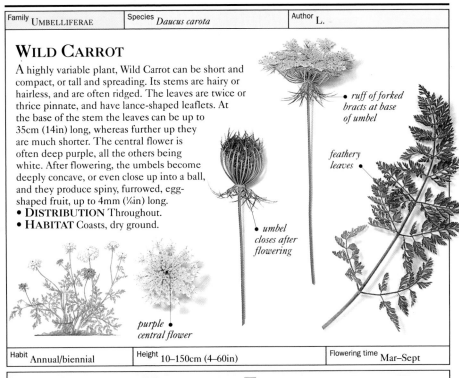

• *ruff of forked bracts at base of umbel*

feathery leaves •

• *umbel closes after flowering*

purple • central flower

Habit Annual/biennial	Height 10–150cm (4–60in)	Flowering time Mar–Sept

HEATHER FAMILY

Family ERICACEAE	Species *Erica cinerea*	Author L.

BELL HEATHER

Bell Heather is a small, dense shrub that is hairless, except on young growth. Its narrow, dark green leaves, up to 6mm (¼in) long, grow in whorls of 3. The urn-shaped flowers, up to 7mm (⅔in) long, form compact clusters at the tips of the stems, with only the stigma projecting beyond the mouth of the flower. The fruit is a small capsule.

• **DISTRIBUTION** N.W. Mediterranean, eastwards to Italy; also N.W. Europe.
• **HABITAT** Dry heaths, maquis, woods; usually on acid soil.
• **REMARK**
There are several other species of *Erica* in the region; many prefer damp ground.

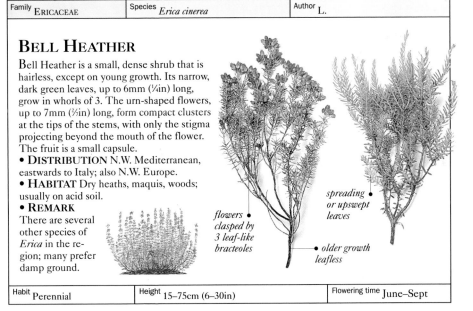

flowers • clasped by 3 leaf-like bracteoles

spreading • or upswept leaves

• *older growth leafless*

Habit Perennial	Height 15–75cm (6–30in)	Flowering time June–Sept

Family ERICACEAE	Species *Erica arborea*	Author L.

TREE HEATH

Tree Heath is one of the tallest European members of the genus *Erica*, regularly reaching a height of 3m (10ft). A densely branching, evergreen shrub with an upswept appearance, its older stems are woody and smooth, and its younger stems are covered in white woolly hairs. Its needle-like leaves, which are up to 5mm (1/5in) long, grow in whorls of 3 or 4. They are hairless, and have downturned edges that almost conceal the undersides. Its tiny, scented, bell-shaped flowers grow in dense clusters. The anthers are a dark red-brown, giving the flowers a dull colour when seen from a distance. The fruit is a small capsule.

• **DISTRIBUTION** Throughout the region, except for the extreme east.

• **HABITAT** Evergreen woods, maquis; on acid soils.

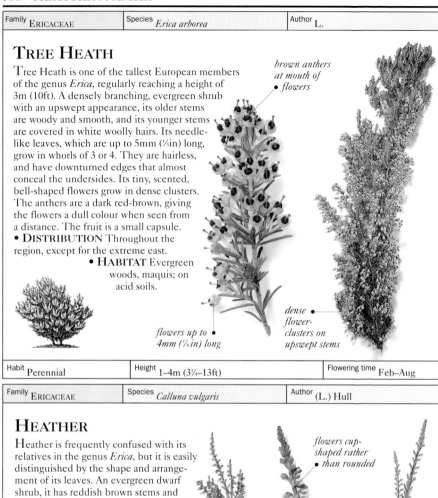

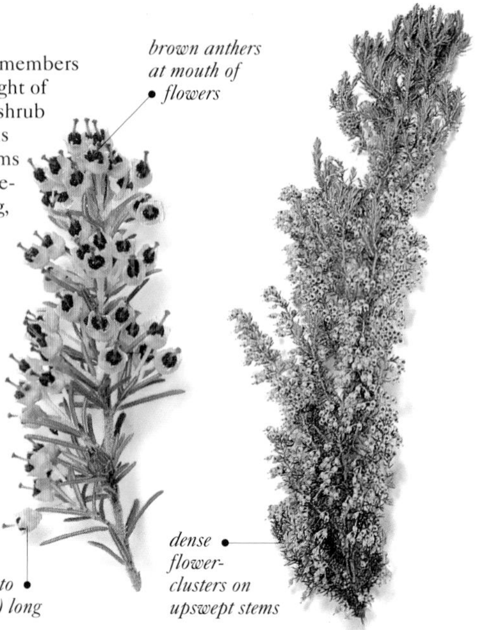
brown anthers at mouth of flowers
flowers up to 4mm (1/6in) long
dense flower-clusters on upswept stems

Habit Perennial	Height 1–4m (3¼–13ft)	Flowering time Feb–Aug

Family ERICACEAE	Species *Calluna vulgaris*	Author (L.) Hull

HEATHER

Heather is frequently confused with its relatives in the genus *Erica*, but it is easily distinguished by the shape and arrangement of its leaves. An evergreen dwarf shrub, it has reddish brown stems and tiny leaves, which grow up to 2mm (1/12in) long and are packed into 4 dense ranks. The flowers are up to 4mm (1/6in) long, and the outermost "petals" are in fact sepals, which are longer than the true petals. The fruit is a small capsule, which is about 2mm (1/8in) long.

• **DISTRIBUTION** W. Mediterranean.

• **HABITAT** Mountainsides and hillsides.

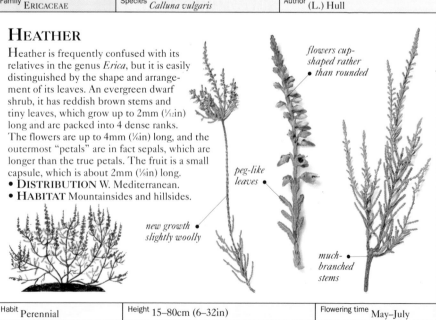

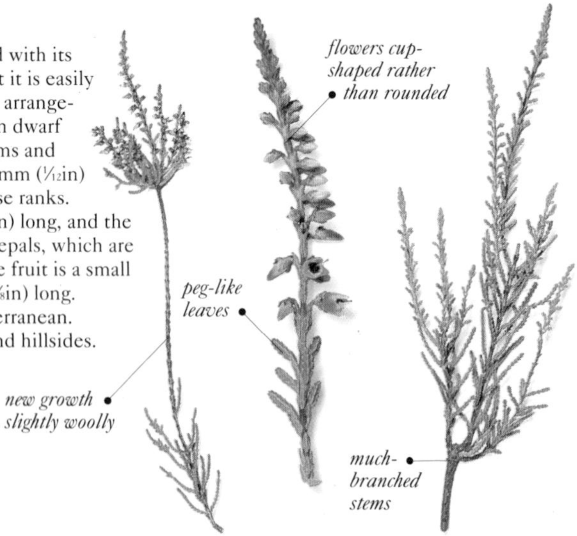
flowers cup-shaped rather than rounded
peg-like leaves
new growth slightly woolly
much-branched stems

Habit Perennial	Height 15–80cm (6–32in)	Flowering time May–July

Family ERICACEAE	Species *Arbutus unedo*	Author L.

STRAWBERRY TREE

In many parts of the region, the Strawberry Tree is an important constituent of dense, evergreen woodland. A shrub or small tree with fissured, flaking, dull red-brown bark, it has alternate leaves, up to 11cm (4¼in) long, which are stalked and elliptic. Its bell-shaped flowers are greenish white or pink, and about 8mm (⅓in) long. The ball-shaped fruit turns red when ripe.

- **DISTRIBUTION** Throughout the region.
- **HABITAT** Maquis, woodland edges, rocky hillsides.

glossy leaves with serrated margins

flowers in drooping clusters

spherical fruit with lobed surface

Habit Perennial	Height 1.5–10m (5–33ft)	Flowering time Oct–Apr

Family ERICACEAE	Species *Arbutus andrachne*	Author L.

GREEK STRAWBERRY TREE

Unlike its more widespread relative (above), the Greek Strawberry Tree has deep red-brown bark, which peels in strips to reveal brighter-coloured young bark beneath. Its leaves are about 10cm (4in) long, and they usually have smooth margins, although they can be toothed on young stems. The flowers are urn-shaped and about 6mm (¼in) long, and are borne in dense clusters on upright stems. The fruit is similar to that of the Strawberry Tree, but is orange rather than red when ripe, and grooved rather than lobed.

- **DISTRIBUTION** E. Mediterranean, westwards to Greece.
- **HABITAT** Rocky hillsides.
- **REMARK** A natural hybrid, *Arbutus x andrachnoides*, is sometimes found in places where *A. unedo* and *A. andrachne* grow close together.

leaves usually untoothed

flowering stems held upright

bark peels on old growth

Habit Perennial	Height Up to 5m (16½ft)	Flowering time Feb–Apr

PRIMROSE FAMILY

Family PRIMULACEAE	Species *Cyclamen balearicum*	Author Willk.

CYCLAMEN BALEARICUM

Like all cyclamens, this spring-flowering species grows from a tuber. In this case, the tuber is up to 25mm (1in) in diameter, and roots from its base. There is no visible stem, and the leaves and flowers grow from the tuber in scattered clusters. The leaves, which are up to 90mm (3⅛in) long, are often slightly lobed, with undulating margins. The flowers have white petals and the flower-stem coils up during fruiting.
• **DISTRIBUTION** Balearic Islands and France.
• **HABITAT** Shady, rocky places; usually on limestone.
• **REMARK** Cyclamens are protected by law throughout much of the region.

white flowers with
• *faint pink veins*

• *petals slightly twisted*

• *slender stems*

• *leaves dull, dark green with silver marbling*

Habit Perennial	Height 5–10cm (2–4in)	Flowering time Feb–Apr

Family PRIMULACEAE	Species *Cyclamen hederifolium*	Author Aiton

IVY-LEAVED SOWBREAD

This autumn-flowering cyclamen grows from a tuber, up to 15cm (6in) across, which roots from its upper surface. The flowers are pink, or sometimes white, with the backswept part of the petals up to 20mm (⅘in) long. The flower-stems coil up during fruiting. The leaves appear as flowering finishes, and are heart-shaped or indented, up to 14cm (5½in) long, with round-toothed margins, marbled green upper sides, and green or purple undersides.
• **DISTRIBUTION** From France eastwards to the Balkans.
• **HABITAT** Cool deciduous woods, shaded ground.
• **REMARK** This species is often cultivated. As with other cyclamens, the sugary-coated seeds are dispersed by ants.

• *ear-like lobes at mouth*

upper surface of leaves marbled •

• *first flowers appear before leaves*

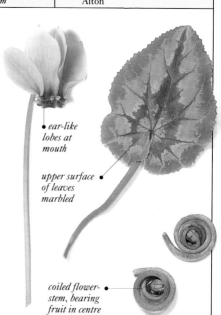

coiled flower-stem, bearing fruit in centre

Habit Perennial	Height 5–10cm (2–4in)	Flowering time Sept–Nov

Family PRIMULACEAE	Species *Cyclamen persicum*	Author Miller

CYCLAMEN PERSICUM

This exceptionally pretty cyclamen is the ancestor of the many large cultivars now grown as house plants. The wild form grows from a tuber, up to 16cm (6¼in) across, which roots from its base, and has heart-shaped leaves, up to 14cm (5½in) long, with thickened, blunt-toothed margins, and marbled upper surfaces. The flowers are white or pale pink with purple markings around their throats. The backswept part of the petals is up to 45mm (1⅘in) long. During fruiting, the flower-stalks arch, but do not coil up.
• **DISTRIBUTION** Aegean region, N. Africa.
• **HABITAT** Rocky hillsides, scrub, and open woods.
• **REMARK** *Cyclamen persicum* is now rare in parts of its range.

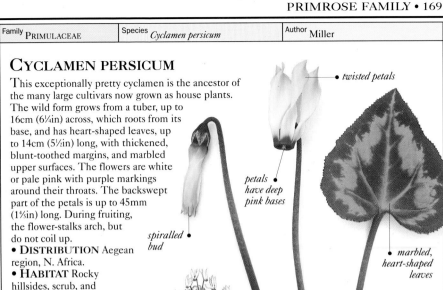

• *twisted petals*

petals have deep pink bases

spiralled bud

• *marbled, heart-shaped leaves*

Habit Perennial	Height 5–15cm (2–6in)	Flowering time Jan–May

Family PRIMULACEAE	Species *Cyclamen repandum*	Author Sibth. & Sm.

SPRING SOWBREAD

This common, spring-flowering cyclamen grows from a tuber, up to 60mm (2⅜in) across, which roots from its base. The heart-shaped leaves are up to 13cm (5in) long. They are highly variable in shape, and have plain green or marbled upper surfaces. The slightly scented flowers are borne on long, slender stalks, and are deep magenta with darker throats and a protruding style. The slightly twisted, backswept part of the petals is up to 30mm (1⅕in) long. The flower-stems coil up during fruiting.
• **DISTRIBUTION** France, eastwards to the Aegean region.
• **HABITAT** Shady places in woods, or among rocks.
• **RELATED SPECIES** *Cyclamen creticum*, found only on Crete, is very similar but has white flowers.

flower throat without lobes •

overlapping • *basal lobes*

leaves toothed or • *deeply lobed*

• *long, slender flower-stalks*

Habit Perennial	Height 6–13cm (2⅖–5in)	Flowering time Mar–May

Family PRIMULACEAE	Species *Anagallis foemina*	Author Miller

BLUE PIMPERNEL

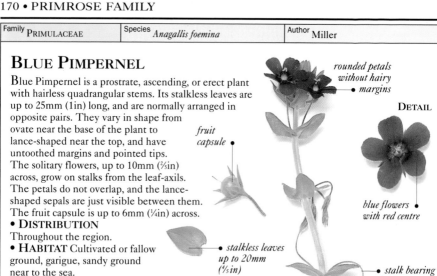

Blue Pimpernel is a prostrate, ascending, or erect plant with hairless quadrangular stems. Its stalkless leaves are up to 25mm (1in) long, and are normally arranged in opposite pairs. They vary in shape from ovate near the base of the plant to lance-shaped near the top, and have untoothed margins and pointed tips. The solitary flowers, up to 10mm (⅖in) across, grow on stalks from the leaf-axils. The petals do not overlap, and the lance-shaped sepals are just visible between them. The fruit capsule is up to 6mm (¼in) across.

rounded petals without hairy margins

DETAIL

blue flowers with red centre

fruit capsule

• **DISTRIBUTION**
Throughout the region.
• **HABITAT** Cultivated or fallow ground, garigue, sandy ground near to the sea.
• **RELATED SPECIES** *Anagallis arvensis*, Scarlet Pimpernel, is very similar and is also found throughout. It has red or blue flowers, and its petals have hairy margins.

stalkless leaves up to 20mm (⅘in)

stalk bearing developing capsule

Habit Annual/biennial	Height 5–50cm (2–20in)	Flowering time Mar–Oct

Family PRIMULACEAE	Species *Coris monspeliensis*	Author L.

CORIS MONSPELIENSIS

From a distance, this small clump-forming plant resembles some kinds of Thyme (see p.198), but a close look reveals that its flowers are not 2-lipped. It has erect or ascending stems, which are woody at the base and densely covered with foliage. The leathery, linear leaves, which grow up to 20mm (⅘in) long, are alternate and stalkless. They may be hairless or hairy, and the highest leaves often have small teeth. The flowers are borne in short, dense clusters, and vary in colour from pink to blue. Each flower measures up to 12mm (½in) across, and has narrow, widely spread petals. The calyx is bell-shaped, and has up to 20 spiny teeth. The spherical capsule is up to 2mm (1/12in) in diameter.

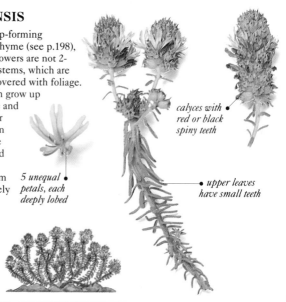

calyces with red or black spiny teeth

5 unequal petals, each deeply lobed

upper leaves have small teeth

• **DISTRIBUTION** W. and C. Mediterranean, including N.W. Africa.
• **HABITAT** Dry coastal areas.

Habit Biennial/perennial	Height 10–30cm (4–12in)	Flowering time Apr–July

THRIFT FAMILY

Family PLUMBAGINACEAE	Species *Limonium vulgare*	Author Miller

COMMON SEA LAVENDER

This leathery-leaved plant has erect, hairless stems growing from a woody base, and surrounded by a rosette of broad, spoon-shaped leaves, up to 15cm (6in) long. The papery flowers grow in small clusters, each up to 20mm (⅘in) long, which are carried on branching leafless stems. Subspecies *serotinum* – the common Mediterranean form – has long branches that often curve downwards.
- **DISTRIBUTION** Throughout the region.
- **HABITAT** Salt marshes.
- **REMARK** This is the most widespread of many sea lavenders that grow in the region.

individual flowers 8mm (⅓in) long

tiny 5-petalled flowers crowded in short spikes

SUBSP. SEROTINUM

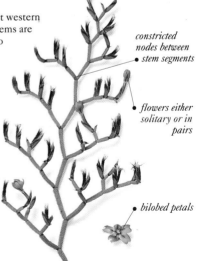

broad leaves grow in a rosette

Habit Perennial	Height 30–70cm (12–28in)	Flowering time July–Oct

Family PLUMBAGINACEAE	Species *Limonium articulatum*	Author (Loisel.) O. Kuntze

LIMONIUM ARTICULATUM

Unlike Common Sea Lavender (above), this compact western species grows on coastal rocks rather than mud. Its stems are hairless, and bear linear or spoon-shaped leaves, up to 35mm (1⅜in) long. These wither before the plant flowers. The flowering stems have a rough texture, and branch near the base of the plant. Their structure is characteristic, with short segments, up to 5mm (⅛in) long, meeting at constricted joints, arranged at angles that give the entire stem a zigzagging appearance. The flowers are about 5mm (⅛in) long, and grow in ones and twos along the side-branches.
- **DISTRIBUTION** Corsica and Sardinia.
- **HABITAT** Seashore rocks.
- **REMARK** Many sea lavenders are similarly localized in their distribution: some are confined to small areas of the mainland; others to archipelagos or even single islands.

constricted nodes between stem segments

flowers either solitary or in pairs

bilobed petals

Habit Perennial	Height 5–15cm (2–6in)	Flowering time June–Sept

Family PLUMBAGINACEAE	Species *Limonium sinuatum*	Author (L.) Miller

WINGED SEA LAVENDER

This eye catching sea lavender is easily identified by its flowers, and by the 3 or 4 narrow wings that run up its erect flowering stems. It has a rosette of bristly, deeply lobed leaves that are up to 20cm (8in) long, and the flowers are borne in compact branching heads composed of clusters of 2 or 3 blooms. Each flower is about 15mm (⅗in) long, and has a conspicuous papery calyx that is usually violet, with joined sepals that create a cup-like rim. The petals are yellowish white or pink.
• **DISTRIBUTION** Throughout.
• **HABITAT** Dry sandy ground, usually near to the sea, but sometimes inland.
• **REMARK** Winged Sea Lavender is frequently cultivated for use as a dried flower.

violet sepals

stem wings up to 3mm (⅛in) wide

yellowish white petals

deeply lobed leaves arranged in a rosette

Habit Perennial	Height 20–40cm (8–16in)	Flowering time Apr–Sept

STORAX FAMILY

Family STYRACACEAE	Species *Styrax officinalis*	Author L.

STORAX

An attractive deciduous shrub or tree, Storax is the only Mediterranean member of a family of plants that has 2 widely separated centres of distribution: Central America and East Asia. Its oval leaves, up to 60mm (2⅜in) long, are bright green above and grey-green beneath. They are alternate, and have stalks about 10mm (⅜in) long. The flowers, about 20mm (⅘in) long, are pleasantly scented, and grow in loose clusters of 3 to 6. Each flower has 5 to 7 petals, joined only at the base, and a hairy, bell-shaped calyx which often lacks teeth. The fruit is dry and single-seeded, with a woolly exterior.
• **DISTRIBUTION** E. Mediterranean, as far west as Italy.
• **HABITAT** Woods, waysides; sometimes cultivated.

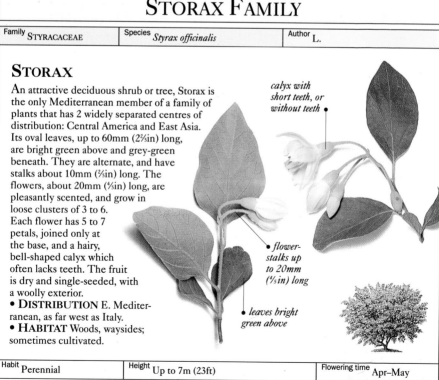

calyx with short teeth, or without teeth

flower-stalks up to 20mm (⅘in) long

leaves bright green above

Habit Perennial	Height Up to 7m (23ft)	Flowering time Apr–May

OLIVE FAMILY

Family OLEACEAE	Species *Olea europaea*	Author L.

OLIVE

No plant is more closely associated with the Mediterranean than this low-growing, often long-lived tree. Its bark is grey and becomes cracked with age, and its leathery leaves, up to 80mm (3⅛in) long, have grey-green upper surfaces and grey, hairy undersides. Its inconspicuous flowers are creamy yellow, with a cup-shaped calyx and 4 spreading petals. The edible fruit has oil-rich flesh surrounding a single seed.
• **DISTRIBUTION** Throughout the region.
• **HABITAT** Woodland, olive groves.

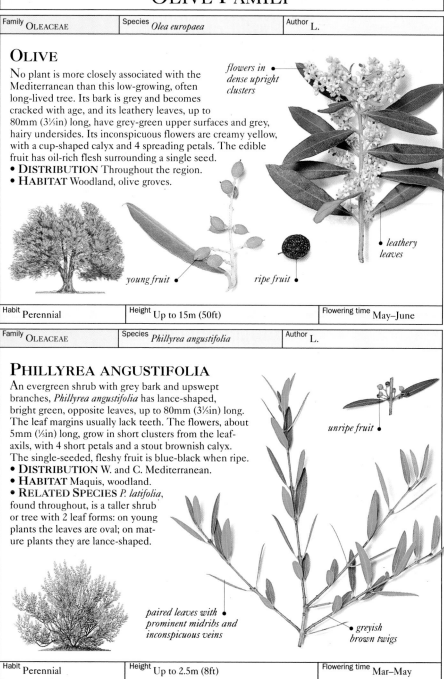

flowers in dense upright clusters

leathery leaves

young fruit

ripe fruit

Habit Perennial	Height Up to 15m (50ft)	Flowering time May–June

Family OLEACEAE	Species *Phillyrea angustifolia*	Author L.

PHILLYREA ANGUSTIFOLIA

An evergreen shrub with grey bark and upswept branches, *Phillyrea angustifolia* has lance-shaped, bright green, opposite leaves, up to 80mm (3⅛in) long. The leaf margins usually lack teeth. The flowers, about 5mm (⅛in) long, grow in short clusters from the leaf-axils, with 4 short petals and a stout brownish calyx. The single-seeded, fleshy fruit is blue-black when ripe.
• **DISTRIBUTION** W. and C. Mediterranean.
• **HABITAT** Maquis, woodland.
• **RELATED SPECIES** *P. latifolia*, found throughout, is a taller shrub or tree with 2 leaf forms: on young plants the leaves are oval; on mature plants they are lance-shaped.

unripe fruit

paired leaves with prominent midribs and inconspicuous veins

greyish brown twigs

Habit Perennial	Height Up to 2.5m (8ft)	Flowering time Mar–May

GENTIAN FAMILY

Family GENTIANACEAE	Species *Blackstonia perfoliata*	Author (L.) Hudson

YELLOW-WORT

Yellow-wort is a variable plant with erect, hairless stems, and stalkless upper leaves that are often fused together. The stems and leaves tend to have a grey-green, waxy appearance. The lowest leaves, up to 30mm (1⅛in) long, are oval and form a rosette. The stem-leaves have broader bases, and either join without a noticeable division, or become narrower where they meet. The flowers are borne in an erect, forked cluster, and can reach up to 35mm (1⅜in) long, although in most plants they are shorter than this. The petals are clasped by a distinctive calyx of narrow, sharply pointed sepals. The fruit is a 2-part capsule.
• **DISTRIBUTION** Throughout the region.
• **HABITAT** Waysides, woods, sandy ground.

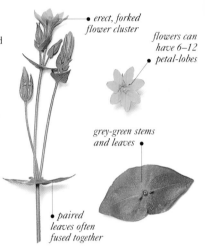

• *erect, forked flower cluster*

flowers can have 6–12 petal-lobes

grey-green stems and leaves •

• *paired leaves often fused together*

Habit Annual	Height 10–60cm (4–24in)	Flowering time Apr–Sept

Family GENTIANACEAE	Species *Centaurium erythraea*	Author Rafn

COMMON CENTAURY

This low-growing and very variable plant is at its most conspicuous in bright sunshine, when its pink or carmine-coloured flowers open wide. It usually has a single hairless stem, which often branches above the midway point, although in some forms it branches nearer the base. The lowest leaves are oval or elliptical, up to 50mm (2in) long, and form a rosette, whereas the stem-leaves are paired and are narrower, with 3 prominent veins. The flowers, about 12mm (½in) across, have 5 petals, which are joined below, and narrow sepals that reach at least halfway along the petal-tube. The fruit is a capsule.
• **DISTRIBUTION** Throughout.
• **HABITAT** Grassland, roadsides.
• **RELATED SPECIES**
Centaurium pulchellum, Lesser Centaury, is a smaller, annual plant without a rosette of leaves, which is found throughout most of Europe.

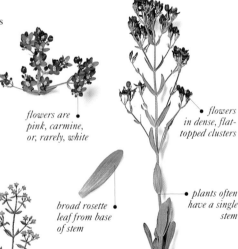

flowers are pink, carmine, or, rarely, white

broad rosette leaf from base of stem

• *flowers in dense, flat-topped clusters*

• *plants often have a single stem*

Habit Biennial	Height 10–50cm (4–20in)	Flowering time May–July

PERIWINKLE FAMILY

Family APOCYNACEAE	Species *Nerium oleander*	Author L.

OLEANDER

The Oleander flowers through the height
of summer, when many other Mediterranean
plants are well past their best. Its green stems
are rather lax and its narrow, leathery leaves grow
in whorls of 3 or 4. The leaves are held at an
acute angle to the stem, giving the plant an
upswept appearance. The flowers, up to
40mm (1⅗in) across, grow in dense clusters
at the stem tips, and produce woody follicles,
which split open to release many feathery seeds.

*flowers may
be red, pink,
or white*

*pointed
sepals*

- **DISTRIBUTION** Throughout.
- **HABITAT** Rocky watercourses;
frequently planted in gardens
and on roadsides.
- **REMARK** The plant's
milky sap is extremely
poisonous.

*ripe follicle
shedding seeds*

*narrow
evergreen leaves
with prominent
midrib*

*leaves have
many lateral
veins*

Habit Perennial	Height Up to 4m (13ft)	Flowering time June–Sept

Family APOCYNACEAE	Species *Vinca difformis*	Author Pourret

INTERMEDIATE PERIWINKLE

erect flowering stems

This glossy-leaved, evergreen plant has a creeping
growth form, but its delicate, pale blue flowers are
held aloft on short, erect stems. The leaves are
paired, and unlike the leaves of *Vinca major*,
Greater Periwinkle (see p.176), they do not
have hairy margins. The flowers are up to
45mm (1⅗in) in diameter, and the petals have
oblique tips. The follicle contains hairless seeds.

- **DISTRIBUTION** S.W. Mediterranean,
including N.W. Africa, eastwards to Italy.
- **HABITAT** Hedges, damp shaded ground,
roadsides, woods.
- **RELATED SPECIES** *V. herbacea*,
Herbaceous Periwinkle, is similar,
but is not evergreen. It is found in
the W. and C. Mediterranean.

*flowers pale
blue or almost
white*

*oval or
lance-shaped
leaves*

Habit Perennial	Stem length Up to 2m (6½ft)	Flowering time Feb–May

Family APOCYNACEAE	Species *Vinca major*	Author L.

GREATER PERIWINKLE

LIKE Intermediate Periwinkle (see p.175), this
creeping plant carries its flowers on short, erect
stems. Its leaves are broad with a blunt base,
and have fine fringing hairs. The flowers are
bluish purple, and their sepals have finely
haired margins.
• **DISTRIBUTION**
Throughout; natur-
alized in the east.
• **HABITAT**
Damp, shady
ground.

• *flowering stems
up to 30cm
(12in) high*

flowers bluish •
*purple with oblique-
tipped petals*

• *glossy
leaves up
to 60mm
(2⅖in) across*

Habit Perennial	Stem length Up to 100cm (40in)	Flowering time Feb–May

MILKWEED FAMILY

Family ASCLEPIADACEAE	Species *Gomphocarpus fruticosus*	Author (L.) Aiton fil.

BRISTLY-FRUITED SILKWEED

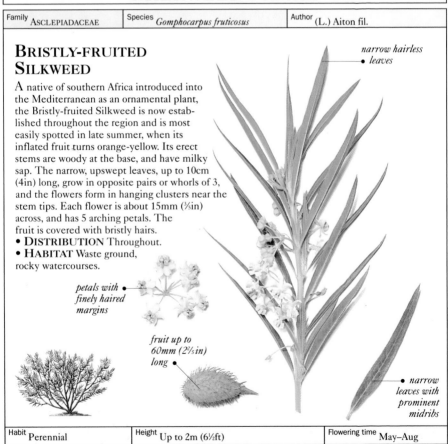

A native of southern Africa introduced into
the Mediterranean as an ornamental plant,
the Bristly-fruited Silkweed is now established throughout the region and is most
easily spotted in late summer, when its
inflated fruit turns orange-yellow. Its erect
stems are woody at the base, and have milky
sap. The narrow, upswept leaves, up to 10cm
(4in) long, grow in opposite pairs or whorls of 3,
and the flowers form in hanging clusters near the
stem tips. Each flower is about 15mm (⅗in)
across, and has 5 arching petals. The
fruit is covered with bristly hairs.
• **DISTRIBUTION** Throughout.
• **HABITAT** Waste ground,
rocky watercourses.

narrow hairless
• *leaves*

petals with •
*finely haired
margins*

*fruit up to
60mm (2⅖in)
long* •

• *narrow
leaves with
prominent
midribs*

Habit Perennial	Height Up to 2m (6½ft)	Flowering time May–Aug

Family ASCLEPIADACEAE	Species *Vincetoxicum hirundinaria*	Author Medicus

SWALLOW-WORT

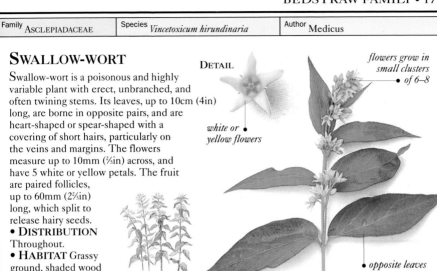

Swallow-wort is a poisonous and highly variable plant with erect, unbranched, and often twining stems. Its leaves, up to 10cm (4in) long, are borne in opposite pairs, and are heart-shaped or spear-shaped with a covering of short hairs, particularly on the veins and margins. The flowers measure up to 10mm (⅜in) across, and have 5 white or yellow petals. The fruit are paired follicles, up to 60mm (2⅜in) long, which split to release hairy seeds.
• **DISTRIBUTION** Throughout.
• **HABITAT** Grassy ground, shaded wood margins.

DETAIL

white or yellow flowers

flowers grow in small clusters of 6–8

opposite leaves with short stalks

Habit Perennial	Height Up to 120cm (48in)	Flowering time May–Sept

BEDSTRAW FAMILY

Family RUBIACEAE	Species *Cruciata laevipes*	Author Opiz

CROSSWORT

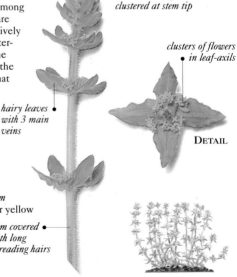

The bedstraw family is one of the largest among flowering plants, but most of its members are found in the tropics or subtropics, and relatively few in temperate regions such as the Mediterranean. Crosswort is a typical member of the family, with downy stems that branch near the base, and leaves, up to 20mm (⅘in) long, that are borne in whorls of 4. The flowers are tiny, up to 3mm (⅛in) long, and have 4 petals. They are packed together in tight clusters at the axils of the leaves. The fruit is rounded and blackish, and is carried on stalks that curve downwards.
• **DISTRIBUTION** Throughout the region, but absent from some islands.
• **HABITAT** Grassland, roadsides.
• **RELATED SPECIES** Bedstraws (*Galium* species) are similar, but often have white or yellow flowers and whorls of up to 12 leaves. Many have fruit with hooked bristles. One of the most widespread species is *G. verum*, Lady's Bedstraw. It has dense clusters of rich yellow flowers.

leaves closely clustered at stem tip

clusters of flowers in leaf-axils

hairy leaves with 3 main veins

DETAIL

stem covered with long spreading hairs

Habit Perennial	Height 20–60cm (8–24in)	Flowering time Apr–June

Family RUBIACEAE	Species *Rubia peregrina*	Author L.

WILD MADDER

Wild Madder is an evergreen, climbing or scrambling plant with 4-angled stems that are woody at their bases. Its leaves, up to 60mm (2⅜in) long, are arranged in whorls of 4 to 8. The leaf margins, midribs, and stem-angles all have sharp, backward-pointing spines that the plant uses for support. The flowers, about 6mm (¼in) across, grow in large clusters. Each flower has 5 sharply pointed, yellow-green petals, and produces a black berry, up to 6mm (¼in) in diameter.

• **DISTRIBUTION** W. and C. Mediterranean.
• **HABITAT** Open woods, rocky ground, field edges.
• **RELATED SPECIES** *R. tinctoria*, Madder, the source of the painter's pigment, is a softer plant with brighter, more rounded petals. It is found throughout the region.

flower-clusters project beyond the leaves

spiny leaf margins

glossy evergreen leaves with a single vein

Habit Perennial	Stem length Up to 2.5m (8ft)	Flowering time Apr–Aug

BINDWEED FAMILY

Family CONVOLVULACEAE	Species *Cuscuta epithymum*	Author (L.) L.

COMMON DODDER

Dodders are parasitic plants that live by extracting water and nutrients from their hosts. Common Dodder lives on many different plants in the Mediterranean region, including *Erica* species and members of the pea family. It frequently swamps its hosts with a tangle of red or yellowish stems that force their way into the host plant's tissues. Its flowers grow in small globular clusters, and are about 2mm (½in) long. They are pinkish or almost transparent, and have 5 petal-lobes and short stamens. The fruit is a capsule. Once a seed has germinated and the resulting plant has located a host, the roots wither away.

• **DISTRIBUTION** Throughout the Mediterranean region.
• **HABITAT** Open ground with shrubs.

flower-cluster

DETAIL

flowering Common Dodder stems parasit-izing a Helianthemum

Habit Annual	Stem length Up to 60cm (24in)	Flowering time June–Sept

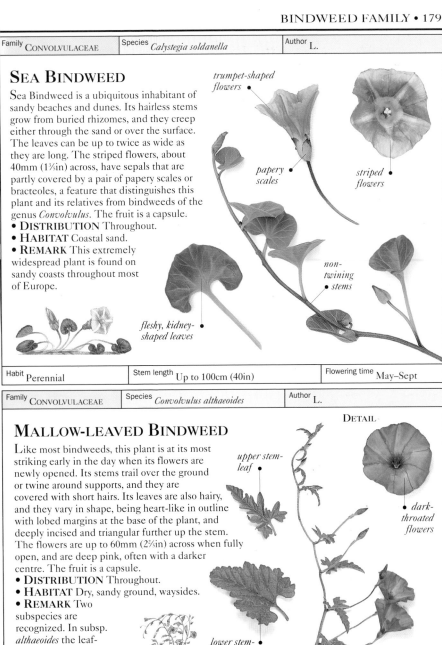

Family CONVOLVULACEAE	Species *Calystegia soldanella*	Author L.

SEA BINDWEED

Sea Bindweed is a ubiquitous inhabitant of
sandy beaches and dunes. Its hairless stems
grow from buried rhizomes, and they creep
either through the sand or over the surface.
The leaves can be up to twice as wide as
they are long. The striped flowers, about
40mm (1⅝in) across, have sepals that are
partly covered by a pair of papery scales or
bracteoles, a feature that distinguishes this
plant and its relatives from bindweeds of the
genus *Convolvulus*. The fruit is a capsule.
• **DISTRIBUTION** Throughout.
• **HABITAT** Coastal sand.
• **REMARK** This extremely
widespread plant is found on
sandy coasts throughout most
of Europe.

trumpet-shaped flowers

papery scales

striped flowers

non-twining stems

fleshy, kidney-shaped leaves

Habit Perennial	Stem length Up to 100cm (40in)	Flowering time May–Sept

Family CONVOLVULACEAE	Species *Convolvulus althaeoides*	Author L.

DETAIL

MALLOW-LEAVED BINDWEED

Like most bindweeds, this plant is at its most
striking early in the day when its flowers are
newly opened. Its stems trail over the ground
or twine around supports, and they are
covered with short hairs. Its leaves are also hairy,
and they vary in shape, being heart-like in outline
with lobed margins at the base of the plant, and
deeply incised and triangular further up the stem.
The flowers are up to 60mm (2⅜in) across when fully
open, and are deep pink, often with a darker
centre. The fruit is a capsule.
• **DISTRIBUTION** Throughout.
• **HABITAT** Dry, sandy ground, waysides.
• **REMARK** Two
subspecies are
recognized. In subsp.
althaeoides the leaf-
lobes are relatively
shallow; in subsp.
tenuissimus they can
reach as far as the
midrib.

upper stem-leaf

dark-throated flowers

lower stem-leaf

stem with short hairs

leaves about 40mm (⅗in) long

Habit Perennial	Stem length Up to 100cm (40in)	Flowering time Apr–July

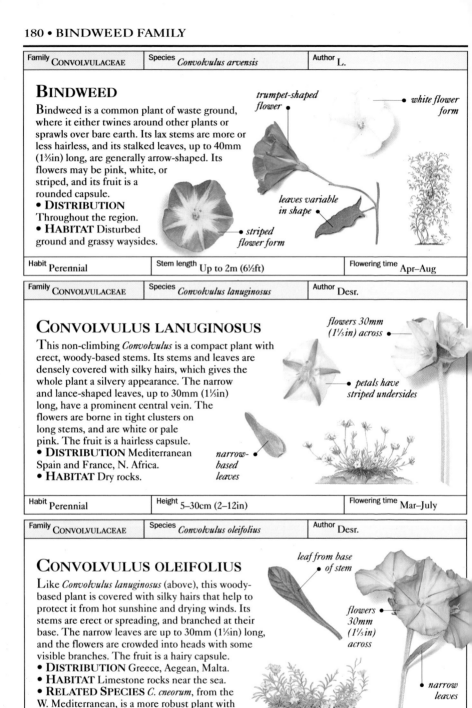

Family CONVOLVULACEAE	Species *Convolvulus arvensis*	Author L.

BINDWEED

Bindweed is a common plant of waste ground, where it either twines around other plants or sprawls over bare earth. Its lax stems are more or less hairless, and its stalked leaves, up to 40mm (1⅗in) long, are generally arrow-shaped. Its flowers may be pink, white, or striped, and its fruit is a rounded capsule.
• **DISTRIBUTION** Throughout the region.
• **HABITAT** Disturbed ground and grassy waysides.

trumpet-shaped flower

white flower form

leaves variable in shape

striped flower form

Habit Perennial	Stem length Up to 2m (6½ft)	Flowering time Apr–Aug

Family CONVOLVULACEAE	Species *Convolvulus lanuginosus*	Author Desr.

CONVOLVULUS LANUGINOSUS

This non-climbing *Convolvulus* is a compact plant with erect, woody-based stems. Its stems and leaves are densely covered with silky hairs, which gives the whole plant a silvery appearance. The narrow and lance-shaped leaves, up to 30mm (1⅕in) long, have a prominent central vein. The flowers are borne in tight clusters on long stems, and are white or pale pink. The fruit is a hairless capsule.
• **DISTRIBUTION** Mediterranean Spain and France, N. Africa.
• **HABITAT** Dry rocks.

flowers 30mm (1⅕in) across

petals have striped undersides

narrow-based leaves

Habit Perennial	Height 5–30cm (2–12in)	Flowering time Mar–July

Family CONVOLVULACEAE	Species *Convolvulus oleifolius*	Author Desr.

CONVOLVULUS OLEIFOLIUS

Like *Convolvulus lanuginosus* (above), this woody-based plant is covered with silky hairs that help to protect it from hot sunshine and drying winds. Its stems are erect or spreading, and branched at their base. The narrow leaves are up to 30mm (1⅕in) long, and the flowers are crowded into heads with some visible branches. The fruit is a hairy capsule.
• **DISTRIBUTION** Greece, Aegean, Malta.
• **HABITAT** Limestone rocks near the sea.
• **RELATED SPECIES** *C. cneorum*, from the W. Mediterranean, is a more robust plant with no visible branches in its flower-heads.

leaf from base of stem

flowers 30mm (1⅕in) across

narrow leaves

Habit Perennial	Height 10–50cm (4–20in)	Flowering time Mar–May

BORAGE FAMILY

Family BORAGINACEAE	Species *Heliotropium europaeum*	Author L.

HELIOTROPE

The Heliotrope is a small and rather variable member of the borage family, with erect or spreading stems which are densely covered with soft hairs, without any coarser spines or bristles. Its elliptical leaves, up to 60mm (2⅜in) long, have conspicuous veins and long stalks. Its flowers grow, in the typical borage-family fashion, with the buds clustered in a coil. As the flowers open, the flowering stem gradually unwinds. Each flower has 5 petals, and is up to 4mm (⅛in) across. The nutlets are borne in clusters of 4.
• **DISTRIBUTION** Throughout the region.
• **HABITAT** Waste ground, fields.

young flowering stem still coiled

flowers with yellow centres

old flowering stem coiled only at tip

soft leaves on long stalks

Habit Annual	Height 5–40cm (2–16in)	Flowering time Apr–Oct

Family BORAGINACEAE	Species *Lithodora fruticosa*	Author (L.) Griseb.

SHRUBBY GROMWELL

This small, densely branched shrub has erect young stems that are covered with short, white hairs. Its older stems have peeling grey bark, and are frequently gnarled and twisted. The leaves, up to 25mm (1in) long, have a covering of flattened hairs, and as they grow older they often develop small raised nodules, or tubercules, particularly near their edges. The flowers, which are about 15mm (⅗in) long, vary in colour from violet to an intense blue, with a long petal tube. The hairy calyx has 5 lobes joined only near the base. The nutlets are up to 4mm (⅛in) long.
• **DISTRIBUTION** Spain, France.
• **HABITAT** Dry ground; usually on limestone.

trumpet-shaped flowers

gnarled, woody older growth

alternate leaves, with downturned margins

Habit Perennial	Height 15–60cm (6–24in)	Flowering time Mar–May

Family BORAGINACEAE	Species *Lithodora hispidula*	Author (Sibth. & Sm.) Griseb.

LITHODORA HISPIDULA

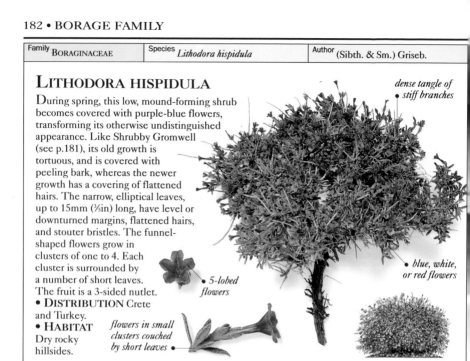

During spring, this low, mound-forming shrub becomes covered with purple-blue flowers, transforming its otherwise undistinguished appearance. Like Shrubby Gromwell (see p.181), its old growth is tortuous, and is covered with peeling bark, whereas the newer growth has a covering of flattened hairs. The narrow, elliptical leaves, up to 15mm (⅗in) long, have level or downturned margins, flattened hairs, and stouter bristles. The funnel-shaped flowers grow in clusters of one to 4. Each cluster is surrounded by a number of short leaves. The fruit is a 3-sided nutlet.

- **DISTRIBUTION** Crete and Turkey.
- **HABITAT** Dry rocky hillsides.

dense tangle of stiff branches

blue, white, or red flowers

5-lobed flowers

flowers in small clusters couched by short leaves

Habit Perennial	Height 10–35cm (4–14in)	Flowering time Mar–May

Family BORAGINACEAE	Species *Onosma taurica*	Author Willd.

GOLDEN DROP

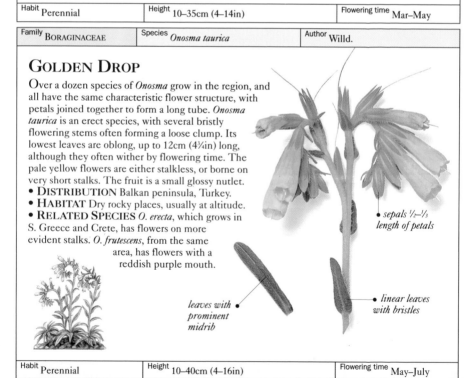

Over a dozen species of *Onosma* grow in the region, and all have the same characteristic flower structure, with petals joined together to form a long tube. *Onosma taurica* is an erect species, with several bristly flowering stems often forming a loose clump. Its lowest leaves are oblong, up to 12cm (4¾in) long, although they often wither by flowering time. The pale yellow flowers are either stalkless, or borne on very short stalks. The fruit is a small glossy nutlet.

- **DISTRIBUTION** Balkan peninsula, Turkey.
- **HABITAT** Dry rocky places, usually at altitude.
- **RELATED SPECIES** *O. erecta*, which grows in S. Greece and Crete, has flowers on more evident stalks. *O. frutescens*, from the same area, has flowers with a reddish purple mouth.

sepals ½–⅓ length of petals

linear leaves with bristles

leaves with prominent midrib

Habit Perennial	Height 10–40cm (4–16in)	Flowering time May–July

Family BORAGINACEAE	Species *Cerinthe major*	Author L.

HONEYWORT

Honeywort is an erect plant with fleshy, almost hairless stems that have a blue-green hue. Its leaves are often dappled with white; the lower are stalked and spoon-shaped, and the upper stalkless and clasping the stem. The tubular flowers are flanked by leafy bracts. The fruit is a shiny black nutlet.
• **DISTRIBUTION** Throughout the region.
• **HABITAT** Waysides, damp ground.

leafy bracts flanking flowers

upper leaves clasp stem

dappled leaves

calyx or entire flower may have purple tinge

Habit Annual	Height 15–60cm (6–24in)	Flowering time Mar–June

Family BORAGINACEAE	Species *Alkanna sartoriana*	Author Boiss. & Heldr.

ALKANNA SARTORIANA

Alkanet members of the genus *Alkanna* are usually low-growing plants with blue or yellow flowers in leafy clusters. This species, which is found only in Greece, has bristly-haired stems and hairy, roughly oblong leaves, up to 12mm (½in) long. The pale yellow flowers, which are about 10mm (⅖in) in diameter, produce small warty nutlets.
• **DISTRIBUTION** S. Greece.
• **HABITAT** Dry, rocky ground.

pale yellow flowers

leafy bracts

bristly-haired stems

Habit Perennial	Height 10–30cm (4–12in)	Flowering time Apr–June

Family BORAGINACEAE	Species *Alkanna tinctoria*	Author (L.) Tausch

DYER'S ALKANET

Named for the dye produced from its roots, this widespread alkanet has prostrate or ascending stems that are covered with downy hairs. Its lower leaves, up to 15cm (6in) long, have stalks and are lance-shaped, whereas its upper leaves are shorter, stalkless, and more linear. The flowers grow in dense, leafy clusters, and the calyx surrounds almost all of the petal-tube. The fruit is a small nutlet with an irregular surface.
• **DISTRIBUTION** Throughout.
• **HABITAT** Sandy or rocky ground, often near to the sea.

flowers about 8mm (⅓in) across

blue flowers

clasping stem-leaves

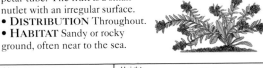

Habit Perennial	Height 10–30cm (4–12in)	Flowering time Feb–June

Family BORAGINACEAE	Species *Echium asperrimum*	Author Lam.

ECHIUM ASPERRIMUM

Buglosses, members of the genus *Echium*, are generally stiff, erect plants covered with bristles or spines. *Echium asperrimum* has elaborately branched stems, with abundant spines. Its lowest leaves are up to 25cm (10in) long and lance-shaped; the stem-leaves are narrower and shorter. The flesh-coloured flowers are up to 18mm (⅝in) long, with projecting stamens, and the fruit is a 3-sided nutlet.
• **DISTRIBUTION** W. Mediterranean, including Italy.
• **HABITAT** Dry ground, waysides.

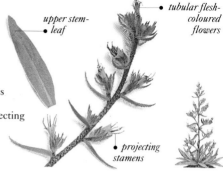

upper stem-leaf

tubular flesh-coloured flowers

projecting stamens

Habit Biennial	Height Up to 100cm (40in)	Flowering time Apr–July

Family BORAGINACEAE	Species *Echium angustifolium*	Author Miller

NARROW-LEAVED BUGLOSS

This variable, red-flowered bugloss is covered with hairs that give the entire plant a grey-green appearance. Its numerous erect stems carry narrow, lance-shaped leaves, up to 60mm (2⅜in) long, and also isolated clusters of red or reddish purple flowers. The flowers are up to 22mm (⅞in) long, with broad throats.
• **DISTRIBUTION** Greece, Crete, Turkey.
• **HABITAT** Waste ground.
• **RELATED SPECIES** *Echium creticum*, which is found in the W. Mediterranean, is another common species with red flowers.

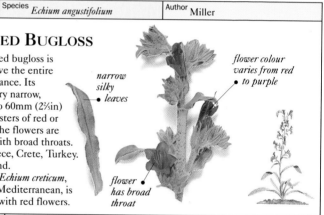

narrow silky leaves

flower colour varies from red to purple

flower has broad throat

Habit Perennial	Height 25–40cm (10–16in)	Flowering time Apr–July

Family BORAGINACEAE	Species *Echium italicum*	Author L.

PALE BUGLOSS

This very widespread bugloss has bristles and softer hairs, and its central flowering stem often has a pyramid of branches, giving it an almost conifer-like outline. The leaves at the base of the stem are lance-shaped, and up to 35cm (14in) long; the stem-leaves are narrower and much shorter. The flowers are up to 12mm (½in) long, with projecting stamens. The flowering stems often persist after the plant dies.
• **DISTRIBUTION** Throughout the region.
• **HABITAT** Roadsides, waste ground, fields.

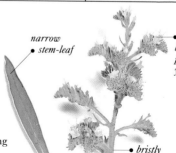

narrow stem-leaf

flowers may be white, pale pink, or pale yellow

bristly stem

Habit Biennial	Height Up to 100cm (40in)	Flowering time Apr–Aug

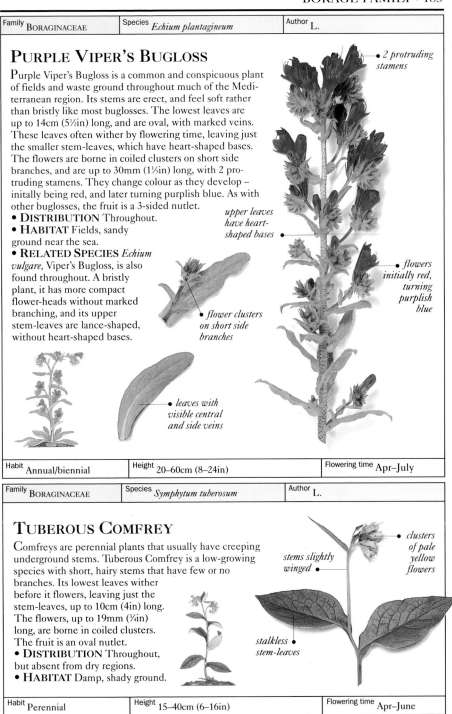

Family BORAGINACEAE	Species *Echium plantagineum*	Author L.

PURPLE VIPER'S BUGLOSS

Purple Viper's Bugloss is a common and conspicuous plant of fields and waste ground throughout much of the Mediterranean region. Its stems are erect, and feel soft rather than bristly like most buglosses. The lowest leaves are up to 14cm (5½in) long, and are oval, with marked veins. These leaves often wither by flowering time, leaving just the smaller stem-leaves, which have heart-shaped bases. The flowers are borne in coiled clusters on short side branches, and are up to 30mm (1⅛in) long, with 2 protruding stamens. They change colour as they develop – initally being red, and later turning purplish blue. As with other buglosses, the fruit is a 3-sided nutlet.
• **DISTRIBUTION** Throughout.
• **HABITAT** Fields, sandy ground near the sea.
• **RELATED SPECIES** *Echium vulgare*, Viper's Bugloss, is also found throughout. A bristly plant, it has more compact flower-heads without marked branching, and its upper stem-leaves are lance-shaped, without heart-shaped bases.

2 protruding stamens

upper leaves have heart-shaped bases

flowers initially red, turning purplish blue

flower clusters on short side branches

leaves with visible central and side veins

Habit Annual/biennial	Height 20–60cm (8–24in)	Flowering time Apr–July

Family BORAGINACEAE	Species *Symphytum tuberosum*	Author L.

TUBEROUS COMFREY

Comfreys are perennial plants that usually have creeping underground stems. Tuberous Comfrey is a low-growing species with short, hairy stems that have few or no branches. Its lowest leaves wither before it flowers, leaving just the stem-leaves, up to 10cm (4in) long. The flowers, up to 19mm (¾in) long, are borne in coiled clusters. The fruit is an oval nutlet.
• **DISTRIBUTION** Throughout, but absent from dry regions.
• **HABITAT** Damp, shady ground.

stems slightly winged

clusters of pale yellow flowers

stalkless stem-leaves

Habit Perennial	Height 15–40cm (6–16in)	Flowering time Apr–June

Family BORAGINACEAE	Species *Anchusa azurea*	Author Miller

LARGE BLUE ALKANET

The alkanet members of the genus *Anchusa* are widespread throughout the Mediterranean region. The Large Blue Alkanet is one of the tallest species, and is a handsome, erect plant with robust, bristly stems that branch throughout their length. Its lowest leaves are up to 30cm (12in) long, and are roughly strap-shaped, whereas the stem-leaves are shorter, narrower, and stalkless. The flowers are purplish or electric-blue, about 20mm (⅘in) across, and have bristly calyces with long teeth. The oblong nutlets, up to 10mm (⅜in) long, are usually borne in groups of 4.
- **DISTRIBUTION** Throughout.
- **HABITAT** Fields, waysides, gardens.
- **REMARK** The Large Blue Alkanet is frequently cultivated outside its native range.
- **RELATED SPECIES**
Anchusa officinalis, Alkanet, is equally widespread, extending northwards to Scandinavia. It has erect, unbranched, bristly stems and lax, coiled clusters of blue or violet flowers. *Anchusa arvensis*, Bugloss, is usually a shorter and more spreading plant, with extremely rough leaves. It is widespread in the region, and throughout Europe as a whole. Several other species are confined to restricted areas.

DETAIL

flowers have white "eyes" formed by hair cluster

bristly stems

stalkless stem-leaves with lobes at base

strap-shaped basal leaf

Habit Perennial	Height 20–150cm (8–60in)	Flowering time Mar–Aug

Family BORAGINACEAE	Species *Anchusa undulata*	Author L.

ANCHUSA UNDULATA

Unlike the Large Blue Alkanet (above), this variable, erect species is usually covered with soft hairs. Its leaves, up to 15cm (6in) long, are oval or lance-shaped. The flowers are often borne on paired branches, which extend to form an upright V. The nutlets are up to 4mm (⅙in) long.
- **DISTRIBUTION** Throughout the Mediterranean region.
- **HABITAT** Cultivated ground, waysides, vineyards.

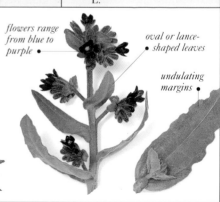

flowers range from blue to purple

oval or lance-shaped leaves

undulating margins

Habit Biennial/perennial	Height 10–50cm (4–20in)	Flowering time Mar–June

Family BORAGINACEAE	Species *Anchusa variegata*	Author (L.) Lehm.

ANCHUSA VARIEGATA

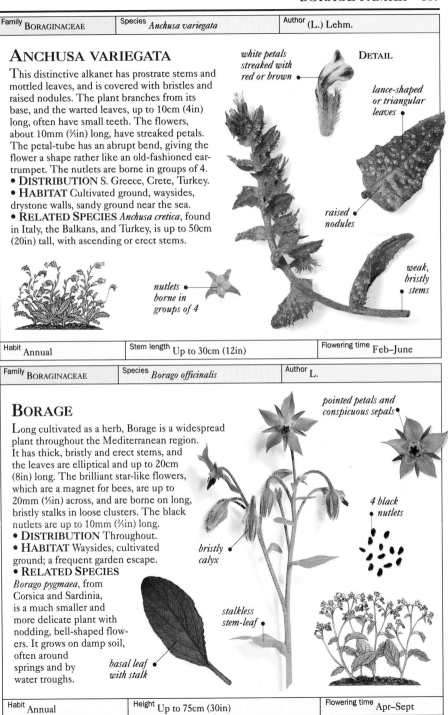

This distinctive alkanet has prostrate stems and mottled leaves, and is covered with bristles and raised nodules. The plant branches from its base, and the warted leaves, up to 10cm (4in) long, often have small teeth. The flowers, about 10mm (⅜in) long, have streaked petals. The petal-tube has an abrupt bend, giving the flower a shape rather like an old-fashioned ear-trumpet. The nutlets are borne in groups of 4.
• **DISTRIBUTION** S. Greece, Crete, Turkey.
• **HABITAT** Cultivated ground, waysides, drystone walls, sandy ground near the sea.
• **RELATED SPECIES** *Anchusa cretica*, found in Italy, the Balkans, and Turkey, is up to 50cm (20in) tall, with ascending or erect stems.

white petals streaked with red or brown •

DETAIL

lance-shaped or triangular leaves

raised • nodules

weak, bristly • stems

nutlets • borne in groups of 4

Habit Annual	Stem length Up to 30cm (12in)	Flowering time Feb–June

Family BORAGINACEAE	Species *Borago officinalis*	Author L.

BORAGE

Long cultivated as a herb, Borage is a widespread plant throughout the Mediterranean region. It has thick, bristly and erect stems, and the leaves are elliptical and up to 20cm (8in) long. The brilliant star-like flowers, which are a magnet for bees, are up to 20mm (⅘in) across, and are borne on long, bristly stalks in loose clusters. The black nutlets are up to 10mm (⅜in) long.
• **DISTRIBUTION** Throughout.
• **HABITAT** Waysides, cultivated ground; a frequent garden escape.
• **RELATED SPECIES** *Borago pygmaea*, from Corsica and Sardinia, is a much smaller and more delicate plant with nodding, bell-shaped flowers. It grows on damp soil, often around springs and by water troughs.

pointed petals and conspicuous sepals •

4 black • nutlets

bristly calyx

stalkless stem-leaf

basal leaf • with stalk

Habit Annual	Height Up to 75cm (30in)	Flowering time Apr–Sept

Family BORAGINACEAE	Species *Cynoglossum columnae*	Author Ten.

CYNOGLOSSUM COLUMNAE

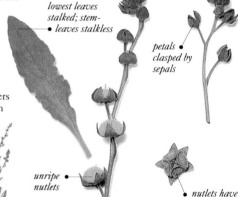

This erect, softly hairy plant is noticeable less for its flowers than for its fruit, which is equipped with small hooks that readily attach to clothing. The leaves are downy and tongue-like (a feature that gives this species and its relatives their common name: hound's-tongues) and they grow up to 15cm (6in) long. The reddish blue flowers are only about 7mm (⅜in) in diameter, with sepals as long as the petals.
The fruit consists of brown nutlets with thickened borders, which are borne in clusters of 4.
• **DISTRIBUTION** C. and E. Mediterranean.
• **HABITAT** Fields, dry ground, stony places.

lowest leaves stalked; stem-leaves stalkless

petals clasped by sepals

unripe nutlets

nutlets have concave hooked surfaces

Habit Annual	Height 25–45cm (10–18in)	Flowering time Mar–July

Family BORAGINACEAE	Species *Cynoglossum creticum*	Author Miller

BLUE HOUND'S-TONGUE

Anyone who walks through the Mediterranean hinterland in summer is likely to become acquainted with this plant – if only as an unwitting carrier of its tenacious seeds. An erect plant with hairy or felty stems, Blue Hound's-tongue has soft leaves up to 20cm (8in) long. It flowers are about 10mm (⅜in) across, and are initially red or pink, becoming blue with age. A distinctive feature of the petals is their net-like veining, in a deeper shade of the background colour. The fruit consists of rounded nutlets, up to 7mm (⅜in) across, borne in clusters of 4, and covered with hooks.
• **DISTRIBUTION** Throughout the region.
• **HABITAT** Open, dry ground, roadsides.
• **RELATED SPECIES** *Cynoglossum cheirifolium*, from the W. Mediterranean, has greyish, densely hairy stems and leaves. It has purple or violet flowers without conspicuous veins.

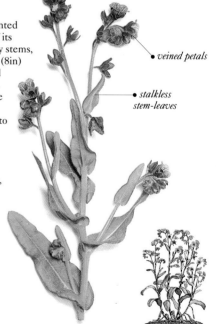

veined petals

stalkless stem-leaves

hooked nutlets hang from dead stems in groups of 4

Habit Biennial	Height 20–60cm (8–24in)	Flowering time Mar–July

VERBENA FAMILY

Family VERBENACEAE	Species *Vitex agnus-castus*	Author L.

CHASTE TREE

Together with Vervain (below), the Chaste Tree is one of the few Mediterranean members of an otherwise mainly tropical family of plants. A deciduous shrub rather than a tree, it has square stems and palmately divided leaves, with narrow, lance-shaped leaflets up to 10cm (4in) long that have densely felted undersides. The flowers are weakly 2-lipped and fragrant, and are borne in whorls forming a long, open spike. The fruit is fleshy, blackish or reddish, and about 2mm (¹⁄₁₂in) long.

- **DISTRIBUTION** Throughout the region.
- **HABITAT** Damp places, roadsides, gardens.
- **REMARK** Chaste Tree is so named for its supposedly anti-aphrodisiac properties, and its seeds were once used by priests and monks. The plant is still used for medicinal drugs.

flowers with protruding stamens

slender leaflets with untoothed margins

berry-like fruit

Habit Perennial	Height 1–6m (3¼–20ft)	Flowering time June–Nov

Family VERBENACEAE	Species *Verbena officinalis*	Author L.

VERVAIN

An erect plant with square, slender stems, Vervain is covered with hairs and has a rough texture. Its leaves are generally lance-shaped, up to 75mm (3in) long, and are deeply cut into lobes, the leaves towards the tops of the stems being less divided than those lower down. The flowers are small – only about 4mm (¹⁄₆in) across – and grow in tall spikes. Each flower has 5 lobes and is cupped by a ribbed, hairy calyx. The fruit divides into 4 one-seeded nutlets, up to 2mm (¹⁄₁₂in) long.

- **DISTRIBUTION** Throughout the region.
- **HABITAT** Waysides, gravelly ground.

flower-spike extends as flowering progresses

DETAIL

flowers with 5 unequal lobes

slender, rigid stems with opposite branches

Habit Perennial	Height 30–60cm (12–24in)	Flowering time May–Sept

MINT FAMILY

Family LABIATAE	Species *Ajuga chamaepitys*	Author (L.) Schreber

GROUND-PINE

Like most members of the mint family, Ground-pine has square stems, leaves in opposite pairs, and flowers with 2 lips. Its stems branch at the base, and are often densely hairy. The plant has a pine-like smell when crushed. The flowers are up to 15mm (⅜in) long. The fruit contains 4 nutlets.
• **DISTRIBUTION** Throughout the region.
• **HABITAT** Fields, vineyards, limestone hills.

3-lobed
• *leaves*

• *yellow flowers*

Habit Annual/perennial	Height 5–30cm (2–12in)	Flowering time Feb–Aug

Family LABIATAE	Species *Ajuga iva*	Author (L.) Schreber

AJUGA IVA

This prostrate or ascending plant has a woody base and a dense covering of hairs. Unlike Ground-pine (above), its leaves are undivided, and are about 15mm (⅜in) long. The flowers, up to 20mm (¼in) long, are borne in clusters of 2 to 4. The flower colour is variable: purple and pink forms are the most common. The plant has a musky smell when crushed.
• **DISTRIBUTION** Throughout.
• **HABITAT** Grassland, stony ground, fields.

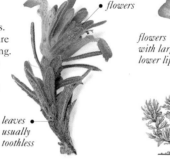

tightly packed • flowers

flowers • with large lower lip

hairy • leaves

leaves • usually toothless

Habit Perennial	Height 5–20cm (2–8in)	Flowering time Apr–Oct

Family LABIATAE	Species *Teucrium divaricatum*	Author Sieber ex Boiss.

TEUCRIUM DIVARICATUM

The members of the genus *Teucrium* – commonly known as germanders – have distinctive flowers, with a 5-lobed lower lip, but no upper lip. This variable, shrubby species has hairy young stems, and oval leaves up to 25mm (1in) long, with shallow lobes or teeth. The pink or purple flowers, about 10mm (⅜in) long, have conspicuous stamens. As with other germanders, the fruit comprises 4 nutlets.
• **DISTRIBUTION** Aegean region.
• **HABITAT** Rocky ground and dry, open places, often near the sea.

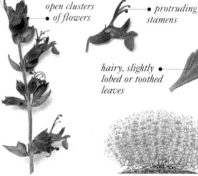

open clusters • of flowers

• protruding stamens

hairy, slightly • lobed or toothed leaves

Habit Perennial	Height 10–30cm (4–12in)	Flowering time Apr–July

Family LABIATAE	Species *Teucrium fruticans*	Author L.

TREE GERMANDER

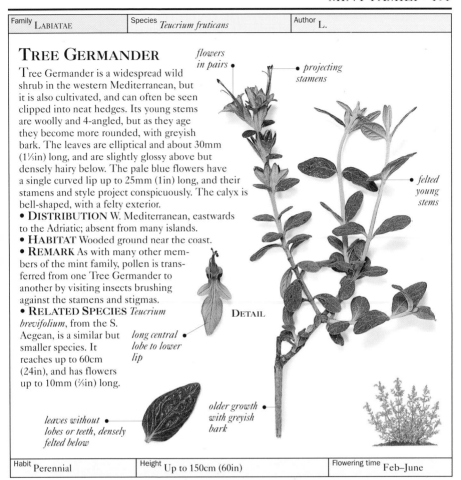

Tree Germander is a widespread wild shrub in the western Mediterranean, but it is also cultivated, and can often be seen clipped into neat hedges. Its young stems are woolly and 4-angled, but as they age they become more rounded, with greyish bark. The leaves are elliptical and about 30mm (1⅛in) long, and are slightly glossy above but densely hairy below. The pale blue flowers have a single curved lip up to 25mm (1in) long, and their stamens and style project conspicuously. The calyx is bell-shaped, with a felted exterior.

- **DISTRIBUTION** W. Mediterranean, eastwards to the Adriatic; absent from many islands.
- **HABITAT** Wooded ground near the coast.
- **REMARK** As with many other members of the mint family, pollen is transferred from one Tree Germander to another by visiting insects brushing against the stamens and stigmas.
- **RELATED SPECIES** *Teucrium brevifolium*, from the S. Aegean, is a similar but smaller species. It reaches up to 60cm (24in), and has flowers up to 10mm (⅖in) long.

flowers in pairs

projecting stamens

felted young stems

DETAIL

long central lobe to lower lip

leaves without lobes or teeth, densely felted below

older growth with greyish bark

Habit Perennial	Height Up to 150cm (60in)	Flowering time Feb–June

Family LABIATAE	Species *Teucrium polium*	Author L.

FELTY GERMANDER

An erect and low-growing plant with a woody base, Felty Germander is densely covered with short, white or golden hairs. Its leaves are up to 25mm (1in) long, and have lobed margins. The flowers are very small, with a single lip, which is about 5mm (⅕in) long. They are either white or red, and grow in domed heads that vary in structure and size.

- **DISTRIBUTION** Throughout.
- **HABITAT** Rocky, sandy ground, often in exposed locations near the coast.

flowers tightly packed in domed head

leaves with lobed margins

Habit Perennial	Height Up to 30cm (12in)	Flowering time May–Aug

Family LABIATAE	Species *Scutellaria columnae*	Author All.

SCUTELLARIA COLUMNAE

Members of the genus *Scutellaria*, known as skullcaps, have generally upright flowers, and a calyx with a characteristic protuberance on its upper surface. *Scutellaria columnae* is an erect species, with stems that are either undivided or branched. Its leaves are up to 80mm (3⅛in) long, oval in outline, with heart-shaped bases. Its flowers are borne in opposite pairs, each flower being flanked by a small bract that looks different from the true leaves. The flowers, up to 22mm (⅞in) long, are purple on the upper lip and pinkish white on the lower.
• **DISTRIBUTION** Corsica, Italy, Balkans.
• **HABITAT** Woodland, shaded ground.
• **RELATED SPECIES**
S. galericulata, Common Skullcap, is a widespread smaller species that has blue flowers. The flowers are borne in widely separated pairs, and the bracts and leaves are very similar.

small green bracts without lobes or teeth

2-lipped calyx

DETAIL

flower of Common Skullcap, S. galericulata

large leaves with lobed margins

Habit Perennial	Height 30–100cm (12–40in)	Flowering time May–July

Family LABIATAE	Species *Prasium majus*	Author L.

PRASIUM MAJUS

Prasium majus is a small, densely branched shrub that is distinguished by its glossy, dark green leaves. Its stems are hairless, and develop a greyish green bark as they age. The paired leaves are usually hairless also, and are up to 50mm (2in) long near the base of the stems, with toothed margins, heart-shaped bases, and a generally nettle-like shape. The flowers grow at the tips of the stems and have a bell-shaped calyx with 2 lips, the upper lip having 3 teeth and the lower having 2. The petals are white or faintly pinkish, with a slightly hooded upper lip, and a lower lip divided into 3 lobes. The flowers produce nutlets that become black when ripe.
• **DISTRIBUTION** Throughout, except France and some islands.
• **HABITAT** Rocky ground, dry-stone walls, hedges; generally near to the sea.

flowers at stem tips

glossy leaves with short stalks

hairless stems

Habit Perennial	Height Up to 100cm (40in)	Flowering time Feb–June

Family LABIATAE	Species *Phlomis fruticosa*	Author L.

JERUSALEM SAGE

Despite its common name, this eye-catching shrub is not a true sage (*Salvia*), but a member of the genus *Phlomis*. Plants in this genus have large, strongly arched flowers and sepals of equal length. Jerusalem Sage is densely branched, and its erect young stems are thickly covered with a crumbly white felt. Its paired leaves, up to 90mm (3⅝in) long, are elliptical or lance-shaped, with abruptly narrowing bases and raised veins on their felted undersides. The striking yellow flowers are borne in clusters of 20 to 30, and form widely separated whorls that are cupped by small, pointed bracts. Each flower is up to 35mm (1⅜in) long, with a domed upper lip and a spreading lower lip. The honeycomb-like dead flower-heads persist until the following year. The fruit contains four 3-sided nutlets.
• **DISTRIBUTION** E. Mediterreanean, as far west as Sardinia.
• **HABITAT** Dry, rocky hillsides in full sun.
• **REMARK** Frequently cultivated in the west, and outside the Mediterranean.

densely packed • flowers

• persistent dead flower-heads

upper lip of flower • hairy

• leaves with white felted undersides

• leaf-margin either untoothed or with rounded teeth

Habit Perennial	Height Up to 125cm (50in)	Flowering time Apr–June

Family LABIATAE	Species *Phlomis lanata*	Author Willd.

PHLOMIS LANATA

Phlomis lanata is similar to Jerusalem Sage (above), but is a smaller shrub with rounded leaves. Nearly all parts of the plant, except its older woody stems, are covered with long, felty hairs. The paired leaves are up to 25mm (1in) long, and the flowers grow in whorls of between 2 and 10 blooms. Each flower is up to 20mm (⅘in) long.
• **DISTRIBUTION** Crete.
• **HABITAT** Stony, open ground at low and moderate altitude.

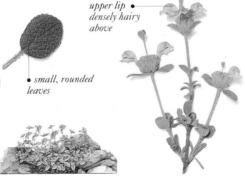

upper lip • densely hairy above

• small, rounded leaves

Habit Perennial	Height Up to 55cm (22in)	Flowering time Mar–May

Family LABIATAE	Species *Phlomis herba-venti*	Author L.

PHLOMIS HERBA-VENTI

Unlike most of its Mediterranean relatives, *Phlomis herba-venti* is a clump-forming herbaceous plant rather than a shrub. Its stems are stiff and erect, and bear pairs of leathery, oval or pointed leaves that may be up to 15cm (6in) long. The leaf-margins usually have rounded teeth. The purple or pink flowers grow in whorls of 2 to 14, and are up to 20mm (⅘in) long, each with a calyx that has narrow, spreading teeth. The fruit contains 4 nuts.
• **DISTRIBUTION** Throughout.
• **HABITAT** Dry, grassy ground.
• **RELATED SPECIES** *P. purpurea*, found in Spain, is a shrub up to 2m (6½ft) high that also has purple flowers. Its leaves have densely woolly undersides.

flowers cupped by a ruff of narrow bracts

leathery, oval or pointed leaves

terminal leaves

rigid stems

leaves usually hairless on upper surfaces

Habit Perennial	Height Up to 70cm (28in)	Flowering time May–July

Family LABIATAE	Species *Phlomis lychnitis*	Author L.

PHLOMIS LYCHNITIS

This small, shrubby plant has erect but rather lax short-haired stems, and narrow, paired leaves up to 10cm (4in) long, but less than 20mm (⅘in) broad. Its flowers are about 25mm (1in) long, and grow in whorls of 4 to 10. Each whorl is clasped by a pair of broad-based bracts that narrow abruptly. The undersides of the bracts are covered with silky hairs. The fruit comprises 4 nutlets.
• **DISTRIBUTION** Spain and France.
• **HABITAT** Garigue, dry, rocky or grassy places.
• **RELATED SPECIES** *Phlomis crinita*, found on mountains in Spain, is taller with broader leaves.

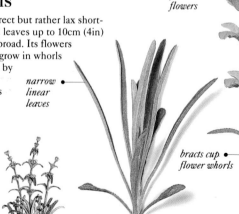

yellow flowers

narrow linear leaves

bracts cup flower whorls

Habit Perennial	Height 25–65cm (10–26in)	Flowering time May–July

Family LABIATAE	Species *Lamium amplexicaule*	Author L.

HENBIT DEADNETTLE

Henbit Deadnettle is a widespread weed of cultivated ground, with erect stems that branch from the base, and sparse or dense hairs. Its lower leaves, up to 25mm (1in) long, are rounded and stalked, with rounded teeth. Its upper leaves have similar margins, but are stalkless and amplexicaul – forming a characteristic collar around the stem. The pinkish purple flowers have a long petal-tube with a slightly pouched lower lip. The fruit has four 3-sided nutlets.

DETAIL

long petal tube

some flowers very short

stalkless stem-leaves meet or overlap

• **DISTRIBUTION**
Throughout the region.
• **HABITAT** Fields,
gardens, waysides.
• **RELATED SPECIES**
Lamium maculatum, Spotted
Deadnettle, is taller, with
pinkish or white flowers.

rounded teeth

Habit Annual	Height Up to 30cm (12in)	Flowering time Jan–July

Family LABIATAE	Species *Ballota acetabulosa*	Author (L.) Bentham

FALSE DITTANY

A highly unusual member of the mint family, False Dittany has erect, woody-based stems, and is completely covered by a dense layer of woolly hairs. Its paired heart-shaped leaves are up to 50mm (2in) long, and have short stalks and round-toothed margins. The flowers are borne in whorls of 6 to 12, and there may be up to 12 whorls on a flowering stem – each one separated from its neighbour by a short gap. The most striking feature of each whorl is its rank of tightly packed calyces, which spread out rather like small cups. Initially, the calyces are small and compact, but as each flower opens, withers, and eventually sets seed, its calyx increases in diameter, until it is up to 20mm (⅘in) across. The relatively inconspicuous petals are white with purple-streaked lips, and are up to 18mm (⅝in) long The fruit contains four 3-sided nutlets.
• **DISTRIBUTION** Greece and the Aegean.
• **HABITAT** Rocky places in full sun.
• **REMARK** False Dittany gets its specific name from the Latin word *acetabulum*, meaning a vinegar cup – a reference to its cup-shaped calyces. It was once used as a source of wicks for oil lamps.

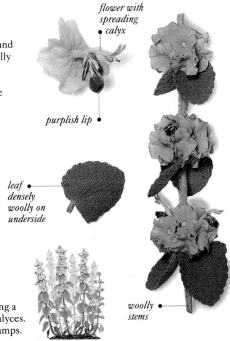

flower with spreading calyx

purplish lip

leaf densely woolly on underside

woolly stems

Habit Perennial	Height Up to 60cm (24in)	Flowering time Apr–June

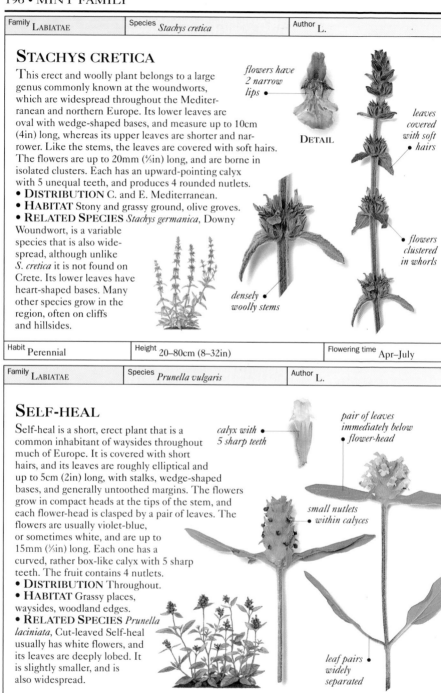

Family LABIATAE	Species *Stachys cretica*	Author L.

STACHYS CRETICA

This erect and woolly plant belongs to a large
genus commonly known at the woundworts,
which are widespread throughout the Mediterranean and northern Europe. Its lower leaves are
oval with wedge-shaped bases, and measure up to 10cm
(4in) long, whereas its upper leaves are shorter and narrower. Like the stems, the leaves are covered with soft hairs.
The flowers are up to 20mm (⅘in) long, and are borne in
isolated clusters. Each has an upward-pointing calyx
with 5 unequal teeth, and produces 4 rounded nutlets.
• **DISTRIBUTION** C. and E. Mediterranean.
• **HABITAT** Stony and grassy ground, olive groves.
• **RELATED SPECIES** *Stachys germanica*, Downy
Woundwort, is a variable
species that is also widespread, although unlike
S. cretica it is not found on
Crete. Its lower leaves have
heart-shaped bases. Many
other species grow in the
region, often on cliffs
and hillsides.

flowers have
2 narrow
lips •

DETAIL

leaves
covered
with soft
• hairs

• flowers
clustered
in whorls

densely •
woolly stems

Habit Perennial	Height 20–80cm (8–32in)	Flowering time Apr–July

Family LABIATAE	Species *Prunella vulgaris*	Author L.

SELF-HEAL

Self-heal is a short, erect plant that is a
common inhabitant of waysides throughout
much of Europe. It is covered with short
hairs, and its leaves are roughly elliptical and
up to 5cm (2in) long, with stalks, wedge-shaped
bases, and generally untoothed margins. The flowers
grow in compact heads at the tips of the stem, and
each flower-head is clasped by a pair of leaves. The
flowers are usually violet-blue,
or sometimes white, and are up to
15mm (⅗in) long. Each one has a
curved, rather box-like calyx with 5 sharp
teeth. The fruit contains 4 nutlets.
• **DISTRIBUTION** Throughout.
• **HABITAT** Grassy places,
waysides, woodland edges.
• **RELATED SPECIES** *Prunella
laciniata*, Cut-leaved Self-heal
usually has white flowers, and
its leaves are deeply lobed. It
is slightly smaller, and is
also widespread.

calyx with •
5 sharp teeth

pair of leaves
immediately below
• flower-head

small nutlets
• within calyces

leaf pairs •
widely
separated

Habit Perennial	Height 10–50cm (4–20in)	Flowering time May–Aug

Family LABIATAE	Species *Satureja montana*	Author L.

WINTER SAVORY

A small, aromatic shrub, Winter Savory has hairy
or hairless stems and narrow, lance-shaped
leaves, up to 30mm (1⅛in) long, with sharp
points. The flowers can be white, pink, or
purple, and are up to 12mm (½in) long. They
are borne in close clusters, and each has a bell-
shaped calyx with pointed teeth. The fruit
has 4 nutlets enclosed by the calyx.
• **DISTRIBUTION** Throughout,
except on most islands.
• **HABITAT** Rocky or
grassy ground.

narrow leaves

bell-shaped calyx

white flower form

Habit Perennial	Height 10–40cm (4–16in)	Flowering time June–Sept

Family LABIATAE	Species *Clinopodium vulgare*	Author L.

WILD BASIL

Wild Basil is an erect plant with hairy stems
and widely separated clusters of purple-pink
flowers. Its leaves, which are up to 65mm
(2⅗in) long, are oval with small teeth and
short stalks. The flowers, which are up
to 22mm (⅞in) long, have curved,
hairy calyces with long teeth.
• **DISTRIBUTION** Throughout.
• **HABITAT** Grassy places, waysides,
usually on limestone.
• **REMARK** The basil used in Mediterranean cooking is *Ocimum basilicum*.

densely packed flower-clusters

lower calyx-teeth longer than upper

leaves with toothed margins

Habit Perennial	Height 30–80cm (12–32in)	Flowering time May–Sept

Family LABIATAE	Species *Origanum onites*	Author L.

POT MARJORAM

Widely used as a culinary herb, Pot Marjoram is
a low-growing, highly aromatic shrub with hairy
stems. Its mid-green leaves, which are are up
to 22mm (⅞in) long, are oval or heart-shaped,
sometimes with toothed margins. Its flowers are
white or pink and grow up to 5mm (⅛in) long.
They are borne in flat-topped clusters, which
are flanked by numerous bracts. The
flowers produce oblong nutlets.
• **DISTRIBUTION** Sicily, Balkan
region, Aegean islands.
• **HABITAT** Scrub, dry, rocky places.

flowers in flattened clusters

downy leaves

Habit Perrenial	Height Up to 60cm (24in)	Flowering time May–Sept

Family LABIATAE	Species *Thymus capitatus*	Author (L.) Hoffmanns. & Link

THYMUS CAPITATUS

More than 30 species of thyme grow in
the Mediterranean region, and of these only
Thymus capitatus can be readily identified from
a distance. This low-growing aromatic shrub has
stiff, erect or spreading branches that are covered
with white felty hairs when young. Its leaves are
narrow and are of 2 markedly different sizes.
The longer leaves, which reach about 10mm
(⅜in), have clusters of much shorter leaves in
their axils, and these shorter leaves are often
the only ones still present on the plant
during the height of summer. The club-
shaped flower-heads are a characteristic
feature of the plant, and they bear
bright purple-pink flowers up to
10mm (⅜in) long. The calyces are
flattened and have 2 lips, and the
fruit contains 4 nutlets.
• **DISTRIBUTION** Throughout,
except in France.
• **HABITAT** Rocky, exposed
ground; usually on limestone.

purple-pink flowers

club-shaped flower-heads

leaves without downturned margins

long leaves often shed in summer

Habit Perennial	Height 20–50cm (8–20in)	Flowering time May–Sept

Family LABIATAE	Species *Thymus vulgaris*	Author L.

COMMON THYME

A widely used culinary herb, this highly aromatic
dwarf shrub has stiff stems that are densely
covered with white hairs towards their tips.
The narrow leaves, up to 8mm (⅓in) long,
have downturned margins and felty
undersides. The flowers vary from
pale purple to almost white. As
in other thymes, they are 2-lipped
with a straight petal-tube, and have
projecting stamens. The calyx is
bell-shaped, with short and
broad upper teeth. The
fruit comprises 4 tiny
nutlets enclosed in
the calyx-tube.
• **DISTRIBUTION**
W. Mediterranean,
eastwards to Italy.
• **HABITAT**
Rocky ground
on limestone
in full sun.

small open flower-heads

pale flowers

flowers with long lower lip

DETAIL

all leaves of roughly equal size

Habit Perennial	Height 10–30cm (4–12in)	Flowering time Apr–July

Family LABIATAE	Species *Rosmarinus officinalis*	Author L.

ROSEMARY

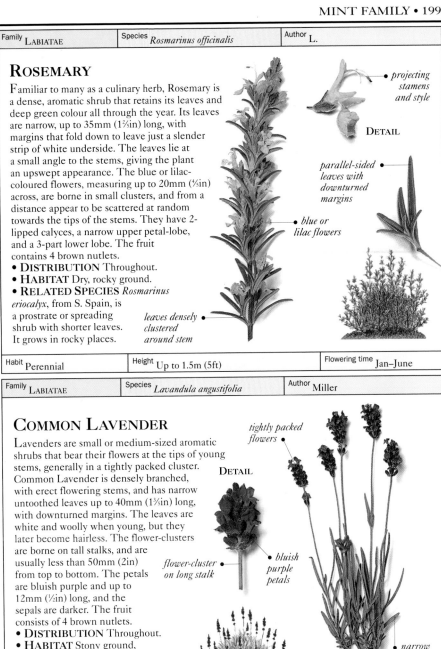

Familiar to many as a culinary herb, Rosemary is a dense, aromatic shrub that retains its leaves and deep green colour all through the year. Its leaves are narrow, up to 35mm (1⅜in) long, with margins that fold down to leave just a slender strip of white underside. The leaves lie at a small angle to the stems, giving the plant an upswept appearance. The blue or lilac-coloured flowers, measuring up to 20mm (⅘in) across, are borne in small clusters, and from a distance appear to be scattered at random towards the tips of the stems. They have 2-lipped calyces, a narrow upper petal-lobe, and a 3-part lower lobe. The fruit contains 4 brown nutlets.
• **DISTRIBUTION** Throughout.
• **HABITAT** Dry, rocky ground.
• **RELATED SPECIES** *Rosmarinus eriocalyx*, from S. Spain, is a prostrate or spreading shrub with shorter leaves. It grows in rocky places.

projecting stamens and style

DETAIL

parallel-sided leaves with downturned margins

blue or lilac flowers

leaves densely clustered around stem

Habit Perennial	Height Up to 1.5m (5ft)	Flowering time Jan–June

Family LABIATAE	Species *Lavandula angustifolia*	Author Miller

COMMON LAVENDER

Lavenders are small or medium-sized aromatic shrubs that bear their flowers at the tips of young stems, generally in a tightly packed cluster. Common Lavender is densely branched, with erect flowering stems, and has narrow untoothed leaves up to 40mm (1⅜in) long, with downturned margins. The leaves are white and woolly when young, but they later become hairless. The flower-clusters are borne on tall stalks, and are usually less than 50mm (2in) from top to bottom. The petals are bluish purple and up to 12mm (½in) long, and the sepals are darker. The fruit consists of 4 brown nutlets.
• **DISTRIBUTION** Throughout.
• **HABITAT** Stony ground, garigue; usually on limestone.
• **REMARK** Common Lavender is the main source of lavender oil, which is used in perfumes.

tightly packed flowers

DETAIL

flower-cluster on long stalk

bluish purple petals

narrow evergreen leaves

Habit Perennial	Height Up to 100cm (40in)	Flowering time June–Aug

Family LABIATAE	Species *Lavandula dentata*	Author L.

TOOTHED LAVENDER

Toothed Lavender is an evergreen aromatic shrub with short-haired stems. It is immediately recognizable by its leaves, which, although narrow, have a neat rank of small teeth or deeper lobes on either margin. Its pale purple flowers are only about 8mm (⅓in) long, and grow in dense heads. As with other lavenders, each flower is clasped by a pointed scale-like bract. Towards the top of the flower-head, the bracts are brightly coloured and up to 15mm (⅗in) long, forming a conspicuous crown.
• **DISTRIBUTION** N.W. Africa, S. and E. Spain, Balearic Islands. Often cultivated outside its native range.
• **HABITAT** Stony ground; usually on limestone.
• **RELATED SPECIES** *Lavandula multifida*, Cut-leaved Lavender, from Spain and S. Italy, has twice-divided leaves, and larger, violet flowers. It lacks a crown of colourful bracts and is only mildly aromatic.

• flower-heads up to 50mm (2in) long on tall stalks

bright purple upper bracts •

pale • flowers

DETAIL

toothed leaves • up to 35mm (1⅖in) long

Habit Perennial	Height 30–100cm (12–40in)	Flowering time Mar–July

Family LABIATAE	Species *Lavandula stoechas*	Author L.

FRENCH LAVENDER

This is undoubtedly the most showy of Mediterranean lavenders, with tall plumes of coloured bracts that are particularly striking when seen against low sunshine early or late in the day. A very aromatic and variable evergreen shrub, it has slightly hairy stems, and narrow leaves up to 40mm (1⅗in) long, with down-turned edges. The flowers grow in dense heads, and the petals are a blackish purple, blending in with the short lower bracts that clasp the flowers. The upper bracts are up to 50mm (2in) long, and are much more conspicuous.
• **DISTRIBUTION** Throughout the Mediterranean. Often cultivated outside its native range.
• **HABITAT** Stony places and pine woods; usually on acid ground.
• **REMARK** There are several subspecies. The widespread subsp. *stoechas* has short flower-stalks. Subsp. *pedunculata*, found in Spain, has flower-stalks that are at least twice as long as the flower-heads.
• **RELATED SPECIES** *Lavandula viridis*, from S. Spain, is similar but has white flowers and green bracts.

bright purple upper bracts •

• small trumpet-like flowers

DETAIL

• flower-heads up to 50mm (2in) long

slightly • hairy stems

SUBSP. STOECHAS

• narrow leaves

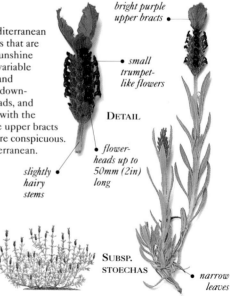

Habit Perennial	Height Up to 100cm (40in)	Flowering time Mar–June

Family LABIATAE	Species *Salvia officinalis*	Author L.

SAGE

The sages, members of the genus *Salvia*, are shrubs or herbaceous plants that usually have flowers in open spikes or racemes. This species – the source of culinary sage – is a low aromatic shrub with erect flowering stems covered with short hairs. Its leaves, up to 50mm (2in) long, have downy undersides. The flowers, up to 35mm (1⅜in) long, are borne in isolated clusters, and as with all sages they have a 2-lipped calyx, with 3 teeth above and 2 below. The petals form a narrow upper hood and a longer, 3-lobed lower lip. The fruit contains brown, oval nutlets.
• **DISTRIBUTION** Spain and S. France, W. Balkans.
• **HABITAT** Stony or grassy ground, dry, open places.

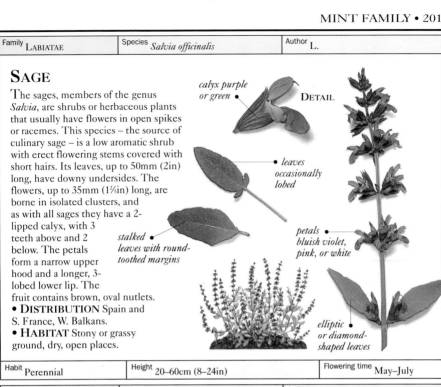

calyx purple or green •

DETAIL

• *leaves occasionally lobed*

stalked leaves with round-toothed margins

petals • *bluish violet, pink, or white*

elliptic • *or diamond-shaped leaves*

Habit Perennial	Height 20–60cm (8–24in)	Flowering time May–July

Family LABIATAE	Species *Salvia sclarea*	Author L.

CLARY

Clary is a robust aromatic biennial that, when flowering, often has a distinctly top-heavy appearance. Its stems are erect and densely branched from about the midway point, and near their bases they carry stalked leaves, up to 80mm (3⅛in) long, that have toothed margins and woolly undersides. Each flower, about 30mm (1⅛in) long, has a narrow, arching upper petal-lobe. Long and often colourful bracts, attached immediately beneath the flower clusters, give the entire inflorescence a dense and rather spiky look. The fruit is 4-seeded.
• **DISTRIBUTION** Throughout the region.
• **HABITAT** Fallow ground, waysides.

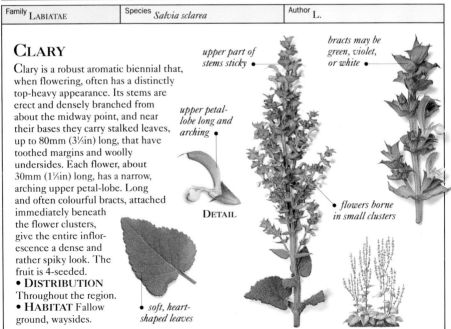

upper part of stems sticky •

bracts may be green, violet, or white •

upper petal-lobe long and arching •

DETAIL

• *flowers borne in small clusters*

• *soft, heart-shaped leaves*

Habit Biennial	Height Up to 100cm (40in)	Flowering time May–Aug

Family LABIATAE	Species *Salvia pomifera*	Author L.

SALVIA POMIFERA

This shrubby sage is at its most conspicuous late in flowering, when its sepals expand to form large, club-like heads. Its young stems are erect and slightly hairy, and bear oval stalked leaves, up to 60mm (2⅜in) long, that have round-toothed margins. The violet-blue flowers, which are about 35mm (1⅜in) long, are each cupped by a papery, reddish calyx. During fruiting, the calyx continues to grow and often becomes folded as it presses against its neighbours.

• **DISTRIBUTION** S. Greece and S. Aegean.

• **HABITAT** Stony ground, waysides.

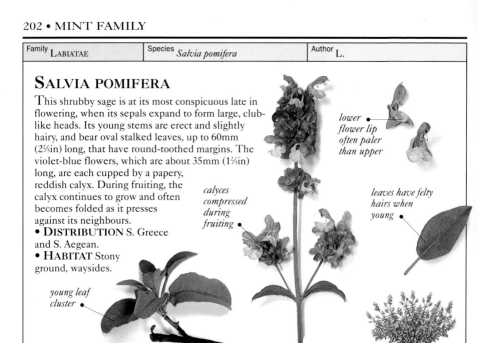

lower flower lip often paler than upper

leaves have felty hairs when young

calyces compressed during fruiting

young leaf cluster

Habit Perennial	Height Up to 120cm (48in)	Flowering time May–July

Family LABIATAE	Species *Salvia triloba*	Author L.

THREE-LOBED SAGE

Three-lobed Sage is a large and robust aromatic shrub from the central part of the Mediterranean region. It has a woody base and erect young stems that are covered with woolly hairs. Towards the top of the plant, the stems are glandular and sticky. The plant's name refers to the shape of its leaves, which are usually – but not invariably – divided into 3 lobes, with a large middle lobe, up to 50mm (2in) long, flanked by a pair of much shorter lobes that are attached at its base. The flowers grow in isolated whorls of about 4 to 6, and are up to 20mm (⅘in) long, with sticky glandular calyces. Unlike *Salvia pomifera* (above), the calyx does not continue to grow during fruiting.

• **DISTRIBUTION** From Sicily eastwards to Crete.

• **HABITAT** Rocky places.

• **REMARK** A highly variable species, particularly in leaf-form.

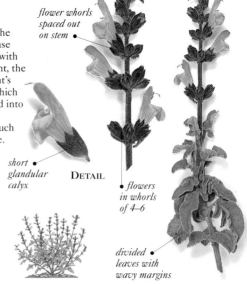

flower whorls spaced out on stem

short glandular calyx

DETAIL

flowers in whorls of 4–6

divided leaves with wavy margins

Habit Perennial	Height Up to 150cm (5ft)	Flowering time Mar–June

POTATO FAMILY

Family SOLANACEAE	Species *Hyoscyamus albus*	Author L.

WHITE HENBANE

The potato family contains many species that have become valuable food plants, along with many more that are extremely poisonous. White Henbane falls into this second category, and is a sticky-haired and often clump-forming plant with erect and sometimes woody-based stems. Its stalked leaves, up to 10cm (4in) long and sometimes almost as wide, have a fresh, light green colour, with jagged teeth. The creamy yellow flowers grow in one-sided clusters, and are up to 30mm (1⅛in) long, with stamens that often protrude. The fruit is a conspicuous capsule, which is cupped by a distinctive elongated calyx.
• **DISTRIBUTION** Throughout the region.
• **HABITAT** Waste ground, rubbish dumps.

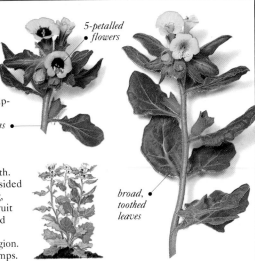

5-petalled flowers

sticky stems

broad, toothed leaves

Habit Annual/perennial	Height 30–90cm (12–36in)	Flowering time Feb–Sept

Family SOLANACEAE	Species *Hyoscyamus aureus*	Author L.

GOLDEN HENBANE

In parts of the eastern Mediterranean, Golden Henbane grows freely on old walls, so its interesting flowers can often be inspected at eye-level. A spreading or hanging plant, it has weak stems and stalked, roughly oval leaves, which are toothed and lobed. Both the stems and leaves are covered with sticky hairs. The almost stalkless flowers, about 25mm (1in) across, have 5 bright yellow, unequal petals that form a hood over the protruding anthers. The fruit capsules form in a double rank along the flowering stems, each one within a cylindrical toothed calyx up to 30mm (1⅛in) long. The entire plant is highly poisonous.
• **DISTRIBUTION** From Crete eastwards.
• **HABITAT** Rocky waste ground, walls.

protruding anthers

purple throat

elongated calyx

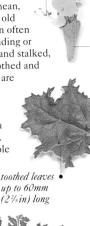

toothed leaves up to 60mm (2⅖in) long

long sticky hairs

Habit Biennial/perennial	Height 30–60cm (12–24in)	Flowering time Mar–June

Family SOLANACEAE	Species *Solanum elaeagnifolium*	Author Cav.

SOLANUM ELAEAGNIFOLIUM

A native of South America, this shrubby plant is one of a number of introduced nightshades that have become established in parts of the Mediterranean region. Erect and only slightly branched, its stems and leaves are densely covered with felt-like hairs, and have small and scattered reddish spines. The leaves are narrow and entire, and are up to 10cm (4in) long, with wavy margins. The purple flowers grow in loose clusters of one to 5, and are about 30mm (1⅛in) across, with 5 pointed petals and dark yellow anthers. The fruit is a small berry that becomes orange-yellow when ripe.
• **DISTRIBUTION** S. Greece, Cyprus.
• **HABITAT** Waste ground.
• **RELATED SPECIES** Other introduced species in the region include *Solanum sodomaeum*, the Sodom Apple, a spiny shrub from southern Africa, which has purple flowers and yellow berries up to 30mm (1⅛in) across. It grows in waste places, frequently close to the sea.

small spines, • particularly at tips of stems

• narrow undivided leaves

berries about • 10mm (⅖in) in diameter

Habit Perennial	Height 30–50cm (12–20in)	Flowering time May–July

Family SOLANACEAE	Species *Mandragora autumnalis*	Author Bertol.

MANDRAKE

The subject of much myth and folklore, Mandrake has a deep and tenacious tap-root that anchors a flat rosette of leathery leaves. The whole plant grows up to 50cm (20in) across, and its flowers are clustered at the centre, growing on separate stalks. Its yellow or orange berries are concealed within enlarged tubular calyces.
• **DISTRIBUTION** S. Mediterranean; absent from France.
• **HABITAT** Cultivated ground, olive groves, waysides, waste ground.
• **RELATED SPECIES** *Mandragora officinarum*, found in N. Italy and Dalmatia, has smaller flowers, and calyces that do not cover its fruit.

flowers up • to 40mm (1⅗in)

• narrow petals

flowers • in clusters

tough • leathery leaves

• leaves have thick midrib

Habit Perennial	Height Up to 20cm (8in)	Flowering time Sep–May

Family SOLANACEAE	Species *Datura stramonium*	Author L.

THORN APPLE

Thorn Apple is a fast-growing, robust, and erect annual with strongly forking, usually hairless, stems. Its leaves, up to 18cm (7in) long, are oval or elliptical in outline, with jagged teeth. The flowers are trumpet-shaped and usually white, and have a long petal-tube, the lower half of which is sheathed by the angled calyx. After flowering, most of the calyx is shed, and this is followed by the development of the "apple" – a spiky, upright capsule. The ripe capsule, up to 60mm (2⅖in) long, splits open to release a large number of rounded black seeds.
• **DISTRIBUTION** Throughout.
• **HABITAT** Waste ground, field edges, roadsides.
• **REMARK** Thorn Apple often appears in quantity in one year, and then vanishes the next. All parts of the plant are highly poisonous.

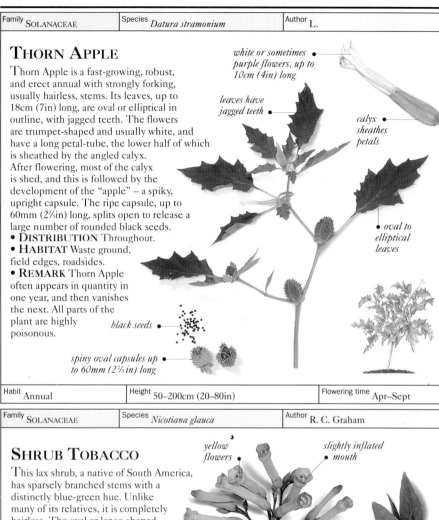

white or sometimes purple flowers, up to 10cm (4in) long

leaves have jagged teeth

calyx sheathes petals

oval to elliptical leaves

black seeds

spiny oval capsules up to 60mm (2⅖in) long

Habit Annual	Height 50–200cm (20–80in)		Flowering time Apr–Sept

Family SOLANACEAE	Species *Nicotiana glauca*	Author R. C. Graham

SHRUB TOBACCO

This lax shrub, a native of South America, has sparsely branched stems with a distinctly blue-green hue. Unlike many of its relatives, it is completely hairless. The oval or lance-shaped leaves, up to 25cm (10in) long, have long stalks, and the yellow, cigarette-shaped flowers grow in loose clusters at the tips of the stems. Each flower, up to 45mm (1⅘in) long, has a slightly inflated mouth, with 5 petal points. The fruit is an oval capsule.
• **DISTRIBUTION** Throughout.
• **HABITAT** Waste ground.
• **RELATED SPECIES** Cigarette tobacco is made from *Nicotiana tabacum*, which has abundant sticky hairs, and is widely cultivated throughout the region.

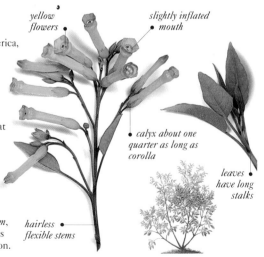

yellow flowers

slightly inflated mouth

calyx about one quarter as long as corolla

leaves have long stalks

hairless flexible stems

Habit Perennial	Height 2–6m (6½–20ft)		Flowering time Mar–Oct

FIGWORT FAMILY

Family SCROPHULARIACEAE	Species *Verbascum sinuatum*	Author L.

VERBASCUM SINUATUM

The Mediterranean region is the home of several dozen
species of *Verbascum*, or mulleins. Many are found only in
the east, but *Verbascum sinuatum* is among the species that
are more widespread. Like many mulleins, it is a stately,
densely hairy plant with tall flowering stems, and has a
rosette of oblong basal leaves, each up to 35cm (14in)
long, with smaller leaves attached to the stem. The
basal leaves are generally stemless, and they have lobed
and wavy margins. The flowering stem has many
ascending branches, and each one carries several small
and isolated clusters of bright yellow flowers, up to
20mm (⅘in) across. As with other mulleins, the flowers
have 5 slightly unequal petals, and 5 stamens with
hairy filaments. In this species, the filament hairs
are violet. The fruit is a capsule that splits to
release large numbers of seeds.
• **DISTRIBUTION** Throughout.
• **HABITAT** Fields, waysides,
grassy places, waste ground.

*flowering stem with
numerous branches*

*stamens with
violet hairs on
filaments*

*basal leaf with
lobes and wavy
margins*

*flowers in clusters
of 2–5, each cluster
clasped by short bract*

*ascending
branches*

Habit Biennial	Height 50–150cm (20–60in)	Flowering time Apr–Aug

Family SCROPHULARIACEAE	Species *Verbascum thapsus*	Author L.

GREAT MULLEIN

This impressive and variable plant is one of a number of mulleins that have densely packed flowers on tall, unbranched stems. The entire plant is covered with greyish or white wool, and its elliptical basal leaves, up to 50cm (20in) long, may or may not have toothed margins. The basal leaves have winged stalks, and the upper leaves have narrow wings that run some distance down the stem. The flowers, up to 35mm (1⅜in) across, have white filament hairs. Each produces an elliptical capsule.
• **DISTRIBUTION** Throughout, but rare in parts of the east.
• **HABITAT** Roadsides, disturbed ground.
• **RELATED SPECIES** *Verbascum pulverulentum*, Hoary Mullein, is covered with very thick wool. *V. rotundifolium*, Round-leaved Mullein, has rounded basal leaves and violet filament hairs.

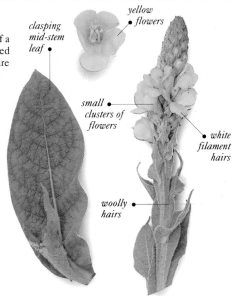

clasping mid-stem leaf

yellow flowers

small clusters of flowers

white filament hairs

woolly hairs

Habit Biennial	Height 30–200cm (12–80in)	Flowering time May–Sept

Family SCROPHULARIACEAE	Species *Verbascum undulatum*	Author Lam.

VERBASCUM UNDULATUM

Like many mulleins, *Verbascum undulatum* is usually a biennial. During its first year, this densely hairy plant forms a large rosette of leaves, each up to 18cm (7in) long. The leaves have deep undulations, and this often gives them a lobed or corrugated appearance. During the second year, the plant produces one or, more usually, several flowering stems, and these bear smaller stem-leaves, sometimes without undulations, and many isolated clusters of flowers. The flowers, up to 50mm (2in) across, have white filament hairs. The many-seeded, elliptical capsule is up to 6mm (¼in) long.
• **DISTRIBUTION** W. Balkans and Greece.
• **HABITAT** Waste ground, stony places, sandy ground.

clusters of unstalked flowers

upper stem-leaf

middle stem-leaf

flowers with white filament hairs

basal leaf

dense hairs

Habit Biennial/perennial	Height 30–120cm (12–48in)	Flowering time Mar–Aug

Family SCROPHULARIACEAE	Species *Scrophularia lucida*	Author L.

SCROPHULARIA LUCIDA

The figworts, members of the genus *Scrophularia*, generally have inconspicuous pouch-like flowers. This hairless species usually has a single erect and 4-angled stem, bearing opposite pairs of pinnately lobed leaves, up to 10cm (4in) long. The greenish red flowers grow in small clusters on lateral stalks. Each flower has 2 erect upper petals and is cupped by rounded sepals. The fruit is a many-seeded capsule.
• **DISTRIBUTION** Greece, Aegean, Italy, S.E. France.
• **HABITAT** Rocky ground, field margins.
• **RELATED SPECIES** *S. canina*, French Figwort, has smaller, purplish flowers.

flowers up to 9mm (⅜in) long

narrow bracts

leaves have toothed lobes

slightly winged stem

Habit Biennial	Height 10–100cm (4–40in)	Flowering time Feb–Apr

Family SCROPHULARIACEAE	Species *Scrophularia auriculata*	Author L.

WATER FIGWORT

Also known as Water Betony, this moisture-loving plant grows from a rhizome and usually has several erect and hairless stems. The stems are 4-angled, and have narrow but distinct wings. The leaves, up to 15cm (6in) long, are oval in outline, with scalloped margins and often 2 small lobes at the base. The flowers grow in open panicles, each flower being up to 9mm (⅜in) long, with green-based petals and purplish brown lips. The rounded fruit, up to 6mm (¼in) long, has a pointed beak.
• **DISTRIBUTION** W. and C. Mediterranean, eastwards to Crete; also north to the British Isles.
• **HABITAT** Stream banks and damp, shady places, often at altitude.
• **REMARK** *Scrophularia nodosa*, Common Figwort, is similar and widespread, but has unwinged stems and toothed, unlobed leaves. It grows in similar habitats.

small flowers

rounded sepals

sepals have papery margins

leaves with crenate margins

winged 4-angled stem

leaves often have 2 small lobes

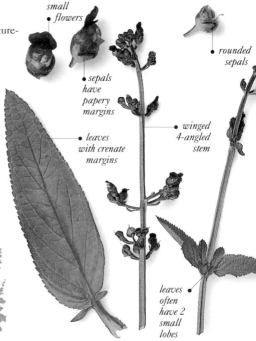

Habit Perennial	Height Up to 100cm (40in)	Flowering time May–Sept

Family SCROPHULARIACEAE	Species *Scrophularia peregrina*	Author L.

NETTLE-LEAVED FIGWORT

Nettle-leaved Figwort is a generally hairless plant with slender, rounded stems. As its name suggests, its leaves, up to 10cm (4in) long, are toothed and nettle-like. They are borne in opposite pairs, and have short stalks. The flowers grow in long-stalked and slightly lax clusters of 2 to 5, and the stalk supporting each cluster is flanked by a bract that has toothed margins like those of the leaves. The flowers, about 8mm (⅓in) long, are dull red or brown. They produce rounded capsules about 6mm (¼in) long.
• **DISTRIBUTION** Throughout.
• **HABITAT** Cultivated ground, waste ground, vineyards.

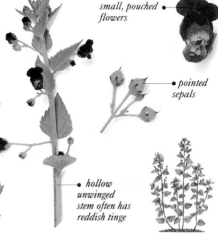

small, pouched flowers

pointed sepals

hollow unwinged stem often has reddish tinge

undivided leaves with toothed margins

Habit Annual	Height 30–90cm (12–36in)	Flowering time Apr–June

Family SCROPHULARIACEAE	Species *Scrophularia trifoliata*	Author L.

SCROPHULARIA TRIFOLIATA

Many figworts have inconspicuous flowers, and are easily overlooked. The same cannot be said of this species, which often grows into a massive and stately plant bearing apricot-coloured blooms the size of thimbles. It is completely hairless, and its stout, erect stems, which branch only from the base, are square in cross-section, with 4 wings. The leaves, up to 20cm (8in) long, grow in opposite pairs and are generally divided into 3, each lobe usually having doubly toothed margins. The flowers grow on short stalks in clusters flanked by leaf-like bracts, and are up to 20mm (⅘in) long, with a marked pouch and rounded sepals. The fruit is a rounded capsule, about 12mm (½in) long.
• **DISTRIBUTION** Corsica, Sardinia, and neighbouring islands.
• **HABITAT** Shady places, often near streams, damp, grassy banks.
• **RELATED SPECIES** *Scrophularia sambucifolia* is a similarly robust but shorter species found in S. Spain. Its leaves are divided nearly as far as the midrib, but are not split into 3 parts.

rounded sepals with wide papery margins

toothed and divided leaves

pouch clasped by sepals

cross-section of stem showing wings

robust, winged stem

Habit Perennial	Height 50–200cm (20–80in)	Flowering time May–Aug

Family SCROPHULARIACEAE	Species *Antirrhinum latifolium*	Author Miller

LARGE SNAPDRAGON

The stems of the Large Snapdragon often branch to produce a number of erect flower-heads, and the whole plant is often densely covered with glandular hairs, a feature that helps to distinguish it from *Antirrhinum majus* (below). The leaves are up to 70mm (2⅓in) long, and are relatively broad. The pale yellow flowers are carried at a narrow angle to the stem; each one has rounded sepals, and is borne on a short stalk flanked by an oval bract. The petals form a 2-lipped tube, the lower lip having a raised fold or "palate" that seals the entrance to the flower. The fruit is an oval and slightly hairy capsule.
• **DISTRIBUTION** N. Spain to Italy.
• **HABITAT** Rocky ground, walls.
• **RELATED SPECIES** Many other *Antirrhinum* species grow in the region, most of them being restricted to the Iberian peninsula. *A. majus*, Snapdragon (see below) is the only one that is widespread. Some species in the genus *Chaenorhinum* have spurred flowers of a similar size, with throats that are only partially closed.

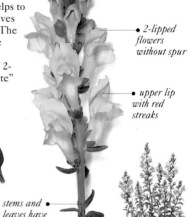

erect flower-head

2-lipped flowers without spur

upper lip with red streaks

leaves 2–3 times as long as wide

stems and leaves have glandular hairs

Habit Biennial/perennial	Height 60–100cm (24–40in)	Flowering time Apr–Sept

Family SCROPHULARIACEAE	Species *Antirrhinum majus*	Author L.

SNAPDRAGON

Although it is frequently cultivated as an annual, the wild Snapdragon is actually a herbaceous perennial with woody-based stems that can grow to a surprising length. The stems are ascending or erect, and they bear narrow, hairless leaves that are up to 70mm (2⅓in) long, but not more than 25mm (1in) wide. The flowers, which are borne on short stalks, are very similar to those of *Antirrhinum latifolium*, the Large Snapdragon (above), but are pink or purple. The fruit is a hairy or hairless capsule up to 14mm (½in) long.
• **DISTRIBUTION** S.W. Mediterranean, eastwards to Sicily.
• **HABITAT** Rocky ground, walls, gardens, cultivated land.
• **REMARK** Snapdragons are pollinated by large insects such as bumblebees, which are strong enough to force open the flower lips to gain access to the inside. Some bees save energy by biting a hole through the base of the petal-tube, before "stealing" the nectar.

flowers on very short stalks

oval bract beneath each flower

leaves at least twice as long as wide

Habit Biennial/perennial	Height Up to 1.5m (5ft)	Flowering time Apr–Oct

Family SCROPHULARIACEAE	Species *Misopates orontium*	Author (L.) Rafin.

LESSER SNAPDRAGON

Also known as Weasel's Snout, this erect annual plant has flowers similar to those of a true snapdragon, but its sepals are quite different. The stem is only slightly branched, and is hairy at least in its upper part. The leaves are narrow and linear, up to 50mm (2in) long, and are arranged in opposite pairs near the base of the stems, and alternately above. The pinkish red flowers grow in an open cluster and are up to 15mm (⅗in) long. They are clasped by 5 narrow sepals of unequal length, the longest exceeding the flower. The fruit is a hairy oval capsule, up to 10mm (⅖in) long.

• **DISTRIBUTION** Throughout.

• **HABITAT** Waysides, cultivated ground, cereal fields.

• **REMARK** A widespread weed throughout much of C. Europe.

• **RELATED SPECIES** *Misopates calycinum* is taller, with white flowers that grow in compact heads.

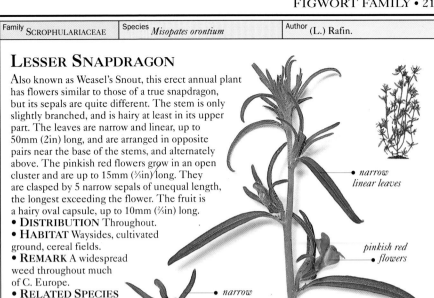

narrow linear leaves

pinkish red flowers

narrow unequal sepals

Habit Annual	Height 20–50cm (8–20in)	Flowering time Mar–Sept

Family SCROPHULARIACEAE	Species *Linaria pelisseriana*	Author (L.) Miller

JERSEY TOADFLAX

This delicate plant is common throughout the region, and reaches its northernmost point in the Channel Islands – hence its common name. Its stems are erect, hairless, and generally unbranched, and for most of their length they carry narrow, linear leaves, up to 40mm (1⅗in) long. At the base of the stems, the leaves are arranged in pairs or whorls, this being particularly apparent in the short non-flowering stem that is the first to appear. The flowers are up to 20mm (⅘in) long, and, as in all toadflaxes, they have a long spur and are clasped by 5 narrow sepals. The fruit is a small capsule.

• **DISTRIBUTION** Throughout the region.

• **HABITAT** Fields and waste ground.

• **RELATED SPECIES** *Linaria pupurea*, Purple Toadflax, a native of C. and S. Italy, is a more robust species with lighter flowers and grey-green leaves. It is widely cultivated and naturalized. There are many other toadflaxes throughout the region, many of them localized.

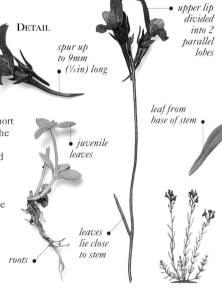

DETAIL

spur up to 9mm (⅜in) long

upper lip divided into 2 parallel lobes

leaf from base of stem

juvenile leaves

leaves lie close to stem

roots

Habit Annual	Height 15–50cm (6–20in)	Flowering time Mar–May

Family SCROPHULARIACEAE	Species *Linaria supina*	Author (L.) Chaz

PROSTRATE TOADFLAX

Prostrate Toadflax has lax, grey-green stems that lie flat and then ascend abruptly, giving the plant a clumped appearance. Its stems are hairless below, but glandular hairy towards their tips. The leaves are up to 20mm (4/5in) long, and are generally not more than 1mm (1/25in) wide. They are arranged in whorls near the base of the stem, and alternately above. The flowers are borne in clusters of about 5 to 10, and are pale yellow, sometimes with a violet tinge. Each flower is up to 20mm (4/5in) long, and has a spur that can be almost as long again. The fruit is a rounded capsule containing blackish winged seeds.
• **DISTRIBUTION** W. Mediterranean, from Spain to N. Italy.
• **HABITAT** Sandy or rocky places.
• **RELATED SPECIES** *Linaria vulgaris*, Common Toadflax, has larger orange flowers, often tinged with yellow. It is widespread throughout N. Europe, but rarer in the Mediterranean.

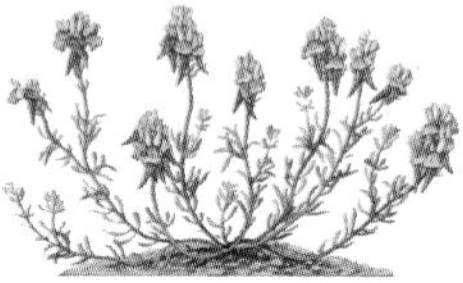

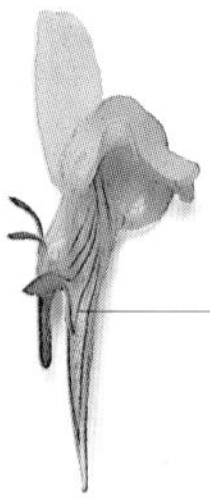
spur up to 15mm (3/5 in) long

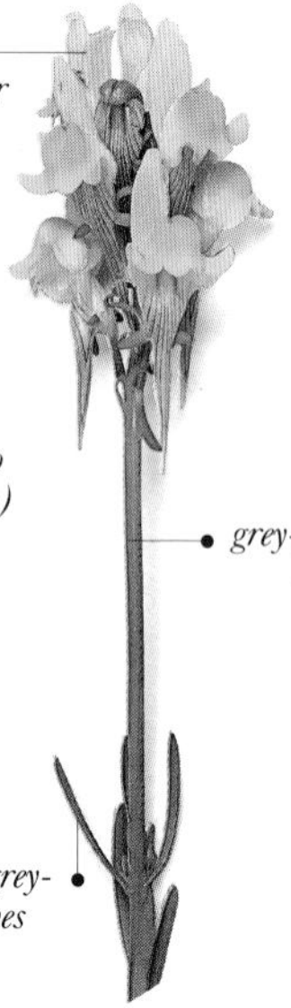
compact flower-cluster
grey-green stems
narrow, grey-green leaves

Habit Annual/perennial	Height 5–30cm (2–12in)	Flowering time May–Aug

Family SCROPHULARIACEAE	Species *Linaria repens*	Author (L.) Miller

PALE TOADFLAX

Pale Toadflax is an elegant plant with sprawling or erect stems that grow from creeping rhizomes. The stems are hairless and grey-green, and they often carry a number of branches from their upper halves. The leaves are narrow and up to 40mm (1 3/5in) long, and are usually arranged in whorls, although they may be alternate above. The flowers are arranged in long spikes, each compact cluster usually containing up to 10 flowers. Each flower is up to 15mm (3/5in) long, with a short spur, white or lilac petals, a yellow patch on the lower lip, and violet veins. The fruit is a small capsule, up to 4mm (1/6in) long, containing grey seeds.
• **DISTRIBUTION** N. Spain to N. Italy.
• **HABITAT** Rocky ground.
• **REMARK** This species is naturalized further north in Europe, including the British Isles, where it forms hybrids with *Linaria purpurea*, Purple Toadflax.

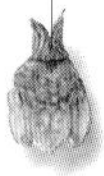
yellow palate

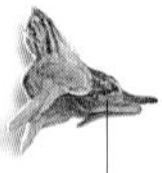
straight spur up to 5mm (1/5 in) long

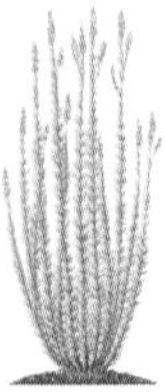

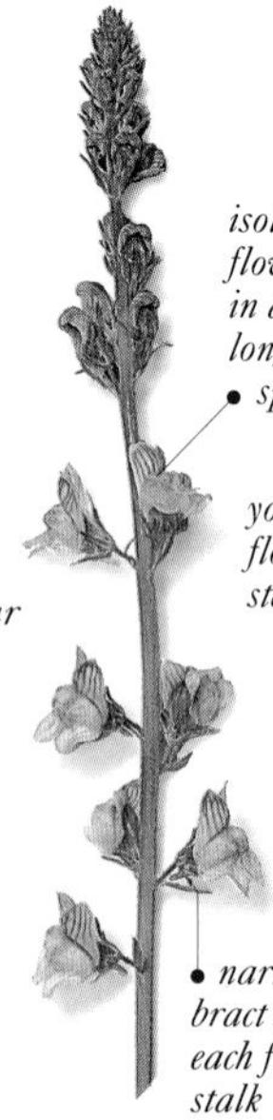
isolated flowers in a long spike
narrow bract beneath each flower-stalk

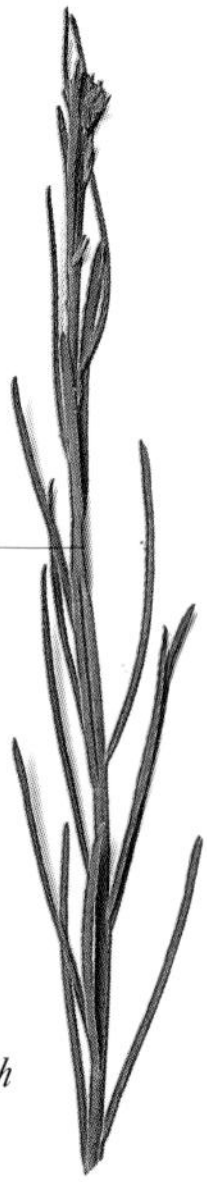
young flower-stem

Habit Perennial	Height 30–120cm (12–48in)	Flowering time May–Aug

| Family SCROPHULARIACEAE | Species *Cymbalaria muralis* | Author P. Gaertner, B. Meyer & Scherb. |

IVY-LEAVED TOADFLAX

This widespread inhabitant of rocks and walls has flowers very much like those of a true toadflax, but very different leaves. Its hairless stems creep or trail, and bear lobed, alternate leaves, about 15mm (⅗in) across. The flowers are violet, lilac, or rarely white, with a yellow patch on the lower lip. The rounded fruit capsule contains black seeds.

• **DISTRIBUTION** Native to Italy and Dalmatia; widely naturalized throughout Europe.

• **HABITAT** Damp rocks and walls; particularly on limestone.

• **REMARK** After flowering, the stalks bearing seed capsules grow away from the light, so the seeds are dispersed in rock crevices.

flowers up to 15mm (⅗in) long

flowers borne singly in leaf-axils

fleshy, kidney-shaped leaves

| Habit Perennial | Stem length Up to 60cm (24in) | Flowering time Mar–Sept |

| Family SCROPHULARIACEAE | Species *Kickxia commutata* | Author (Bernh. ex Reichenb.) Fritsch |

KICKXIA COMMUTATA

Commonly known as fluellens, members of the genus *Kickxia* have creeping or climbing stems and broad leaves. In this species, numerous pro-strate stems fan out from a central point, and are covered with glandular hairs. The alternately arranged leaves are rounded or oval at the base of the stems, and up to 30mm (1⅛in) long; the leaves towards the stem tips are much smaller and arrow-shaped. The flowers are either white with a pink flush, or blue and yellow with a purple-spotted lip. The flowers are held away from the stems on stiff, hairless stalks. Each flower is up to 15mm (⅗in) long, and has a spotted lower lip and long spur. The fruit is a rounded capsule.

• **DISTRIBUTION** Throughout.

• **HABITAT** Sandy ground.

• **RELATED SPECIES** *Kickxia lanigera* is similar, but is covered with long hairs. It has heart-shaped leaves, and violet and white flowers. Although widespread, it is rarely abundant.

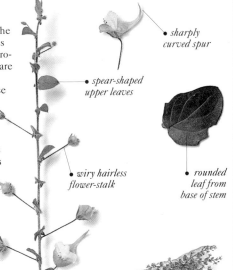

sharply curved spur

spear-shaped upper leaves

wiry hairless flower-stalk

rounded leaf from base of stem

| Habit Perennial | Height 20–70cm (8–28in) | Flowering time June–Sept |

Family SCROPHULARIACEAE	Species *Veronica cymbalaria*	Author Bodard

PALE SPEEDWELL

Unlike most speedwells, which have blue or lilac flowers, this widespread species is white-flowered. A hairy, low-growing plant with several sprawling stems, it has stalked fan-like leaves, up to 15mm (⅝in) long, which are divided into 5 to 9 unequal lobes. The flowers are borne singly on long stalks; as in all speedwells, they have 4 petals, and just 2 stamens, which protrude from the flower. The fruit is a 2-lobed capsule.
• **DISTRIBUTION** Throughout.
• **HABITAT** Cultivated ground, rocks, roadsides, bases of walls.
• **RELATED SPECIES** Many other speedwells are found in the region – Spain alone, for example, has more than 30 species. *Veronica persica*, Common Field Speedwell, is one of the most widespread blue-flowered species. Introduced from S.W. Asia, it is now a common weed throughout Europe. The widespread *Veronica anagallis-aquatica* has racemes of blue flowers, and grows in damp places.

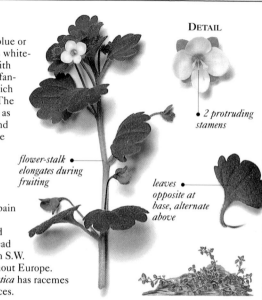

DETAIL

2 protruding stamens

flower-stalk elongates during fruiting

leaves opposite at base, alternate above

Habit Annual	Height 10–60cm (4–24in)	Flowering time Feb–Mar

Family SCROPHULARIACEAE	Species *Parentucellia latifolia*	Author (L.) Caruel

SOUTHERN RED BARTSIA

An erect and usually unbranched plant, Southern Red Bartsia frequently grows in open clumps. Its stems, leaves, and sepals are covered with glandular hairs, and the stems often have a reddish tinge. The triangular or oval leaves are opposite and stalkless, up to 12mm (½in) long, and deeply toothed. The reddish purple flowers grow in a dense, leafy head, and each one projects only a little way beyond its clasping sepals. The fruit is a hairless capsule.
• **DISTRIBUTION** Throughout.
• **HABITAT** Sandy and stony ground, roadsides, grassy places.
• **REMARK** Bartsias are hemi-parasites. Unlike true parasites such as Dodder (see p.178) or broomrapes (see p.218), they have green leaves, and can carry out photosynthesis. However, they obtain water and minerals by tapping into the root systems of neighbouring plants.

dense flower-head with leafy bracts

inconspicuous flowers up to 10mm (⅖in) long

deeply toothed leaves

reddish stem

Habit Annual	Height 5–20cm (2–8in)	Flowering time Mar–June

Family SCROPHULARIACEAE	Species *Parentucellia viscosa*	Author (L.) Caruel

YELLOW BARTSIA

Yellow Bartsia is a taller and generally more striking plant than its relative *Parentucellia latifolia*, Southern Red Bartsia (opposite). Erect and generally unbranched, it is covered with glandular hairs that give it a sticky texture. Its leaves are opposite and stalkless, and are toothed but undivided, reaching a length of 45mm (1⅛in). The bright yellow or, rarely, white flowers, up to 25mm (1in) long, grow in dense heads. Each flower is clasped by a calyx with narrow teeth. The upper flowerlip is undivided, whereas the longer lower lip is split into 3 spreading lobes. The fruit is a hairy, oblong capsule.

• **DISTRIBUTION** Throughout the region.
• **HABITAT** Damp pastures, ditch banks, sandy ground near to the sea.

dense flower-head
• with leafy bracts

divided lower
lip of flower
longer than
upper lip •

toothed
• margins

lance-
shaped
leaves •

Habit Annual	Height 10–70cm (4–28in)	Flowering time Apr–Sept

Family SCROPHULARIACEAE	Species *Bellardia trixago*	Author (L.) All.

BELLARDIA TRIXAGO

In suitable conditions, *Bellardia trixago* can be a handsome plant, with a pyramid-shaped head of conspicuous flowers. Its stem is erect and generally undivided – although some plants have lateral branches – and is covered with sticky glandular hairs. The opposite leaves, up to 90mm (3½in) long, are narrow with toothed margins. The flowers are usually purple and white, or more rarely yellow, and grow in a 4-sided spike. Each flower, up to 25mm (1in) long, has an undivided domed upper lip, a flaring lower lip split into 3 broad lobes, and a bell-shaped calyx with short teeth. The fruit is a rounded capsule.

• **DISTRIBUTION** Throughout the Mediterranean region.
• **HABITAT** Pastures, way-sides, olive groves.
• **REMARK** Like the bartsias (above and opposite), this plant is a hemiparasite.

large, toothed
• bracts

narrow, stalkless,
• toothed leaves

flowers
up to
25mm
(1in) long

Habit Annual	Height 15–70cm (6–28in)	Flowering time Apr–July

Family SCROPHULARIACEAE	Species *Lathraea clandestina*	Author L.

PURPLE TOOTHWORT

Purple Toothwort is a completely parasitic plant that "steals" nutrients from the roots of broadleaved trees, chiefly willows (*Salix* species), poplars (*Populus*) and alders (*Alnus*). Its stems are subterranean, and bear stalkless, scale-like, white leaves. The hooded violet flowers, which are up to 50mm (2in) long, grow in dense clumps at the surface, and produce seeds in oval capsules.
• **DISTRIBUTION** N. Spain to Italy, also northwards to Belgium.
• **HABITAT** Damp woodland, plantations, wooded riverbanks.

upper lip of flower curved and claw-like

subterranean stem with scale-like leaves

Habit Perennial	Height Up to 80mm (3⅛in)	Flowering time Apr–July

GLOBULARIA FAMILY

Family GLOBULARIACEAE	Species *Globularia alypum*	Author L.

SHRUBBY GLOBULARIA

Shrubby Globularia is a highly branched, evergreen shrub with brownish bark. Its leathery, spoon-shaped leaves are about 20mm (⅘in) long, and are borne singly or in small clusters. The bright blue flowers grow in dense rounded heads, up to 25mm (1in) across, each head being cupped by ranks of pointed, oval bracts that overlap like roof tiles. The fruit is dry, and is enclosed by the calyx.
• **DISTRIBUTION** Throughout.
• **HABITAT** Maquis, garigue, exposed stony ground.
• **REMARK** Members of the globularia family look superficially similar to some members of the daisy family, particularly knapweeds (*Centaurea* species). However, they can be distinguished by their 5 unequal petals.
• **RELATED SPECIES** A number of shrubby species are found in mountains. *Globularia punctata*, Globularia, is a widespread herbaceous species in the north of the region.

flower-clusters at tips of stems

closely packed tubular flowers with unequal petals

small, pointed, leathery leaves, sometimes toothed

alternate leaves

Habit Perennial	Height Up to 100cm (40in)	Flowering time Jan–June

ACANTHUS FAMILY

Family ACANTHACEAE	Species *Acanthus mollis*	Author L.

BEAR'S BREECH

This stately herbaceous perennial is an
inhabitant of cool, shady places and often
decorates waysides and gardens in wooded,
hilly ground. Its generally hairless leaves are
attached mainly at ground level, and they form
a cluster of large, deeply divided blades up to
60cm (24in) long, each on a long stalk. The
flowers, up to 50mm (2in) long, are borne in a
tall cylindrical spike, each flower having a single
visible lip with 3 white lobes tinged with purple,
and a long calyx with a hooded
upper lip. The flowers are
flanked by large oval bracts
with spiny teeth, and the fruit
contains black, pea-sized seeds.
• **DISTRIBUTION** W. and C.
Mediterranean, east to Dalmatia.
• **HABITAT** Shady places,
waysides, often cultivated.

*flowers up
to 50mm
(2in) long*

*soft glossy
leaves divided
almost to
the midrib*

Habit Perennial	Height 25–100cm (10–40in)	Flowering time May–July

Family ACANTHACEAE	Species *Acanthus spinosus*	Author L.

SPINY BEAR'S BREECH

Unlike its soft-leaved relative (above), Spiny
Bear's Breech often grows in dry and quite
exposed situations. An eye-catching plant
when in flower, it has erect stems that are
often covered with short hairs, and thistle-
like leaves up to 60cm (24in) long, mainly
attached at ground level. The leaves are
doubly divided almost as far as the
midrib, and their teeth end with hard,
sharp spines. The flowers grow in a tall,
cylindrical spike and are very similar to those
of Bear's Breech, but their bracts are often more
sharply spined. The fruit is a capsule containing
a few large seeds.
• **DISTRIBUTION** C. Mediterranean,
from S.E. Italy to the Aegean.
• **HABITAT** Waysides, fallow ground,
olive groves, stony pasture.
• **REMARK** The leaves of *Acanthus*
species are believed to have inspired
the decorative foliage on the capitals
of Corinthian pillars in classical Greece.

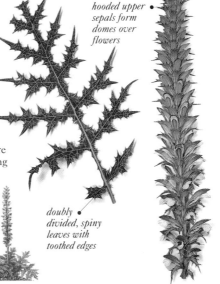

*hooded upper
sepals form
domes over
flowers*

*doubly
divided, spiny
leaves with
toothed edges*

Habit Perennial	Height 25–100cm (10–40in)	Flowering time May–June

BROOMRAPE FAMILY

Family OROBANCHACEAE	Species *Orobanche crenata*	Author Forskål

OROBANCHE CRENATA

DETAIL

The broomrape family is made up entirely of parasitic plants that lack chlorophyll – the green pigment that most plants use to harness the energy in sunlight. *Orobanche crenata* is a particularly widespread species that parasitizes plants in the pea family. The visible part of the plant consists of the erect and slightly hairy flowering stem. Towards its base it has narrow, scale-like leaves, up to 25mm (1in) long, and above it bears densely packed, slightly fragrant 2-lipped flowers. The fruit is a many-seeded capsule.
• **DISTRIBUTION** Throughout the region.
• **HABITAT** Fields, gardens; a common weed in plots of broad beans and peas.
• **REMARK** There are many similar species. Some have a wide range of hosts, whereas others grow only on specific species.

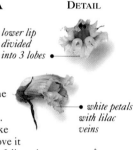

lower lip divided into 3 lobes •

• white petals with lilac veins

• each flower up to 30mm (1⅕in) long

• narrow, pointed sepals

• unbranched flowering stem

Habit Annual/perennial	Height Up to 80cm (32in)	Flowering time Feb–Aug

Family OROBANCHACEAE	Species *Orobanche ramosa*	Author L.

BRANCHED BROOMRAPE

DETAIL

This variable plant is one of the relatively small number of broomrapes that have branching stems. It is covered with glandular hairs, and its stems are up to 4mm (⅙in) in diameter, with a wider base usually just below ground level. The scale-like leaves are widely scattered, and not more than 8mm (⅓in) long. The flowers, up to 22mm (⅞in) long, vary in number, and may be borne in open or dense spikes. They are blue and white, with a distinct curve.
• **DISTRIBUTION** Throughout.
• **HABITAT** Cultivated fields, fallow ground, waysides, banks, and hedges.
• **REMARK** This species grows on a wide range of plants, including cultivated members of the potato family, such as potatoes themselves and tobacco.
• **RELATED SPECIES** *Orobanche lavandulacea* also has white and blue flowers, and is often branched. It frequently grows on *Psoralea bituminosa*, Pitch Trefoil, (see p.93) and is widespread.

• upper lobe of flower notched

• curved petal-tube

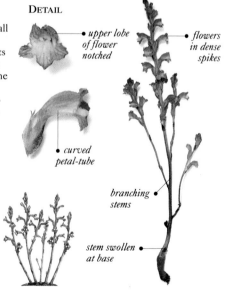

• flowers in dense spikes

branching stems

stem swollen • at base

Habit Perennial	Height 5–30cm (2–12in)	Flowering time Apr–June

PLANTAIN FAMILY

Family PLANTAGINACEAE	Species *Plantago lanceolata*	Author L.

RIBWORT PLANTAIN

Ribwort Plantain is a widespread and highly variable plant that can be hairy or hairless, usually with several rosettes of leaves. The leaves vary in shape from linear to almost elliptical, and are up to 30cm (12in) long (including the stalk, if present), with toothed or entire margins. The leafless stalks supporting the flower-heads are about twice as long as the leaves, and have 5 pronounced furrows. The flowers are brown and about 4mm (⅙in) long, and have hanging pale yellow anthers. The fruit is a capsule containing 2 boat-shaped seeds.
• **DISTRIBUTION** Throughout the Mediterranean region.
• **HABITAT** Fields, grassy ground, waste ground, roadsides.

small wind-pollinated flowers

compact heads

pronounced parallel leaf veins

leaf upperside

Habit Perennial	Height Up to 60cm (24in)	Flowering time Apr–Oct

Family PLANTAGINACEAE	Species *Plantago lagopus*	Author L.

HARE'S-FOOT PLANTAIN

This generally annual plantain has a rosette of lance-shaped leaves, up to 30cm (12in) long, and rounded or oblong flower-heads that are about 10mm (⅖in) high. The flower-heads are carried on furrowed stalks about 3 times as long as the leaves. The tiny flowers often have hairy lobes, and these, together with the hairy sepals and bracts, give the entire flower-head a soft, almost furry texture – hence the hare's-foot of its common name. The fruit is a rounded capsule.
• **DISTRIBUTION** Throughout.
• **HABITAT** Fields, sandy waste ground, roadsides.
• **RELATED SPECIES**
Several other species with leaves in rosettes grow in the region. *Plantago media*, Hoary Plantain, which is widespread on the Mediterranean mainland, is a typical perennial species with downy leaves and lilac anthers.

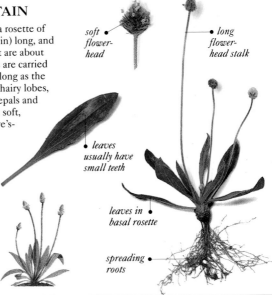

soft flower-head

long flower-head stalk

leaves usually have small teeth

leaves in basal rosette

spreading roots

Habit Annual/perennial	Height 10–40cm (4–16in)	Flowering time Apr–June

Family PLANTAGINACEAE	Species *Plantago afra*	Author L.

PLANTAGO AFRA

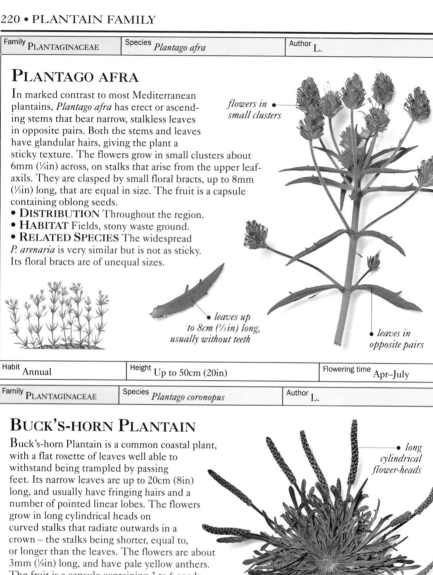

In marked contrast to most Mediterranean plantains, *Plantago afra* has erect or ascending stems that bear narrow, stalkless leaves in opposite pairs. Both the stems and leaves have glandular hairs, giving the plant a sticky texture. The flowers grow in small clusters about 6mm (¼in) across, on stalks that arise from the upper leaf-axils. They are clasped by small floral bracts, up to 8mm (⅓in) long, that are equal in size. The fruit is a capsule containing oblong seeds.
• **DISTRIBUTION** Throughout the region.
• **HABITAT** Fields, stony waste ground.
• **RELATED SPECIES** The widespread *P. arenaria* is very similar but is not as sticky. Its floral bracts are of unequal sizes.

flowers in small clusters

leaves up to 8cm (⅓in) long, usually without teeth

leaves in opposite pairs

Habit Annual	Height Up to 50cm (20in)	Flowering time Apr–July

Family PLANTAGINACEAE	Species *Plantago coronopus*	Author L.

BUCK'S-HORN PLANTAIN

Buck's-horn Plantain is a common coastal plant, with a flat rosette of leaves well able to withstand being trampled by passing feet. Its narrow leaves are up to 20cm (8in) long, and usually have fringing hairs and a number of pointed linear lobes. The flowers grow in long cylindrical heads on curved stalks that radiate outwards in a crown – the stalks being shorter, equal to, or longer than the leaves. The flowers are about 3mm (⅛in) long, and have pale yellow anthers. The fruit is a capsule containing 3 to 6 seeds.
• **DISTRIBUTION** Throughout the region.
• **HABITAT** Rocky or sandy ground near the coast; occasionally inland.

long cylindrical flower-heads

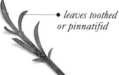

leaves toothed or pinnatifid

leaves in flat rosette

Habit Biennial/perennial	Height Up to 25cm (10in)	Flowering time Feb–Sept

HONEYSUCKLE FAMILY

Family CAPRIFOLIACEAE	Species *Sambucus ebulus*	Author L.

DWARF ELDER

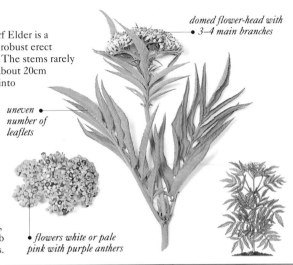

domed flower-head with 3–4 main branches

Also known as Danewort, Dwarf Elder is a herbaceous plant that produces robust erect stems from a creeping rhizome. The stems rarely branch. Its opposite leaves are about 20cm (8in) long. Each one is divided into between 5 and 13 lance-shaped leaflets with toothed margins. The 5-petalled flowers, in heads up to 16cm (6¼in) across, produce black berries, containing 3 to 5 seeds.

uneven number of leaflets

• **DISTRIBUTION**
Throughout the region.
• **HABITAT** Damp ground, riverbanks, hedges.
• **RELATED SPECIES**
Sambucus nigra, Common Elder, is a widespread deciduous shrub or small tree with edible berries.

flowers white or pale pink with purple anthers

Habit Perennial	Height 60–200cm (2–6½ft)	Flowering time June–July

Family CAPRIFOLIACEAE	Species *Viburnum tinus*	Author L.

LAURUSTINUS

clusters of white or pinkish white flowers

This frequently cultivated evergreen shrub or small tree flowers over a long period, and its flowers and fruit are often present at the same time. Its old growth is clad in grey bark, whereas the young stems have a reddish tinge, and are often slightly hairy. The leathery, oval leaves, up to 10cm (4in) long, are borne in opposite pairs. The small 5-petalled flowers grow in loose, domed heads up to 90mm (3⅗in) across, and are white or white tinged with pink. They produce clusters of blue-black fruit with a metallic sheen. Each fruit contains a single stone.

leaves dark green above, lighter below

• **DISTRIBUTION**
Throughout, except in the extreme east, Crete, and many smaller islands in the region.
• **HABITAT** Maquis, shady woods on hillsides, gardens.
• **REMARK** The fruit is poisonous.

fruit-cluster

oval untoothed leaves

Habit Perennial	Height Up to 7m (23ft)	Flowering time Jan–June

Family CAPRIFOLIACEAE	Species *Lonicera etrusca*	Author G. Santi

ETRUSCAN HONEYSUCKLE

Etruscan Honeysuckle is a deciduous woody climber that
twines around other plants, or sprawls over surrounding
vegetation. Its leaves are arranged in opposite pairs,
and the lowest are spoon-shaped and up to 80mm
(3⅛in) long. They are generally blunt-tipped. The
leaf-stalks become progessively shorter up the
stem, and the highest leaves are joined together.
The fragrant flowers grow in long-stalked
heads, and are up to 45mm (1⅛in) long.
Each flower is tubular and 2-lipped, the
upper lip having 4 lobes. The fruit is a red
berry that grows in small clusters.
• **DISTRIBUTION** Throughout.
• **HABITAT** Woodland, scrub,
waysides, hedgebanks.
• **RELATED SPECIES**
Lonicera periclymenum,
Common Honeysuckle
of N. Europe, is a similar
species and is also wide-
spread. However, its leaves
are never joined at their bases.

*flower-
heads single
or in groups
of up to 3*

*leaves usually •
blunt-tipped*

*uppermost •
leaves joined
at base*

Habit Perennial	Height Up to 2.5m (8ft)	Flowering time May–July

Family CAPRIFOLIACEAE	Species *Lonicera implexa*	Author Aiton

LONICERA IMPLEXA

This evergreen honeysuckle has hairless, slightly
waxy young stems, and leathery, oblong or oval
leaves with white undersides. The leaves
are up to 80mm (3⅛in) long, and though
variable in shape, those on the upper
parts of the stems are generally
stalkless and frequently joined.
Unlike Etruscan Honeysuckle
(above), this species has flowers
that grow in stalkless clusters of 2 to
6, cupped by the leaves. The flowers
are 2-lipped and up to 45mm (1⅛in)
long, with very short calyces. The
orange or red berries are cupped
by the leaves, and look rather
like eggs in a nest.
• **DISTRIBUTION**
Throughout the region.
• **HABITAT** Maquis, open ground.
• **REMARK** Several shrubby *Lonicera*
species grow in mountains bordering the
Mediterranean region, particularly in S. Spain.

*flowers in small •
stalkless clusters*

*leaves with pale
• undersides*

*• leaves joined
around stem*

Habit Perennial	Height Up to 2m (6½ft)	Flowering time May–July

VALERIAN FAMILY

Family VALERIANACEAE	Species *Centranthus ruber*	Author (L.) DC.

RED VALERIAN

Red Valerian is a conspicuous plant with clustered stems growing from an underground rhizome. Its stems and leaves are hairless, and have a blue-green hue and a slightly fleshy texture. The oval or lance-shaped leaves, up to 80mm (3⅛in) long, are arranged in opposite pairs. The lowest leaves are stalked, whereas the uppermost are stalkless and often toothed. The flowers are red, pink, or sometimes white, and grow in crowded clusters. Each flower, about 10mm (⅜in) long, is tubular and has a 5-lobed mouth, and a slender backward-pointing spur near the base of the tube. The fruit is a single-seeded nut with a parachute of feathery hairs.
• **DISTRIBUTION** Throughout; introduced and naturalized in many parts of C. and N.W. Europe, including the British Isles.
• **HABITAT** Rocky ground, walls; frequently cultivated.
• **REMARK** The pink form is the most common, although red and white forms are often scattered among pink-flowered plants.

• *cluster of parallel flowers*

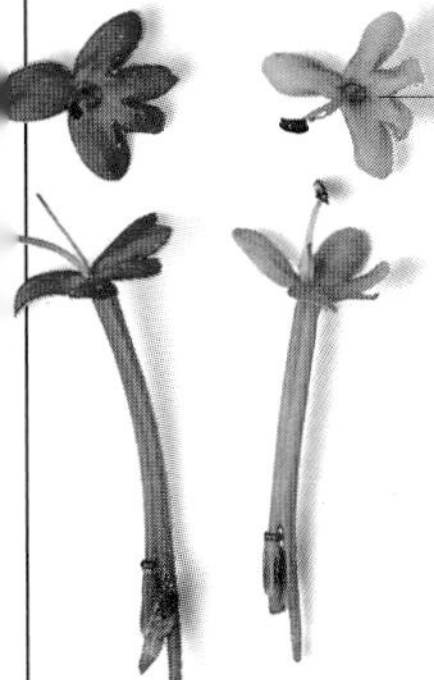

• *5-lobed mouth*

• *spur*

• *stem and leaves have waxy surfaces*

• *stalkless upper leaves clasp the stem*

• *lower stem-leaf*

Habit Perennial	Height 30–80cm (12–32in)	Flowering time Apr–Aug

Family VALERIANACEAE	Species *Valeriana tuberosa*	Author L.

VALERIANA TUBEROSA

As its name suggests, this widespread valerian grows from tuberous roots. Its hairless stem is usually solitary, and is surrounded at its base by a rosette of elliptical leaves, up to 10cm (4in) long. By contrast, the stem-leaves have a compound appearance: the lowest have long wedge-shaped lobes; the highest have widely spaced linear lobes. The flowers, about 5mm (⅕in) long, are similar to those of Red Valerian (see p.223), but are spurless, and are borne in smaller domed heads. The flowers have 5 slightly unequal petal-lobes and 3 protruding stamens. The fruit has a feathery tuft formed by its attached calyx.
• **DISTRIBUTION** Throughout, except on most islands.
• **HABITAT** Dry grassland, grassy places among rocks.
• **REMARK** Several similar species can be found in the region, particularly in damp ground at altitude.

pink flowers

compact flower-head

upper leaf with linear lobes

DETAIL

single unbranched stem

spoon-shaped basal leaf

Habit Perennial	Height Up to 50cm (20in)	Flowering time Apr–July

TEASEL FAMILY

Family DIPSACACEAE	Species *Scabiosa graminifolia*	Author L.

GRASS-LEAVED SCABIOUS

Unlike most Mediterranean plants, scabiouses often flower until well into summer, creating welcome colour in sunbaked open ground. Grass-leaved Scabious is a slender, woody-based species with opposite, linear leaves, up to 80mm (3⅛in) long. The leaves have a silky texture produced by a dense covering of hairs. As with other members of the teasel family, the individual flowers or florets are packed into a dense flower-head. The flat or domed heads are up to 40mm (1⅜in) across. The tubular florets have a cup-shaped calyx with 5 teeth.
• **DISTRIBUTION** Mediterranean France and Spain.
• **HABITAT** Rocky ground.
• **RELATED SPECIES** Many other blue-flowered teasel species occur in the region. Some belong to the genus *Scabiosa*, others to the genus *Knautia*.

DETAIL

single flower-head

long stalk

outer florets have large lobes

silky grass-like

Habit Perennial	Height Up to 40cm (16in)	Flowering time Apr–July

Family DIPSACACEAE	Species *Scabiosa prolifera*	Author L.

CARMEL DAISY

This early-flowering scabious is restricted to the extreme east of the region, and is a common roadside plant in parts of Israel and the Lebanon. Its stout, hairy stems repeatedly divide into equal branches, with a flower-head, up to 40mm (1⅝in) across, tucked in each fork. The leaves are oblong or oval, often with wavy edges. The florets are pale yellow, with the outermost having large, flaring lower lobes. As with all members of this genus, each floret has a second calyx or involucel. After the flowers have withered, a spherical fruiting head develops, with the papery involucels forming chambers like cells in a honeycomb. Eventually, the head breaks up, with the involucels acting like sails that catch the wind and bear the seeds away.
• **DISTRIBUTION** From Turkey and Cyprus eastwards.
• **HABITAT** Fields, roadsides, waste ground; usually on limestone.

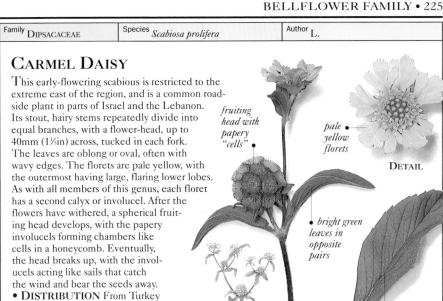

fruiting head with papery "cells"

pale • yellow florets

DETAIL

• bright green leaves in opposite pairs

• undivided leaves

Habit Annual	Height Up to 30cm (12in)	Flowering time Feb–Apr

BELLFLOWER FAMILY

Family CAMPANULACEAE	Species *Campanula saxatilis*	Author L.

CAMPANULA SAXATILIS

Like most of its relatives, *Campanula saxatilis* has conspicuous violet-blue flowers that are shaped like 5-lobed bells. Its spreading or ascending stems grow from a thick rhizome, and carry hairless leaves; those near the base have long stalks. The flowers, up to 20mm (⅘in) long, have pointed sepals, and produce capsules that split open to release their seeds.
• **DISTRIBUTION** S. Greece, Crete.
• **HABITAT** Rocky slopes, walls.
• **RELATED SPECIES** There are many very similar species, especially in the Aegean region. Some, including *C. tubulosa* (see p.226), are restricted to small areas of the mainland or to individual islands.

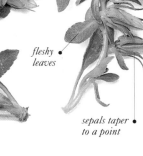

violet-blue • flowers

fleshy • leaves

sepals taper • to a point

stems snap • easily if bent

Habit Perennial	Height Up to 20cm (8in)	Flowering time Apr–July

Family CAMPANULACEAE	Species *Campanula tubulosa*	Author Lam.

CAMPANULA TUBULOSA

Unlike *Campanula saxatilis* (see p.225), this plant is covered with coarse hairs, and has a rough texture. Its stems are spreading or ascending, and grow by repeatedly dividing in two. The lower leaves have long stalks and toothed or scalloped margins, the leaf and stalk together being up to 10cm (4in) long. The upper leaves are stalkless. The velvety flower-tube is up to 20mm (⅘in) long, and is clasped by pointed sepals. The base of each sepal has 2 lobe-like appendages – a characteristic feature of some *Campanula* species. The fruit is a capsule that splits open to release its seeds.
• **DISTRIBUTION** W. Crete.
• **HABITAT** Damp rock crevices, gullies.

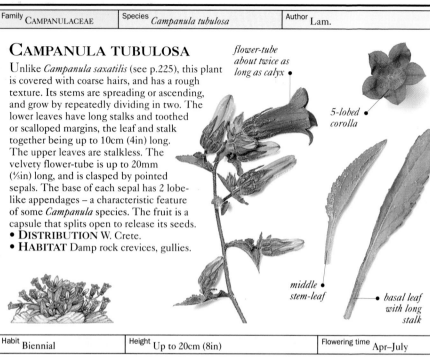

flower-tube about twice as long as calyx

5-lobed corolla

middle stem-leaf

basal leaf with long stalk

Habit Biennial	Height Up to 20cm (8in)	Flowering time Apr–July

Family CAMPANULACEAE	Species *Legousia pentagonia*	Author (L.) Druce

LEGOUSIA PENTAGONIA

Legousia pentagonia belongs to a small genus of annuals that frequently grow as weeds on cultivated ground. Its finely haired stems are densely branched near the base, and bear stalked lower leaves that grow up to 20mm (⅘in) long. The upper leaves are smaller and stalkless. The violet flowers grow in open racemes, and each is cup-shaped, and up to 25mm (1in) in diameter when fully open. Like other members of the genus, this species has extremely long and narrow cylindrical ovaries, which look at first glance like slightly thickened flower-stalks. The ripe ovary produces a seed capsule up to 30mm (1⅕in) long.
• **DISTRIBUTION** Aegean region, including Greece, Crete, and Turkey.
• **HABITAT** Fields, olive groves, fallow ground, usually in open situations.

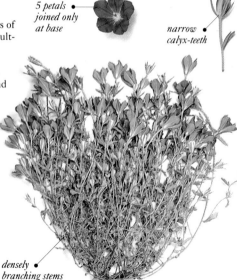

5 petals joined only at base

narrow calyx-teeth

densely branching stems

Habit Annual	Height 10–40cm (4–16in)	Flowering time Mar–June

Family CAMPANULACEAE	Species *Legousia hybrida*	Author (L.) Delarbre

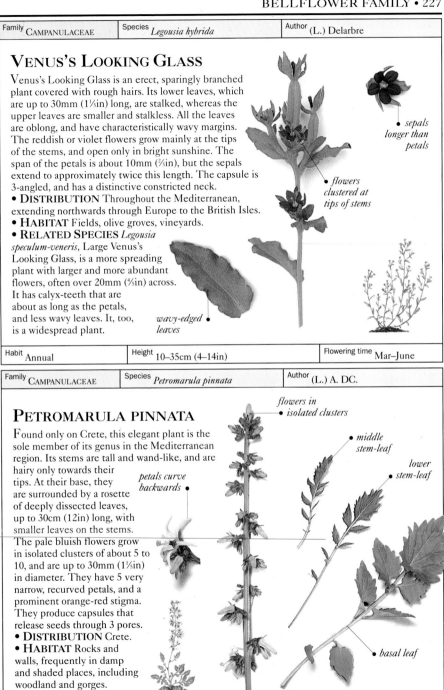

VENUS'S LOOKING GLASS

Venus's Looking Glass is an erect, sparingly branched plant covered with rough hairs. Its lower leaves, which are up to 30mm (1⅛in) long, are stalked, whereas the upper leaves are smaller and stalkless. All the leaves are oblong, and have characteristically wavy margins. The reddish or violet flowers grow mainly at the tips of the stems, and open only in bright sunshine. The span of the petals is about 10mm (⅜in), but the sepals extend to approximately twice this length. The capsule is 3-angled, and has a distinctive constricted neck.
• **DISTRIBUTION** Throughout the Mediterranean, extending northwards through Europe to the British Isles.
• **HABITAT** Fields, olive groves, vineyards.
• **RELATED SPECIES** *Legousia speculum-veneris*, Large Venus's Looking Glass, is a more spreading plant with larger and more abundant flowers, often over 20mm (⅘in) across. It has calyx-teeth that are about as long as the petals, and less wavy leaves. It, too, is a widespread plant.

sepals longer than petals

flowers clustered at tips of stems

wavy-edged leaves

Habit Annual	Height 10–35cm (4–14in)	Flowering time Mar–June

Family CAMPANULACEAE	Species *Petromarula pinnata*	Author (L.) A. DC.

PETROMARULA PINNATA

Found only on Crete, this elegant plant is the sole member of its genus in the Mediterranean region. Its stems are tall and wand-like, and are hairy only towards their tips. At their base, they are surrounded by a rosette of deeply dissected leaves, up to 30cm (12in) long, with smaller leaves on the stems. The pale bluish flowers grow in isolated clusters of about 5 to 10, and are up to 30mm (1⅛in) in diameter. They have 5 very narrow, recurved petals, and a prominent orange-red stigma. They produce capsules that release seeds through 3 pores.
• **DISTRIBUTION** Crete.
• **HABITAT** Rocks and walls, frequently in damp and shaded places, including woodland and gorges.

flowers in isolated clusters

middle stem-leaf

lower stem-leaf

petals curve backwards

basal leaf

Habit Perennial	Height Up to 125cm (50in)	Flowering time Apr–May

DAISY FAMILY

Family COMPOSITAE	Species *Bellis perennis*	Author L.

DAISY

This low-growing plant is among the most familiar members of the world's largest family of flowering plants. Its leaves grow in a basal rosette and are hairy, particularly when young. They have a spoon-shaped outline, with or without teeth, and are up to 60mm (2⅜in) long. Each "flower" is actually a cluster of tiny florets – a feature shared by all plants in this family. The inner disc-florets are tubular and yellow, while the outer ray-florets have a single, petal-like flap. The fruit is a small achene.
• **DISTRIBUTION** Throughout.
• **HABITAT** Roadsides, grassy ground.
• **REMARK** Its common name – a corruption of "day's eye"– derives from its habit of opening only in sunshine.
• **RELATED SPECIES** *Bellis annua*, Annual Daisy, is a smaller plant with a more distinct stem and shorter leaves.

cluster of yellow disc-florets

ray-florets often tipped with purple

leaf-stalk roughly as long as blade

thick roots

Habit Perennial	Height 15cm (6in)	Flowering time Feb–June

Family COMPOSITAE	Species *Aster tripolium*	Author L.

SEA ASTER

The Sea Aster is a late-flowering inhabitant of damp, salty ground, and often forms dense stands in low-lying parts of the coastline, both around the Mediterranean and elsewhere in Europe. Its stems are erect or ascending, and are generally hairless, branching at the base. The fleshy leaves are lance-shaped or linear, and up to 12cm (4¾in) long. Only the lower leaves have stalks. The flower-heads measure about 20mm (⅘in) across, and each is clasped by blunt, overlapping flower-bracts. Most plants have blue or mauve ray-florets, but in the west of the region, some plants have disc-florets only. The fruit is a brown achene with a tuft of feathery hairs.
• **DISTRIBUTION** Throughout the region.
• **HABITAT** Salt marshes, lagoons, saline places inland.

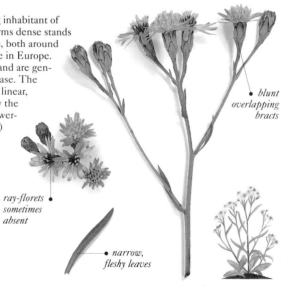

blunt overlapping bracts

ray-florets sometimes absent

narrow, fleshy leaves

Habit Annual/perennial	Height 20–60cm (8–24in)	Flowering time Sept–Nov

Family COMPOSITAE	Species *Helichrysum italicum*	Author (Roth) G. Don fil.

HELICHRYSUM ITALICUM

Over a dozen species of *Helichrysum* grow in the region, most being low, aromatic subshrubs in dry, exposed places. *Helichrysum italicum* is among the more widespread examples. It has a woody base, and spreading and ascending branches that are covered with felty hairs when young. The narrow, stalkless leaves, up to 30mm (1⅕in) long, have downturned margins. As in other species of *Helichrysum*, the florets are all tubular, and are packed into small flower-heads which are themselves clustered in larger groups, up to 80mm (3⅕in) across. The flower-heads are clasped by papery bracts. The fruit is a small achene.

• **DISTRIBUTION** Throughout the region.
• **HABITAT** Dry, rocky ground; sandy areas near to the sea.
• **REMARK** The "everlasting" flower-heads are used in dried-flower arrangements, for they retain their colour after being picked and allowed to dry.

each flower-head is clasped by stiff papery bracts

spreading branches bearing clusters of flower-heads

Habit Perennial	Height 20–50cm (8–20in)	Flowering time Apr–May

Family COMPOSITAE	Species *Helichrysum stoechas*	Author (L.) Moench

HELICHRYSUM STOECHAS

Helichrysum stoechas can often be identified by a powerful, curry-like aroma produced when its stems or leaves are crushed. A variable and generally dense subshrub, it has ascending branches that are densely covered with hairs, which also extend over its narrow leaves. Its flowers are borne in small heads about 5mm (⅕in) across, each head being clasped by loosely overlapping flower-bracts. The fruit is a small achene with white glands.

• **DISTRIBUTION** Throughout.
• **HABITAT** Garigue, sandy and rocky ground near the coast.
• **REMARK** Subsp. *stoechas*, which is found from Dalmatia westwards, is strongly aromatic. Subsp. *barrelieri*, which is found from Sicily to Turkey, has very little smell.
• **RELATED SPECIES** *H. sanguineum*, which is found from Turkey eastwards, has bright red flower-bracts.

flower-heads in rounded or flattened clusters

flower-head after fruiting

narrow felted leaves, up to 25mm (1in) long

Habit Perennial	Height 10–50cm (4–20in)	Flowering time Apr–July

Family COMPOSITAE	Species *Phagnalon graecum*	Author Boiss. & Heldr.

PHAGNALON GRAECUM

Phagnalon graecum belongs to a genus of dwarf shrubs that, although sometimes widespread, are rarely objects of outstanding beauty. This species has ascending or erect stems which bear alternate leaves for much of their length. The leaves, up to 25mm (1in) long, are narrow with wavy margins and are densely hairy, particularly beneath. The flower-heads are borne singly, and are composed entirely of tubular, yellow florets. Each flower-head is up to 20mm (⅘in) in diameter, and its florets barely project out of the narrow bracts. The fruit is a cylindrical achene.
• **DISTRIBUTION** Italy, Balkans, Crete.
• **HABITAT** Dry, rocky ground, garigue, and roadsides.
• **REMARK** This species is also known as *P. rupestre*, the subsp. *graecum* (shown here) being slightly shorter with narrower bracts.

solitary flower-heads

narrow bracts

tubular florets

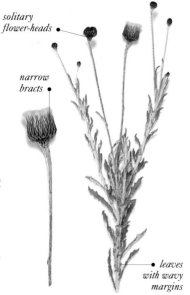

leaves with wavy margins

Habit Perennial	Height 10–30cm (4–12in)	Flowering time Apr–May

Family COMPOSITAE	Species *Phagnalon sordidum*	Author (L.) Reichenb.

PHAGNALON SORDIDUM

Even during the height of its flowering season, *Phagnalon sordidum* is scarcely an alluring sight. A low and straggling dwarf shrub, it has narrow, white-felted leaves, which are up to 30mm (1⅛in) long, with downturned margins. Its spindly, ascending stems carry stalkless, flask-shaped flower-heads. Each flower-head measures approximately 15mm (⅗in) long, and has scaly, brown bracts and barely projecting florets. Unlike the majority of of its relatives, this species bears its flower-heads in small clusters, with 2 to 6 flower-heads growing on each stem.
• **DISTRIBUTION** Spain, eastwards to C. Italy.
• **HABITAT** Rocks, walls, and dry, rocky roadsides.
• **REMARK** This species often forms hybrids with 2 other western species, *P. graecum* (above) and *P. saxatile*.

stalkless cone-shaped flower-heads

clustered flower-heads

spindly stems

narrow leaves

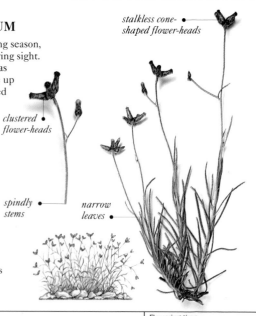

Habit Perennial	Height 15–30cm (6–12in)	Flowering time May–July

Family COMPOSITAE	Species *Inula crithmoides*	Author L.

GOLDEN SAMPHIRE

Like many members of the daisy family, Golden Samphire begins to flower at the height of summer, and continues flowering well into autumn. A robust, woody-based, and hairless plant, it branches mainly at its base, and has a number of leafy, ascending or erect stems. The stalkless leaves are up to 45mm (1⅘in) long, and are narrow and fleshy. They broaden slightly towards their tips, which often have 3 teeth. The flower-heads are up to 25mm (1in) in diameter. Each one has a hemispherical involucre with narrow bracts, orange disc-florets, and yellow ray-florets. The downy fruit is up to 3mm (⅛in) long, with a tuft of white hairs.
• **DISTRIBUTION** Throughout, and northwards to the British Isles.
• **HABITAT** Rocky and sandy coasts, salt marshes; occasionally inland.
• **REMARK** Although predominantly coastal, Golden Samphire is found inland in E. Spain.

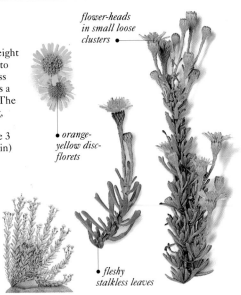

flower-heads in small loose clusters

orange-yellow disc-florets

fleshy stalkless leaves

Habit Perennial	Height Up to 100cm (40in)	Flowering time Aug–Oct

Family COMPOSITAE	Species *Dittrichia viscosa*	Author (L.) W. Greuter

AROMATIC INULA

In some parts of the Mediterranean, Aromatic Inula is one of the most conspicuous plants of late summer, flowering in immense profusion along roadsides, in vineyards, and on waste ground. A woody-based shrubby plant, it has erect, leafy stems covered with glands, and is extremely sticky, with a resin-like smell. Its leaves, up to 70mm (2⅘in) long, are narrow and pointed, the lower leaves being stalked, and the upper leaves clasping the stem. The flower-heads are about 15mm (⅗in) across, and have bright yellow ray-florets, which are long and usually well separated, and slightly darker disc-florets. The fruit is about 2mm (¹⁄₁₂in) long, with a narrow tuft of hair attached at the base.
• **DISTRIBUTION** Throughout.
• **HABITAT** Garigue, pine woods, fields, vineyards, waste ground, and roadsides.
• **REMARK** This plant is also known as *Inula viscosa*.

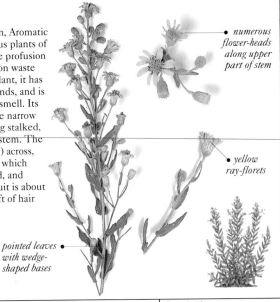

numerous flower-heads along upper part of stem

yellow ray-florets

pointed leaves with wedge-shaped bases

Habit Perennial	Height 40–125cm (16–50in)	Flowering time Aug–Nov

Family COMPOSITAE	Species *Pallenis spinosa*	Author (L.) Cass.

PALLENIS SPINOSA

A widespread weed of waste ground, *Pallenis spinosa* has woody-based stems and a characteristic way of branching, with its side-branches becoming much longer than its central ones. Its leaves are oval or spoon-shaped, and up to 80mm (3⅕in) long. The lower leaves have stalks, but the upper leaves are stalkless and partly clasp the stem. The flower-heads are about 25mm (1in) in diameter. They have have long ray-florets, each with 3 sharp teeth, and a ruff of narrow, leafy bracts. The outer bracts are much the longest, with spiny tips. The fruit is a flattened achene, which is about 2.5mm (⅒in) long.
• **DISTRIBUTION** Throughout.
• **HABITAT** Fields, waste ground.
• **REMARK** *Pulicaria dysenterica*, Common Fleabane, has rather similar flowers but lacks the long bracts. A softly hairy plant, it grows in damp places throughout the region.

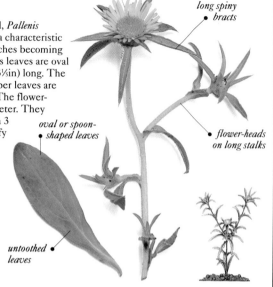

long spiny bracts

oval or spoon-shaped leaves

flower-heads on long stalks

untoothed leaves

Habit Annual/biennial	Height Up to 60cm (24in)	Flowering time Apr–July

Family COMPOSITAE	Species *Asteriscus aquaticus*	Author (L.) Less.

ASTERISCUS AQUATICUS

Similar in structure to *Pallenis spinosa* (above), this low-growing plant also has conspicuous leafy bracts, but in this case they lack spiny tips. The stem usually branches only towards its tip, and bears oblong leaves, up to 60mm (2⅜in) long. The lower leaves are stalked, but the upper leaves are stalkless and clasping. The flower-heads are borne singly, and have a ring of relatively short, bright yellow ray-florets which are far exceeded by the longest bracts. The fruit is a small achene with silky hairs.
• **DISTRIBUTION** Throughout.
• **HABITAT** Fallow fields, damp places, sandy ground near the sea.
• **RELATED SPECIES** *Asteriscus maritimus* is a low-growing shrub with flower-bracts that are often not much longer than the ray-florets. It grows in rocky places near the sea, from Greece westwards.

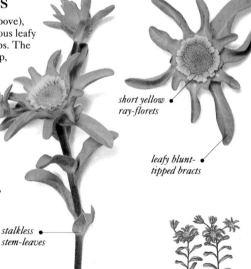

short yellow ray-florets

leafy blunt-tipped bracts

stalkless stem-leaves

Habit Annual	Height 10–50cm (4–20in)	Flowering time Apr–July

Family COMPOSITAE	Species *Xanthium strumarium*	Author L.

COCKLEBUR

The Cocklebur is an erect, branching annual that has roughly triangular leaves up to 15cm (6in) long. The leaves are borne on long stalks, and have heart-shaped or wedge-shaped bases and a rough texture. The flowers are small and inconspicuous, and are borne in groups of a single sex, with the male flowers above the female ones. The female flowers grow in pairs, surrounded by an oval involucre. This forms a spiny or hooked outer case to the fruiting head, which is up to 35mm (1⅜in) long when ripe.
• **DISTRIBUTION** Throughout the region.
• **HABITAT** Disturbed ground, marshy places, waysides, sandy beaches.
• **RELATED SPECIES**
Xanthium spinosum, Spiny Cocklebur, native to South America, is widely naturalized throughout the Mediterranean region. It has a similar shape, but has stalkless leaves and sharp, yellow spines.

toothed leaves with long stalks

ripe fruiting head with hooks or spines

Habit Annual	Height 20–120cm (8–48in)	Flowering time July–Sept

Family COMPOSITAE	Species *Santolina chamaecyparissus*	Author L.

COTTON LAVENDER

Cotton Lavender is a doubly misleading name, because this attractive and aromatic dwarf shrub is neither a form of cotton nor a lavender, but a typical member of the daisy family. It branches at its base, and its young growth is covered with a silvery grey down. The narrow leaves are alternately arranged, and rarely more than 30mm (1⅛in) long. They have neat ranks of teeth or lobes, and may be downy. The bright yellow, button-like flower-heads measure about 20mm (⅘in) in diameter, and consist solely of tubular florets. The fruit is an oblong achene, without a tuft of hair.
• **DISTRIBUTION** W. and C. Mediterranean, eastwards to Dalmatia.
• **HABITAT** Dry ground, gardens.
• **REMARK** A widely cultivated species, often used in dwarf flowering hedges.
• **RELATED SPECIES** *Santolina rosmarinifolia*, which grows in Spain and S. France, is similar, but its rosemary-like leaves are often entirely without lobes.

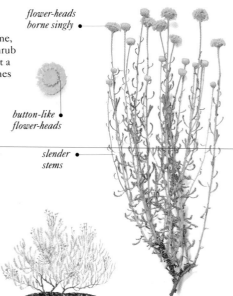

flower-heads borne singly

button-like flower-heads

slender stems

Habit Perennial	Height 10–50cm (4–20in)	Flowering time June–Sept

Family COMPOSITAE	Species *Anthemis chia*	Author L.

ANTHEMIS CHIA

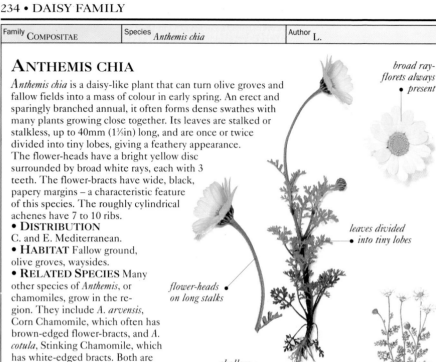

Anthemis chia is a daisy-like plant that can turn olive groves and fallow fields into a mass of colour in early spring. An erect and sparingly branched annual, it often forms dense swathes with many plants growing close together. Its leaves are stalked or stalkless, up to 40mm (1⅜in) long, and are once or twice divided into tiny lobes, giving a feathery appearance. The flower-heads have a bright yellow disc surrounded by broad white rays, each with 3 teeth. The flower-bracts have wide, black, papery margins – a characteristic feature of this species. The roughly cylindrical achenes have 7 to 10 ribs.

- **DISTRIBUTION**
C. and E. Mediterranean.
- **HABITAT** Fallow ground, olive groves, waysides.
- **RELATED SPECIES** Many other species of *Anthemis*, or chamomiles, grow in the region. They include *A. arvensis*, Corn Chamomile, which often has brown-edged flower-bracts, and *A. cotula*, Stinking Chamomile, which has white-edged bracts. Both are common throughout Europe.

broad ray-florets always present

leaves divided into tiny lobes

flower-heads on long stalks

shallow roots

Habit Annual	Height 5–40cm (2–16in)	Flowering time Feb–Apr

Family COMPOSITAE	Species *Anthemis rigida*	Author (Sibth. & Sm.) Boiss. & Heldr.

ANTHEMIS RIGIDA

Like many shore plants, this small mat-forming chamomile has stout stems and tough, slightly fleshy leaves. Its stems are usually numerous but unbranched, and have a covering of hairs. The leaves are once or twice divided, with plump lobes, and are often no more than 20mm (⅘in) long. The flower-heads are borne on short stalks, and normally lack ray-florets. Each one has a relatively deep, conical involucre, with hairy triangular or lance-shaped bracts. The fruit is an achene without apparent ribs.

- **DISTRIBUTION**
Aegean region.
- **HABITAT** Sandy beaches.

ray-florets usually absent

flower-heads borne on short stalks

dense fleshy foliage

divided leaves

Habit Annual	Stem length Up to 15cm (6in)	Flowering time Mar–May

Family COMPOSITAE	Species *Achillea millefolium*	Author L.

YARROW

Members of the genus *Achillea* are sometimes mistaken for plants in the carrot family, because their flowers grow in flat or domed clusters. However, a close look reveals that each cluster is composed not of individual flowers, but of small flower-heads each containing a number of florets. Yarrow, or Milfoil, is a variable and often downy species with alternate, highly divided, feathery leaves. Its flower-heads have both ray-florets and tubular disc-florets. The fruit is a flattened achene, without a tuft of hair.

• **DISTRIBUTION** Widespread, but absent from many islands and parts of the south.

• **HABITAT** Grassy areas.

• **RELATED SPECIES** There are many other similar species in the region. *A. tomentosa*, Yellow Milfoil, found eastwards to Italy, has bright yellow flower-heads.

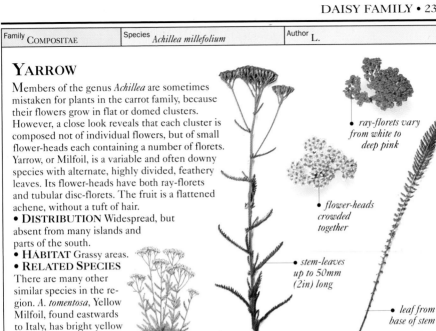

• *ray-florets vary from white to deep pink*

• *flower-heads crowded together*

• *stem-leaves up to 50mm (2in) long*

• *leaf from base of stem*

Habit Perennial	Height Up to 60cm (24in)	Flowering time June–Aug

Family COMPOSITAE	Species *Chamaemelum mixtum*	Author (L.) All.

CHAMAEMELUM MIXTUM

This aromatic and daisy-like plant has a characteristic branching growth, the side-branches being held at a wide angle to the main stem. The whole plant is often covered in fine hairs, and has alternately arranged, stalkless leaves, up to 80mm (3⅛in) long. The leaves are oblong in outline; those near the base of the stem are once or twice divided, whereas those higher up are divided once, or just toothed. The flower-heads are about 25mm (1in) across, with broad, white rays. The fruit is an achene, without a tuft of hair.

• **DISTRIBUTION** Throughout.

• **HABITAT** Sandy ground, roadsides.

• **RELATED SPECIES** *Chamaemelum nobile*, Chamomile, is similar, but is a perennial species with very fine, feathery leaves and a creeping growth. It is found in the west of the Mediterranean region, and has been spread widely by cultivation.

• *flower-heads borne singly*

• *white ray-florets with yellow bases*

• *branches at a wide angle to stem*

• *toothed upper stem-leaf*

Habit Annual	Height 15–60cm (6–24in)	Flowering time June–Sept

Family COMPOSITAE	Species *Anacyclus clavatus*	Author (Desf.) Pers.

ANACYCLUS CLAVATUS

Anacyclus clavatus is a widespread plant of waste places, equally at home on sandy ground near the coast or along the dusty verges of busy roads. Erect and often bushy, it branches near its base, and its leaves, up to 10cm (4in) long, are twice or thrice divided, giving a feathery appearance. The flower-heads are solitary, up to 40mm (1⅗in) in diameter, and their flower-bracts are silky, with white or purple margins. The fruit is an achene, without a tuft of hair.
• **DISTRIBUTION** Throughout.
• **HABITAT** Disturbed ground, roadsides.

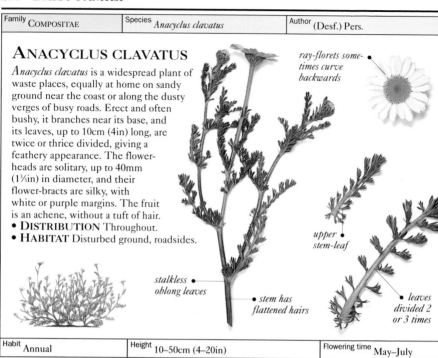

ray-florets some-
times curve
backwards

upper
stem-leaf

stalkless •
oblong leaves

• stem has
flattened hairs

• leaves
divided 2
or 3 times

Habit Annual	Height 10–50cm (4–20in)	Flowering time May–July

Family COMPOSITAE	Species *Otanthus maritimus*	Author (L.) Hoffmanns. & Link

COTTONWEED

Cottonweed is a sprawling plant of dunes and sandy beaches. The dense, silver-grey felt on its stems and leaves protects it from the drying coastal wind, and also from the heat that is reflected upwards by the surrounding sand. The plant branches from its base, and has numerous woody-based stems. The leaves are stalkless and generally no more than 15mm (⅗in) long, with an oblong outline and toothed or untoothed margins. The flower-heads grow in small clusters on short stalks, and are about 10mm (⅖in) across. They lack ray-florets, and have oval flower-bracts. The fruit is a curved and fairly large achene, about 4mm (⅙in) long.
• **DISTRIBUTION**
Throughout; also widespread on coasts in N.W. Europe.
• **HABITAT** Sandy beaches and dunes; occasionally seen on shingle beaches.

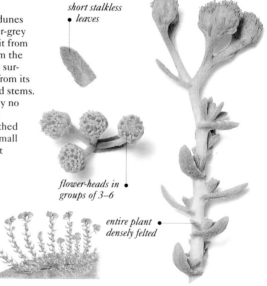

short stalkless
• leaves

flower-heads in •
groups of 3–6

entire plant •
densely felted

Habit Perennial	Stem length Up to 50cm (20in)	Flowering time June–Sept

Family COMPOSITAE	Species *Chrysanthemum coronarium*	Author L.

CROWN DAISY

This tall, eye-catching annual has large
flower-heads up to 60mm (2⅜in) across,
and it frequently grows in abundance,
creating a mass of colour against a background of feathery foliage. Its stems are
erect and hairless, and carry numerous
branches. The oblong or lance-shaped
leaves can be over 10cm (4in) long,
and are usually doubly divided, *thickened*
with toothed, lance-shaped *flower-stalk*
lobes. The flower-heads are
supported by thickened stalks,
and have a central disc of yellow,
tubular florets, surrounded by
broad ray-florets. The ray-florets
may be entirely yellow, or yellow
towards their bases and white
towards their tips. The fruit is
an achene, without a tuft of hairs.
• **DISTRIBUTION** Throughout,
but more common in the east.
• **HABITAT** Fields, waste ground.

*ray-florets can
have yellow
bases •*

*white and •
yellow form*

*finely •
divided
leaves*

Habit Annual	Height 20–75cm (8–30in)	Flowering time Mar–Sept

Family COMPOSITAE	Species *Chrysanthemum segetum*	Author L.

CORN MARIGOLD

Unlike its larger relative, the Crown Daisy
(above), Corn Marigold is an erect but only
sparingly branched plant, with oblong leaves that
are often deeply cut but never wholly divided. The
entire plant is hairless, and has a blue-green hue and
a slightly fleshy texture. The lower leaves can be up
to 80mm (3⅛in) long with long lobes, whereas the
upper leaves are much shorter, without lobes and
sometimes without teeth as well. The flower-
heads average about 45mm (1¾in) across, and are
always entirely yellow. The achenes produced
by the innermost florets have 10 distinct ribs.
• **DISTRIBUTION** Greece and Crete; widely
naturalized as far north as
Scandinavia.
• **HABITAT** Fallow or
arable ground, waysides.
• **REMARK** This is one of
several species that are in
decline as a result of the
more widespread use of
herbicides.

*disc- and •
ray-florets
both yellow*

*• swollen
stalk supporting
flower-head*

*• lobed,
slightly fleshy
leaves*

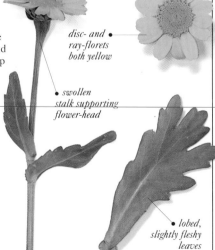

Habit Annual	Height 20–60cm (8–24in)	Flowering time Mar–May

Family COMPOSITAE	Species *Cotula coronopifolia*	Author L.

BUTTONWEED

Although native to southern Africa, this small
but distinctive plant is naturalized in many
other parts of the world, including the Mediterranean. Entirely hairless and rather fleshy, it
sometimes grows in dense, low swathes that
resemble bright green turf. Its
branching stems are clasped by
stalkless leaves, up to 50mm (2in)
long, with margins that are either
entire, or lobed or toothed
towards the leaf tip. The
flower-heads, up to 10mm (⅜in)
across, grow singly on long stalks.
They do not have ray-florets.
• **DISTRIBUTION**
W. Mediterranean.
• **HABITAT** Damp, salty ground
near the sea, muddy quaysides.

DETAIL

flower-heads •
on long stalks

• button-like
flower-heads

fleshy leaves,
sometimes
• lobed

• erect
stems

narrow
stalkless
leaves

Habit Annual	Height Up to 30cm (12in)	Flowering time Apr–July

Family COMPOSITAE	Species *Senecio cineraria*	Author DC.

SILVER RAGWORT

The ragworts make up one of the largest
genera of flowering plants, with over 2,000
species worldwide. The number of species
that can be found in the Mediterranean
runs into many dozens, and nearly all
have yellow flower-heads in flattish
clusters, or corymbs, and produce tufted
seeds that are dispersed by the wind. Silver
Ragwort is a decorative, densely felted shrub
from the west and centre of the region. Its stems
have woody bases, and branch mainly at their
base. They bear very variable leaves, up to 15cm
(6in) long, that are divided into narrow lobes. The
flower-heads grow in stalked clusters, and are up to
15mm (⅜in) across. They have yellow-orange disc-
florets and clearer yellow ray-florets, and produce
achenes with a tuft of white hairs.
• **DISTRIBUTION**
W. and C. Mediterranean.
• **HABITAT** Rocky ground
near to the coast, beaches,
waste ground, gardens.
• **REMARK** Sometimes
classified as a subspecies of
Senecio bicolor; Silver Ragwort
is often cultivated for its foliage.

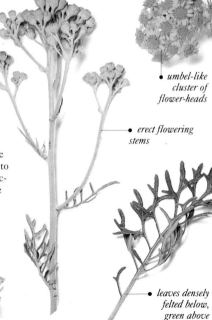

• umbel-like
cluster of
flower-heads

• erect flowering
stems

• leaves densely
felted below,
green above

Habit Perennial	Height 25–60cm (10–24in)	Flowering time May–Aug

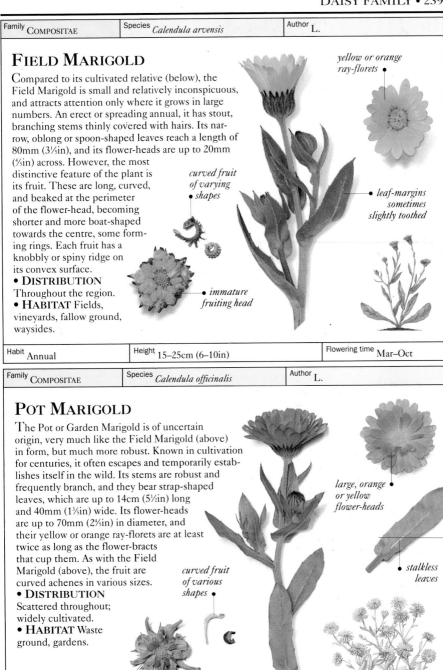

Family COMPOSITAE	Species *Calendula arvensis*	Author L.

FIELD MARIGOLD

Compared to its cultivated relative (below), the
Field Marigold is small and relatively inconspicuous,
and attracts attention only where it grows in large
numbers. An erect or spreading annual, it has stout,
branching stems thinly covered with hairs. Its narrow, oblong or spoon-shaped leaves reach a length of
80mm (3⅛in), and its flower-heads are up to 20mm
(⅘in) across. However, the most
distinctive feature of the plant is
its fruit. These are long, curved,
and beaked at the perimeter
of the flower-head, becoming
shorter and more boat-shaped
towards the centre, some forming rings. Each fruit has a
knobbly or spiny ridge on
its convex surface.
• **DISTRIBUTION**
Throughout the region.
• **HABITAT** Fields,
vineyards, fallow ground,
waysides.

*yellow or orange
ray-florets*

*curved fruit
of varying
shapes*

*leaf-margins
sometimes
slightly toothed*

*immature
fruiting head*

Habit Annual	Height 15–25cm (6–10in)	Flowering time Mar–Oct

Family COMPOSITAE	Species *Calendula officinalis*	Author L.

POT MARIGOLD

The Pot or Garden Marigold is of uncertain
origin, very much like the Field Marigold (above)
in form, but much more robust. Known in cultivation
for centuries, it often escapes and temporarily establishes itself in the wild. Its stems are robust and
frequently branch, and they bear strap-shaped
leaves, which are up to 14cm (5½in) long
and 40mm (1⅗in) wide. Its flower-heads
are up to 70mm (2⅘in) in diameter, and
their yellow or orange ray-florets are at least
twice as long as the flower-bracts
that cup them. As with the Field
Marigold (above), the fruit are
curved achenes in various sizes.
• **DISTRIBUTION**
Scattered throughout;
widely cultivated.
• **HABITAT** Waste
ground, gardens.

*large, orange
or yellow
flower-heads*

*curved fruit
of various
shapes*

*stalkless
leaves*

*immature
fruiting head*

Habit Annual/perennial	Height 20–50cm (8–20in)	Flowering time Mar–June

Family COMPOSITAE	Species *Carlina corymbosa*	Author L.

CARLINA CORYMBOSA

Carlina corymbosa is a variable and extremely spiny plant that grows from a creeping underground stem. Its leaves are up to 90mm (3⅝in) long, and are lance-shaped in outline, and deeply lobed or toothed. Its straw-coloured flower-heads reach a diameter of about 30mm (1⅛in), and are surrounded by sharp bracts. The fruit is an achene with a tuft-like ring of hairs.
• **DISTRIBUTION** Throughout.
• **HABITAT** Stony places, waysides, dry pastures, open woodland.
• **RELATED SPECIES** *C. acanthifolia*, which is found in mountains eastwards to the Balkans region, is a stemless species with a spectacular single flower-head measuring up to 70mm (2⅜in) in diameter, surrounded by petal-like bracts. It is often used as a decoration.

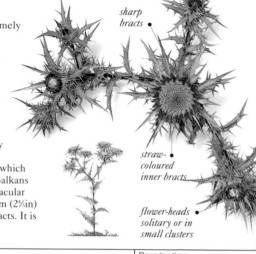

sharp bracts

straw-coloured inner bracts

flower-heads solitary or in small clusters

Habit Biennial/perennial	Height 20–50cm (8–20in)	Flowering time June–Sept

Family COMPOSITAE	Species *Atractylis cancellata*	Author L.

ATRACTYLIS CANCELLATA

This small and slender thistle can be recognized not so much by its flower-heads but by its outer bracts, which form a delicate curved cage around the florets. Its erect and often hairless stems bear narrow leaves, up to 50mm (2in) long, with teeth and soft spines. The flower-heads, borne on short stalks in open clusters, are about 15mm (⅝in) across, with purple florets. The inner bracts are lance-shaped, but the outer bracts have narrow segments, and curve around the almost spherical involucre. The fruit has a tuft of white hairs.
• **DISTRIBUTION** Throughout the region.
• **HABITAT** Dry, stony ground, fallow fields.
• **REMARK** Two subspecies are recognized. Subsp. *gaditana*, from S.W. Spain, grows in much damper ground than the more wide-spread subsp. *cancellata*.
• **RELATED SPECIES** *Atractylis humilis* is a perennial species, found in Spain and S.E. France, with fewer bract segments. *A. gummifera*, Pine Thistle, found throughout the Mediterranean region except in the extreme east, is a stemless species with a rosette of much longer leaves. It has conspicuous purple flower-heads, up to 70mm (2⅜in) across, surrounded by a rosette of leaf-like outer bracts.

cage of finely divided outer bracts

leaves bear soft spines

stem often hairless

narrow, toothed leaves

Habit Annual	Height Up to 25cm (10in)	Flowering time Apr–July

Family COMPOSITAE	Species *Echinops ritro*	Author L.

GLOBE THISTLE

The Globe Thistle is a variable, erect, and usually unbranched plant, with hairy or hairless stems, and spiny lobed leaves that are densely woolly beneath and sometimes sticky above. Its blue flowers grow in heads that each contain a single floret surrounded by stiff greenish blue bracts, while the heads are themselves arranged in a ball. The fruit has a tuft of bristly hairs.
• **DISTRIBUTION** Throughout.
• **HABITAT** Dry fields, stony ground, garigue.
• **RELATED SPECIES** There are several similar species in the region. One of the largest is *Echinops spinosissimus*, which has pale flower-clusters up to 70mm (2⅛in) across. It grows eastwards from Sicily.

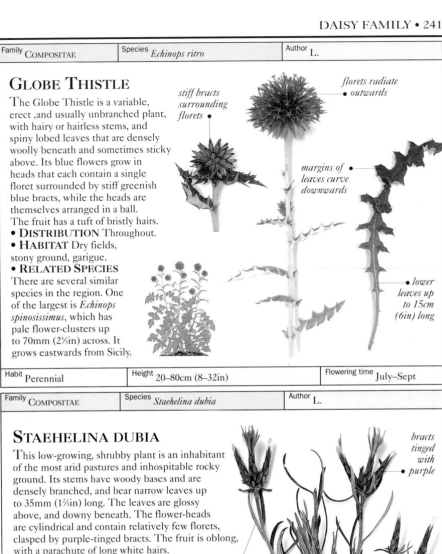

stiff bracts surrounding florets

florets radiate outwards

margins of leaves curve downwards

lower leaves up to 15cm (6in) long

Habit Perennial	Height 20–80cm (8–32in)	Flowering time July–Sept

Family COMPOSITAE	Species *Staehelina dubia*	Author L.

STAEHELINA DUBIA

This low-growing, shrubby plant is an inhabitant of the most arid pastures and inhospitable rocky ground. Its stems have woody bases and are densely branched, and bear narrow leaves up to 35mm (1⅜in) long. The leaves are glossy above, and downy beneath. The flower-heads are cylindrical and contain relatively few florets, clasped by purple-tinged bracts. The fruit is oblong, with a parachute of long white hairs.
• **DISTRIBUTION** S.W. Mediterranean, eastwards to Italy.
• **HABITAT** Dry, rocky ground.
• **RELATED SPECIES** Two much larger species grow in the east of the Mediterranean region: *Staehelina arborea*, which grows up to 100cm (40in) tall, is found only in Crete, whereas *S. fruticosa* also grows in mainland Greece. Both of these species are dense shrubs with compact clusters of white or pink flower-heads.

bracts tinged with purple

flower-heads solitary or in small clusters

narrow, linear leaves

Habit Perennial	Height 20–40cm (8–16in)	Flowering time June–July

Family COMPOSITAE	Species *Carduus pycnocephalus*	Author L.

CARDUUS PYCNOCEPHALUS

This slender thistle has narrow, winged stems that are covered in felty hairs. Its leaves are lobed and spiny, and those at the base of the plant reach 20cm (8in) or more. The flower-heads, up to 20mm (⅝in) across, grow singly or in groups of 2 to 3, on stalks of varying length. The fruit, as with all *Carduus* thistles, is an achene with a tuft of undivided hairs.
• **DISTRIBUTION** Throughout the region.
• **HABITAT** Waste ground, waysides.
• **REMARK** Many other *Carduus* species grow in the region. All have winged stems.

spiny flower-bracts

purple tubular florets

leaves with 2–5 pairs of spiny lobes

Habit Annual/biennial	Height 20–80cm (8–32in)	Flowering time Mar–June

Family COMPOSITAE	Species *Notobasis syriaca*	Author (L.) Cass.

SYRIAN THISTLE

Despite its common name, this extremely spiny annual is a native Mediterranean plant, and is widespread as far west as Spain and Portugal. Its tall and rigid stems often have a slightly metallic bluish tinge towards their tips, where they frequently branch. The basal leaves are up to 30cm (12in) long, with stalks and deep, spine-tipped lobes, while the leaves further up the stem become narrower and more divided – the highest leaves forming ruffs of stiff spines around the flower-heads. The flower-heads grow singly, or in small clusters, and are up to 25mm (1in) long, with purple florets. The dark brown achene has a tuft of feathery hairs.
• **DISTRIBUTION** Throughout the Mediterranean, except France and northerly parts of the region.
• **HABITAT** Fields, waste ground, roadsides.
• **RELATED SPECIES** Thistles in the genus *Cirsium* also have feathery haired fruit.

long spines surrounding flower-heads

leaves have white veins or marbling

stiff, ribbed stems

Habit Annual	Height 20–100cm (8–40in)	Flowering time Mar–June

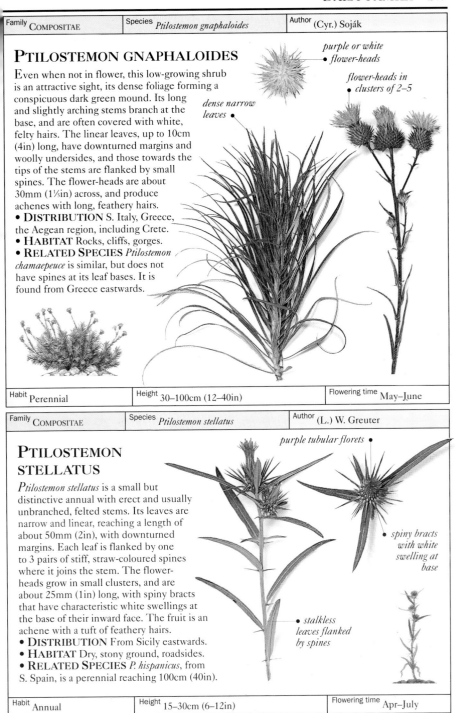

Family COMPOSITAE	Species *Ptilostemon gnaphaloides*	Author (Cyr.) Soják

PTILOSTEMON GNAPHALOIDES

Even when not in flower, this low-growing shrub is an attractive sight, its dense foliage forming a conspicuous dark green mound. Its long and slightly arching stems branch at the base, and are often covered with white, felty hairs. The linear leaves, up to 10cm (4in) long, have downturned margins and woolly undersides, and those towards the tips of the stems are flanked by small spines. The flower-heads are about 30mm (1⅛in) across, and produce achenes with long, feathery hairs.
• **DISTRIBUTION** S. Italy, Greece, the Aegean region, including Crete.
• **HABITAT** Rocks, cliffs, gorges.
• **RELATED SPECIES** *Ptilostemon chamaepeuce* is similar, but does not have spines at its leaf bases. It is found from Greece eastwards.

purple or white
• flower-heads

flower-heads in
• clusters of 2–5

dense narrow
leaves •

Habit Perennial	Height 30–100cm (12–40in)	Flowering time May–June

Family COMPOSITAE	Species *Ptilostemon stellatus*	Author (L.) W. Greuter

PTILOSTEMON STELLATUS

Ptilostemon stellatus is a small but distinctive annual with erect and usually unbranched, felted stems. Its leaves are narrow and linear, reaching a length of about 50mm (2in), with downturned margins. Each leaf is flanked by one to 3 pairs of stiff, straw-coloured spines where it joins the stem. The flower-heads grow in small clusters, and are about 25mm (1in) long, with spiny bracts that have characteristic white swellings at the base of their inward face. The fruit is an achene with a tuft of feathery hairs.
• **DISTRIBUTION** From Sicily eastwards.
• **HABITAT** Dry, stony ground, roadsides.
• **RELATED SPECIES** *P. hispanicus*, from S. Spain, is a perennial reaching 100cm (40in).

purple tubular florets •

• spiny bracts with white swelling at base

• stalkless leaves flanked by spines

Habit Annual	Height 15–30cm (6–12in)	Flowering time Apr–July

Family COMPOSITAE	Species *Galactites tomentosa*	Author Moench

GALACTITES TOMENTOSA

This erect, thistle-like plant is a common sight on roadsides throughout the region. It branches above, and its rigid stems are covered with a white felt, as are the undersides of its leaves. The leaves, about 15cm (6in) long, are lobed or more deeply divided, with sharp spines. The flower-heads have a flattened appearance, the large outer florets radiating to form a ring. Each flower-head is surrounded by bracts that narrow to form outward-pointing spines. The fruit is an achene, with a tuft of long, feathery hairs.

outer florets much larger than those in centre

- **DISTRIBUTION** Throughout the region.
- **HABITAT** Roadsides, pastures, fallow land.

flower-heads solitary or in small clusters

leaves have white veins or marbling on upper surfaces

Habit Annual/biennial	Height 15–100cm (6–40in)	Flowering time Apr–Aug

Family COMPOSITAE	Species *Onopordum illyricum*	Author L.

ONOPORDUM ILLYRICUM

The genus *Onopordum* includes the tallest, bulkiest, and most formidably armed thistles that grow in the region. *Onopordum illyricum* is a widespread species with an erect stem, branched above, that has densely packed, spiny wings and often a covering of felt-like hairs. Its leaves, up to 15cm (6in) long, are stalkless and narrow in outline, with deep spine-tipped lobes. The flower-heads, up to 60mm (2⅜in) across, have a brush-like tuft of purple florets. The stiff bracts surrounding the flower-heads are up to 7mm (⅜in) wide at their bases but narrow to a spine; the outer bracts turn downwards. The fruit is a plump achene.

purple tubular florets

flower-heads on branching stems

- **DISTRIBUTION** Throughout the region.
- **HABITAT** Rocky ground, waysides.

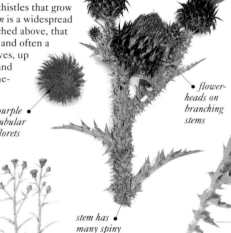

stem has many spiny wings

narrow spiny leaves

Habit Biennial	Height 30–150cm (12–60in)	Flowering time June–July

Family COMPOSITAE	Species *Onopordum argolicum*	Author Boiss.

ONOPORDUM ARGOLICUM

Onopordum argolicum is a particularly imposing thistle with an erect winged stem that branches towards its tip. The wings are spiny, and not more than 8mm (⅓in) wide. The leaves are oblong or lance-shaped in outline, up to 25cm (10in) long, and are deeply cut into 10 to 12 pairs of connected spine-tipped lobes. The flower-heads have a bun-sized tuft of crowded, tubular purple florets, cupped by overlapping spine-tipped bracts – the outer-most bracts being turned down. The fruit is a brownish grey achene with a tuft of rough hairs.
• **DISTRIBUTION** S. Greece, Malta, Sardinia, Sicily.
• **HABITAT** Dry waste ground, roadsides, field margins.
• **RELATED SPECIES** *O. nervosum*, found in Spain, is a spectacular grey-green plant with a candelabra-like arrangement of spreading branches, and very broad, spiny wings. It frequently grows to over 2.5m (8ft), and is sometimes cultivated as a specimen plant.

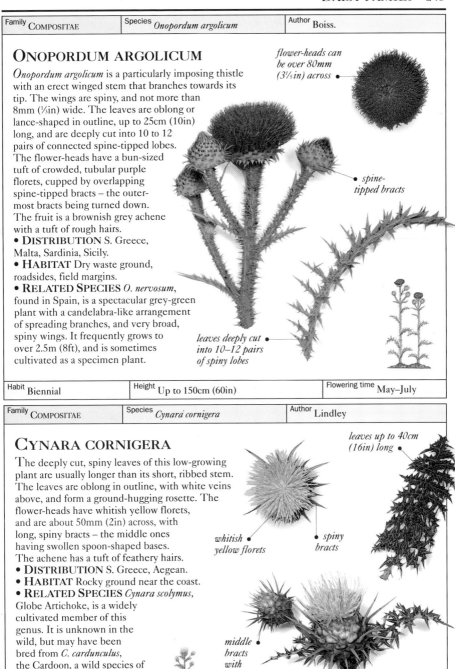

flower-heads can be over 80mm (3⅓in) across

spine-tipped bracts

leaves deeply cut into 10–12 pairs of spiny lobes

Habit Biennial	Height Up to 150cm (60in)	Flowering time May–July

Family COMPOSITAE	Species *Cynara cornigera*	Author Lindley

CYNARA CORNIGERA

The deeply cut, spiny leaves of this low-growing plant are usually longer than its short, ribbed stem. The leaves are oblong in outline, with white veins above, and form a ground-hugging rosette. The flower-heads have whitish yellow florets, and are about 50mm (2in) across, with long, spiny bracts – the middle ones having swollen spoon-shaped bases. The achene has a tuft of feathery hairs.
• **DISTRIBUTION** S. Greece, Aegean.
• **HABITAT** Rocky ground near the coast.
• **RELATED SPECIES** *Cynara scolymus*, Globe Artichoke, is a widely cultivated member of this genus. It is unknown in the wild, but may have been bred from *C. cardunculus*, the Cardoon, a wild species of the W. and C. Mediterranean.

leaves up to 40cm (16in) long

whitish yellow florets

spiny bracts

middle bracts with swollen bases

Habit Perennial	Height Up to 30cm (12in)	Flowering time May–June

Family COMPOSITAE	Species *Silybum marianum*	Author (L.) Gaertner

MILK THISTLE

During its first year, the Milk or Holy Thistle's slightly fleshy, strikingly veined leaves form a rosette that can be over 80cm (32in) across. The leaves are deeply cut into spiny-tipped lobes. The branched flowering stem, which appears in the second year, carries smaller leaves, and large solitary flower-heads, up to 80mm (3⅛in) across. The bracts clasping the flower-head broaden into a spiny-edged cup before narrowing again to form a long, grooved spine. The achenes are black with a tuft of rough white hairs.

grooved radiating spines

purple tubular florets

dead flower-head

leaves with spiny and wavy margins

• **DISTRIBUTION**
Throughout the region.
• **HABITAT** Waste ground, roadsides.
• **REMARK** The young leaves are edible.
• **RELATED SPECIES**
Silybum eburneum, which grows in N. Africa and E. Spain, is similar, but has roughly haired basal leaves, and bracts with longer spines.

Habit Biennial	Height 20–150cm (8–60in)	Flowering time Apr–July

Family COMPOSITAE	Species *Leuzea conifera*	Author (L.) DC.

LEUZEA CONIFERA

Leuzea conifera is instantly recognizable by its flower-heads, which look like small, glossy pine-cones set in a bed of leaves. Its stems bear narrowly lobed leaves up to 80mm (3⅛in) long, and the undersides of the leaves, like the stems, have a covering of woolly hairs. The flower-heads are about 50mm (2in) long, and have purple florets, and broad, incurved papery bracts. After flowering, the bracts open wide to release black achenes with long white hairs.

bracts open wide after flowering

stems short and usually unbranched

narrowly lobed leaves

• **DISTRIBUTION**
Eastwards to Italy.
• **HABITAT** Dry, rocky ground, gar-igue, pine woods.

Habit Perennial	Height 5–30cm (2–12in)	Flowering time May–Aug

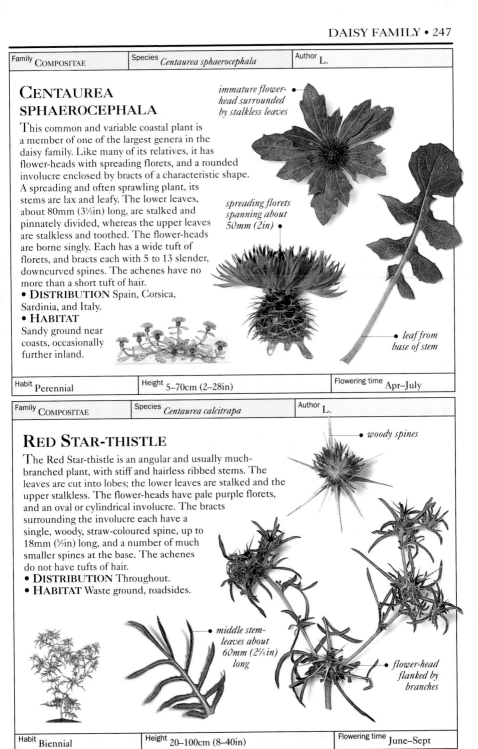

Family COMPOSITAE	Species *Centaurea sphaerocephala*	Author L.

CENTAUREA SPHAEROCEPHALA

This common and variable coastal plant is a member of one of the largest genera in the daisy family. Like many of its relatives, it has flower-heads with spreading florets, and a rounded involucre enclosed by bracts of a characteristic shape. A spreading and often sprawling plant, its stems are lax and leafy. The lower leaves, about 80mm (3⅛in) long, are stalked and pinnately divided, whereas the upper leaves are stalkless and toothed. The flower-heads are borne singly. Each has a wide tuft of florets, and bracts each with 5 to 13 slender, downcurved spines. The achenes have no more than a short tuft of hair.
• **DISTRIBUTION** Spain, Corsica, Sardinia, and Italy.
• **HABITAT** Sandy ground near coasts, occasionally further inland.

immature flower-head surrounded by stalkless leaves

spreading florets spanning about 50mm (2in)

leaf from base of stem

Habit Perennial	Height 5–70cm (2–28in)	Flowering time Apr–July

Family COMPOSITAE	Species *Centaurea calcitrapa*	Author L.

RED STAR-THISTLE

The Red Star-thistle is an angular and usually much-branched plant, with stiff and hairless ribbed stems. The leaves are cut into lobes; the lower leaves are stalked and the upper stalkless. The flower-heads have pale purple florets, and an oval or cylindrical involucre. The bracts surrounding the involucre each have a single, woody, straw-coloured spine, up to 18mm (⅝in) long, and a number of much smaller spines at the base. The achenes do not have tufts of hair.
• **DISTRIBUTION** Throughout.
• **HABITAT** Waste ground, roadsides.

woody spines

middle stem-leaves about 60mm (2⅖in) long

flower-head flanked by branches

Habit Biennial	Height 20–100cm (8–40in)	Flowering time June–Sept

Family COMPOSITAE	Species *Centaurea melitensis*	Author L.

MALTESE STAR-THISTLE

Maltese Star-thistle is an erect plant, branched
above, with stems that are winged towards their tips.
Its bright green leaves are often lobed at
the base of the plant and lance-shaped
above. The flower-heads grow singly,
or in groups of 2 to 3. The involucre is
round, and each bract has a long central
spine, flanked by one to 3 pairs of much
smaller spines. The fruit is an achene,
with a seed and hair-tuft of equal length.
• **DISTRIBUTION** Throughout.
• **HABITAT** Roadsides, waste ground.

bright yellow florets

spiny bracts

upper stem-leaves rarely more than 20mm (⅘in) long

Habit Annual/biennial	Height 25–60cm (10–24in)	Flowering time Apr–Aug

Family COMPOSITAE	Species *Centaurea solstitialis*	Author L.

YELLOW STAR-THISTLE

Yellow Star-thistle is usually a slender
and highly branched plant, with grey-
felted winged stems. The lower leaves
are lance-shaped and pinnately lobed;
the upper leaves are stalkless, narrow,
and untoothed. The solitary flower-
heads have yellow florets and a round
involucre, with bracts that each end
in a long straw-coloured spine. The
fruit is a black achene, with a tuft of
hair twice the length of the seed.
• **DISTRIBUTION** Throughout.
• **HABITAT** Waste ground, fields.

flower-head about 20mm (⅘in) across

radiating spines

pinnately lobed basal leaf

Habit Annual/biennial	Height 30–100cm (12–40in)	Flowering time July–Sept

Family COMPOSITAE	Species *Crupina crupinastrum*	Author (Moris) Vis.

CRUPINA CRUPINASTRUM

This slender plant is leafy only
on its lower half, the upper half
consisting of fine branches, each
carrying a single flower-head. The
stem-leaves have narrow lobes.
The flower-heads have a spindle-
shaped involucre, and produce
achenes with a tuft of golden hairs.
• **DISTRIBUTION** Throughout,
except mainland France.
• **HABITAT** Rocky ground.

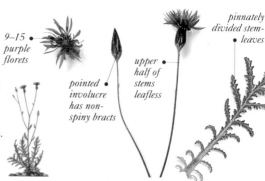

9–15 purple florets

pointed involucre has non-spiny bracts

pinnately divided stem-leaves

upper half of stems leafless

Habit Annual	Height 20–50cm (8–20in)	Flowering time May–July

Family COMPOSITAE	Species *Carthamus lanatus*	Author L.

CARTHAMUS LANATUS

Carthamus lanatus is a variable thistle-like plant with a strong smell, and stiff branching stems that are often covered with cobwebby hairs. The entire plant is leafy: the lower leaves are toothed and oval in outline, whereas the upper leaves have narrow lobes and partly clasp the stem. The flower-heads grow singly at the tips of the stems, and are about 30mm (1⅛in) long. They have bright yellow florets, spreading outwards to form a tuft, and are surrounded by a cluster of spiny leaves. The fruit is a dark brown achene that has scales fringed with hairs.
- **DISTRIBUTION** Throughout.
- **HABITAT** Fields, waste ground, roadsides.
- **RELATED SPECIES**
C. arborescens, from S. Spain, also has yellow flowers, but is a much larger, densely branched perennial.

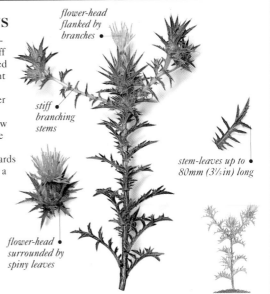

flower-head flanked by branches •

stiff • branching stems

stem-leaves up to • 80mm (3⅕in) long

flower-head • surrounded by spiny leaves

Habit Annual	Height 30–70cm (12–28in)	Flowering time June–Aug

Family COMPOSITAE	Species *Carduncellus caeruleus*	Author (L.) C. Presl

CARDUNCELLUS CAERULEUS

Many spiny-leaved members of the daisy family have purple or yellow flower-heads, but the lilac-blue colour of this plant is a little more unusual. Although very variable, it generally has stout, unbranched stems, each carrying a single flower-head, and its stems and the undersides of its leaves, which are about 10cm (4in) long, are often covered with woolly hairs. The lowest leaves are stalked, but the strap-like stem-leaves are stalkless, with spiny teeth. The flower-heads are clasped by spiny, leaf-like outer bracts, and they produce achenes with several rows of hairs.
- **DISTRIBUTION** Throughout, except Dalmatia.
- **HABITAT** Fields, waysides.
- **RELATED SPECIES**
Carduncellus monspelliensium, which grows in Spain, France, and Italy, is shorter or frequently stemless.

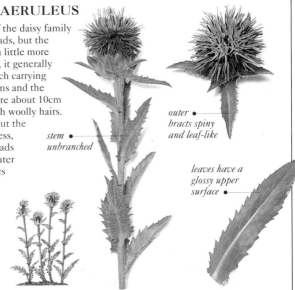

outer • bracts spiny and leaf-like

stem • unbranched

leaves have a glossy upper surface •

Habit Perennial	Height 30–60cm (12–24in)	Flowering time May–July

Family COMPOSITAE	Species *Scolymus hispanicus*	Author L.

SPANISH OYSTER PLANT

During the height of summer, the Spanish Oyster Plant's bright green leaves and yellow flowers stand out vividly against the scorched vegetation of sandy ground. A stout-looking, angular plant, it has irregularly branching stems that bear spiny, deeply cut, wavy-edged leaves. The stem-leaves reach a length of about 80mm (3⅛in), and merge with spiny wings that run a short distance down the stem. The flower-heads grow in the leaf-axils, with several being in flower on each stem. They have conspicuous ray-florets, and are clasped by spiny-tipped bracts. The fruit has short bristles, and it often has wing-like flaps.

• **DISTRIBUTION** Throughout.

• **HABITAT** Waste ground, coastal sand.

• **RELATED SPECIES** *Scolymus grandiflorus*, from the west of the region, is smaller but has larger flowers, couched by 3 very spiny, hairy bracts. The upper parts of its stems are continuously winged.

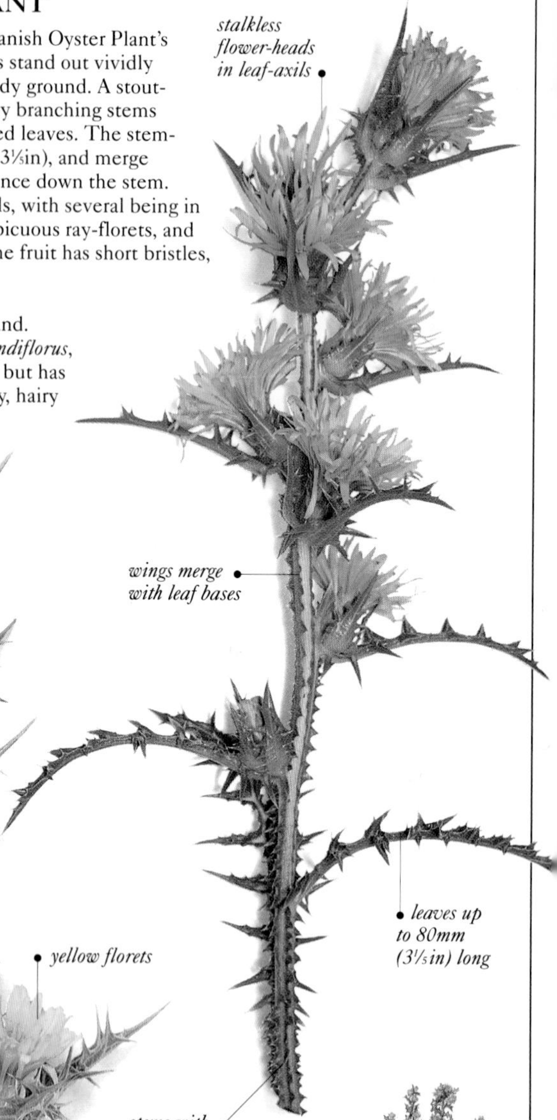

stalkless flower-heads in leaf-axils

wings merge with leaf bases

leaves up to 80mm (3⅛in) long

yellow florets

stems with short wings

bright green leaves

Habit Biennial/perennial	Height 20–80cm (8–32in)	Flowering time June–Sept

Family COMPOSITAE	Species *Cichorium intybus*	Author L.

CHICORY

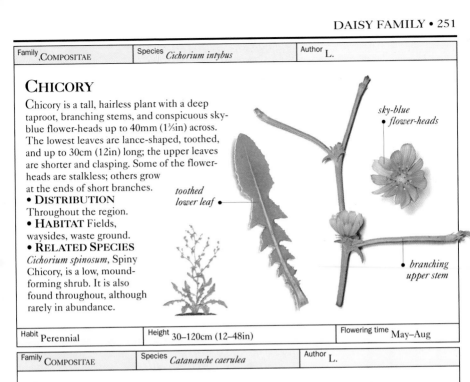

Chicory is a tall, hairless plant with a deep taproot, branching stems, and conspicuous sky-blue flower-heads up to 40mm (1⅜in) across. The lowest leaves are lance-shaped, toothed, and up to 30cm (12in) long; the upper leaves are shorter and clasping. Some of the flower-heads are stalkless; others grow at the ends of short branches.
• **DISTRIBUTION** Throughout the region.
• **HABITAT** Fields, waysides, waste ground.
• **RELATED SPECIES** *Cichorium spinosum*, Spiny Chicory, is a low, mound-forming shrub. It is also found throughout, although rarely in abundance.

sky-blue flower-heads

toothed lower leaf

branching upper stem

Habit Perennial	Height 30–120cm (12–48in)	Flowering time May–Aug

Family COMPOSITAE	Species *Catananche caerulea*	Author L.

CUPIDONE

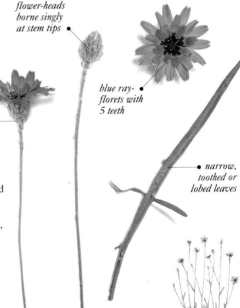

Although often grown as a garden flower, this elegant member of the daisy family is a wild plant of dry grassland in the western Mediterranean. Its leaves are linear and up to 30cm (12in) long, often with 2 to 4 narrow lobes or teeth. Almost all of them are clustered around the base of the fine, sparingly branched stems, which carry deep blue flower-heads, composed entirely of ray-florets. When fully open, the flower-heads measure about 60mm (2⅜in) across. The base of each flower-head is surrounded by paper-thin, silvery bracts, and similar but smaller scales extend some way down the stem. The fruit is an achene, with a row of narrow scales.
• **DISTRIBUTION** Eastwards to Italy.
• **HABITAT** Dry grassland, roadsides; particularly on limestone.
• **RELATED SPECIES** *Catananche lutea*, from the E. Mediterranean, is an annual species with yellow flowers. Its leaves are also clustered around the base of the stems.

flower-heads borne singly at stem tips

flower-head surrounded by translucent bracts

blue ray-florets with 5 teeth

narrow, toothed or lobed leaves

Habit Perennial	Height 20–90cm (8–36in)	Flowering time June–Sept

Family COMPOSITAE	Species *Hyoseris radiata*	Author L.

HYOSERIS RADIATA

Hyoseris radiata is one of a number of Mediterranean plants that are often dismissed as "dandelions". Like a dandelion, it has broad yellow flower-heads and leaves that form a rosette. However, instead of being flat, its leaves are narrow and deeply cut, and their overlapping lobes produce an almost corrugated appearance. The flower-heads are carried singly on leafless stems. They consist entirely of ray-florets, and measure about 40mm (1⅝in) in diameter when fully open. The outermost florets are often streaked with green or purple beneath, and the bracts cupping the florets are in 2 ranks, those in the inner rank being much the longest. The fruit is a brown achene with scales and stiff hairs.
• **DISTRIBUTION** Throughout.
• **HABITAT** Grassy ground, roadsides.
• **RELATED SPECIES** *H. scabra*, which is found throughout the Mediterranean region, is an annual species with flower-heads that are borne on lax, short stalks.

• *flower-head cupped by 2 rows of bracts*

ray-florets only

• *narrow lobed leaves up to 25cm (10in) long*

Habit Perennial	Height Up to 35cm (14in)	Flowering time All year round

Family COMPOSITAE	Species *Urospermum dalechampii*	Author (L.) Scop. ex F. W. Schmidt

UROSPERMUM DALECHAMPII

In good conditions, *Urospermum dalechampii* is a handsome plant, with numerous pale yellow flower-heads that can be 60mm (2⅜in) across. Its stems are covered with fine, downy hairs, and are surrounded by a rosette of pinnately divided lance-shaped leaves, up to 19cm (7½in) long. The stems also bear smaller leaves that are often untoothed, and these are stalkless and clasping. The flower-heads grow singly, and the hollow supporting stem broadens as it approaches the downy, cup-shaped involucre, which has a single row of broad bracts joined at the base. The flower-heads consist of ray-florets only, and those around the edge generally have a streak of red on their undersides. The fruit is a black achene with an oblique beak, and a tuft of dark, feathery hairs – unlike the "parachutes" formed by similar-looking dandelions (*Taraxacum* species).
• **DISTRIBUTION** W. Mediterranean, eastwards to Dalmatia.
• **HABITAT** Grassy ground, roadsides, field edges.

florets with 5 tiny teeth, sometimes black-tipped

downy stems •

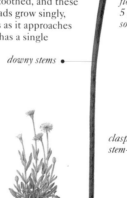

clasping stem-leaf •

• *divided basal leaf*

Habit Perennial	Height 25–40cm (10–16in)	Flowering time Mar–Aug

Family COMPOSITAE	Species *Tragopogon hybridus*	Author L.

TRAGOPOGON HYBRIDUS

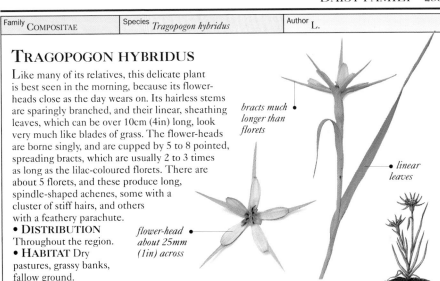

Like many of its relatives, this delicate plant is best seen in the morning, because its flower-heads close as the day wears on. Its hairless stems are sparingly branched, and their linear, sheathing leaves, which can be over 10cm (4in) long, look very much like blades of grass. The flower-heads are borne singly, and are cupped by 5 to 8 pointed, spreading bracts, which are usually 2 to 3 times as long as the lilac-coloured florets. There are about 5 florets, and these produce long, spindle-shaped achenes, some with a cluster of stiff hairs, and others with a feathery parachute.

bracts much longer than florets

linear leaves

- **DISTRIBUTION** Throughout the region.
- **HABITAT** Dry pastures, grassy banks, fallow ground.

flower-head about 25mm (1in) across

Habit Annual	Height 20–40cm (8–16in)	Flowering time Apr–June

Family COMPOSITAE	Species *Tragopogon porrifolius*	Author L.

SALSIFY

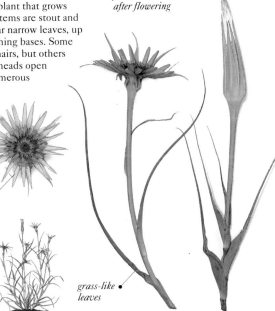

Salsify is a variable, grassy looking plant that grows from a long and tenacious root. Its stems are stout and occasionally branched, and they bear narrow leaves, up to 15cm (6in) long, with wide sheathing bases. Some plants are covered with cobwebby hairs, but others are practically hairless. The flower-heads open for just a few hours, and contain numerous florets that vary in colour from pale lilac to a deep reddish purple. They are cupped by narrow pointed bracts, which can be up to twice as long as the florets. After flowering, the bracts close up, but they later reopen to reveal a conspicuous spherical "clock" of achenes, each with a feathery parachute.

flower-head closes after flowering

florets lilac to reddish purple

- **DISTRIBUTION** Throughout; often cultivated.
- **HABITAT** Grassy ground, waysides, and road verges.
- **REMARK** The root is edible, and has a mild nutty flavour.

grass-like leaves

Habit Biennial	Height 20–125cm (8–50in)	Flowering time Apr–July

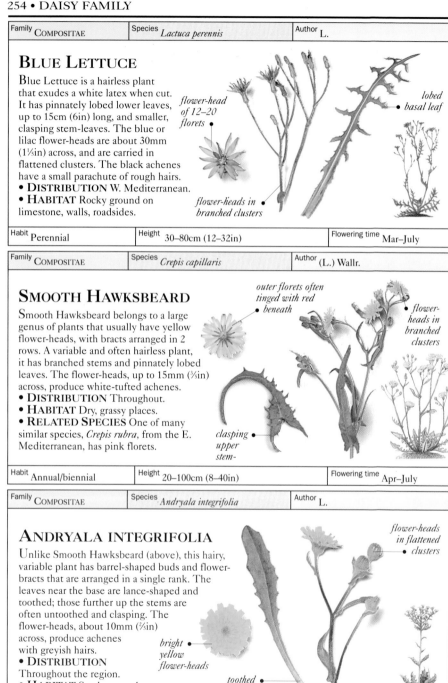

Family COMPOSITAE	Species *Lactuca perennis*	Author L.

BLUE LETTUCE

Blue Lettuce is a hairless plant that exudes a white latex when cut. It has pinnately lobed lower leaves, up to 15cm (6in) long, and smaller, clasping stem-leaves. The blue or lilac flower-heads are about 30mm (1⅕in) across, and are carried in flattened clusters. The black achenes have a small parachute of rough hairs.
• **DISTRIBUTION** W. Mediterranean.
• **HABITAT** Rocky ground on limestone, walls, roadsides.

flower-head of 12–20 florets

lobed basal leaf

flower-heads in branched clusters

Habit Perennial	Height 30–80cm (12–32in)	Flowering time Mar–July

Family COMPOSITAE	Species *Crepis capillaris*	Author (L.) Wallr.

SMOOTH HAWKSBEARD

Smooth Hawksbeard belongs to a large genus of plants that usually have yellow flower-heads, with bracts arranged in 2 rows. A variable and often hairless plant, it has branched stems and pinnately lobed leaves. The flower-heads, up to 15mm (⅗in) across, produce white-tufted achenes.
• **DISTRIBUTION** Throughout.
• **HABITAT** Dry, grassy places.
• **RELATED SPECIES** One of many similar species, *Crepis rubra*, from the E. Mediterranean, has pink florets.

outer florets often tinged with red beneath

flower-heads in branched clusters

clasping upper stem-

Habit Annual/biennial	Height 20–100cm (8–40in)	Flowering time Apr–July

Family COMPOSITAE	Species *Andryala integrifolia*	Author L.

ANDRYALA INTEGRIFOLIA

Unlike Smooth Hawksbeard (above), this hairy, variable plant has barrel-shaped buds and flower-bracts that are arranged in a single rank. The leaves near the base are lance-shaped and toothed; those further up the stems are often untoothed and clasping. The flower-heads, about 10mm (⅖in) across, produce achenes with greyish hairs.
• **DISTRIBUTION** Throughout the region.
• **HABITAT** Sandy ground.

flower-heads in flattened clusters

bright yellow flower-heads

toothed basal leaf

Habit Annual/perennial	Height 13–80cm (5–32in)	Flowering time Apr–July

MONOCOTYLEDONS

POSIDONIA FAMILY

Family POSIDONIACEAE	Species *Posidonia oceanica*	Author (L.) Delile

POSIDONIA OCEANICA

Posidonia oceanica is an abundant plant throughout much of the Mediterranean, but it is rarely seen as it grows entirely submerged in seawater. It forms dense "meadows" on the seabed, and its presence offshore is often indicated by mounds of strap-like scales, frequently mistaken for seaweed, that are washed up on beaches. It is also the source of *pelotes de mer* – round or oval balls of tiny fibres that are created by the rolling action of the waves and cast ashore. The plant grows from a creeping stem, and has strap-shaped leaves, up to 60cm (24in) long. Its flowers are green, and grow in clusters of 3 to 5. Unusually for a flowering plant, it is pollinated under water, and it produces fleshy fruit, about 10mm (⅜in) across.
- **DISTRIBUTION** Circum-Mediterranean.
- **HABITAT** Marine, growing in water up to 30m (100ft) deep.
- **RELATED SPECIES** The family includes only 2 other species, both of which grow off the coast of S. Australia.

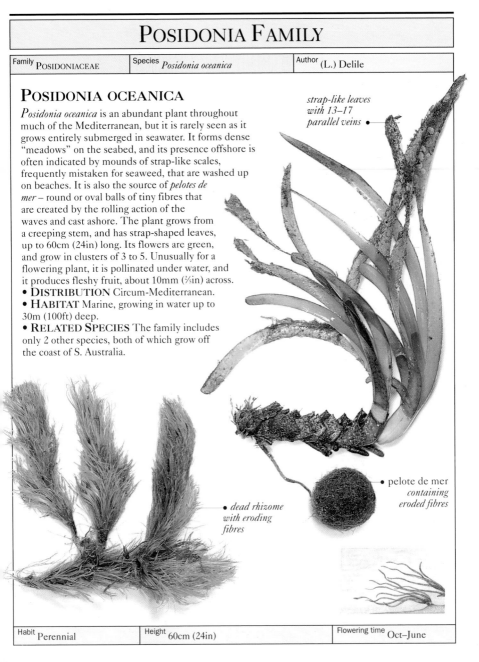

strap-like leaves with 13–17 parallel veins •

• *dead rhizome with eroding fibres*

• pelote de mer *containing eroded fibres*

Habit Perennial	Height 60cm (24in)	Flowering time Oct–June

LILY FAMILY

Family LILIACEAE	Species *Asphodelus fistulosus*	Author L.

HOLLOW-STEMMED ASPHODEL

The lily family includes a large and diverse collection of plants in the Mediterranean region, among them some species that have become rare as a result of unscrupulous collection. However, the asphodels are under no such threat. These robust, hairless plants are widespread, and can be seen on open ground of all kinds, particularly where there is overgrazing, or where the soil has been disturbed. The Hollow-stemmed Asphodel is a short-lived species with fibrous roots that often grows in dense swathes. It has hollow stems and leaves and, like most members of the lily family, its white flowers have 6 petal-like segments, or tepals. The flowers are borne singly on branching stems, and measure about 30mm (1⅛in) across. The fruit is a round capsule about 5mm (⅓in) in diameter.

• **DISTRIBUTION** Throughout.

• **HABITAT** Garigue, grassy banks, sandy ground, waysides; on poor, non-calcareous soils.

striped buds

DETAIL

• *tepals have a dark brown or pink central vein*

hollow • cylindrical leaves

• *flowering stems either branched or unbranched*

leaves all arise • from base of plant

Habit Perennial	Height Up to 75cm (30in)	Flowering time Feb–June

Family LILIACEAE	Species *Asphodelus aestivus*	Author Brot.

COMMON ASPHODEL

Common Asphodel is a tough, hairless perennial with
a grey-green hue that grows from thickened roots. Its
leaves, which are up to 30mm (1⅛in) across and
45cm (18in) long, all arise from the plant's base,
and are V-shaped and pointed, with a slightly
raised midrib on the underside. The flowers
are borne on a tall stem with numerous branches.
Each flower has a short stalk and is up to 40mm
(1⅝in) across, with white tepals that have a
reddish brown central vein. The fruit is a
round capsule about 7mm (⅜in) across.
• **DISTRIBUTION** Throughout.
• **HABITAT** Rocky ground, garigue, pasture.
• **REMARK** Common Asphodel is one of a
number of plants that have benefited greatly
from man-made changes in the Mediterranean
region. It is avoided by browsing animals, and
frequently increases to vast numbers where goats
or cattle keep other vegetation in check. Its starchy
roots are tasteless but edible, although they are not
used as food nowadays. They were at one time
gathered for use in the production of glue.

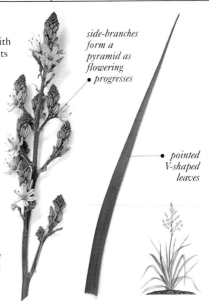

*side-branches
form a
pyramid as
flowering
• progresses*

*• pointed
V-shaped
leaves*

Habit Perennial	Height 50–150cm (20–60in)	Flowering time Feb–June

Family LILIACEAE	Species *Asphodelus albus*	Author Miller

WHITE ASPHODEL

Similar in form to Common Asphodel
(above), this species is distinguished by
its flowering stem, which rarely has any
branches, and by its long bracts, which
often give the young flower-heads a dark
appearance. Its leaves are usually channelled,
and measure up to 20mm (⅘in) across and 60cm
(24in) long. Its flowers have white tepals with a
dark brown or green central vein, and they grow
on short stalks that are exceeded in length by
the accompanying bracts. Each flower measures
up to 60mm (2⅜in) across, and produces a
capsule up to 25mm (1in) across.
• **DISTRIBUTION** W. and C. Mediterranean, as far east as Greece, but absent from
most islands; also C. and N.W. Europe.
• **HABITAT** Woods, grassy ground,
waysides, mountains.
• **REMARK** White
Asphodel is generally
less abundant than the
Common Asphodel.

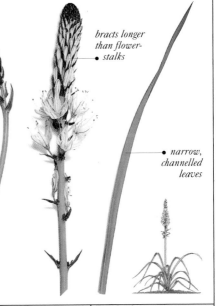

*bracts longer
than flower-
• stalks*

*• narrow,
channelled
leaves*

*unbranched •
flowering stem*

Habit Perennial	Height 50–125cm (20–50in)	Flowering time Apr–June

| Family LILIACEAE | Species *Asphodeline lutea* | Author (L.) Reichenb. |

YELLOW ASPHODEL

Like the Common Asphodel, *Asphodelus aestivus* (see p.257), this conspicuous plant is often a sign of overgrazed land. It, too, has fleshy roots, but its thick stems are leafy for their entire length. The basal leaves are 35cm (14in) long, whereas the leaves further up the stem are progessively shorter. The deep yellow flowers grow on short stalks and have 6 narrow, slightly unequal tepals. The fruit capsule contains black, 3-sided seeds.
• **DISTRIBUTION** C. and E. Mediterranean, N.W. Africa.
• **HABITAT** Rocky hillsides, garigue.
• **RELATED SPECIES** *A. liburnica*, found in the Balkans, Crete, and S. Italy, is a shorter species, with narrower leaves.

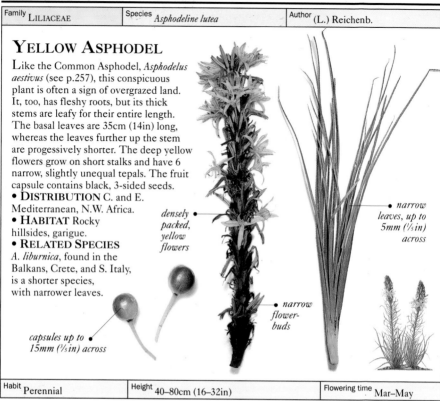

densely packed, yellow flowers

narrow flower-buds

narrow leaves, up to 5mm (¹/₅in) across

capsules up to 15mm (⁵/₈in) across

| Habit Perennial | Height 40–80cm (16–32in) | Flowering time Mar–May |

| Family LILIACEAE | Species *Aphyllanthes monspeliensis* | Author L. |

APHYLLANTHES MONSPELIENSIS

When not in flower, *Aphyllanthes monspeliensis* looks deceptively like a dense clump of rushes. Its stems are hairless, stiff, and ridged, and its leaves are reduced to narrow sheaths that clasp each stem at its base. When the plant does flower, its true identity becomes apparent. The flowers grow in clusters of one to 3 at the stem tips, and are clasped by papery bracts. They are generally pale blue, or very occasionally white, and have 6 blunt-tipped tepals, each with a dark central vein. They produce capsules containing 3 black seeds.
• **DISTRIBUTION** W. Mediterranean, eastwards to N. Italy.
• **HABITAT** Garigue, grassy places, waysides, and road verges.

flowers about 25mm (1in) across

non-flowering stem

papery bracts beneath flowers

narrow, rush-like stems

| Habit Perennial | Height 20–50cm (8–20in) | Flowering time Apr–July |

Family LILIACEAE	Species *Colchicum autumnale*	Author L.

AUTUMN CROCUS

Also known as Meadow Saffron, this attractive but poisonous plant flowers in autumn, when its leaves have yet to develop. It grows from an underground corm, and its flowers appear either singly or in clusters of up to 6. They have 6 tepals, joined to form a long tube, and 6 stamens. The fruit is a green capsule, about 30mm (1⅛in) long, which is clasped at ground level by the glossy, strap-shaped leaves.
• **DISTRIBUTION** W. and C. Mediterranean, eastwards to Greece; also north to British Isles.
• **HABITAT** Meadows, grassy ground, waysides, open woods.

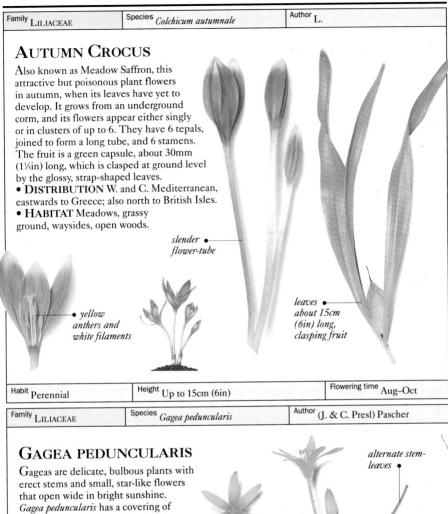

slender •
flower-tube

• *yellow anthers and white filaments*

leaves •
about 15cm
(6in) long,
clasping fruit

Habit Perennial	Height Up to 15cm (6in)	Flowering time Aug–Oct

Family LILIACEAE	Species *Gagea peduncularis*	Author (J. & C. Presl) Pascher

GAGEA PEDUNCULARIS

Gageas are delicate, bulbous plants with erect stems and small, star-like flowers that open wide in bright sunshine. *Gagea peduncularis* has a covering of short hairs, and 2 thread-like basal leaves. Its stem-leaves are broader and alternate, and sometimes have hairy margins. The flowers are bright yellow above, greenish below, and are about 25mm (1in) across when fully open. They have downy stalks, and grow in clusters of one to 3. The fruit is a small capsule.
• **DISTRIBUTION** Balkans, Aegean region, including Crete.
• **HABITAT** Hillsides, stony ground.
• **REMARK** There are many similar species of *Gagea* in the region. They are known collectively as yellow stars of Bethlehem.

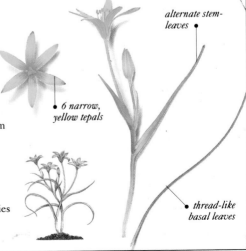

alternate stem-leaves •

• *6 narrow, yellow tepals*

• *thread-like basal leaves*

Habit Perennial	Height Up to 10cm (4in)	Flowering time Jan–Apr

Family LILIACEAE	Species *Gagea graeca*	Author (L.) A. Terracc.

GAGEA GRAECA

Formerly classified as *Lloydia graeca*, this slender and hairless plant is easily distinguished from most other gageas (see p.259) by its white, trumpet-shaped flowers. It grows from a small bulb, and has 2 to 4 linear basal leaves, while the stem carries a small number of lance-shaped leaves, arranged alternately. The flowers are stalked, and grow in loose clusters of 3 to 5. Each one has 6 separate tepals, up to 15mm (⅝in) long and streaked with purple on the outside, and these overlap to form a funnel. The flowers are initially nodding, but they turn upwards as they open. The fruit is a many-seeded capsule.
• **DISTRIBUTION** S. Greece, Aegean region, including Crete.
• **HABITAT** Rocky ground, rough hill pasture, cliffs, walls, waysides.
• **RELATED SPECIES** *Gagea trinervia*, from N. Africa and Sicily, has solitary white flowers.

tepals with round lobes

flowers streaked with purple

funnel-shaped flowers

stem-leaves arranged alternately

Habit Perennial	Height 5–25cm (2–10in)	Flowering time Apr–May

Family LILIACEAE	Species *Tulipa biflora*	Author Pallas

TULIPA BIFLORA

Tulips are bulbous perennials with showy flowers, and relatively few but often rather broad leaves. Over a dozen species are native to the European part of the Mediterranean region, but in addition to these, others have been introduced into cultivation from further afield. As a wild plant, *Tulipa biflora* barely touches on the borders of the Mediterranean, but it is sometimes seen in cultivation. It has just 2 leaves, which are deeply channelled and sometimes wavy-edged, and it produces between one and 4 star-shaped flowers on short stems. The flowers open widely in bright sunshine. They have narrow, lance-shaped tepals, which are reddish green below, and white above with a yellow base. The fruit is a small capsule.
• **DISTRIBUTION** C. Balkans, extending to C. Asia.
• **HABITAT** Open, rocky or grassy ground.

yellow stamens

1–4 flowers

2 leaves only

narrow tepals white and yellow above

Habit Perennial	Height Up to 18cm (7in)	Flowering time Apr–June

Family LILIACEAE	Species *Tulipa clusiana*	Author DC.

LADY TULIP

Although native to the region from Iran to northern Pakistan, the Lady Tulip has been cultivated in the Mediterranean region for several hundred years, and has become naturalized in some areas. It has up to 5 narrow, channelled leaves, up to 30cm (12in) long. The flowers, up to 60mm (2⅜in) long, grow singly on slender stalks. Their tepals are white, the outermost 3 being slightly larger and suffused with red on the outside, and all 6 have a purple blotch at the base of the inward face. The stamens are dark purple and hairless. The fruit is a capsule, which is about 10mm (⅜in) long.
• **DISTRIBUTION** Sporadic in France, Italy, and Greece.
• **HABITAT** In and near cultivated ground.
• **REMARK** Many other species of tulip have been introduced into the region, particularly from C. Asia, and have been used to produce today's large-flowered hybrids. Few of these are established in the wild.

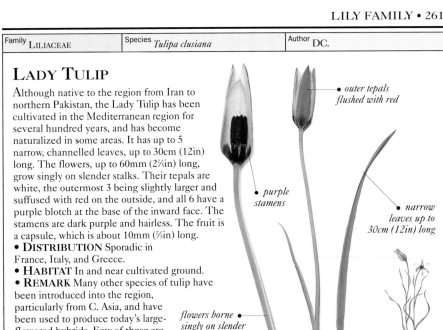

• *outer tepals flushed with red*

• *purple stamens*

• *narrow leaves up to 30cm (12in) long*

flowers borne singly on slender stalks

Habit Perennial	Height Up to 35cm (14in)	Flowering time Mar–May

Family LILIACEAE	Species *Tulipa orphanidea*	Author Boiss. ex Heldr.

TULIPA ORPHANIDEA

In some parts of the Mediterranean, tulips are weeds of cultivation, and they bring a blaze of colour to fields before dying back for the summer. Changing farming practices mean that this mass flowering is an increasingly rare sight, but in some places *Tulipa orphanidea* still blooms in abundance for a few weeks each spring. This variable plant has up to 7 channelled, linear leaves, and one to 3 orange or reddish flowers, up to 50mm (2in) long, which often remain tinged with green on the outside. The tepals usually have a dark patch at the base of the interior face.
• **DISTRIBUTION** Balkans, W. Crete, Turkey.
• **HABITAT** Rocky ground, cultivated fields.
• **RELATED SPECIES** *T. boetica*, sometimes known as *T. undulatifolia*, also grows in fields in the Balkans and Turkey, although not in Crete. It has wavy-edged leaves, and dark bases on the outside of the tepals. Its tepals have sharp points.

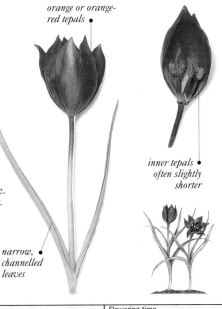

orange or orange-red tepals •

inner tepals • often slightly shorter

narrow, • channelled leaves

Habit Perennial	Height Up to 30cm (12in)	Flowering time Mar–May

Family LILIACEAE	Species *Tulipa saxatilis*	Author Sieber ex Sprengel

TULIPA SAXATILIS

This exceptionally attractive tulip has 2 to 3 strap-shaped leaves, up to 40cm (16in) long, with distinctively glossy upper surfaces. The flowers are borne either singly or in a group of up to 3, and have lilac-coloured tepals flushed with yellow towards their bases. This species rarely forms seeds, and instead spreads vegetatively by means of white blunt-tipped stolons which grow from the base of the bulb. Each one forms a new bulb some distance from the parent plant.
• **DISTRIBUTION** Crete and Turkey.
• **HABITAT** Rocky ground, stony places, meadows.
• **RELATED SPECIES** *Tulipa cretica* is similar and also spreads by means of stolons, but it has non-glossy, channelled leaves. It is found only in Crete.

lilac tepals with yellow bases

leaves have glossy upper surfaces

yellow anthers

Habit Perennial	Height Up to 25cm (10in)	Flowering time Mar–May

Family LILIACEAE	Species *Tulipa sylvestris*	Author L.

WILD TULIP

Of all the tulips found in the region, this species is the most widespread. It can be seen in large numbers on some rocky hillsides, although it is always sporadic and is absent from many areas. It has 2 to 4 narrow and channelled leaves, up to 30cm (12in) long, often with a blue-green hue. The flowers are generally solitary, and are nodding when in bud. They have yellow, pointed tepals up to 70mm (2⅜in) long, the outer 3 usually being flushed with green or red on the outside. As with other tulips, the overall appearance of the flowers depends very much on the weather. In cool or windy conditions, the flowers look bullet-shaped, but in still and hot weather they open out until they are star-like, with the outer tepals sometimes curving back. Like *Tulipa saxatilis* (above), this species often spreads by stolons.
• **DISTRIBUTION** Throughout.
• **HABITAT** Rocky hillsides, woods, waysides; often cultivated.

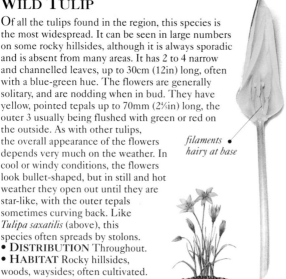

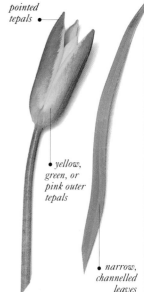

pointed tepals

filaments hairy at base

yellow, green, or pink outer tepals

narrow, channelled leaves

Habit Perennial	Height 10–45cm (4–18in)	Flowering time Apr–May

Family LILIACEAE	Species *Fritillaria messanensis*	Author Rafin.

FRITILLARIA MESSANENSIS

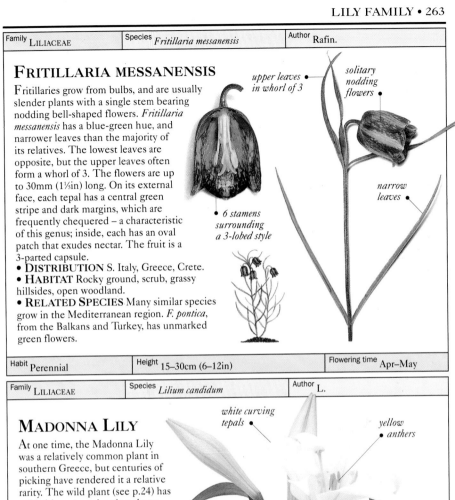

Fritillaries grow from bulbs, and are usually slender plants with a single stem bearing nodding bell-shaped flowers. *Fritillaria messanensis* has a blue-green hue, and narrower leaves than the majority of its relatives. The lowest leaves are opposite, but the upper leaves often form a whorl of 3. The flowers are up to 30mm (1⅛in) long. On its external face, each tepal has a central green stripe and dark margins, which are frequently chequered – a characteristic of this genus; inside, each has an oval patch that exudes nectar. The fruit is a 3-parted capsule.

- **DISTRIBUTION** S. Italy, Greece, Crete.
- **HABITAT** Rocky ground, scrub, grassy hillsides, open woodland.
- **RELATED SPECIES** Many similar species grow in the Mediterranean region. *F. pontica*, from the Balkans and Turkey, has unmarked green flowers.

upper leaves in whorl of 3

solitary nodding flowers

narrow leaves

6 stamens surrounding a 3-lobed style

Habit Perennial	Height 15–30cm (6–12in)	Flowering time Apr–May

Family LILIACEAE	Species *Lilium candidum*	Author L.

MADONNA LILY

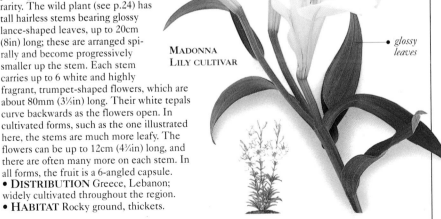

At one time, the Madonna Lily was a relatively common plant in southern Greece, but centuries of picking have rendered it a relative rarity. The wild plant (see p.24) has tall hairless stems bearing glossy lance-shaped leaves, up to 20cm (8in) long; these are arranged spirally and become progressively smaller up the stem. Each stem carries up to 6 white and highly fragrant, trumpet-shaped flowers, which are about 80mm (3⅛in) long. Their white tepals curve backwards as the flowers open. In cultivated forms, such as the one illustrated here, the stems are much more leafy. The flowers can be up to 12cm (4¾in) long, and there are often many more on each stem. In all forms, the fruit is a 6-angled capsule.

- **DISTRIBUTION** Greece, Lebanon; widely cultivated throughout the region.
- **HABITAT** Rocky ground, thickets.

white curving tepals

yellow anthers

MADONNA LILY CULTIVAR

glossy leaves

Habit Perennial	Height Up to 100cm (40in)	Flowering time May–June

Family LILIACEAE	Species *Ornithogalum arabicum*	Author L.

ORNITHOGALUM ARABICUM

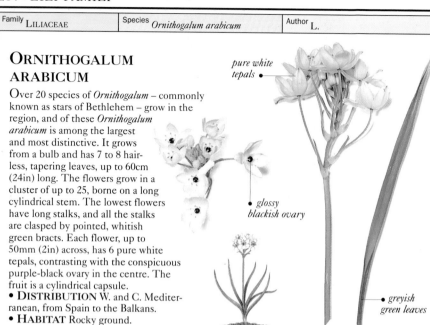

pure white tepals •

• glossy blackish ovary

• greyish green leaves

Over 20 species of *Ornithogalum* – commonly known as stars of Bethlehem – grow in the region, and of these *Ornithogalum arabicum* is among the largest and most distinctive. It grows from a bulb and has 7 to 8 hairless, tapering leaves, up to 60cm (24in) long. The flowers grow in a cluster of up to 25, borne on a long cylindrical stem. The lowest flowers have long stalks, and all the stalks are clasped by pointed, whitish green bracts. Each flower, up to 50mm (2in) across, has 6 pure white tepals, contrasting with the conspicuous purple-black ovary in the centre. The fruit is a cylindrical capsule.
• **DISTRIBUTION** W. and C. Mediterranean, from Spain to the Balkans.
• **HABITAT** Rocky ground.

Habit Perennial	Height 30–80cm (12–32in)	Flowering time Apr–May

Family LILIACEAE	Species *Ornithogalum narbonense*	Author L.

ORNITHOGALUM NARBONENSE

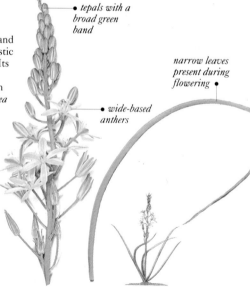

• tepals with a broad green band

narrow leaves present during flowering •

• wide-based anthers

Ornithogalum narbonense is a widespread and easily recognized plant, with a characteristic spire of 20 to 50 greenish white flowers. Its flowering stems are surrounded by 4 to 6 linear and channelled leaves, up to 16mm (⅝in) wide. Unlike the much taller *Urginea maritima* (opposite), its leaves are always present during flowering. The flowers, about 25mm (1in) across, have white tepals with a broad green stripe. Initially, the flower-stalks are held outwards, but as the fruit begins to form, they close up against the stem.
• **DISTRIBUTION** Throughout.
• **HABITAT** All kinds of open ground, from rocky scrub and grassy hillsides to fields, vineyards, and roadsides.
• **RELATED SPECIES** *O. pyrenaicum*, Bath Asparagus, has yellowish green flowers, and its leaves usually wither before the flowers appear.

Habit Perennial	Height Up to 60cm (24in)	Flowering time May–July

Family LILIACEAE	Species *Ornithogalum umbellatum*	Author L.

STAR OF BETHLEHEM

The Star of Bethlehem is a common wayside plant, with an umbel-like cluster of up to 20 flowers. Its hairless leaves are up to 5mm (⅕in) wide, and have a thin white stripe on the upper surfaces. The flowers, up to 40mm (1⅗in) across, have white uppersides and a broad green stripe on the underside. In dull weather, they quickly close. The fruit is an oval capsule.

• **DISTRIBUTION** Throughout, extending northwards through Europe, and naturalized in Scandinavia and the British Isles.

• **HABITAT** Rocky or grassy ground, fallow ground, road verges; frequently cultivated.

• **RELATED SPECIES** *Ornithogalum collinum*, a similar and widespread species, has a very short flowering stem, barely rising above ground level.

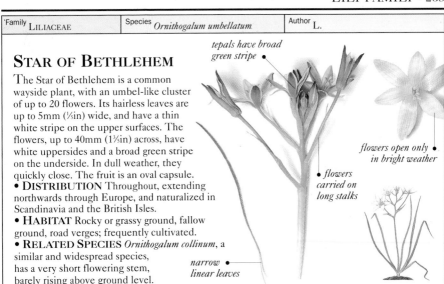

tepals have broad green stripe •

flowers open only • in bright weather

• flowers carried on long stalks

narrow • linear leaves

Habit Perennial	Height 20–30cm (8–12in)	Flowering time Mar–May

Family LILIACEAE	Species *Urginea maritima*	Author (L.) Baker

SEA SQUILL

The Sea Squill is one of the Mediterranean's most characteristic plants, flowering in late summer after its leaves have died away. It grows from a huge bulb, up to 15cm (6in) across, which is often only half-buried in the ground. The leaves are up to 100cm (40in) long and 10cm (4in) wide. By early summer they wither away and, from late July onwards, a single flowering stem, up to 150cm (60in) high, gradually develops. This bears several hundred star-like flowers, up to 15mm (⅗in) across, each with 6 white tepals that have a dark central stripe. The fruit is a 3-sided capsule containing winged seeds. Both the bulbs and leaves are poisonous.

• **DISTRIBUTION** Throughout.

• **HABITAT** Open rocky, sandy, or fallow ground, usually near the coast.

• **REMARK** The Sea Squill often dominates large areas of coastal land. Its leaves are avoided by browsing goats. Extracts from the bulbs were once used as medicines and rat poison.

glossy, strap-like leaves •

star-shaped • flowers

thick roots •

• bulb often protrudes above ground

Habit Perennial	Height Up to 150cm (60in)	Flowering time July–Oct

Family LILIACEAE	Species *Scilla autumnalis*	Author L.

AUTUMN SQUILL

This widespread plant is one of the few autumn-flowering squills in the region. It has 5 to 10 narrow and channelled hairless leaves, up to 15cm (6in) long, which begin to grow as the flowers appear. The bell-shaped flowers grow in a raceme containing 6 to 20 blooms, and are about 5mm (⅛in) long, with upward pointing stalks. The fruit is a small capsule containing black seeds.
• **DISTRIBUTION** Throughout.
• **HABITAT** Rocky and grassy ground, cultivated ground, waysides, and road verges.

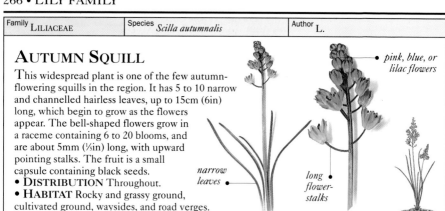

pink, blue, or lilac flowers

narrow leaves

long flower-stalks

Habit Perennial	Height 5–20cm (2–8in)	Flowering time Sept–Nov

Family LILIACEAE	Species *Scilla peruviana*	Author L.

SCILLA PERUVIANA

Despite its exotic appearance and name, this very variable squill is native to the western Mediterranean. Its grows from a large bulb, and has linear and rather lax leaves up to 60cm (24in) long and 40mm (1⅜in) wide. Its flowers grow in a dense conical raceme, containing 20 to 100 blooms. The lowest have long stalks with noticeable bracts, while the uppermost are almost stalkless. Its fruit is a capsule with a pointed beak.
• **DISTRIBUTION** W. Mediterranean, from N. Africa to Italy; absent from Balearic Islands and Corsica.
• **HABITAT** Grassy ground, woodland, waysides.

flowers blue or, rarely, white

strap-like leaves

slight channel

Habit Perennial	Height Up to 50cm (20in)	Flowering time Mar–May

Family LILIACEAE	Species *Muscari armeniacum*	Author Leichtlin ex Baker

MUSCARI ARMENIACUM

This variable grape hyacinth, with its sky-blue flowers, is the parent of many cultivated varieties. It has 3 to 5 narrow, linear leaves, up to 30cm (12in) long, and its flowers grow in a densely packed raceme, up to 50mm (2in) high. Each flower is barrel-shaped, with a white or pale rim that has 5 small and spreading teeth. The fruit capsule has 3 flattened valves.
• **DISTRIBUTION** Balkans, Turkey.
• **HABITAT** Rocky and grassy ground, open woodland.

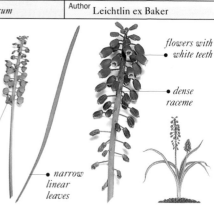

flowers with white teeth

dense raceme

fruiting head

narrow linear leaves

Habit Perennial	Height 10–40cm (4–16in)	Flowering time Feb–May

Family LILIACEAE	Species *Muscari comosum*	Author (L.) Miller

TASSEL HYACINTH

The Tassel Hyacinth is a distinctive, widespread plant, easily recognized by its purple or electric-blue "tassel", which is made of small infertile flowers with long stalks. The plant has 3 to 5 linear and channelled leaves, up to 40cm (16in) long, these usually being shorter than the flower-stalk. The flower-head is often over 20cm (8in) long, and has an open appearance. The fertile flowers are brown with pale greenish yellow teeth, and are widely separated. As they mature, they droop downwards. The infertile flowers, at the top of the flower-head, are more densely crowded, and have upswept stalks. The fruit is a 3-valved capsule, which is up to 15mm (⅗in) long.

• **DISTRIBUTION** Throughout.

• **HABITAT** Scrub and grassy ground; common on grassy banks and road verges.

• **RELATED SPECIES** A number of other species also have brownish fertile flowers. They include *Muscari cycladicum*, from the Aegean region, and *M. gussonei*, from Italy and Sicily. Both have short-stalked fertile flowers, and much smaller tassels.

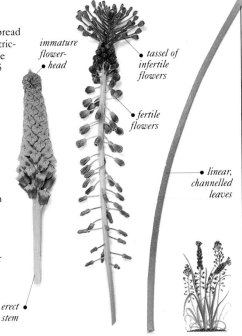

immature flower-head •

• tassel of infertile flowers

• fertile flowers

• linear, channelled leaves

erect • stem

Habit Perennial	Height 15–50cm (6–20in)	Flowering time Mar–May

Family LILIACEAE	Species *Muscari neglectum*	Author Guss. ex Ten.

COMMON GRAPE HYACINTH

Although variable in colour, the Common Grape Hyacinth is usually much darker than *Muscari armeniacum* (opposite). It has 3 to 6 linear and channelled leaves, which are up to 40cm (16in) long, and a compact flower-head. The uppermost flowers are usually light blue, small, and sterile, whereas the flowers below are blackish blue with white recurved teeth. It is only these lower flowers that form fruit.

• **DISTRIBUTION** Throughout the region.

• **HABITAT** Rocky and grassy ground, olive groves, open scrub, waysides.

• **RELATED SPECIES** *M. commutatum*, also shown here, is very similar, but lacks white teeth. It is found in Italy and the Balkans.

light blue • sterile flowers

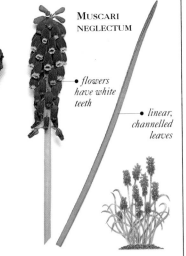

MUSCARI NEGLECTUM

• flowers have white teeth

• linear, channelled leaves

MUSCARI COMMUTATUM

Habit Perennial	Height Up to 30cm (12in)	Flowering time Feb–May

Family LILIACEAE	Species *Allium roseum*	Author L.

ROSY GARLIC

Like all its numerous relatives in the genus *Allium*, Rosy Garlic grows from a bulb, and produces a strong and lingering smell when crushed. Its hairless flowering stems are sheathed near their bases by 2 to 4 narrow leaves. These are up to 35cm (14in) long, and are often glossy, sometimes with rough margins. As with other onions and garlics, the flowers grow in dense umbels, which are initially enclosed by papery spathes. In this species, the umbels are hemispherical, and up to 70mm (2⅜in) across. Each one contains 5 to 30 pale pink, bell-shaped blooms up to 12mm (½in) long, on long stalks. In some plants, the umbels also contain small bulbils, which eventually fall to produce new plants. The fruit is a small capsule containing black seeds.
• **DISTRIBUTION**
Throughout the region.
• **HABITAT** Grassy open ground, roadsides.

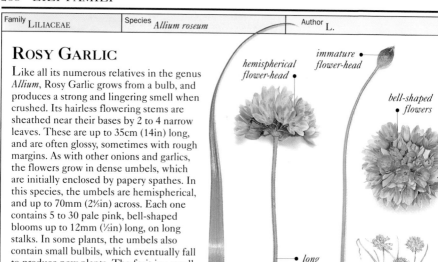

hemispherical flower-head

immature flower-head

bell-shaped flowers

long stalk

narrow leaves without keel

Habit Perennial	Height Up to 65cm (26in)	Flowering time Mar–June

Family LILIACEAE	Species *Allium neapolitanum*	Author Cyr.

NAPLES GARLIC

This mild-smelling species is one of the most widespread white-flowered garlics in the Mediterranean region. Its flowering stems have a distinctive cross-section, with 2 wings separating a roughly flat face from one that is more rounded. The leaves, usually 2 to 3 in number, are up to 35cm (14in) long. They sheathe the stem for about a quarter of its length, and each has a prominent keel on its underside. The star-shaped flowers are up to 20mm (⅘in) long, and are borne in a roughly hemispherical umbel up to 90mm (3½in) across. Initially, the flower-head is enclosed by a single papery spathe, and this remains attached after the flowers have opened. The fruit capsules are surrounded by the dried tepals, and the dead flower-heads often persist for many months.
• **DISTRIBUTION**
Throughout the region.
• **HABITAT** Grassy ground, fields, roadsides, woodland edges, gardens.

star-shaped flowers

flowering stems with 2 wings

spathe splits as flowers open

flat leaves with keel

Habit Perennial	Height 20–50cm (8–20in)	Flowering time Feb–May

Family LILIACEAE	Species *Allium subhirsutum*	Author L.

ALLIUM SUBHIRSUTUM

A smaller and more delicate plant than Naples Garlic (opposite), this species can be recognized by its leaves, which have spreading hairs along their margins. The hairs are very fine, but are easily visible when a leaf is seen against the light. The leaves are narrow and keeled, and up to 45cm (18in) long, and they sheathe the base of the stem. The flowers grow in a sparse umbel up to 70mm (2⅘in) across, with the papery spathe attached. Each flower has a long stalk, white tepals, and brown or yellow anthers. The fruit is a small capsule, up to 3mm (⅛in) long.

• **DISTRIBUTION** Throughout the region.

• **HABITAT** Open forests, scrub, garigue, often near the coast; also cultivated.

• **RELATED SPECIES** *Allium trifoliatum*, from the C. and E. Mediterranean, also has leaves with hairy margins, but its flowers are often streaked with pink. *A. subvillosum*, which grows in Spain, the Balearic Islands, and N. Africa, has densely packed umbels of white flowers. It is usually found on sandy ground near the coast.

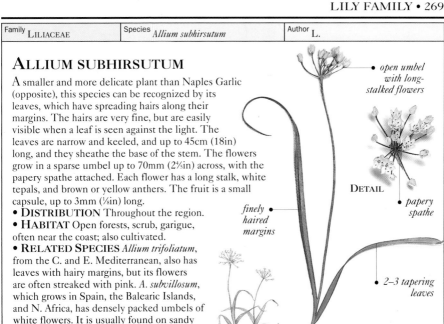

open umbel with long-stalked flowers

DETAIL

papery spathe

finely haired margins

2–3 tapering leaves

Habit Perennial	Height Up to 30cm (12in)	Flowering time Apr–June

Family LILIACEAE	Species *Allium triquetrum*	Author L.

THREE-CORNERED LEEK

The Three-cornered Leek frequently grows in large swathes, and from a distance often looks more like a white-flowered bluebell than a member of the genus *Allium*. However, its strong smell when crushed soon reveals its real identity. The flowering stems are distinctive, with a triangular cross-section and 3 sharp wings. The stems are sheathed at the base by 2 to 3 flat, tapering leaves, up to 40cm (16in) long, which are narrow and keeled. The 3 to 15 flowers are white with green central streaks, relatively narrow, and up to 18mm (⅗in) long. Their tepals are pointed, and the stamens hidden within the flower. Instead of forming a domed flower-head, they grow in a characteristic lopsided umbel with a persistent spathe.

• **DISTRIBUTION** W. Mediterranean, from Spain to Italy. Naturalized as far north as southern Great Britain.

• **HABITAT** Woods, grassy ground, waysides, road verges, usually where damp; also cultivated.

• **RELATED SPECIES** *A. pendulinum*, from the C. Mediterranean, is a similar species with smaller flowers.

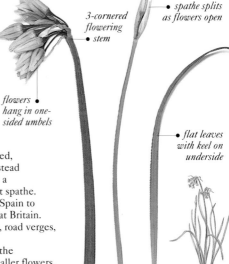

3-cornered flowering stem

spathe splits as flowers open

flowers hang in one-sided umbels

flat leaves with keel on underside

Habit Perennial	Height 10–45cm (4–18in)	Flowering time Mar–May

Family LILIACEAE	Species *Allium ampeloprasum*	Author L.

WILD LEEK

The Wild Leek is a very variable plant, with an overall bluish green tinge. Some specimens are extremely robust and reach head height, but others are much smaller. The leaves, up to 50cm (20in) long, sheathe the lower half or third of the stem, and are flat and tapering. They are arranged alternately, and have minute white teeth, both on the keel and along their margins. Up to 500 flowers, about 5mm (⅕in) long, are packed into a dense ball-shaped head, which can be 80mm (3⅛in) across. Initially, the flower-head is covered by a papery spathe, but this splits and then falls away as the flowers open. The flowers range in colour from white and pink to a deep red, and they produce small capsules with black seeds.
• **DISTRIBUTION** Throughout the region.
• **HABITAT** Fields, waysides, disturbed ground.
• **REMARK** This species is believed to be the ancestor of the cultivated leek, *Allium ampeloprasum* var. *porrum*, or *A. porrum*.

spathe shed as flower-head develops

flowers tightly packed in dense umbel

thick stem

tapering leaves with toothed margins

Habit Perennial	Height 45–180cm (18–72in)	Flowering time May–Aug

Family LILIACEAE	Species *Allium nigrum*	Author L.

ALLIUM NIGRUM

This majestic *Allium* is often seen in cultivated ground, particularly in olive groves in the east of the region. Its 3 to 6 leaves are flat and strap-like, the largest being up to 50cm (20in) long and 80mm (3⅛in) across. They surround the base of the stem, and are attached at or below ground level. The flower-head is carried on a tall cylindrical stem, and is up to 10cm (4in) in diameter. It is densely packed, and is either hemispherical or shaped like an inverted cone. The flowers range in colour from white to lilac. Their tepals are narrow and elliptical, and have green mid-veins, and their ovaries are either black or dark green. The flowers produce capsules up to 8mm (⅓in) long.
• **DISTRIBUTION** Throughout the region.
• **HABITAT** Fields, olive groves, fallow ground.
• **RELATED SPECIES** *A. atropurpureum*, which grows in the N. Balkans and Turkey, is similar but smaller, with purple flower-heads which are up to 70mm (2⅘in) in diameter.

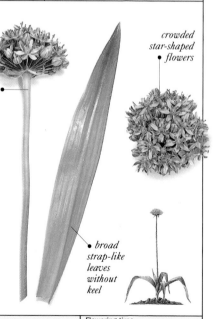

crowded star-shaped flowers

cylindrical flowering stem

broad strap-like leaves without keel

Habit Perennial	Height 60–90cm (24–36in)	Flowering time May–June

Family LILIACEAE	Species *Asparagus acutifolius*	Author L.

ASPARAGUS ACUTIFOLIUS

Asparaguses grow from rhizomes, and generally have straggling stems and a feathery appearance. *Asparagus acutifolius* is one of several woody species in the region. Its pale stems bear what appear to be needle-like leaves, up to 8mm (⅓in) long, in clusters of 10 to 30. As with other asparaguses, these "leaves" are actually cladodes – short, slender stems that have taken over the function of leaves – and the true leaves are reduced to small scales. The small yellowish flowers, about 4mm (⅛in) long, are roughly tubular and have 6 tepals, fused almost to their tips. Male and female flowers grow on separate plants, the female flowers producing berries that turn black when ripe.
• **DISTRIBUTION** Throughout the region.
• **HABITAT** Woods, maquis, garigue.
• **RELATED SPECIES** *A. albus*, found in N. Africa, Spain, and the Balkans, is similar, but has white stems.

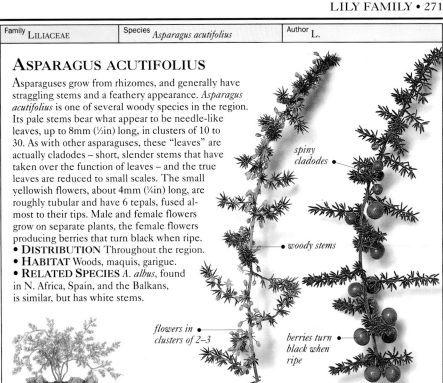

spiny cladodes

woody stems

flowers in clusters of 2–3

berries turn black when ripe

Habit Perennial	Height Up to 200cm (80in)	Flowering time Apr–June

Family LILIACEAE	Species *Asparagus officinalis*	Author L.

COMMON ASPARAGUS

Long cultivated for its edible shoots, this widespread and variable plant has herbaceous rather than woody stems. Its soft, leaf-like cladodes grow in bunches of 4 to 15, and are up to 25mm (1in) long. They are usually pressed close to the stem. The pale yellow or green flowers, up to about 6mm (¼in) long, are normally arranged in pairs. Unlike the flowers of *Asparagus acutifolius* (above), they are generally separated from the cladodes, rather than scattered among them. The fruit is a red berry.
• **DISTRIBUTION** Throughout the region.
• **HABITAT** Garigue, grassy road verges, sandy ground near the sea; often cultivated.
• **RELATED SPECIES** *A. maritimus*, Maritime Asparagus, which grows in the centre and east of the Mediterranean region, is similar but has striated stems.

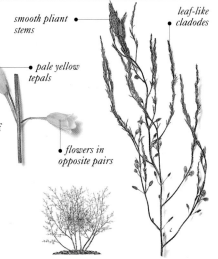

smooth pliant stems

leaf-like cladodes

pale yellow tepals

flowers in opposite pairs

Habit Perennial	Height 40–200cm (16–80in)	Flowering time June–Sept

| Family LILIACEAE | Species *Ruscus aculeatus* | Author L. |

BUTCHER'S BROOM

Butcher's Broom grows from underground rhizomes, and every year produces a fresh growth of stiff brush-like shoots. Each of these appears to bear alternately arranged, elliptical, and spine-tipped leaves, up to 40mm (1⅜in) long. However, the "leaves" are in fact cladodes, or modified stems, the true leaves being reduced to tiny papery scales. The flowers grow directly on the upper surface of the cladodes, and are greenish, star-shaped, and about 5mm (⅛in) across. Male and female flowers grow on different plants, and the female flowers produce round, red berries.
• **DISTRIBUTION** Throughout; also northwards to the British Isles.
• **HABITAT** Shaded ground in woods, scrub, hedges; usually in dry, fertile soil.

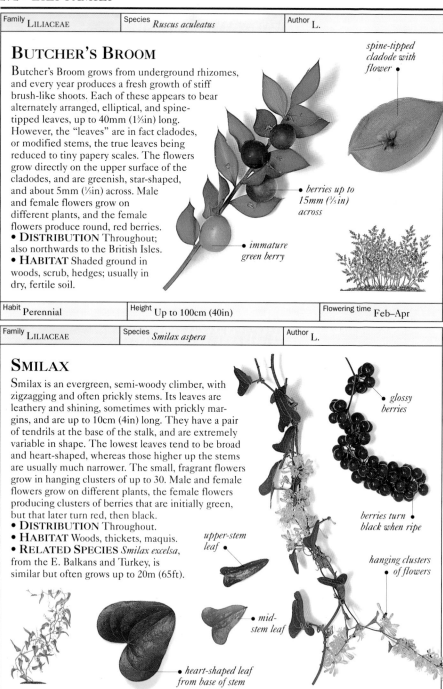

spine-tipped cladode with flower

berries up to 15mm (⅔in) across

immature green berry

| Habit Perennial | Height Up to 100cm (40in) | Flowering time Feb–Apr |

| Family LILIACEAE | Species *Smilax aspera* | Author L. |

SMILAX

Smilax is an evergreen, semi-woody climber, with zigzagging and often prickly stems. Its leaves are leathery and shining, sometimes with prickly margins, and are up to 10cm (4in) long. They have a pair of tendrils at the base of the stalk, and are extremely variable in shape. The lowest leaves tend to be broad and heart-shaped, whereas those higher up the stems are usually much narrower. The small, fragrant flowers grow in hanging clusters of up to 30. Male and female flowers grow on different plants, the female flowers producing clusters of berries that are initially green, but that later turn red, then black.
• **DISTRIBUTION** Throughout.
• **HABITAT** Woods, thickets, maquis.
• **RELATED SPECIES** *Smilax excelsa*, from the E. Balkans and Turkey, is similar but often grows up to 20m (65ft).

glossy berries

berries turn black when ripe

hanging clusters of flowers

upper-stem leaf

mid-stem leaf

heart-shaped leaf from base of stem

| Habit Perennial | Height Up to 15m (50ft) | Flowering time Aug–Nov |

AGAVE FAMILY

Family AGAVACEAE	Species *Agave americana*	Author L.

CENTURY PLANT

The Century Plant is a native of Mexico, and was introduced into the Mediterranean region in the 16th century. It has a rosette of large and very robust grey-blue leaves, up to 2m (6½ft) long, each with a long dark spine at the tip. The flowering stem appears when the plant is about 10 years old, and reaches a height of about 8m (26ft). It has 20 to 30 horizontal branches, each bearing a plate-sized cluster of fragrant yellow, 6-tepalled flowers, which produce 3-sided capsules. After flowering, the plant dies, but it is often survived by young plants produced by stolons.
• **DISTRIBUTION** Throughout.
• **HABITAT** Steep, rocky ground near the coast; often cultivated.
• **REMARK** Some cultivated forms have variegated leaves.

towering panicle of yellow flowers

spiny-toothed margins

fleshy, stiff, spine-tipped leaves

Habit Perennial	Height Up to 8m (26ft)	Flowering time June–Aug

DAFFODIL FAMILY

Family AMARYLLIDACEAE	Species *Sternbergia lutea*	Author (L.) Ker-Gawler ex Sprengel

STERNBERGIA

Like all members of the daffodil family, this attractive autumn-flowering plant grows from a bulb. Its leaves, up to 15mm (⅜in) wide, are present at the same time as the flowers. The flowers are up to 50mm (2in) long, and are borne individually on short stalks, with a papery spathe at the base of each flower. The fleshy fruit is slightly berry-like, with numerous seeds.
• **DISTRIBUTION** N. Africa, W. and C. Mediterranean; but absent from France and many Mediterranean islands.
• **HABITAT** Stony ground, scrub, pastures; frequently cultivated.
• **REMARK** Although similar to some crocuses (see p.280), Sternbergia has 6 and not 3 stamens.

6 anthers

6 equal, golden yellow tepals

papery spathe

short flowering stem

dark green, linear leaves

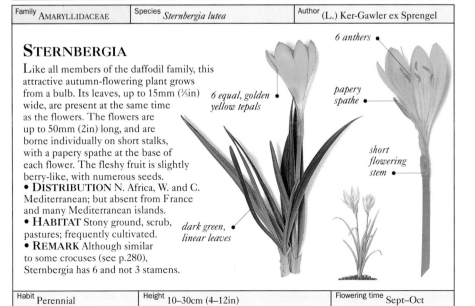

Habit Perennial	Height 10–30cm (4–12in)	Flowering time Sept–Oct

Family AMARYLLIDACEAE	Species *Leucojum aestivum*	Author L.

SUMMER SNOWFLAKE

Snowflakes grow from bulbs, and usually have several flowers in a drooping umbel. The Summer Snowflake is a robust species, with a 2-angled flowering stem and vivid green leaves up to 25cm (10in) long. Its bell-shaped flowers, up to 25mm (1in) long, grow in clusters of 2 to 5. They have white tepals with a distinctive green spot, and bright yellow anthers. The fruit is a slightly fleshy capsule containing numerous seeds.
• **DISTRIBUTION** C. Mediterranean, from France to Turkey; north to Britain.
• **HABITAT** Marshes, meadows, damp, grassy ground; often cultivated.
• **RELATED SPECIES** There are several similar species in the region. *Leucojum autumnale*, Autumn Snowflake, flowers from August to October, and its leaves appear after its flowers. It is a more delicate plant, with fewer flowers, and grows on rocky ground in the west. *L. roseum*, from Corsica and Sardinia, is a pink, autumn-flowering species.

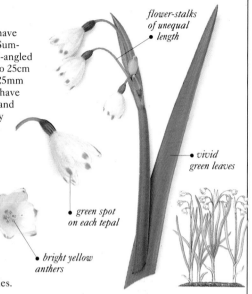

flower-stalks of unequal length

vivid green leaves

green spot on each tepal

bright yellow anthers

Habit Perennial	Height 35–60cm (14–24in)	Flowering time Apr–July

Family AMARYLLIDACEAE	Species *Narcissus poeticus*	Author L.

PHEASANT'S EYE NARCISSUS

Narcissi are familiar garden plants, and many forms now in cultivation are descended from Mediterranean species. Like its relatives, the Pheasant's Eye Narcissus grows from a bulb. Its flowering stem has 2 ridges, and it has 3 to 5 flat and often slightly twisted leaves, up to 40cm (16in) long. The flowers, up to 60mm (2⅜in) across, are usually solitary, with white tepals that are frequently backswept in wild plants. The short cylindrical corona has a finely toothed rim, often marked by a red ring that forms the distinctive "pheasant's eye". The fruit is a capsule with 3 compartments.
• **DISTRIBUTION** Throughout the region, except on most islands.
• **HABITAT** Grassy ground and woodland edges, often at altitude; frequently cultivated.
• **RELATED SPECIES** The widespread, autumn-flowering *Narcissus serotinus* is quite similar but far more delicate, without a red-rimmed corona. Its thread-like leaves appear in spring.

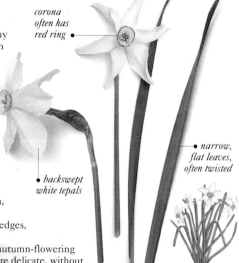

corona often has red ring

narrow, flat leaves, often twisted

backswept white tepals

Habit Perennial	Height 20–60cm (8–24in)	Flowering time Apr–June

Family AMARYLLIDACEAE	Species *Narcissus jonquilla*	Author L.

COMMON JONQUIL

Despite its small size, the Common Jonquil produces an extraordinarily intense fragrance. Its leaves are 2–4mm (¹⁄₁₂–¹⁄₆in) wide, dark green and grooved, and it has 2–6 flowers. Each flower has a straight, cylindrical tube, about 20mm (⅝in) long, and spreading or slightly reflexed tepals and a shallow cup-like corona. The tepals and corona are the same colour.
• **DISTRIBUTION** Spain; frequently cultivated, and naturalized in France, Italy, and parts of the Balkans.
• **HABITAT** Meadows, gardens.

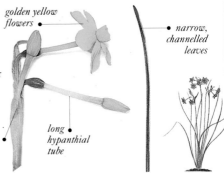

golden yellow flowers

narrow, channelled leaves

papery spathe

long hypanthial tube

Habit Perennial	Height Up to 20cm (8in)	Flowering time Mar–May

Family AMARYLLIDACEAE	Species *Narcissus requienii*	Author M. J. Roemer

RUSH-LEAVED NARCISSUS

A more slender plant than the Common Jonquil (above), this species has glossy, grooved leaves, only 2mm (¹⁄₁₂in) wide at most, and does not have a strong fragrance. The flowers grow singly or in pairs, and have straight tubes up to 18mm (⅝in) long. The shallow corona is usually about half the length of the spreading tepals.
• **DISTRIBUTION** S. France, Spain.
• **HABITAT** Rocky and grassy hillsides.
• **REMARK** Also known as *Narcissus juncifolius*.
• **RELATED SPECIES** *N. gaditanus*, from S. Spain, has 2 to 5 flowers, each with a curved tube.

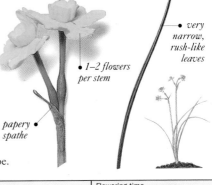

very narrow, rush-like leaves

1–2 flowers per stem

papery spathe

Habit Perennial	Height Up to 15cm (6in)	Flowering time Mar–May

Family AMARYLLIDACEAE	Species *Narcissus bulbocodium*	Author L.

HOOP PETTICOAT DAFFODIL

This distinctive narcissus is a plant of mountain slopes bordering the region. Its leaves are dark green and usually less than 2mm (¹⁄₁₂in) wide, with 2 to 4 on a single plant. The solitary flowers are light or golden yellow, often tinged with green. They have a cone-shaped corona, up to 20mm (⅝in) long, surrounded by 6 small, pointed, and often recurved tepals.
• **DISTRIBUTION** N. Africa, Spain, S. France.
• **HABITAT** Rocky ground, pastures, often at altitudes above 1,000m (3,300ft), sandy hillsides.
• **RELATED SPECIES** *Narcissus cantabricus*, White Hoop Petticoat Daffodil, from S. Spain, has white flowers.

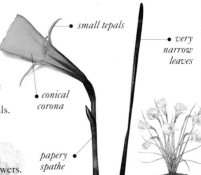

small tepals

very narrow leaves

conical corona

papery spathe

Habit Perennial	Height Up to 40cm (16in)	Flowering time Mar–May

Family AMARYLLIDACEAE	Species *Narcissus tazetta*	Author L.

POLYANTHUS NARCISSUS

With its distinctive clustered heads of bicoloured blooms, the Polyanthus Narcissus is one of the most attractive flowers of early spring. This variable plant has 3 to 6 blue-green linear leaves, which are up to 50cm (20in) long, with a keel on the lower surface. The flowers are fragrant, and grow in clusters of 3 to 15. Each one is up to 40mm (1⅜in) across, with broad white tepals, which usually overlap, and a wide orange-yellow corona. The flower-stalks are of unequal length, and they are surrounded at the base by a papery spathe. Several differing subspecies are recognized.

• **DISTRIBUTION** Throughout the region, but absent from many islands.

• **HABITAT** Grassy ground, meadows, cultivated ground, margins of fields and olive groves, gardens.

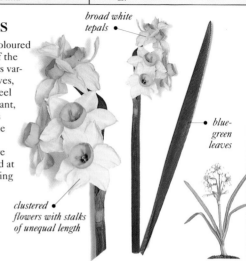

broad white tepals •

• blue-green leaves

clustered • flowers with stalks of unequal length

Habit Perennial	Height 25–60cm (10–24in)	Flowering time Feb–May

Family AMARYLLIDACEAE	Species *Pancratium illyricum*	Author L.

ILLYRIAN SEA LILY

Despite its name, this handsome plant is a native not of the ancient region of Illyria, but of Corsica and Sardinia. It grows from a large bulb, and has several flat, strap-shaped leaves up to 50cm (20in) long and 30mm (1⅛in) wide. Its flowers are borne on a long stalk, and are initially enclosed in a papery spathe that has 2 parts. Each flower-head has 12 or more pure white blooms, the flowers being up to 90mm (3⅓in) long, with narrow, pointed tepals that are at least twice as long as the corona and longer than the flower's tube. The fruit is a 3-sided capsule, which splits when ripe to release a number of shiny black seeds.

• **DISTRIBUTION** Corsica, Sardinia, Capri.

• **HABITAT** Mainly on rocky ground near to the sea, but also on grassy hillsides and forest edges away from the coast, particularly in Corsica.

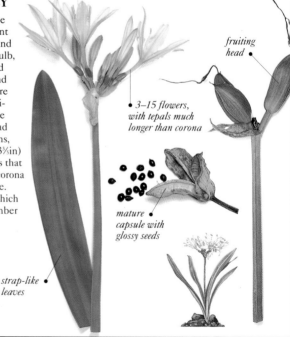

fruiting head •

• 3–15 flowers, with tepals much longer than corona

mature • capsule with glossy seeds

strap-like • leaves

Habit Perennial	Height Up to 60cm (24in)	Flowering time May–July

Family AMARYLLIDACEAE	Species *Pancratium maritimum*	Author L.

SEA DAFFODIL

The Sea Daffodil is one of the most striking plants of the Mediterranean shoreline, with pure white flowers that appear from July onwards. Its grows from a deeply buried bulb, and has numerous erect grey-green leaves. The leaves, which often appear with the onset of winter, are not more than 20mm (⅜in) broad, and they often have a distinctive spiral twist. The flowers grow in clusters of 3 to 15, and their slender tepals are up to 50mm (2in) long. Unlike the flowers of Illyrian Sea Lily (opposite), Sea Daffodils have large trumpet-shaped coronas and a long green flower-tube. The 3-sided fruit capsule releases large black seeds.

• **DISTRIBUTION** Throughout the region.

• **HABITAT** Sandy beaches, dunes.

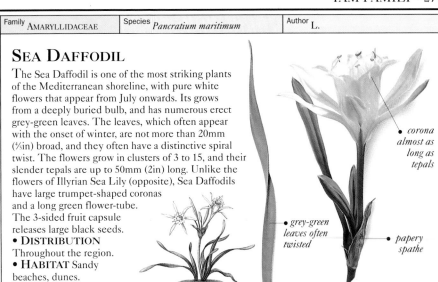

corona almost as long as tepals

grey-green leaves often twisted

papery spathe

Habit Perennial	Height Up to 50cm (20in)	Flowering time July–Oct

YAM FAMILY

Family DIOSCOREACEAE	Species *Tamus communis*	Author L.

BLACK BRYONY

Black Bryony is one of the few European members of a largely tropical family of plants. It grows from a large underground tuber, and produces vigorous twining stems. Its leaves have long stalks, and are heart-shaped, glossy above, and up to 15cm (6in) long. By contrast, the greenish yellow flowers are small and inconspicuous. Each one is up to 6mm (¼in) across, and male and female flowers grow on separate plants. The female flowers produce clusters of round, poisonous red berries, about 10mm (⅜in) in diameter, which often persist for several months after the stems have died.

• **DISTRIBUTION** Throughout, extending northwards to Great Britain.

• **HABITAT** Scrub, hedges, roadsides.

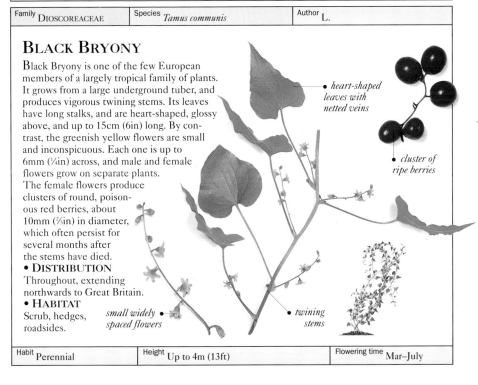

heart-shaped leaves with netted veins

cluster of ripe berries

small widely spaced flowers

twining stems

Habit Perennial	Height Up to 4m (13ft)	Flowering time Mar–July

IRIS FAMILY

Family IRIDACEAE	Species *Hermodactylus tuberosus*	Author (L.) Miller

SNAKE'S HEAD IRIS

Also known as the Widow Iris, this sombre but sweet-smelling member of the iris family grows from a collection of tubers, and has narrow, 4-angled leaves, up to 3mm (⅛in) across, which are usually longer than the flowering stems. Its solitary flowers have parts arranged in threes. From the centre, these are the erect and petal-like styles, the pale yellow inner tepals or "standards", and the curved outer tepals or "falls", which have a velvety brown external face. The fruit is a 3-parted capsule.
• **DISTRIBUTION** C. Mediterranean, from S.E. France to Turkey.
• **HABITAT** Rocky and grassy hillsides, garigue, waysides.

flowers often held at angle to stem

brown face on fall

4-angled, grass-like leaves

Habit Perennial	Height 20–40cm (8–16in)	Flowering time Feb–Apr

Family IRIDACEAE	Species *Iris unguicularis*	Author Poiret

ALGERIAN IRIS

When not in flower, this variable iris looks very much like a clump of coarse grass, with arching linear leaves that are usually not more than 5mm (⅕in) wide. It grows from rhizomes, and produces a number of pale or dark purple flowers, each borne separately on what appear to be short stems, up to 20cm (8in) long. Each "stem" is actually a flower-tube, with the flower's ovary near or below ground level – an arrangement reminiscent of crocuses (see p.280). The flower's standards are plain purple, while the falls have a white centre with an orange stripe and purple veins. The fruit forms near ground level, and the seeds are dispersed by ants.
• **DISTRIBUTION** N.W. Africa, E. Mediterranean including Greece, Crete, and Turkey.
• **HABITAT** Open woodland, hillsides, maquis, wooded road-sides; often cultivated.

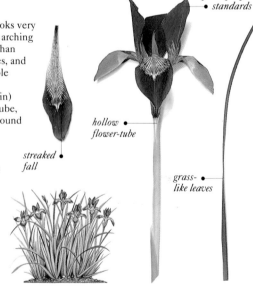

plain purple standards

streaked fall

hollow flower-tube

grass-like leaves

Habit Perennial	Height 10–50cm (4–20in)	Flowering time Dec–Apr

Family IRIDACEAE	Species *Iris germanica* var. *florentina*	Author Dykes

WHITE GERMAN IRIS

The German Iris has been cultivated since ancient times, and may be seen both in its bluish violet form, and in the white-flowered form shown here. Both forms grow from thick rhizomes and have flat, spear-shaped leaves, up to 40mm (1⅜in) wide, growing in the same plane. The fragrant flowers grow in groups of about 3 to 4 on stout branching stems, each flower being cupped by a papery spathe. The flowers are large and impressive, with incurved standards and flaring falls that each have a yellow "beard" along the centre line. The fruit is a capsule containing pear-shaped seeds.

• **DISTRIBUTION** Throughout.
• **HABITAT** Rocky ground, field margins, roadsides; frequently cultivated
• **RELATED SPECIES** The widely cultivated *Iris albicans* is very similar, but is generally smaller and has spathes that remain green throughout flowering.

raised central "beard"

flat leaves up to 70cm (28in) long

robust stems

Habit Perennial	Height 40–90cm (16–36in)	Flowering time Apr–June

Family IRIDACEAE	Species *Iris lutescens*	Author Lam.

IRIS LUTESCENS

Despite its delicate appearance, this small iris thrives on wind-battered hillsides. Its leaves are flat and spear-shaped, like those of the German Iris (above), but are only 30cm (12in) long. Its flowers may be yellow, an intense purple, or bicoloured, with plants of different colours often growing together. The capsule contains pear-shaped seeds.

• **DISTRIBUTION** W. Mediterranean, from Spain to Italy.
• **HABITAT** Dry hillsides, pine woods.
• **RELATED SPECIES** *Iris attica*, from the Balkans, is similar, but the flowers often have blue "beards" rather than yellow or white.

flowers grow singly or in pairs

purple flower form

curved fall with yellow or white "beard"

spreading, spear-shaped leaves

Habit Perennial	Height 10–40cm (4–16in)	Flowering time Mar–Apr

| Family IRIDACEAE | Species *Gynandriris sisyrinchium* | Author (L.) Parl. |

BARBARY NUT

This common and widespread iris-like plant grows from a corm – hence the "nut" in its common name. It rarely has more than 2 leaves, and these are thin, arching, and thread-like, and up to about 50cm (20in) long. At its base, each one is covered by a long sheath. The pale purplish blue flowers are up to 40mm (1⅜in) high, and develop from torpedo-shaped buds enclosed by brown papery spathes. Each stem produces about one to 6 flowers, and these have spreading falls, often held almost horizontally, with a white patch that is sometimes speckled. The flowers usually open one at a time, and are short-lived – appearing at about midday and withering by the evening. They produce brown pear-shaped seeds.
• **DISTRIBUTION** Throughout.
• **HABITAT** Stony, sandy, and grassy ground, field margins, waysides.
• **RELATED SPECIES** *Iris xiphium*, Spanish Iris, is a much more robust plant with fewer flowers. It grows in the west, and is widely cultivated.

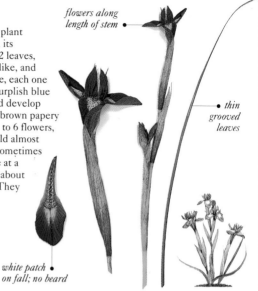

flowers along length of stem •

• thin grooved leaves

white patch • on fall; no beard

| Habit Perennial | Height 5–50cm (2–20in) | Flowering time Feb–May |

| Family IRIDACEAE | Species *Crocus biflorus* | Author Miller |

CROCUS BIFLORUS

True crocuses – as opposed to members of the genus *Colchicum* (see p.259) – have 3 stamens, and their inner and outer tepals are frequently differently coloured. Like other crocuses, this extremely variable species grows from a small corm, and has narrow leaves up to 2.5mm (⅒in) wide with a central white stripe. The leaves grow from the base before flowering begins. There are one to 3 white or pale lilac flowers. The ovaries are below ground.
• **DISTRIBUTION** C. and E. Mediterranean, from Italy eastwards.
• **HABITAT** Stony and grassy ground.
• **REMARK** There are many other species of crocus in the region, often confined to small areas.

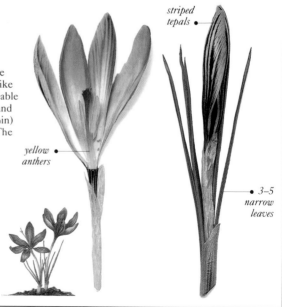

striped tepals •

yellow • anthers

• 3–5 narrow leaves

| Habit Perennial | Height Up to 10cm (4in) | Flowering time Feb–Apr |

Family IRIDACEAE	Species *Crocus versicolor*	Author Ker-Gawler

CROCUS VERSICOLOR

Like many Mediterranean crocuses, this western species is found only in a relatively small area. Its 3 to 6 grey-green leaves appear before the flowers. The flowers are white, lilac, or purple, and have conspicuous feather-edged stripes on the outside of the tepals, which are about 30mm (1⅛in) long. The anthers are yellow, and the style has 3 short lobes. As with other crocuses, the flower-tube base is enclosed by a papery spathe, and the ovaries are below ground level.
• **DISTRIBUTION** S.E. France, N.W. Italy.
• **HABITAT** Rocky and grassy ground, woodland; frequently cultivated.
• **RELATED SPECIES** A number of similar species are found in the west of the region. *Crocus corsicus*, which is found only in Corsica, is a very similar spring-flowering species with narrower leaves. *C. cambessedesii* grows only in pinewoods and hillsides in the Balearic Islands. It also has narrow leaves, and flowers from late autumn to early spring.

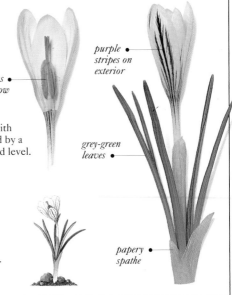

purple stripes on exterior

3 stamens with yellow anthers

grey-green leaves

papery spathe

Habit Perennial	Height Up to 20cm (8in)	Flowering time Jan–May

Family IRIDACEAE	Species *Romulea bulbocodium*	Author (L.) Sebastiani & Mauri

ROMULEA BULBOCODIUM

Romuleas grow from corms, and are small crocus-like plants with 6 equal tepals and a pair of narrow basal leaves. In *Romulea bulbocodium* the basal leaves are up to 30cm (12in) long. The star-like flowers, unlike those of crocuses (above), are borne on a stem. In this species, the stem carries one to 6 flowers, up to 25mm (1in) across, which vary from white to violet. The capsule contains numerous brown seeds.
• **DISTRIBUTION** Throughout, except on some islands.
• **HABITAT** Rocky, grassy, and sandy places, usually at low altitude.
• **RELATED SPECIES** Many of the dozen or so romuleas in the region have smaller purple or violet flowers. The widespread *R. columnae*, Sand Crocus, has purple or lilac flowers on very slender stalks.

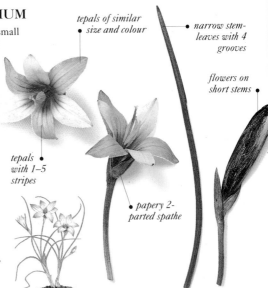

tepals of similar size and colour

narrow stem-leaves with 4 grooves

flowers on short stems

tepals with 1–5 stripes

papery 2-parted spathe

Habit Perennial	Height Up to 10cm (4in)	Flowering time Feb–May

Family IRIDACEAE	Species *Gladiolus illyricus*	Author Koch

GLADIOLUS ILLYRICUS

3–10 flowers

Gladioli grow from corms, and have flat, almost grass-like leaves that, at the base at least, grow in the same plane. In this relatively low-growing species, the largest leaves reach about 40cm (16in) in length. The reddish purple flowers are up to 45mm (1⅛in) long, and usually grow in a single spike containing 3 to 10 blooms. Each flower has 6 unequal tepals, the 3 lowest being streaked with white and red, with adjacent flowers tending to point in alternate directions. The fruit capsule contains winged seeds.

anthers shorter than supporting filaments

• **DISTRIBUTION** From Spain and N.W. Africa, eastwards to Greece.
• **HABITAT** Open woodland, scrub, grassy places.
• **RELATED SPECIES** *Gladiolus communis*, found in the same area, is taller and has up to 20 flowers, often on branched stems.

narrow, blade-like leaves

Habit Perennial	Height 20–50cm (8–20in)	Flowering time Apr–July

Family IRIDACEAE	Species *Gladiolus italicus*	Author Miller

FIELD GLADIOLUS

lower leaves broadest

This robust gladiolus is a remarkably beautiful weed that is rarely seen far from cultivated ground. It has from 3 to 5 leaves, the longest reaching about 65cm (26in) in length, and up to 16mm (⅝in) wide. The flowers are up to 50mm (2in) long and, as in *Gladiolus illyricus* (above), tend to point in alternating directions. The 3 lowest tepals usually have a central pale streak, surrounded by a darker border. The fruit is a capsule that contains unwinged seeds.

dark-bordered streaks on lower tepals

• **DISTRIBUTION** Throughout.
• **HABITAT** Cultivated fields, olive groves, grassy ground, rocky hillsides.
• **REMARK** Several Mediterranean species of gladioli are cultivated, together with gladioli that originate from southern Africa. The latter species are usually more robust than those native to the Mediterranean, and their cultivars have a wide variety of colours, some distinctly garish.

anthers longer than their supporting filaments

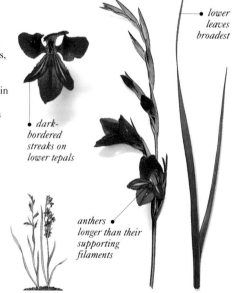

Habit Perennial	Height 50–100cm (20–40cm)	Flowering time Mar–June

GRASS FAMILY

Family GRAMINEAE	Species *Cynosurus echinatus*	Author L.

ROUGH DOG'S TAIL

Grasses generally have small, rather drab flowers that are pollinated by the wind. No other plant family is so widespread, either in the Mediterranean region, or in the world as a whole. Rough Dog's Tail is a low-growing, hairless species that often forms small clumps. Its leaves have a rough surface and are up to 10mm (⅜in) wide. The egg-shaped flower-heads are always held above the leaves, and are up to 40mm (1⅜in) long, excluding the projecting awns. As with most grasses, the fruit is a caryopsis or grain.

oval flower-head with projecting awns

• **DISTRIBUTION**
Throughout the region.
• **HABITAT** Rocky ground, fields, waysides, grassy places. Common in gardens and waste ground in towns.

flat leaves with rough upper surfaces

Habit Annual	Height 20–60cm (8–24in)	Flowering time Apr–July

Family GRAMINEAE	Species *Briza maxima*	Author L.

LARGE QUAKING GRASS

The scaly, fish-like flower-heads of this plant make it one of the most easily identified of Mediterranean grasses. An erect and slender plant, it has narrow, hairless leaves up to 20cm (8in) long. Its flowering stems divide above into about a dozen branches, each bearing a flattened flower-head, or spikelet. The spikelets, which are up to 25mm (1in) long, have pointed tips and 3 to 10 pairs of papery, overlapping scales. The fruit is a grain that has one rounded face and one flattened face.

1–12 flower-heads on each stem

flower-head with overlapping scales

• **DISTRIBUTION** Throughout.
• **HABITAT** Dry hillsides, garigue, waysides, gardens.
• **REMARK** The flower-heads tremble in the breeze. This plant is collected for use in decorative dried flower arrangements.
• **RELATED SPECIES** *Briza media*, Quaking Grass, is a widespread and similar perennial species.

slender stems

Habit Annual	Height 10–60cm (4–24in)	Flowering time Apr–June

Family GRAMINEAE	Species *Elymus farctus*	Author (Viv.) Runem. ex Meld.

SAND COUCH

Sand Couch is one of the characteristic grasses of exposed coastal sand. Several distinct subspecies exist – the most common Mediterranean form having stiff, erect stems that grow from a long rhizome which creeps below the surface. Its leaves are grey-green, about 5mm (⅕in) wide, and usually strongly inrolled. The flowering stems are rigid, and carry a spike of flowers 10–35cm (4–14in) long, each spike being made up of short spikelets with up to 10 flowers. The spikelets are arranged in 2 opposite and alternating ranks, and fold outwards from recesses in the stem.

• **DISTRIBUTION** Throughout.
• **HABITAT** Beach sand, dunes.
• **REMARK** Subspecies *rechingeri*, which grows on rocky coasts around the Aegean region, does not have a creeping rhizome.

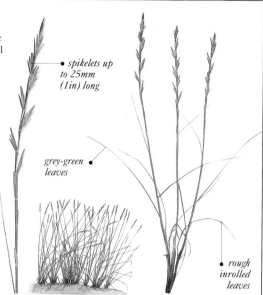

spikelets up to 25mm (1in) long •

grey-green • leaves

• rough inrolled leaves

Habit Perennial	Height 50–80cm (20–32in)	Flowering time June–Aug

Family GRAMINEAE	Species *Aegilops neglecta*	Author Reg. ex Bertol.

AEGILOPS NEGLECTA

This low, clump-forming grass can be recognized by its small flower-heads and spiky awns, which fold outwards as the flower-head matures. It has numerous stems, which branch from the base. The leaves have sparse fine hairs, and their blades, about 5mm (⅕in) wide, are attached to long sheaths that loosely surround the stems. The flower-heads, about 30mm (1⅕in) long, consist of 2 to 3 barrel-shaped fertile spikelets, with spreading awns of roughly equal size.

• **DISTRIBUTION** Throughout the region.
• **HABITAT** Waysides, dry grassy ground, olive groves.
• **REMARK** The grasses in this genus are close relatives of wheats. A species that grows in the Balkans, *Aegilops speltoides*, is thought to be an ancestor of cultivated wheat.

spreading awns •

gradually • tapering flower-head

many stems branching • from base

Habit Annual	Height 10–40cm (4–16cm)	Flowering time Apr–July

Family GRAMINEAE	Species *Avena sterilis*	Author L.

WINTER WILD OAT

Winter Wild Oat is tall and rather sparse grass, with several stems branching from the base. Its leaves are flat, up to 60cm (24in) long and 12mm (½in) wide, and have a rough texture. The flower-heads develop in a roughly pyramidal cluster, about 20–40cm (8–16in) long, and they hang from spreading and widely spaced branches. Each flower-head is up to 40mm (1⅜in) long, and has 3 to 4 fertile flowers and 2 conspicuous elbowed awns. The mature fruiting heads detach easily, and often work their way into the clothing of people passing by.

• **DISTRIBUTION** Throughout the region.
• **HABITAT** Dry fields, waste ground, waysides.
• **REMARK** This plant is a common weed of cultivated ground.

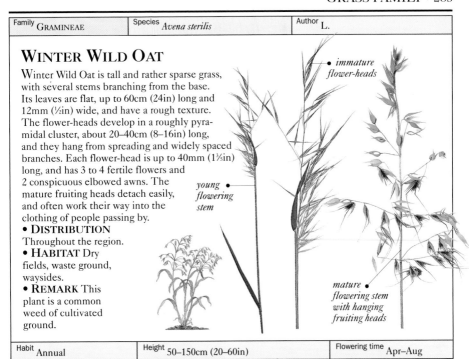

immature flower-heads

young flowering stem

mature flowering stem with hanging fruiting heads

Habit Annual	Height 50–150cm (20–60in)	Flowering time Apr–Aug

Family GRAMINEAE	Species *Lagurus ovatus*	Author L.

HARE'S TAIL

In summer, the bobbing flower-heads of Hare's Tail are a common sight on the margins of Mediterranean beaches. This small and attractive grass has a cluster of stems bearing soft, downy leaves that are up to 10mm (⅜in) wide. The flower-heads are roughly egg-shaped, and up to 20mm (⅔in) long, and each one contains tightly packed single-flowered spikelets with silky awns that project to form a fine "fur" around the entire flower-head. Only the upper spikelets produce seeds.

• **DISTRIBUTION** Throughout.
• **HABITAT** Dry, sandy places, usually near the sea but sometimes further inland; often cultivated.
• **REMARK** This species is one of a number of Mediterranean grasses that are frequently used as decorative dried flowers.

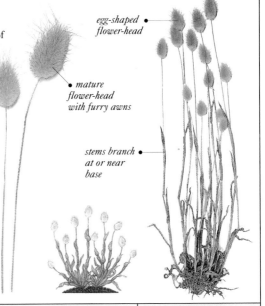

egg-shaped flower-head

mature flower-head with furry awns

stems branch at or near base

Habit Annual	Height 10–50cm (4–20in)	Flowering time Apr–June

Family GRAMINEAE	Species *Ammophila arenaria*	Author (L.) Link

MARRAM

Marram is the dominant grass of sand-dunes. Its creeping rhizomes and long roots bind sand grains together, and help to stabilize dunes against coastal winds. An erect, clump-forming plant, it has hairless stems and narrow, sharply pointed leaves. The leaves are about 50cm (20in) long, and are tightly inrolled – a feature that helps to prevent water loss. The flower-heads are dense and cylindrical, and up to 20cm (8in) long. Each one is composed of closely packed, single-flowered spikelets, up to 14mm (⅗in) long.

cylindrical flower-head

• **DISTRIBUTION** Throughout the region; also common on coasts throughout Europe, as far north as Norway.

• **HABITAT** Sand dunes.

• **REMARK** Marram usually follows Sand Couch (see p.284), growing slightly further inland and creating taller dunes.

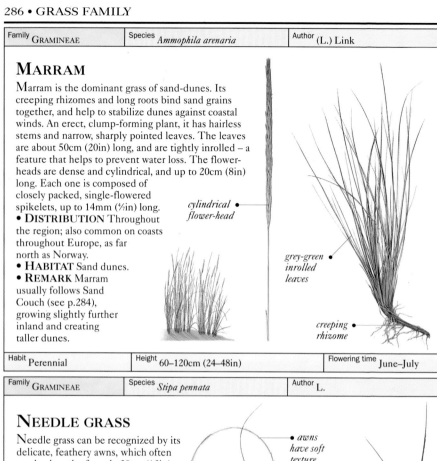

grey-green inrolled leaves

creeping rhizome

Habit Perennial	Height 60–120cm (24–48in)	Flowering time June–July

Family GRAMINEAE	Species *Stipa pennata*	Author L.

NEEDLE GRASS

Needle grass can be recognized by its delicate, feathery awns, which often reach a length of nearly 30cm (12in). A clumped perennial, it has rigid stems and very narrow, almost thread-like leaves. The leaves have inrolled margins, and are usually less than 2mm (¹⁄₁₂in) wide. The flower-heads are up to 10cm (4in) long, and contain relatively few flowers. Their conspicuous awns are spiralled towards their base, and have feathery hairs.

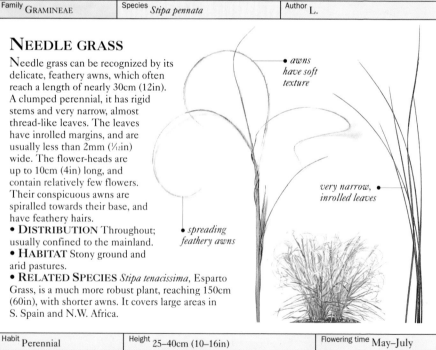

awns have soft texture

very narrow, inrolled leaves

spreading feathery awns

• **DISTRIBUTION** Throughout; usually confined to the mainland.

• **HABITAT** Stony ground and arid pastures.

• **RELATED SPECIES** *Stipa tenacissima*, Esparto Grass, is a much more robust plant, reaching 150cm (60in), with shorter awns. It covers large areas in S. Spain and N.W. Africa.

Habit Perennial	Height 25–40cm (10–16in)	Flowering time May–July

Family GRAMINEAE	Species *Arundo donax*	Author L.

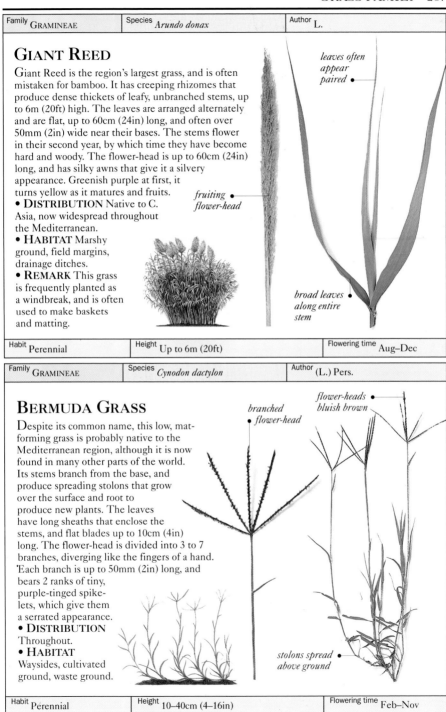

GIANT REED

Giant Reed is the region's largest grass, and is often mistaken for bamboo. It has creeping rhizomes that produce dense thickets of leafy, unbranched stems, up to 6m (20ft) high. The leaves are arranged alternately and are flat, up to 60cm (24in) long, and often over 50mm (2in) wide near their bases. The stems flower in their second year, by which time they have become hard and woody. The flower-head is up to 60cm (24in) long, and has silky awns that give it a silvery appearance. Greenish purple at first, it turns yellow as it matures and fruits.

• **DISTRIBUTION** Native to C. Asia, now widespread throughout the Mediterranean.

• **HABITAT** Marshy ground, field margins, drainage ditches.

• **REMARK** This grass is frequently planted as a windbreak, and is often used to make baskets and matting.

leaves often appear paired •

*fruiting •
flower-head*

*broad leaves •
along entire
stem*

Habit Perennial	Height Up to 6m (20ft)	Flowering time Aug–Dec

Family GRAMINEAE	Species *Cynodon dactylon*	Author (L.) Pers.

BERMUDA GRASS

Despite its common name, this low, mat-forming grass is probably native to the Mediterranean region, although it is now found in many other parts of the world. Its stems branch from the base, and produce spreading stolons that grow over the surface and root to produce new plants. The leaves have long sheaths that enclose the stems, and flat blades up to 10cm (4in) long. The flower-head is divided into 3 to 7 branches, diverging like the fingers of a hand. Each branch is up to 50mm (2in) long, and bears 2 ranks of tiny, purple-tinged spike-lets, which give them a serrated appearance.

• **DISTRIBUTION** Throughout.

• **HABITAT** Waysides, cultivated ground, waste ground.

*branched
• flower-head*

*flower-heads •
bluish brown*

*stolons spread •
above ground*

Habit Perennial	Height 10–40cm (4–16in)	Flowering time Feb–Nov

ARUM FAMILY

Family ARACEAE	Species *Arum italicum*	Author Miller

ITALIAN ARUM

Arums are fleshy, hairless perennials that grow
from underground tubers. This variable and widespread species has arrow-shaped leaves up to 35cm
(14in) long, which appear in the autumn. Their upper
surfaces are glossy, and are often mottled with white.
The flowers are small, and grow at the base of a
column or spadix that is partially enclosed by a
hood, or spathe. In this species, the spathe is
up to 40cm (16in) long, and the club-like
extension of the spadix is yellow, sometimes tinged with purple. The fruit is
a berry that turns red when ripe.
• **DISTRIBUTION** Throughout.
• **HABITAT** Woods, hedges,
shaded places, gardens.
• **RELATED
SPECIES** *Arum
dioscoridis*, which
grows in the extreme
east, has a purple
spadix, and the inside of
its spathe is spattered
with purple blotches.

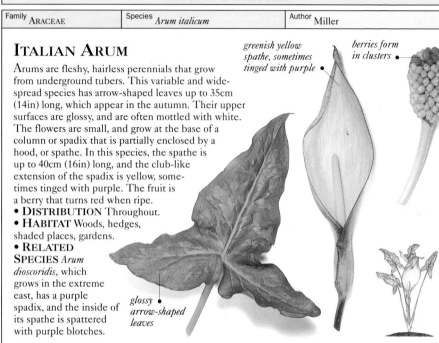

*greenish yellow
spathe, sometimes
tinged with purple* •

*berries form
in clusters* •

*glossy •
arrow-shaped
leaves*

Habit Perennial	Height 25–50cm (10–20in)	Flowering time Apr–May

Family ARACEAE	Species *Arisarum vulgare*	Author Targ.-Tozz.

FRIAR'S COWL

This common but intriguing arum-like plant
has a cluster of oval or spear-shaped leaves,
up to 12cm (4¾in) long, and solitary flower-
heads on stems that are usually as long as
the leaf-stalks. The spathe, or "cowl", is
striped with greenish purple. In the most
widespread form of the plant, the spathe
is usually bent forwards, with the brownish spadix projecting from its mouth.
The fruit is a greenish berry.
• **DISTRIBUTION** Throughout.
• **HABITAT** Grassy and rocky ground,
garigue, field margins.
• **RELATED SPECIES** *Arisarum
proboscideum*, Mouse Plant, from
S. Spain and S. Italy, has a long
curling tip to its spathe, which
looks like a mouse's tail.

*striped spathe,
usually bent* •

*• streaked
flower-stems*

*glossy plain •
green leaves*

Habit Perennial	Height 20–40cm (8–16in)	Flowering time Oct–May

| Family ARACEAE | Species *Dracunculus vulgaris* | Author Schott |

DRAGON ARUM

The Dragon Arum is a striking and sinister-looking plant that produces an overpowering stench of rotting meat when in flower. This odour, together with the plant's carrion-like hue, attracts the flies that pollinate its flowers. Its erect stem is clasped by mottled brown and white leaf bases, and the leaf blades, which are up to 35cm (14in) long, are divided into 9 to 15 wavy-edged lobes. The spathe also has wavy margins, and is mainly green on the outside, but blood-red within. The base of the spadix bears numerous small flowers, and its pointed and slightly flattened upper part often extends beyond the spathe. The fruit is an orange-red berry.

• **DISTRIBUTION** C. and E. Mediterranean, from Corsica and Sardinia eastwards.

• **HABITAT** Scrub, rocky ground; common around rocks and walls used for shelter by goats and sheep.

• **REMARK** As in other members of the arum family, the spadix produces heat by chemical reactions. The warmth helps to vaporize the substances that attract pollinating flies. The flies enter the cup at the base of the spathe, and are trapped by a tiny ring of downward-pointing hairs. Here they brush any pollen they may be carrying onto the female flowers. When the male flowers mature, the flies collect pollen from them. The hairs then wither, and the flies escape.

spadix with spathe removed

wavy-edged spathe

cluster of male and female flowers hidden inside base of spathe

wavy margins

leaves with twisted lobes

mottled leaf-bases clasping stem

| Habit Perennial | Height Up to 100cm (40in) | Flowering time Apr–June |

ORCHID FAMILY

Family ORCHIDACEAE	Species *Epipactis helleborine*	Author (L.) Crantz

BROADLEAVED HELLEBORINE

The orchid family is the second largest family of flowering plants, containing over 18,000 species worldwide. Many tropical orchids are epiphytes – plants that perch on other plants – but the Mediterranean's orchids are all terrestrial. The Broad-leaved Helleborine is a predominantly woodland species that grows from a short rhizome. Its stout stem is downy above, and is clasped by up to 10 broad, oval leaves up to 15cm (6in) long, which are arranged in a spiral. The flowers grow in a largely one-sided spike, which contains 15 to 50 blooms. They vary in colour from green to deep red, and have large petals and sepals, and a lip with a pronounced central fold. As with other orchids, the fruit is a capsule that splits open to release large numbers of dust-like seeds. These are dispersed by the wind.

• **DISTRIBUTION** Throughout, northwards to Scandinavia.
• **HABITAT** Open broadleaved or coniferous woodland, scrub, and dunes.
• **REMARK** Pollination is carried out by wasps that are attracted by the flowers' subtle odour. The flowers do not produce nectar, only a glossy nectar-like wax.

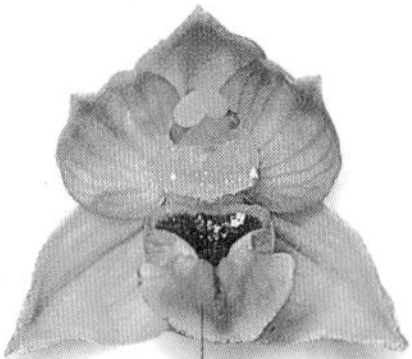

15–50 flowers on short stalks

flowers up to 20mm (⅘in) wide

stout stem

pink flower form

green flower form

broad oval leaves

clasping leaves

leaves spiral around stem

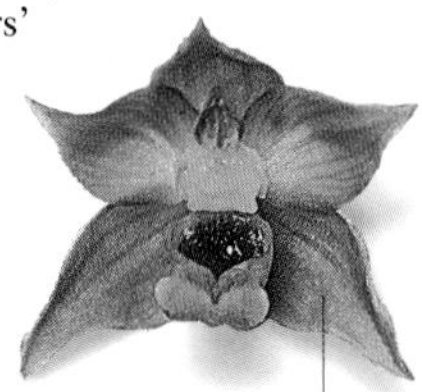

Habit Perennial	Height 35–100cm (14–40in)	Flowering time June–Aug

Family ORCHIDACEAE	Species *Cephalanthera rubra*	Author (L.) L. C. M. Richard

RED HELLEBORINE

This rather slender orchid grows from a creeping rhizome. Its stem is slightly hairy above, often slightly kinked, and bears 5 to 8 leaves that are arranged alternately along its entire length. The leaves are lance-shaped and channelled, and those in the middle of the stem reach a length of 12cm (4¾in). The flowers, about 20mm (⅝in) long, are extremely attractive and conspicuous, with spreading pointed sepals and a white lip.
• **DISTRIBUTION** Throughout.
• **HABITAT** Open woodland, road verges; usually on calcareous ground.
• **RELATED SPECIES** *Cephalanthera longifolia*, Narrow-leaved Helleborine, which is also widespread, has white flowers and much narrower leaves. Both species occur northwards to Britain and Scandinavia.

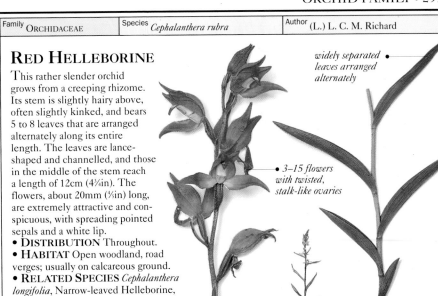

widely separated leaves arranged alternately

3–15 flowers with twisted, stalk-like ovaries

slender stem

Habit Perennial	Height 20–60cm (8–24in)	Flowering time All year round

Family ORCHIDACEAE	Species *Limodorum abortivum*	Author (L.) Swartz

VIOLET BIRD'S NEST ORCHID

Also known as the Violet Limodore, this striking orchid has no green leaves. It grows from a short rhizome with thickened roots, and produces stout erect stems that have numerous dark purple scales. The stems are either solitary, or in clumps of up to 4. Each stem carries 5 to 25 flowers, and these are up to 45mm (1⅛in) across, with broad sepals, narrower petals, and a slightly curved tubular spur, which is about as long the ovary. Four of the flower-lobes spread laterally, while one forms a hood, and another an upwardly arching lip patterned with yellow.
• **DISTRIBUTION** Throughout the region.
• **HABITAT** Grassland and scrub on calcareous ground; always near pines.
• **REMARK** This orchid is generally thought to be a saprophyte – a plant that lives on decaying organic matter in the soil. However, it may possibly be a parasite, feeding on the tissues of living host plants.
• **RELATED SPECIES** *Neottia nidus-avis*, Bird's Nest Orchid, is also a saprophyte found throughout the region. It has shorter, brownish yellow flower-heads.

flowers in a lax cluster

large lip marked with yellow

DETAIL

Habit Perennial	Height 40–80cm (16–32in)	Flowering time Apr–July

Family ORCHIDACEAE	Species *Platanthera chlorantha*	Author (Custer) Reichenb.

GREATER BUTTERFLY ORCHID

This moth-pollinated orchid has flowers with extremely long, curved spurs. It grows from a double tuber and has 2 large, oval or elliptical leaves, up to 15cm (6in) long, near the base of its stem, and smaller leaves on the stem itself. Each flower has a hood formed by 2 petals and a sepal. The spur is usually horizontal with a swollen tip.

• **DISTRIBUTION** Throughout, except on some islands.

• **HABITAT** Open woodland, scrub, grassy ground.

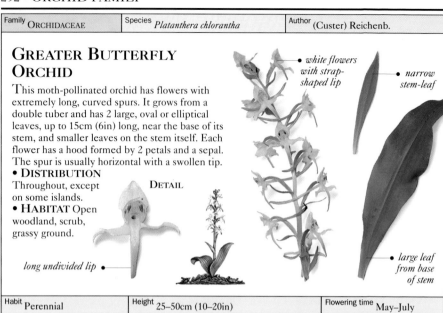

white flowers with strap-shaped lip

narrow stem-leaf

DETAIL

long undivided lip

large leaf from base of stem

Habit Perennial	Height 25–50cm (10–20in)	Flowering time May–July

Family ORCHIDACEAE	Species *Orchis papilionacea*	Author L.

PINK BUTTERFLY ORCHID

The genus *Orchis* includes over 20 species in the Mediterranean region. Although this particular species has relatively few flowers, it is one of the most conspicuous. Like almost all its relatives, it grows from a pair of rounded tubers that sustain it during the summer drought. Its stems are often leafy and, although sometimes slender, can be as thick as a pencil. The leaves are lance-shaped, channelled, and unspotted, and up to about 10cm (4in) long. The flowers grow in a lax head of about 3 to 8 blooms, each flower being clasped by a reddish bract that is longer than the stalk-like ovary. The sepals and petals form a dark open hood; the lip is broad and rounded, up to 16mm (⅝in) long, and usually pale pink.

• **DISTRIBUTION** Throughout.

• **HABITAT** Open woodland, maquis, rocky hillsides, fields and rough pasture, roadsides; often in considerable numbers.

• **REMARK** This is one of the most widespread and variable Mediterranean orchids. In some plants, the lip is dark and heavily streaked; in others it is pale and plain.

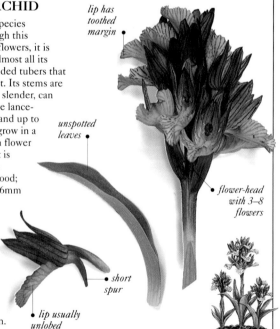

lip has toothed margin

unspotted leaves

flower-head with 3–8 flowers

short spur

lip usually unlobed

Habit Perennial	Height 20–40cm (8–16in)	Flowering time Feb–May

Family ORCHIDACEAE	Species *Orchis morio*	Author L.

GREEN-WINGED ORCHID

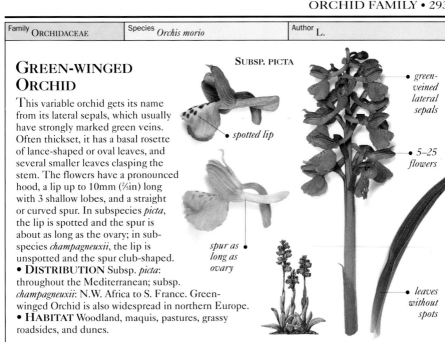

SUBSP. PICTA

- green-veined lateral sepals

spotted lip

- 5–25 flowers

This variable orchid gets its name from its lateral sepals, which usually have strongly marked green veins. Often thickset, it has a basal rosette of lance-shaped or oval leaves, and several smaller leaves clasping the stem. The flowers have a pronounced hood, a lip up to 10mm (⅜in) long with 3 shallow lobes, and a straight or curved spur. In subspecies *picta*, the lip is spotted and the spur is about as long as the ovary; in subspecies *champagneuxii*, the lip is unspotted and the spur club-shaped.

spur as long as ovary

- leaves without spots

• **DISTRIBUTION** Subsp. *picta*: throughout the Mediterranean; subsp. *champagneuxii*: N.W. Africa to S. France. Green-winged Orchid is also widespread in northern Europe.
• **HABITAT** Woodland, maquis, pastures, grassy roadsides, and dunes.

Habit Perennial	Height 5–50cm (2–20in)	Flowering time Feb–May

Family ORCHIDACEAE	Species *Orchis coriophora*	Author L.

BUG ORCHID

SUBSP. FRAGRANS

sharply pointed hood

The Bug Orchid is usually a compact plant with sharply pointed, linear or lance-shaped, unspotted leaves, up to 10cm (4in) long. Most of the leaves form a rosette around the base; smaller leaves sheathe the stem as far as the flower-head. The flower-head is dense and cylindrical, and its tightly packed flowers, about 8mm (⅓in) wide, have pointed hoods, and 3-lobed lips. In the subspecies *fragrans* – the most common Mediterranean form – the flowers are fragrant, either maroon or greenish, with red spots, and the central lobe of the lip is longer than the side lobes.

leaves reach as far as flower-head

densely packed flowers

• **DISTRIBUTION** Subsp. *fragrans*: throughout, except parts of the east.
• **HABITAT** Damp grassland and sand, hillsides, waysides.

long central lobe

Habit Perennial	Height 15–40cm (6–16in)	Flowering time Mar–May

Family ORCHIDACEAE	Species *Orchis lactea*	Author Poiret

ORCHIS LACTEA

This generally pale orchid has a stout
stem, and oblong or lance-shaped leaves
without spots. About 3 to 4 leaves spread
from the base of the stem, whereas the
upper leaves are clasping. The flowers
grow in a compact oval spike and, as in
many orchids, each flower has a twisted
stalk-like ovary, so that it is effectively
upside down. The flowers are clasped
by short bracts, and have short,
downward-pointing spurs, and
greenish hoods with sharply pointed
sepals. The lip is 3-lobed and about
10mm (⅜in) long, and has purple spots
over a white or cream background.
• **DISTRIBUTION** Throughout the region.
• **HABITAT** Garigue, grassy ground, waysides.
• **RELATED SPECIES** *Orchis lactea* is sometimes classified as a subspecies of *O. tridentata*,
Toothed Orchid. This widespread species is similar
but frequently larger, and has a distinctive triangular
central lobe to its lip.

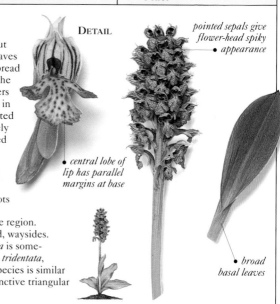

DETAIL

*pointed sepals give
flower-head spiky
appearance*

*central lobe of
lip has parallel
margins at base*

*broad
basal leaves*

Habit Perennial	Height 10–20cm (4–8in)	Flowering time Feb–Apr

Family ORCHIDACEAE	Species *Orchis italica*	Author Poiret

WAVY-LEAVED MONKEY ORCHID

Also known as the Italian Man
Orchid, this common and eye-
catching plant has a dense, oval
head of long-lobed flowers. Its
roughly oblong leaves have distinctive
wavy margins, and often have purple
blotches. About 5 to 8 of the leaves,
which can be over 12cm (4¾in) long,
form a basal rosette, and smaller leaves
sheathe the stem. The flowers are
usually pale pink, and each has a
pointed, open hood, a conspicuous
"man-like" lip, and a short spur.
• **DISTRIBUTION** Throughout, except
in France and some islands in the west.
• **HABITAT** Pine woodland, scrub, grassy
places, field margins.
• **RELATED SPECIES** *Orchis simia*, Monkey
Orchid, is very similar but has curled lip-lobes,
and does not have wavy leaves. It is found
throughout, except most islands in the west.

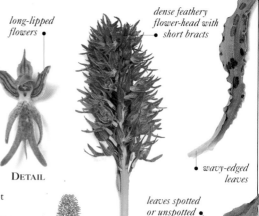

*long-lipped
flowers*

*dense feathery
flower-head with
short bracts*

DETAIL

*wavy-edged
leaves*

*leaves spotted
or unspotted*

Habit Perennial	Height 20–40cm (8–16in)	Flowering time Mar–May

Family ORCHIDACEAE	Species *Orchis purpurea*	Author Hudson

LADY ORCHID

Given suitable conditions, the Lady Orchid can be an impressive plant, with glossy foliage and a dense flower-head. Its leaves, which can reach over 20cm (8in) long, are roughly elliptic with a slightly fleshy feel. The young flower-head has a striking purple coloration – almost as if it has been dipped in ink – created by the numerous dark hoods of the tightly packed flowers. As the flowers develop, their paler lips become apparent. These are 3-lobed, very broad, and up to 15mm (⅗in) long. They have a white or pale pink background colour above, with tufts of purple hairs that look like spots, and are often washed with purple below.

• **DISTRIBUTION** N.W. and C. Mediterranean, eastwards to Turkey. Absent from most islands in the east.

• **HABITAT** Woodland, particularly with pines, scrub, grassy ground; often in large groups.

flower-bracts shorter than the stalk-like ovaries

glossy unspotted leaves

flowers have broad lips and short spurs

DETAIL

robust stem

Habit Perennial	Height 30–80cm (12–32in)	Flowering time Apr–June

Family ORCHIDACEAE	Species *Orchis saccata*	Author Ten.

ORCHIS SACCATA

Although widespread, this early-flowering orchid is uncommon throughout much of its range. Its stems are short but usually rather stout – often with a brownish purple hue. The oval or oblong leaves are up to 10cm (4in) long, with 2 to 4 forming a basal rosette, and the others sheathing the stem as far as the flower-head. The 2 to 15 flowers each have a dark bract which can be longer than the stalk-like ovary. The lateral sepals are held upright, and are greenish or purplish. The lip, up to 12mm (½in) long, is white, flushed with pink or purple.

• **DISTRIBUTION** Throughout. the region.

• **HABITAT** Dry, rocky ground, scrub, garigue.

unlobed lip and swollen sac-like spur

DETAIL

leaves with or without spots

flowers widely spaced

Habit Perennial	Height 12–35cm (4¾–14in)	Flowering time Feb–Mar

Family ORCHIDACEAE	Species *Orchis mascula*	Author L.

EARLY PURPLE ORCHID

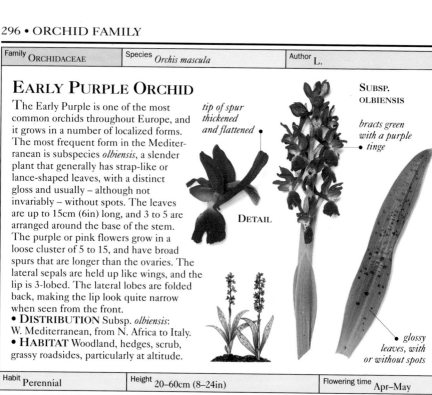

tip of spur thickened and flattened

SUBSP. OLBIENSIS

bracts green with a purple tinge

The Early Purple is one of the most common orchids throughout Europe, and it grows in a number of localized forms. The most frequent form in the Mediterranean is subspecies *olbiensis*, a slender plant that generally has strap-like or lance-shaped leaves, with a distinct gloss and usually – although not invariably – without spots. The leaves are up to 15cm (6in) long, and 3 to 5 are arranged around the base of the stem. The purple or pink flowers grow in a loose cluster of 5 to 15, and have broad spurs that are longer than the ovaries. The lateral sepals are held up like wings, and the lip is 3-lobed. The lateral lobes are folded back, making the lip look quite narrow when seen from the front.
• **DISTRIBUTION** Subsp. *olbiensis*: W. Mediterranean, from N. Africa to Italy.
• **HABITAT** Woodland, hedges, scrub, grassy roadsides, particularly at altitude.

DETAIL

glossy leaves, with or without spots

Habit Perennial	Height 20–60cm (8–24in)	Flowering time Apr–May

Family ORCHIDACEAE	Species *Orchis provincialis*	Author Balbis

PROVENCE ORCHID

This attractive and slender orchid is one of the few yellow-flowered members of its genus. Its leaves are lance-shaped or strap-like, up to 15cm (6in) long, and have conspicuous dark spots. There are 3 to 20 flowers, with bracts usually as long as their stalk-like ovaries. Each flower has a long upcurved spur, spreading upper sepals, and a 3-lobed lip up to 12mm (½in) long. The lip is darker than the rest of the flower.
• **DISTRIBUTION** W. Mediterranean, from N.W. Africa to Greece; absent from Balearic Islands.
• **HABITAT** Grassy ground, scrub, open woodland, maquis.

spotted leaves

long flower-bracts with 1–3 veins

dark lip, often with small darker spots

DETAIL

Habit Perennial	Height 15–35cm (6–14in)	Flowering time Apr–June

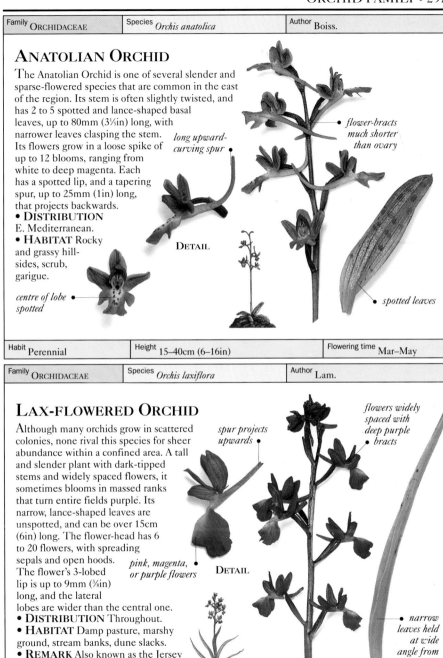

Family ORCHIDACEAE	Species *Orchis anatolica*	Author Boiss.

ANATOLIAN ORCHID

The Anatolian Orchid is one of several slender and sparse-flowered species that are common in the east of the region. Its stem is often slightly twisted, and has 2 to 5 spotted and lance-shaped basal leaves, up to 80mm (3⅛in) long, with narrower leaves clasping the stem. Its flowers grow in a loose spike of up to 12 blooms, ranging from white to deep magenta. Each has a spotted lip, and a tapering spur, up to 25mm (1in) long, that projects backwards.
• **DISTRIBUTION**
E. Mediterranean.
• **HABITAT** Rocky and grassy hill-sides, scrub, garigue.

long upward-curving spur

flower-bracts much shorter than ovary

DETAIL

centre of lobe spotted

spotted leaves

Habit Perennial	Height 15–40cm (6–16in)	Flowering time Mar–May

Family ORCHIDACEAE	Species *Orchis laxiflora*	Author Lam.

LAX-FLOWERED ORCHID

Although many orchids grow in scattered colonies, none rival this species for sheer abundance within a confined area. A tall and slender plant with dark-tipped stems and widely spaced flowers, it sometimes blooms in massed ranks that turn entire fields purple. Its narrow, lance-shaped leaves are unspotted, and can be over 15cm (6in) long. The flower-head has 6 to 20 flowers, with spreading sepals and open hoods. The flower's 3-lobed lip is up to 9mm (⅜in) long, and the lateral lobes are wider than the central one.
• **DISTRIBUTION** Throughout.
• **HABITAT** Damp pasture, marshy ground, stream banks, dune slacks.
• **REMARK** Also known as the Jersey Orchid, this species is found northwest to the Channel Islands.

spur projects upwards

flowers widely spaced with deep purple bracts

pink, magenta, or purple flowers

DETAIL

narrow leaves held at wide angle from stem

Habit Perennial	Height 30–120cm (12–48in)	Flowering time Apr–June

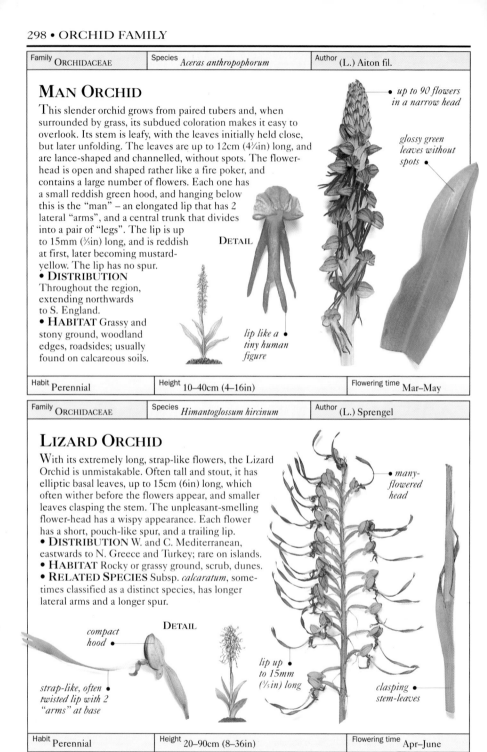

Family ORCHIDACEAE	Species *Aceras anthropophorum*	Author (L.) Aiton fil.

MAN ORCHID

This slender orchid grows from paired tubers and, when surrounded by grass, its subdued coloration makes it easy to overlook. Its stem is leafy, with the leaves initially held close, but later unfolding. The leaves are up to 12cm (4¾in) long, and are lance-shaped and channelled, without spots. The flower-head is open and shaped rather like a fire poker, and contains a large number of flowers. Each one has a small reddish green hood, and hanging below this is the "man" – an elongated lip that has 2 lateral "arms", and a central trunk that divides into a pair of "legs". The lip is up to 15mm (⅝in) long, and is reddish at first, later becoming mustard-yellow. The lip has no spur.

• **DISTRIBUTION** Throughout the region, extending northwards to S. England.

• **HABITAT** Grassy and stony ground, woodland edges, roadsides; usually found on calcareous soils.

DETAIL

up to 90 flowers in a narrow head

glossy green leaves without spots

lip like a tiny human figure

Habit Perennial	Height 10–40cm (4–16in)	Flowering time Mar–May

Family ORCHIDACEAE	Species *Himantoglossum hircinum*	Author (L.) Sprengel

LIZARD ORCHID

With its extremely long, strap-like flowers, the Lizard Orchid is unmistakable. Often tall and stout, it has elliptic basal leaves, up to 15cm (6in) long, which often wither before the flowers appear, and smaller leaves clasping the stem. The unpleasant-smelling flower-head has a wispy appearance. Each flower has a short, pouch-like spur, and a trailing lip.

• **DISTRIBUTION** W. and C. Mediterranean, eastwards to N. Greece and Turkey; rare on islands.

• **HABITAT** Rocky or grassy ground, scrub, dunes.

• **RELATED SPECIES** Subsp. *calcaratum*, sometimes classified as a distinct species, has longer lateral arms and a longer spur.

DETAIL

many-flowered head

compact hood

strap-like, often twisted lip with 2 "arms" at base

lip up to 15mm (⅗in) long

clasping stem-leaves

Habit Perennial	Height 20–90cm (8–36in)	Flowering time Apr–June

Family ORCHIDACEAE	Species *Barlia robertiana*	Author (Loisel.) W. Greuter

GIANT ORCHID

Although not the tallest orchid in the Mediterranean region, this early-flowering species is certainly the bulkiest. It grows from paired tubers, and has a stout stem that is often flushed with purple. The leaves are glossy, unspotted, and oval or elliptic, those near the base being up to 25cm (10in) long and 10cm (4in) wide. Its intensely fragrant flowers eventually form a column-like head that can be longer than the supporting stem. Each flower has a bract that is much longer than its ovary, 2 cupped, lateral sepals, a small hood, and a broad 3-lobed lip. The lip is up to 20mm (⅘in) long, and is either greenish or rusty pink, with spots or streaks, and a wavy margin. The long side lobes are arm-like, and the central lobe is divided into 2 leg-like flaps.
• **DISTRIBUTION** Throughout, except for the extreme east.
• **HABITAT** Grassy ground, open woodland, scrub, roadsides.

DETAIL

• *light-flowered form, with greenish lip*

• *dark bracts usually twice as long as ovaries*

flower-head elongates to form a column •

dark-flowered form, • with rusty pink lip

DETAIL

• *upper leaves clasp stem*

fleshy, glossy • leaves without spots

• *spreading lower leaves*

Habit Perennial	Height 30–80cm (12–32in)	Flowering time Dec–Mar

Family ORCHIDACEAE	Species *Anacamptis pyramidalis*	Author (L.) L. C. M. Richard

PYRAMIDAL ORCHID

The Pyramidal Orchid is widespread throughout the whole of Europe, and in parts of the Mediterranean can be seen in large numbers. It grows from paired tubers, and has a slender stem, leafy all the way to the flower-head. The lower leaves, up to 25cm (10in) long, are linear or lance-shaped and channelled, whereas the upper leaves are reduced to small clasping scales. Initially, the flower-head is always conical. The flowers are usually pink, and up to 10mm (⅜in) across. Each has a narrow bract about as long as its ovary, 2 spreading lateral sepals, a small hood, and a lip with 3 roughly equal lobes. A long, fine spur projects backwards and downwards.
• **DISTRIBUTION** Throughout.
• **HABITAT** Grassy ground, scrub, maquis, roadsides; usually on calcareous ground.
• **REMARK** This species is pollinated by butterflies and moths, whose long tongues can reach to the end of the spur.

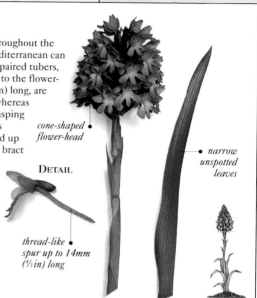

cone-shaped flower-head

DETAIL

narrow unspotted leaves

thread-like spur up to 14mm (½in) long

Habit Perennial	Height 20–60cm (8–24in)	Flowering time Mar–May

Family ORCHIDACEAE	Species *Serapias cordigera*	Author L.

HEART-FLOWERED SERAPIAS

This is the tallest of the tongue orchids, a small and particularly distinctive genus of Mediterranean plants. It grows from tuberous roots, and has narrow, channelled leaves, often reaching 13cm (5in) long, which clasp the stem as far as the flowers. The flower-head has 4 to 10 flowers, clustered closely together. Each flower has an almost cylindrical mouth, and is flanked by a dark bract that is much longer than the ovary. The lateral lobes of the lip form the sides of the mouth, while the central lobe forms a projecting heart-shaped tongue, about 25mm (1in) long, which is usually maroon or blood-red. This has dark hairs near its base.
• **DISTRIBUTION** W. and C. Mediterranean, eastwards to Turkey.
• **HABITAT** Damp grassy ground, heathland, scrub, sandy places.

bract and sepals similar in colour

central lobe of lip heart-shaped

DETAIL

narrow, channelled leaves

Habit Perennial	Height 15–45cm (6–18in)	Flowering time Mar–May

Family ORCHIDACEAE	Species *Serapias lingua*	Author L.

TONGUE ORCHID

Like its relatives, the Tongue Orchid often grows in scattered colonies, and in some places is a common roadside plant. It has slender stems and 4 to 5 narrow, lance-shaped leaves, with higher leaves clasping the stem. The flower-head contains 2 to 8 flowers and, unlike the Heart-flowered Serapias' (opposite), its flowers are well spread out. Each flower has a boat-shaped flanking bract, and sepals of the same reddish colour and veining form the hood. The hood is usually horizontal, and the flower has a sharply bent lip, which can be yellowish, pink, or red. The lateral lobes of the lip are always much darker than the projecting tongue. A characteristic feature of this species is a single swelling at the base of the lip.
• **DISTRIBUTION** W. and C. Mediterranean, from N.W. Africa to Greece.
• **HABITAT** Grassy ground, marshy areas, damp sand near the coast.

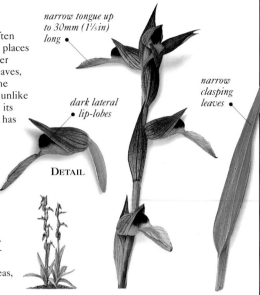

narrow tongue up to 30mm (1⅕in) long •

dark lateral • lip-lobes

narrow clasping leaves •

DETAIL

Habit Perennial	Height 10–30cm (4–12in)	Flowering time Mar–May

Family ORCHIDACEAE	Species *Serapias parviflora*	Author Parl.

SMALL TONGUE ORCHID

The Small Tongue Orchid is usually a rather drab plant, with narrow and channelled lance-shaped leaves that have a marked curve. The flower-head contains about 3 to 10 reddish green flowers, and each is 20mm (⅘in) long at the most. The flower-lip is reddish, with 2 darker lateral lobes that are normally hidden inside the flower's cylindrical mouth. The projecting tongue is narrow, and is sharply folded back so that it lies next to the flower's stalk-like ovary – a characteristic feature of this species.
• **DISTRIBUTION** W. and C. Mediterranean, from N.W. Africa eastwards to Turkey.
• **HABITAT** Grassland, olive groves, dune slacks, roadsides.
• **REMARK** The base of the flower's central lobe has 2 dark swellings – a feature that helps to distinguish this plant from the Tongue Orchid (above), which has just one.

small drab • flowers

narrow curved leaves •

DETAIL

• narrow lip folded back

Habit Perennial	Height 10–35cm (4–14in)	Flowering time Mar–May

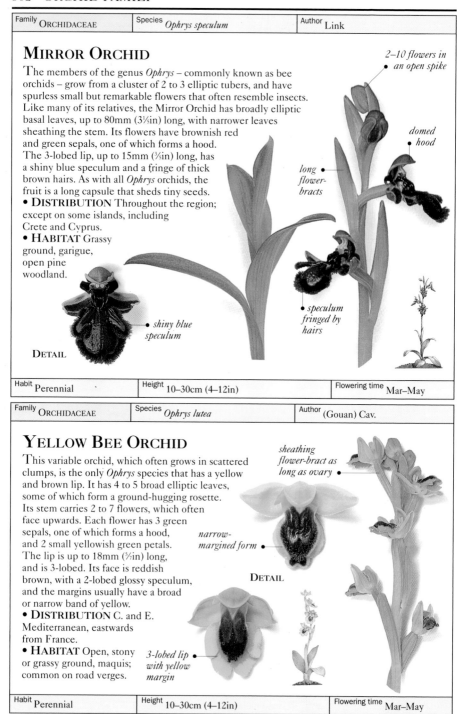

| Family ORCHIDACEAE | Species *Ophrys speculum* | Author Link |

MIRROR ORCHID

The members of the genus *Ophrys* – commonly known as bee orchids – grow from a cluster of 2 to 3 elliptic tubers, and have spurless small but remarkable flowers that often resemble insects. Like many of its relatives, the Mirror Orchid has broadly elliptic basal leaves, up to 80mm (3⅛in) long, with narrower leaves sheathing the stem. Its flowers have brownish red and green sepals, one of which forms a hood. The 3-lobed lip, up to 15mm (⅝in) long, has a shiny blue speculum and a fringe of thick brown hairs. As with all *Ophrys* orchids, the fruit is a long capsule that sheds tiny seeds.
• **DISTRIBUTION** Throughout the region; except on some islands, including Crete and Cyprus.
• **HABITAT** Grassy ground, garigue, open pine woodland.

2–10 flowers in an open spike

domed hood

long flower-bracts

speculum fringed by hairs

shiny blue speculum

DETAIL

| Habit Perennial | Height 10–30cm (4–12in) | Flowering time Mar–May |

| Family ORCHIDACEAE | Species *Ophrys lutea* | Author (Gouan) Cav. |

YELLOW BEE ORCHID

This variable orchid, which often grows in scattered clumps, is the only *Ophrys* species that has a yellow and brown lip. It has 4 to 5 broad elliptic leaves, some of which form a ground-hugging rosette. Its stem carries 2 to 7 flowers, which often face upwards. Each flower has 3 green sepals, one of which forms a hood, and 2 small yellowish green petals. The lip is up to 18mm (⅝in) long, and is 3-lobed. Its face is reddish brown, with a 2-lobed glossy speculum, and the margins usually have a broad or narrow band of yellow.
• **DISTRIBUTION** C. and E. Mediterranean, eastwards from France.
• **HABITAT** Open, stony or grassy ground, maquis; common on road verges.

sheathing flower-bract as long as ovary

narrow-margined form

DETAIL

3-lobed lip with yellow margin

| Habit Perennial | Height 10–30cm (4–12in) | Flowering time Mar–May |

Family ORCHIDACEAE	Species *Ophrys fusca*	Author Link

SOMBRE BEE ORCHID

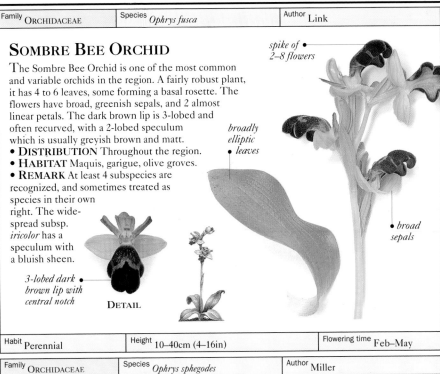

spike of 2–8 flowers

The Sombre Bee Orchid is one of the most common and variable orchids in the region. A fairly robust plant, it has 4 to 6 leaves, some forming a basal rosette. The flowers have broad, greenish sepals, and 2 almost linear petals. The dark brown lip is 3-lobed and often recurved, with a 2-lobed speculum which is usually greyish brown and matt.

broadly elliptic leaves

- **DISTRIBUTION** Throughout the region.
- **HABITAT** Maquis, garigue, olive groves.
- **REMARK** At least 4 subspecies are recognized, and sometimes treated as species in their own right. The widespread subsp. *iricolor* has a speculum with a bluish sheen.

broad sepals

3-lobed dark brown lip with central notch

DETAIL

Habit Perennial	Height 10–40cm (4–16in)	Flowering time Feb–May

Family ORCHIDACEAE	Species *Ophrys sphegodes*	Author Miller

EARLY SPIDER ORCHID

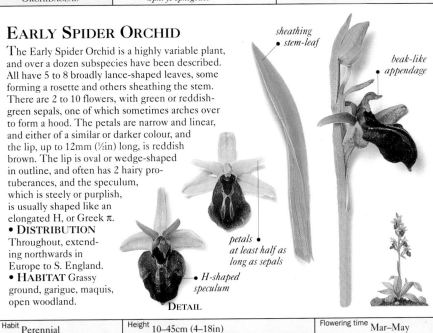

sheathing stem-leaf

beak-like appendage

The Early Spider Orchid is a highly variable plant, and over a dozen subspecies have been described. All have 5 to 8 broadly lance-shaped leaves, some forming a rosette and others sheathing the stem. There are 2 to 10 flowers, with green or reddish-green sepals, one of which sometimes arches over to form a hood. The petals are narrow and linear, and either of a similar or darker colour, and the lip, up to 12mm (½in) long, is reddish brown. The lip is oval or wedge-shaped in outline, and often has 2 hairy protuberances, and the speculum, which is steely or purplish, is usually shaped like an elongated H, or Greek π.

- **DISTRIBUTION** Throughout, extending northwards in Europe to S. England.
- **HABITAT** Grassy ground, garigue, maquis, open woodland.

petals at least half as long as sepals

H-shaped speculum

DETAIL

Habit Perennial	Height 10–45cm (4–18in)	Flowering time Mar–May

Family ORCHIDACEAE	Species *Ophrys ferrum-equinum*	Author Desf.

HORSESHOE ORCHID

This elegant orchid has lance-shaped basal leaves, often over 12cm (4¾in) long, with a few smaller leaves sheathing the stem. Although normally less than 40cm (16in) tall, specimens in shady woods can sometimes reach 60cm (24in). The stem carries 2 to 5 flowers with very conspicuous purple or pink sepals. These are roughly equal, with the uppermost one arching forwards over the flower. The reddish brown lip is up to 12mm (½in) long, and is either unlobed, or very slightly lobed, with a velvety texture. The plant takes its name from its bluish purple speculum, which is either shaped like a horseshoe, or reduced to 2 parallel lines.
• **DISTRIBUTION** S. Greece, Crete, Aegean region, Turkey.
• **HABITAT** Grassy or rocky ground, open pine woodland.

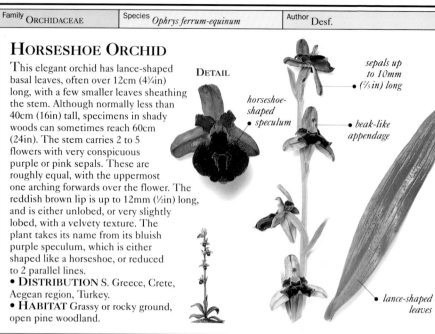

DETAIL

horseshoe-shaped • speculum

sepals up to 10mm (⅖in) long

beak-like appendage

lance-shaped leaves

Habit Perennial	Height 15–40cm (6–16in)	Flowering time Mar–May

Family ORCHIDACEAE	Species *Ophrys argolica*	Author Fleischm.

EYED BEE ORCHID

This variable and low-growing orchid has 4 to 6 lance-shaped leaves, and a stem that carries 2 to 8 flowers. Each flower has pink, purple, or rarely white sepals, up to 12mm (½in) long, which are rather narrow, with the uppermost sepal often curving forwards. The petals are wedge-shaped with broad bases, and are about half as long as the petals. The deep maroon lip is up to 12mm (½in) long, with a velvety surface. Its base is often light yellow, and the speculum is usually horseshoe- or H-shaped and generally indistinct, except for 2 prominent yellow "eyes".
• **DISTRIBUTION** E. Mediterranean, including S. Greece, Crete, and Turkey. Absent westward.
• **HABITAT** Scrub, grassy hillsides, olive groves.
• **REMARK** In subsp. *elegans*, the lip is 3-lobed; subsp. *flavescens* has white sepals and a very pale lip.

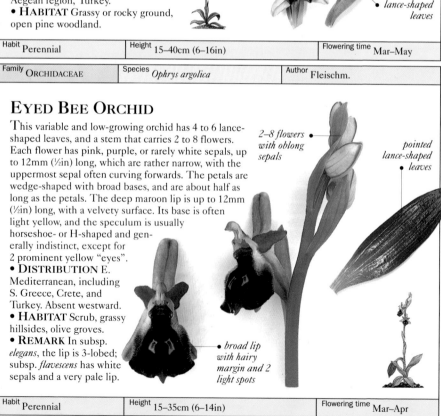

2–8 flowers with oblong sepals

pointed lance-shaped leaves

broad lip with hairy margin and 2 light spots

Habit Perennial	Height 15–35cm (6–14in)	Flowering time Mar–Apr

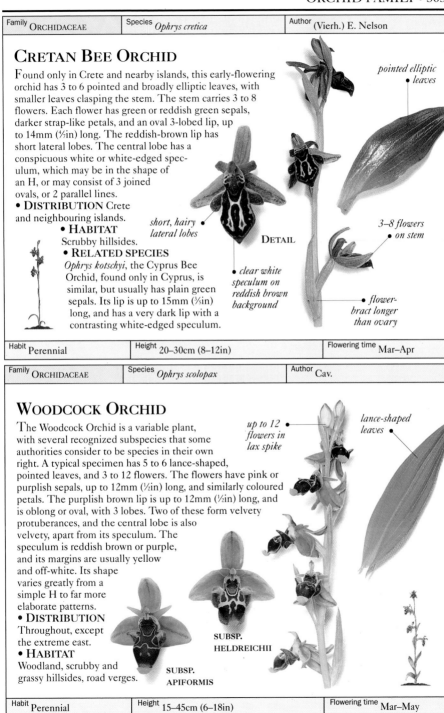

Family ORCHIDACEAE	Species *Ophrys cretica*	Author (Vierh.) E. Nelson

CRETAN BEE ORCHID

Found only in Crete and nearby islands, this early-flowering orchid has 3 to 6 pointed and broadly elliptic leaves, with smaller leaves clasping the stem. The stem carries 3 to 8 flowers. Each flower has green or reddish green sepals, darker strap-like petals, and an oval 3-lobed lip, up to 14mm (½in) long. The reddish-brown lip has short lateral lobes. The central lobe has a conspicuous white or white-edged speculum, which may be in the shape of an H, or may consist of 3 joined ovals, or 2 parallel lines.

• **DISTRIBUTION** Crete and neighbouring islands.

　　• **HABITAT** Scrubby hillsides.

　　• **RELATED SPECIES** *Ophrys kotschyi*, the Cyprus Bee Orchid, found only in Cyprus, is similar, but usually has plain green sepals. Its lip is up to 15mm (⅗in) long, and has a very dark lip with a contrasting white-edged speculum.

pointed elliptic leaves

short, hairy lateral lobes

DETAIL

3–8 flowers on stem

clear white speculum on reddish brown background

flower-bract longer than ovary

Habit Perennial	Height 20–30cm (8–12in)	Flowering time Mar–Apr

Family ORCHIDACEAE	Species *Ophrys scolopax*	Author Cav.

WOODCOCK ORCHID

The Woodcock Orchid is a variable plant, with several recognized subspecies that some authorities consider to be species in their own right. A typical specimen has 5 to 6 lance-shaped, pointed leaves, and 3 to 12 flowers. The flowers have pink or purplish sepals, up to 12mm (½in) long, and similarly coloured petals. The purplish brown lip is up to 12mm (½in) long, and is oblong or oval, with 3 lobes. Two of these form velvety protuberances, and the central lobe is also velvety, apart from its speculum. The speculum is reddish brown or purple, and its margins are usually yellow and off-white. Its shape varies greatly from a simple H to far more elaborate patterns.

• **DISTRIBUTION** Throughout, except the extreme east.

• **HABITAT** Woodland, scrubby and grassy hillsides, road verges.

up to 12 flowers in lax spike

lance-shaped leaves

SUBSP. HELDREICHII

SUBSP. APIFORMIS

Habit Perennial	Height 15–45cm (6–18in)	Flowering time Mar–May

Family ORCHIDACEAE	Species *Ophrys fuciflora*	Author (F. W. Schmidt) Moench

LATE SPIDER ORCHID

Also known as *Ophrys holoserica*, the Late Spider Orchid is a highly variable, widespread plant, with over 6 recognized subspecies in the region. Most plants have 4 to 7 broadly lance-shaped leaves, some clasping the stem. The number of flowers ranges from 2 to 14. Each flower has broad and roughly equal sepals, and these can be pink or pinkish white, often with a green central line. The petals, about half the length of the sepals, are of the same colour. The lip is variable in shape, but is normally broad and unlobed, giving the flower a "square-jawed" appearance. The speculum usually has a yellow margin, and is very variable in shape.
• **DISTRIBUTION**
Throughout, apart from the extreme east; also found in C. and N.W. Europe, just extending to S. England.
• **HABITAT** Grassy and scrubby ground, garigue.

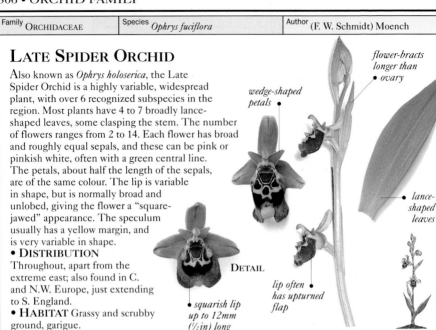

flower-bracts longer than • ovary

wedge-shaped petals •

• lance-shaped leaves

DETAIL

lip often • has upturned flap

• squarish lip up to 12mm (½in) long

Habit Perennial	Height 15–50cm (6–20in)	Flowering time Apr–May

Family ORCHIDACEAE	Species *Ophrys tenthredinifera*	Author Willd.

SAWFLY ORCHID

This handsome and vigorous orchid is often seen on stony or grassy ground near the coast. It has up to 9 broadly lance-shaped leaves, many of which clasp the stem, and bears about 3 to 8 flowers in an open spike. The sepals are usually rounded, and are often an intense lilac-pink. However, in some plants – such as the one shown here – they can be pale green, and in others they are whitish. The petals are triangular, with blunt tips. The flower-lip is up to 14mm (⅝in) long, and is usually unlobed with a distinctive rectangular shape. The lip margins are usually yellow, although they may be green or light brown. The speculum has a C- or W-shaped outline.
• **DISTRIBUTION**
W. and C. Mediterranean, from N. Africa to Turkey.
• **HABITAT** Scrub, grassy or stony ground, often close to the coast.

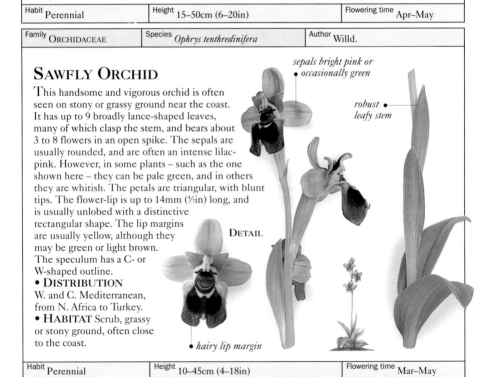

sepals bright pink or • occasionally green

robust • leafy stem

DETAIL

• hairy lip margin

Habit Perennial	Height 10–45cm (4–18in)	Flowering time Mar–May

Family ORCHIDACEAE	Species *Ophrys apifera*	Author Hudson

BEE ORCHID

One of the most widespread *Ophrys* species, the Bee Orchid
is found not only in the Mediterranean but also as far north
as the Scottish borders. A variable plant, it has oval or lance-
shaped basal leaves, and narrower leaves clasping the stem.
There are 2 to 9 flowers, each having broad sepals up
to 15mm (⅗in) long. The sepals are usually pale pink,
although they are sometimes white. The pinkish petals
are much shorter than the sepals, and the lip is up
to 13mm (½in) long, often with a pronounced
"beak". The lip is generally reddish brown,
with 2 stumpy lateral lobes, and a
rounded central lobe. The speculum
normally has a yellowish margin.
• **DISTRIBUTION** Throughout.
• **HABITAT** Woodland, maquis,
scrub, garigue, dune slacks.
• **REMARK** Widespread
varieties include *O. apifera* var.
chlorantha, which has whitish sepals
and a greenish lip, and *O. apifera* var.
trollii, Wasp Orchid, which has a
yellowish lip, with a sharp tip.

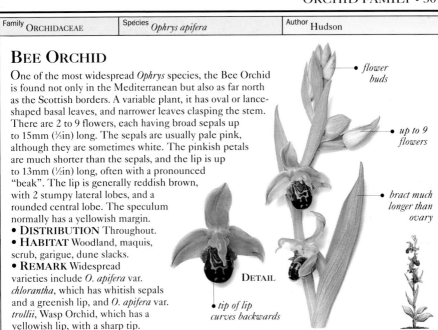

• *flower buds*

• *up to 9 flowers*

• *bract much longer than ovary*

DETAIL

• *tip of lip curves backwards*

Habit Perennial	Height 15–50cm (6–20in)	Flowering time Apr–May

Family ORCHIDACEAE	Species *Ophrys bombyliflora*	Author Link

BUMBLEBEE ORCHID

The Bumblebee Orchid is one of the smallest and
least conspicuous of all Mediterranean
orchids. It has a rosette of broadly lance-
shaped leaves, the lowest hugging the
ground and the upper ones clasping the
stem. The flowers are often less than 20mm (⅘in)
across. Their sepals are rounded and green, while
the 2 petals are short and triangular, and are also
green except for their dark bases. The lip is
dull brown, and is up to 8mm (⅓in)
long. It has 3 lobes, the lateral 2
hairy and pointing backwards.
The central lobe has a small
terminal point, and has a
roughly X- or H-shaped
speculum, but this is
often indistinct.
• **DISTRIBUTION**
Scattered localities
throughout.
• **HABITAT** Rough
grassland, olive groves.

spike of 1–5 blooms

rounded green sepals •

upper leaves clasp stem •

brown, 3-lobed lip • **DETAIL**

bract shorter than ovary

Habit Perennial	Height 7–25cm (2⅘–10in)	Flowering time Mar–May

GLOSSARY

Terms for parts of a plant are explained on pp.12–19. Below, words printed in **bold** type refer to entries elsewhere in the glossary.

• **AWN**
In grasses, a bristle-like structure projecting from the **flower-head**.

• **AXIL**
The angle between the stem and a lateral branch or leaf.

• **BIPINNATE**
Pinnate but with divisions that are themselves pinnate.

• **BRACT**
A leaf-like structure, often growing below a flower.

• **BRACTEOLE**
A secondary **bract**, either above a bract or on a lateral branch.

• **BULB**
A food-storage organ formed by a compact cluster of fleshy leaf bases.

• **BULBIL**
A small **bulb**, often located in the **axil** of a leaf or **bract**.

• **CALCAREOUS**
Having a high calcium content; refers to rocks and soils.

• **CALYX**
The outermost **whorl** of a flower, containing the sepals.

• **CARPEL**
A female seed-producing unit in a flower, consisting of an ovary connected by a style to a stigma.

• **COROLLA**
An inner **whorl** of a flower, containing the petals.

• **CORONA**
A collection of petal-like flaps, often drawn out to form a tube.

• **CRENATE**
Having minutely round-toothed or scalloped margins.

• **DECIDUOUS**
Shedding leaves and/or other organs annually.

• **DISC-FLORET**
A **floret** in the disc-like centre of a **flower-head**.

• **EPICALYX**
A secondary **calyx**, outside the true calyx.

• **FLORET**
A small flower in a **flower-head**; often refers to daisy flowers.

• **FLOWER-HEAD**
A group of flowers or **florets** having a characteristic and recognizable form.

• **GLAND**
A small superficial organ that secretes oils or other substances.

• **GLANDULAR HAIR**
A hair that contains a **gland**.

• **HEMIPARASITIC**
Living partly on nutrients abstracted from other plants.

• **HERBACEOUS**
Dying down to ground level at the end of each growing season.

• **HYPANTHIAL TUBE**
A tube formed by the extension of the **receptacle** below a flower.

• **INFLORESCENCE**
A group of flowers arising from a common stem.

• **INTRODUCED**
Brought into a region by human activity – accidentally or otherwise.

• **INVOLUCRE**
A ring of crowded bracts encircling a **flower-head**.

• **INVOLUCRAL BRACT**
A bract that forms part of an involucre.

• **KEEL**
In flowers of the pea family, a basal pair of petals that are joined to form a hull-shaped structure.

• **LATEX**
Viscous, milky sap.

• **LIP**
A substantial lobe formed by parts of a flower.

• **MEALY**
Having a flour-like texture.

• **NATIVE**
Belonging to a region through natural circumstances.

• **NATURALIZED**
Introduced into a region, and subsequently surviving naturally.

• **NECTARY**
Nectar-secreting organ: usually formed by a modified flower-part.

• **NODE**
The point on a stem where one or more leaves are attached.

• **PARASITIC**
Deriving nutrients entirely from another plant.

• **PINNATE**
Having leaflets arranged on two sides of a common stalk.

• **RAY-FLORET**
A strap-like **floret**, often around the circumference of a **flower-head**.

• **RECEPTACLE**
The part of a stem that has flower-parts attached to it.

• **RECURVED**
Bent backwards.

• **RHIZOME**
A creeping underground stem that often acts as a food-storage organ.

• **RUNNER**
A **stolon** that grows above ground.

• **SAPROPHYTE**
A plant that derives its nutrients from dead organic matter.

• **SEPTUM**
A partition; often refers to walls within a fruit.

• **SPATHE**
In monocots, a bract that may completely surround an inflorescence.

• **SPECULUM**
A mirror-like patch found on the **lip** of certain orchids.

• **SPUR**
A hollow pouch, formed by petals or sepals, projecting from a flower.

• **STAMINODE**
A sterile stamen, often modified into a petal or **nectary**.

• **STANDARD**
In flowers of the pea family, the uppermost petal, which is often large and **recurved**.

• **STOLON**
A stem that grows horizontally, either above or below ground.

• **SHRUBLET**
A small woody perennial, usually less than 50cm (20in) high.

• **SUCCULENT**
Fleshy; a plant with fleshy leaves.

• **SUTURE**
A seam along which a pod or other fruit splits open.

• **TAPROOT**
A strong main root that grows vertically downwards.

• **TEPAL**
An outer segment in a monocot flower; tepals are not clearly differentiated into petals and sepals.

• **TUBER**
A food-storage organ formed by a swollen underground stem.

• **TUBERCLE**
A small warty protuberance.

• **VALVE**
One of several parts of a fruit that become fully or partly separated.

• **WHORL**
A collection of organs encircling a stem.

• **WING**
In flowers of the pea family, a lateral petal.

INDEX

A

Acacia karoo 84
Acacia retinodes 84
Acanthaceae 217
Acanthus family 217
Acanthus mollis 217
Acanthus spinosus 217
Aceras anthropophorum 298
Achene 18
Achillea millefolium 235
Achillea tomentosa 235
Actinomorphic flowers 17
Adenocarpus complicatus 88
Adenocarpus telonensis 88
Adonis annua 59
Adonis microcarpa 59
Aegilops neglecta 284
Aegilops speltoides 284
Agavaceae 273
Agave americana 273
Agave family 273
Agrostemma githago 49
Agrostemma gracilis 49
Aizoaceae 47
Ajuga chamaepitys 190
Ajuga iva 190
Alcea pallida 142
Alcea rosea 142
Alexanders 159
Alexanders, Perfoliate 159
Alfalfa 104
Algerian Iris 278
Alkanet 186
Alkanet, Dyer's 183
Alkanet, Large Blue 186
Alkanna sartoriana 183
Alkanna tinctoria 183
Allium ampeloprasum 270
Allium atropurpureum 270
Allium neapolitanum 268
Allium nigrum 270
Allium pendulinum 269
Allium roseum 268
Allium subhirsutum 269
Allium subvillosum 269
Allium trifoliatum 269

Allium triquetrum 269
Althaea officinalis 141
Alyssum, Golden 74
Alyssum saxatile 74
Amaranthaceae 44
Amaranth family 44
Amaranthus cruentus 44
Amaryllidaceae 273
American Pokeweed 46
Ammophila arenaria 286
Anacamptis pyramidalis 300
Anacardiaceae 134
Anacyclus clavatus 236
Anagallis arvensis 170
Anagallis foemina 170
Anagyris foetida 85
Anatolian Orchid 297
Anchusa arvensis 186
Anchusa azurea 186
Anchusa cretica 187
Anchusa officinalis 186
Anchusa undulata 186
Anchusa variegata 187
Andryala integrifolia 254
Anemone coronaria 56
Anemone, Crown 56
Anemone heldreichii 57
Anemone hortensis 58
Anemone pavonina 57
Animal dispersal 19
Annual Daisy 228
Annual Lavatera 141
Annual Nettle 37
Annual Scorpion Vetch 114
Annual Yellow Vetchling 97
Anthemis arvensis 234
Anthemis chia 234
Anthemis cotula 234
Anthemis rigida 234
Anthyllis cytisoides 111
Anthyllis hermanniae 112
Anthyllis tetraphylla 111
Anthyllis vulneraria 112
Antirrhinum latifolium 210
Antirrhinum majus 210
Aphyllanthes monspeliensis 258

Apocynaceae 175
Apple, Sodom 204
Apple, Thorn 205
Arabis recta 73
Arabis verna 73
Araceae 288
Arbutus andrachne 167
Arbutus x *andrachnoides* 167
Arbutus unedo 167
Arisarum proboscideum 288
Arisarum vulgare 288
Aristolochiaceae 39
Aristolochia clematitis 40
Aristolochia cretica 39
Aristolochia pistolochia 39
Aristolochia rotunda 41
Aristolochia sempervirens 40
Aromatic Inula 231
Artichoke, Globe 245
Arum dioscoridis 288
Arum, Dragon 289
Arum family 288
Arum, Italian 288
Arum italicum 288
Arundo donax 287
Asclepiadaceae 176
Asparagus acutifolius 271
Asparagus albus 271
Asparagus, Bath 264
Asparagus, Common 271
Asparagus maritimus 271
Asparagus officinalis 271
Asphodel, Common 257
Asphodel, Hollow-leaved 256
Asphodeline liburnica 258
Asphodeline lutea 258
Asphodelus aestivus 257
Asphodelus alba 257
Asphodelus fistulosus 256
Asphodel, White 257
Asphodel, Yellow 258
Asteriscus aquaticus 232
Asteriscus maritimus 232

Aster, Sea 228
Aster tripolium 228
Astragalus hamosus 92
Astragalus massiliensis 92
Astragalus monspessulanus 93
Atractylis cancellata 240
Atractylis gummifera 240
Atractylis humilis 240
Aubrieta 73
Aubrieta deltoidea 73
Autumn Crocus 259
Autumn Snowflake 274
Autumn Squill 266
Avena sterilis 285

B

Ballota acetabulosa 195
Balsam family 135
Balsaminaceae 135
Balsam, Kashmir 135
Barbary Nut 280
Barberry family 63
Barlia robertiana 299
Bartsia, Southern Red 214
Bartsia, Yellow 215
Basil, Cow 51
Basil, Wild 197

Bath Asparagus 264
Bear's Breech 217
Bear's Breech, Spiny 217
Bedstraw family 177
Bedstraw, Lady's 177
Bee Orchid 307
Bee Orchid, Cretan 305
Bee Orchid, Cyprus 305
Bee Orchid, Eyed 304
Bee Orchid, Sombre 303
Bee Orchid, Yellow 302
Bellardia trixago 215
Bellflower family 225
Bell Heather 165
Bellis annua 228
Bellis perennis 228
Berberidaceae 63
Bermuda Buttercup 120
Bermuda Grass 287
Berries 19
Betony, Water 208
Bindweed 180
Bindweed family 178
Bindweed, Mallow-leaved 179
Bindweed, Sea 179
Bird's-foot, Orange 113
Bird's-foot Trefoil, Common 108
Bird's-foot Trefoil, Greater 108
Bird's Nest Orchid 291
Bird's Nest Orchid, Violet 291
Birthwort 40
Birthwort family 39
Birthwort, Round-leaved 41
Biscutella didyma 76
Black Bryony 277
Blackstonia perfoliata 174
Bladder Campion 50
Bladder Senna 91
Bladder Vetch 111
Blue Eryngo 157
Blue Hound's-tongue 188
Blue Lettuce 254
Blue Pimpernel 170
Bokhara Clover 101

Bongardia chrysopogon 63
Borage 187
Borage family 181
Boraginaceae 181
Borago officinalis 187
Borago pygmaea 187
Botanist's equipment 24
Bougainvillea 45
Bouganvillea glabra 45
Box 136
Box family 136
Branched Broomrape 218
Bristly-fruited Silkweed 176
Briza maxima 283
Briza media 283
Broad-leaved Everlasting Pea 99
Broad-leaved Helleborine 290
Broadleaved woodland 21
Broom, Butcher's 272
Broomrape, Branched 218
Broomrape family 218
Broom, Spanish 87
Broom, Thorny 86
Bryonia alba 153
Bryonia cretica 153
Bryony, Black 277
Bryony, White 153
Buck's-horn Plantain 220
Buckthorn Family 136
Buckthorn, Mediterranean 136
Bugloss 186
Bugloss, Narrow-leaved 184
Bugloss, Pale 184
Bugloss, Purple Viper's 185
Bugloss, Viper's 185
Bug Orchid 293
Bulb 12
Bumblebee Orchid 307
Bupleurum flavum 161
Bupleurum fruticosum 161
Bupleurum gibraltaricum 161
Burnet, Thorny 82

Butcher's Broom 272
Buttercup, Bermuda 120
Buttercup family 54
Buttercup, Turban 60
Butterfly Orchid, Greater 292
Butterfly Orchid, Pink 292
Buttonweed 238
Buxus sempervirens 136

C

Cactaceae 154
Cactus family 154
Cakile màritima 77
Calendula arvensis 239
Calendula officinalis 239
Calicotome spinosa 86
Calicotome villosa 85
Calluna vulgaris 166
Caltrop family 123
Caltrops, Small 123
Calystegia soldanella 179
Campanulaceae 225
Campanula saxatilis 225
Campanula tubulosa 226
Campion, Bladder 50
Campion, White 50
Candytuft 75
Caper 69
Caper family 69
Capitulum 16
Capparidaceae 69
Capparis ovata 69
Capparis spinosa 69
Caprifoliaceae 221
Capsule 18
Cardaria draba 76
Cardoon 245
Carduncellus caeruleus 249
Carduncellus monspelliensium 249
Carduus pycnocephalus 242

Carlina acanthifolia 240
Carlina corymbosa 240
Carmel Daisy 225
Carob 83
Carpobrotus edulis 47
Carrot family 157
Carrot, Wild 165
Carthamus arborescens 249
Carthamus lanatus 249
Caryophyllaceae 48
Cashew family 134
Castor Oil Plant 126
Catacanche caerulea 251
Catacanche lutea 251
Catchfly, Small-flowered 50
Celandine, Lesser 61
Centaurea calcitrapa 247
Centaurea melitensis 248
Centaurea solstitialis 248
Centaurea sphaerocephala 247
Centaurium erythraea 174
Centaurium pulchellum 174
Centaury, Common 174
Centaury, Lesser 174
Centranthus ruber 223
Century Plant 273
Cephalanthera longifolia 291
Cephalanthera rubra 291
Ceratonia siliqua 83
Cercis siliquastrum 83
Cerinthe major 183
Chamaemelum mixtum 235

Chamaemelum nobile 235
Chamomile 235
Chamomile, Corn 234
Chamomile, Stinking 234
Chaste Tree 189
Cheiranthus cheiri 71
Chenopodiaceae 43
Chicory 251
Chicory, Spiny 251
Chrysanthemum coronarium 237
Chrysanthemum segetum 237
Cichorium intybus 251
Cichorium spinosa 251
Cistaceae 146
Cistus albidus 146
Cistus, Grey-leaved 146
Cistus incanus 147
Cistus ladanifer 148
Cistus monspeliensis 149
Cistus, Narrow-leaved 149
Cistus populifolius 149
Cistus, Sage-leaved 149
Cistus salvifolius 149
Clary 201
Clematis flammula 58
Clematis, Fragrant 58
Clematis viticella 59
Climate 6
Climbing plants 14
Clinopodium vulgare 197
Clover, Bokhara 101
Clover, Narrow leaved Crimson 105
Clover, Star 105
Clypeola jonthlaspi 75
Cneorum family 132
Cneorum tricoccon 132
Cocklebur 233
Cocklebur, Spiny 233
Cock's-comb Sainfoin 118
Colchicum autumnale 259
Colutea arborescens 91
Comfrey, Tuberous 185
Common Asparagus 271
Common Asphodel 257

Common Bird's-foot Trefoil 108
Common Centaury 174
Common Dodder 178
Common Elder 221
Common Field Speedwell 214
Common Figwort 208
Common Fleabane 232
Common Fumitory 68
Common Grape Hyacinth 267
Common Honeysuckle 222
Common Jonquil 275
Common Juniper 34
Common Lavender 199
Common Mallow 137
Common Peony 63
Common Poppy 65
Common Sea Lavender 171
Common Skullcap 192
Common Thyme 198
Common Toadflax 212
Common Vetch 95
Compositae 228
Compound leaves 15
Coniferous woodland 21
Conifers 34
Consolida ambigua 55
Consolida orientalis 55
Consolida regalis 55
Convolvulaceae 178
Convolvulus althaeoides 179
Convolvulus arvensis 180
Convolvulus cneorum 180
Convolvulus lanuginosus 180
Convolvulus oleifolius 180
Coris monspeliensis 170
Corm 12
Corn Chamomile 234
Corncockle 49
Corn Marigold 237
Coronilla cretica 116
Coronilla emerus 114
Coronilla globosa 115
Coronilla juncea 113
Coronilla scorpioides 114

Coronilla valentina 114
Coronilla varia 115
Corymb 16
Cotinus coggygria 134
Cotton Lavender 233
Cottonweed 236
Cotula coronopifolia 238
Couch, Sand 284
Cow Basil 51
Cranesbill, Tuberous 121
Crassulaceae 79
Crepis capillaris 254
Crepis rubra 254
Cress family 70
Cress, Disc 75
Cress, Hoary 76
Cretan Bee Orchid 305
Crithmum maritimum 160
Crocus, Autumn 259
Crocus biflorus 280
Crocus cambessedesii 281
Crocus corsicus 281
Crocus, Sand 281
Crocus versicolor 281
Crosswort 177
Crown Anemone 56
Crown Daisy 237
Crown Vetch 115
Cruciata laevipes 177
Cruciferae 70
Crupina crupinastrum 248
Cucumber, Squirting 153
Cucurbitaceae 153
Cultivated Flax 124
Cultivated ground 23
Cupidone 251
Cupressaceae 34
Cuscuta epithymum 178
Cut-leaved Lavender 200
Cut-leaved Self-heal 196
Cyclamen balearicum 168
Cyclamen creticum 169
Cyclamen hederifolium 168
Cyclamen persicum 169
Cyclamen repandum 169
Cymbalaria muralis 213
Cyme 16
Cynara cardunculus 245
Cynara cornigera 245
Cynara scolymus 245
Cynodon dactylon 287

Cynoglossum cheirifolium 188
Cynoglossum columnae 188
Cynoglossum creticum 188
Cynosurus echinatus 283
Cypress family 34
Cypress Spurge 129
Cyprus Bee Orchid 305
Cytinus hypocistis 41
Cytisus villosus 86

D

Daffodil family 273
Daffodil, Hoop Petticoat 275
Daffodil, Sea 277
Daffodil, White Hoop Petticoat 275
Daisy 228
Daisy, Annual 228
Daisy, Carmel 225
Daisy, Crown 237
Daisy family 228
Danewort 221
Daphne family 143
Daphne gnidium 143
Daphne laureola 144
Daphne sericea 143
Datura stramonium 205
Daucus carota 165
Deadnettle, Henbit 195
Deadnettle, Spotted 195
Dehiscent fruits 18
Dianthus carthusianorum 53
Dianthus sylvestris 53
Dicotyledons 36
Dicotyledons, identification 25
Dioscoreaceae 277
Dipsacaceae 224
Disc Cress 75
Dissected leaves 15
Dittany, False 195
Dittrichia viscosa 231
Dock family 42
Dock, Horned 42
Dodder, Common 178
Dog Rose 81
Dorycnium hirsutum 107
Dorycnium pentaphyllum 107

Downy
 Woundwort 196
Dracunculus vulgaris
 289
Dragon Arum 289
Dragon's Teeth 109
Dwarf Elder 221
Dwarf Mallow 139
Dyer's Alkanet 183

E

Early Purple Orchid
 296
Early Spider Orchid
 303
Ebenus cretica 119
Ecballium elaterium 153
Echinophora spinosa
 158
Echinops ritro 241
Echinops spinosissimus
 241
Echium angustifolium
 184
Echium asperrimum 184
Echium creticum 184
Echium italicum 184
Echium plantagineum
 185
Echium vulgare 185
Elder, Common 221
Elder, Dwarf 221
Elymus farctus 284
Ephedraceae 35
Ephedra distachya 35
Ephedra fragilis 35
Ephedra major 35
Epipactis helleborine 290
Erect plants 14
Ericaceae 165

Erica arborea 166
Erica cinerea 165
Erodium gruinum 122
Erodium malacoides 122
Erodium moschatum
 123
Erodium petraeum 121
Eruca vesicaria 76
Eryngium amethystinum
 157
Eryngium campestre 157
Eryngium maritimum
 157
Eryngo, Blue 157
Eryngo, Field 157
Esparto Grass 286
Etruscan Honeysuckle
 222
Eucalyptus
 camaldulensis 155
Euphorbia
 acanthothamnos 128
Euphorbiaceae 126
Euphorbia characias
 127
Euphorbia cyparissias
 129
Euphorbia dendroides
 129
Euphorbia helioscopia
 128
Euphorbia maculata
 131
Euphorbia paralias 130
Euphorbia peplis 131
Euphorbia peplus 131
Euphorbia pithyusa 130
Euphorbia rigida 130
Euphorbia spinosa 128
Evening Primrose,
 Large-flowered 156
Everlasting Pea,
 Broadleaved 99
Eyed Bee Orchid 304
Fagaceae 36

F

False Dittany 195
Fat Hen family 43
Felty Germander 191
Fennel 160
Fennel, Giant 162
Ferula communis 162
Ferulago asparagifolia
 163
Ferulago nodosa 163
Ferula tingitana 162
Ficus carica 36

Field Eryngo 157
Field Gladiolus 282
Field Marigold 239
Field Speedwell,
 Common 214
Fig 36
Fig, Hottentot 47
Figwort, Common 208
Figwort family 206
Figwort, French 208
Figwort, Nettle-leaved
 209
Figwort, Water 208
Flax, Cultivated 124
Flax family 124
Flax, Pale 124
Flax, Upright Yellow
 125
Flax, White 125
Fleabane, Common
 232
Flowering 11
Flowers 13
Flower types 16
Fluellen 213
Foeniculum vulgare 160
Follicle 18
Forking Larkspur 55
Four O'clock
 family 45
Four O'clock Plant 45
Fragrant Clematis 58
Frankeniaceae 152
Frankenia laevis 152
French Figwort 208
French Lavender 200
Friar's Cowl 288
Fringed Rue 132
Fritillaria messanensis
 263
Fritillaria pontica 263
Fruits 13
Fruit types 18
Fumaria capreolata 68
Fumaria officinalis 68
Fumitory, Common 68
Fumitory, Ramping 68

G

Gagea graeca 260
Gagea peduncularis 259
Gagea trinerva 260
Galactites tomentosa 244
Galium verum 177
Garden Marigold 239
Garigue 22
Garlic, Naples 268
Garlic, Rosy 268

Genista cinerea 87
Genista scorpius 87
Gentianaceae 174
Gentian family 174
Geraniaceae 121
Geranium family 121
Geranium tuberosum
 121
Germander, Felty 191
Germander, Tree 191
German Iris, White
 279
Germination 10
Giant Fennel 162
Giant Orchid 299
Giant Reed 287
Gladiolus communis 282
Gladiolus, Field 282
Gladiolus illyricus 282
Gladiolus italicus 282
Glasswort 43
Glaucium corniculatum
 66
Glaucium flavum 66
Globe Artichoke 245
Globe Thistle 241
Globularia 216
Globularia alypum 216
Globulariaceae 216
Globularia family 216
Globularia punctata 216
Globularia, Shrubby
 216
Golden Drop 182
Golden Henbane 203
Golden Samphire 231
Gomphocarpus fruticosus
 176
Gourd family 153
Gramineae 283
Grape Hyacinth,
 Common 267
Grass, Bermuda 287
Grass, Esparto 286
Grass family 283
Grass, Large Quaking
 283
Grass-leaved Scabious
 224
Grass, Needle 286
Grassy ground habitat
 23
Greater Bird's-foot
 Trefoil 108
Greater Butterfly
 Orchid 292
Greater Periwinkle
 176
Great Mullein 207

Greek Spiny Spurge 128
Greek Strawberry Tree 167
Green-winged Orchid 293
Grey-leaved Cistus 146
Gromwell, Shrubby 181
Ground-pine 190
Growth habit 14
Gum Cistus 148
Gum, Red 155
Guttiferae 145
Gynandriris sisyrinchium 280

H

Habitats 20
Hairy Yellow Vetch 94
Halimione portulacoides 43
Halimium halimifolium 150
Hare's Ear, Shrubby 161
Hare's-foot Plantain 219
Hare's Tail 285
Hawksbeard, Smooth 254
Heart-flowered Serapias 300
Heather 166
Heather, Bell 165
Heather family 165
Heath, Sea 152
Heath, Tree 166
Hedge-parsley, Spreading 164
Hedysarum coronarium 117
Hedysarum spinosissimum 117
Helianthemum apenninum 151
Helianthemum lavandulifolium 151
Helichrysum italicum 229
Helichrysum sanguineum 229
Helichrysum stoechas 229
Heliotrope 181
Heliotropium europaeum 181

Hellebore, Stinking 54
Helleborine, Broad-leaved 290
Helleborine, Narrow-leaved 291
Helleborine, Red 291
Helleborus cyclophyllus 54
Helleborus foetidus 54
Helleborus lividus 54
Henbane, Golden 203
Henbane, White 203
Henbit Deadnettle 195
Herbaceous Periwinkle 175
Hermodactylus tuberosus 278
Hibiscus 142
Hibiscus rosa-sinensis 142
Himantoglossum hircinum 298
Hippocrepis unisiliquosa 116
Hoary Cress 76
Hoary Mullein 207
Hoary Plantain 219
Hoary Stock 72
Hollow-leaved Asphodel 256
Hollyhock 142
Holly, Sea 157
Holy Thistle 246
Honesty 74
Honeysuckle, Common 222
Honeysuckle, Etruscan 222
Honeysuckle family 221
Honeywort 183
Hoop Petticoat Daffodil 275
Hoop Petticoat Daffodil, White 275
Hop Trefoil 106
Horned Dock 42
Horseshoe Orchid 304
Hottentot Fig 47
Hound's-tongue, Blue 188
Hyacinth, Common Grape 267
Hyacinth, Tassel 267
Hyoscyamus albus 203
Hyoscyamus aureus 203

Hyoseris radiata 252
Hyoseris scabra 252
Hypecoum imberbe 67
Hypecoum procumbens 67
Hypericum empetrifolium 145
Hypericum perforatum 145

I

Iberis amara 75
Identification 25
Illyrian Sea Lily 276
Impatiens balfourii 135
Indehiscent fruits 18
Indian Bead Tree 133
Inflorescence types 16
Intermediate Periwinkle 175
Inula, Aromatic 231
Inula crithmoides 231
Iridaceae 278
Iris albicans 279
Iris, Algerian 278
Iris attica 279
Iris family 278
Iris germanica var. *florentina* 279
Iris lutescens 279
Iris, Snake's Head 278
Iris, Spanish 280
Iris unguicularis 278
Iris, White German 279
Iris, Widow 278
Iris xiphium 280
Irregular flowers 17
Isatis tinctoria 70
Italian Arum 288
Italian Man Orchid 294
Italian Sainfoin 117
Ivy-leaved Sowbread 168
Ivy-leaved Toadflax 213

J

Japanese Pittosporum 80
Jersey Orchid 297
Jersey Toadflax 211
Jerusalem Sage 193
Joint Pine 35
Joint Pine family 35
Jonquil, Common 275

Judas Tree 83
Juniper, Common 34
Juniper, Phoenician 34
Juniper, Prickly 34
Juniperus communis 34
Juniperus oxycedrus 34
Juniperus phoenicea 34

K

Kashmir Balsam 135
Kermes Oak 36
Kickxia commutata 213
Kickxia lanigera 213
Kidney Vetch 112
Knotgrass, Sea 42

L

Labiatae 190
Lactuca perennis 254
Lady Orchid 295
Lady's Bedstraw 177
Lady Tulip 261
Lagoecia cuminoides 158
Lagurus ovatus 285
Lamium amplexicaule 195
Lamium maculatum 195
Landscape history 7
Large Blue Alkanet 186
Large Disc Medick 103
Large-flowered Evening Primrose 156
Large Mediterranean Spurge 127
Large Quaking Grass 283

Large Snapdragon 210
Large Venus's Looking
Glass 227
Large Yellow
Rest-harrow 100
Larkspur, Forking 55
Late Spider Orchid
306
Lathraea clandestina
216
Lathyrus annuus 97
Lathyrus aphaca 97
Lathyrus articulatus 98
Lathyrus cicera 98
Lathyrus clymenum 98
Lathyrus latifolius 99
Lathyrus sylvestris 99
Laurel, Spurge 144
Laurustinus 221
Lavandula angustifolia
199
Lavandula dentata 200
Lavandula multifida
200
Lavandula stoechas 200
Lavandula viridis 200
Lavatera, Annual 141
Lavatera arborea 138
*Lavatera
bryoniifolia* 139
Lavatera cretica
139

Lavatera maritima 140
Lavatera trimestris 141
Lavender, Common
199
Lavender, Common
Sea 171
Lavender, Cotton 233
Lavender, Cut-leaved
200
Lavender, French 200
Lavender, Toothed
200
Lavender, Winged Sea
172
Lax-flowered Orchid
297
Leaf types 15
Leek, Three-cornered
269
Leek, Wild 270
Legousia hybrida 227
Legousia pentagonia 226
*Legousia speculum-
veneris* 227
Leguminosae 83
Lentisc 134
Leontice 63
Leontice leontopetalum
63
Lesser Celandine 61
Lesser Centaury 174
Lesser
Sea-spurrey 48
Lesser
Snapdragon 211
Lettuce, Blue 254
Leucojum aestivum 274
Leucojum autumnale
274
Leucojum roseum 274
Leuzea conifera 246
Liliaceae 256
Lilium candidum 263
Lily family 256
Lily, Illyrian Sea 276
Lily, Madonna 263
Limodorum abortivum
291
Limonium articulatum
171
Limonium sinuatum
172
Limonium vulgare 171
Linaceae 124
Linaria pelisseriana
211
Linaria purpurea 211
Linaria repens 212
Linaria supina 212

Linaria vulgaris 212
Linum bienne 124
Linum narbonense 124
Linum strictum 125
Linum suffruticosum 125
Linum tenuifolium 125
Linum trigynum 125
Linum usitatissimum
124
Lithodora fruticosa 181
Lithodora hispidula 182
Lizard Orchid 298
Lobularia maritima 75
Lomentum 18
Long-beaked
Storksbill 122
Long-headed Poppy
65
Lonicera etrusca 222
Lonicera implexa 222
Lonicera periclymenum
222
Loosestrife family 154
Lotus corniculatus 108
Lotus cytisoides 108
Lotus edulis 109
Lotus uliginosus 108
Love-in-a-Mist 55
Lucerne 104
Lunaria annua 74
Lupin, Narrow-leaved
89
Lupinus albus 89
Lupinus angustifolius
89
Lupinus micranthus 90
Lupinus varius 90
Lupin, White 89
Lythraceae 154
Lythrum acutangulum
154
Lythrum junceum 154

M

Madder 178
Madder, Wild 178
Madonna Lily 263
Mahogany family 133
Malcolmia flexuosa 70
Malcolmia maritima 70
Mallow, Common 137
Mallow, Dwarf 139
Mallow family 137
Mallow-leaved
Bindweed 179
Mallow-leaved
Storksbill 122
Mallow, Marsh 141

Mallow, Sea 140
Mallow, Small Tree
139
Mallow, Tree 138
Maltese Cross 123
Maltese Star-thistle
248
Malvaceae 137
Malva cretica 137
Malva neglecta 139
Malva sylvestris 137
Mandragora autumnalis
204
*Mandragora
officinarum* 204
Mandrake 204
Man Orchid 298
Maquis 22
Marigold, Corn 237
Marigold, Field 239
Marigold, Garden 239
Marigold, Pot 239
Maritime Asparagus
271
Marjoram, Pot 197
Marram 286
Marsh Mallow 141
Mastic Tree 134
Matthiola fruticulosa
71
Matthiola incana 72
Matthiola tricuspidata
72
Meadow Saffron 259
Mechanical dispersal
19
Medicago arborea 102
Medicago marina 103
*Medicago
orbicularis* 103
Medicago rugosa 103
Medicago sativa 104
Medicago scutellata 104
Medick, Large Disc
103
Medick, Sea 103
Medick, Tree 102
Mediterranean
Buckthorn 136
Mediterranean
landscape 7
Melia azederach 133
Meliaceae 133
Melilot, Small 101
Melilotus alba 101
Melilotus indica 101
Melilotus neapolitana
102
Melilot, White 101

Mesembryanthemum
Family 47
Mignonette family 78
Mignonette, White 78
Mignonette, Wild 78
Milfoil 235
Milfoil, Yellow 235
Milk Thistle 246
Milk-vetch,
Montpellier 93
Milkweed family 176
Milkwort family 133
Milkwort, Nicean 133
Mint family 190
Mirabilis jalapa 45
Mirror Orchid 302
Misopates calycinum
211
Misopates orontium 211
Monkey Orchid 294
Monkey Orchid,
Wavy-leaved 294
Monocot flowers 17
Monocot leaves 15
Monocotyledons 255
Monocotyledons,
identification 25
Montpellier Milk-
vetch 93
Moraceae 36
Mouse Plant 288
Mulberry family 36
Mullein, Great 207
Mullein, Hoary 207
Mullein, Round-
leaved 207
Muscari armeniacum
266
Muscari comosum 267
Muscari commutatum
267
Muscari cycladicum 267
Muscari gussonei 267
Muscari neglectum 267
Myrtaceae 155
Myrtle 155
Myrtle family 155
Myrtus communis 155

N

Naples Garlic 268
Narcissus bulbocodium
275
Narcissus cantabricus
275
*Narcissus
gaditanus* 275
Narcissus jonquilla 275

Narcissus, Pheasant's-
eye 274
Narcissus poeticus 274
Narcissus, Polyanthus
276
Narcissus requienii 275
Narcissus, Rush-
leaved 275
Narcissus serotinus 274
Narcissus tazetta 276
Narrow-leaved
Bugloss 184
Narrow-leaved Cistus
149
Narrow-leaved
Crimson Clover 105
Narrow-leaved
Helleborine 291
Narrow-leaved Lupin
89
Navelwort 79
Needle Grass 286
Neottis nidus-avis 291
Nerium oleander 175
Nettle, Annual 37
Nettle family 37
Nettle-leaved Figwort
209
Nettle, Roman 37
Nicean Milkwort 133
Nicotiana glauca 205
Nicotiana tabacum 205
Nigella arvensis 55
Nigella damascena 55
Notobasis syriaca 242
Nut 19
Nyctaginaceae 45

O

Oak family 36
Oak, Kermes 36
Ocimum basilicum
197
Oenothera erythrosepala
156
Oenothera suaveolens
156
Oleaceae 173
Olea europaea 173
Oleander 175
Olive 173
Olive family 173
Olive region 6
Onagraceae 156
Onobrychis aequidentata
118
Onobrychis caput-galli
118

Onobrychis crista-galli
118
*Onobrychis
viciifolia* 119
Ononis natrix 100
Ononis spinosa 100
Onopordium argolicum
245
Onopordium illyricum
244
Onopordium nervosum
245
Onosma erecta 182
Onosma frutescens 182
Onosma taurica 182
Ophrys apifera 307
Ophrys argolica 304
Ophrys bombyliflora 307
Ophrys cretica 305
Ophrys ferrum-equinum
304
Ophrys fuciflora 306
Ophrys fusca 303
Ophrys kotschyi 305
Ophrys lutea 302
Ophrys scolopax 305
Ophrys speculum 302
Ophrys sphegodes 303
Ophrys tenthredinifera
306
Opium Poppy 64
Opuntia maxima 154
Orange Bird's-foot 113
Orchidaceae 290
Orchid, Anatolian 297
Orchid, Bee 307
Orchid, Bug 293
Orchid, Bumblebee
307
Orchid, Cretan Bee
305
Orchid, Cyprus Bee
305
Orchid, Early
Purple 296
Orchid, Early Spider
303
Orchid, Eyed Bee 304
Orchid family 290
Orchid, Giant 299
Orchid, Greater
Butterfly 292
Orchid, Green-winged
293
Orchid, Horseshoe 304
Orchid, Italian Man
294
Orchid, Jersey 297
Orchid, Lady 295

Orchid, Late Spider
306
Orchid, Lax-flowered
297
Orchid, Lizard 298
Orchid, Man 298
Orchid, Mirror 302
Orchid, Monkey 294
Orchid, Pink Butterfly
292
Orchid, Provence 296
Orchid, Pyramidal
300
Orchid, Sawfly 306
Orchid, Small Tongue
301
Orchid, Sombre Bee
303
Orchid, Tongue 301
Orchid, Toothed 294
Orchid, Wasp 307
Orchid, Wavy-leaved
Monkey 294
Orchid, Woodcock 305
Orchid, Yellow Bee
302
Orchis anatolica 297
Orchis coriophora 293
Orchis italica 294
Orchis lactea 294
Orchis laxiflora 297
Orchis mascula 296
Orchis morio 293
*Orchis
papilionacea* 292
Orchis provincialis 296
Orchis purpurea 295
Orchis saccata 295
Orchis simia 294
Orchis tridentata 294
Origanum onites 197
Ornithogalum arabicum
264
Ornithogalum collinum
265
*Ornithogalum
narbonense* 264
*Ornithogalum
pyrenaicum* 264
*Ornithogalum
umbellatum* 265
Ornithopus compressus
113
Ornithopus pinnatus
113
Orobanchaceae 218
Orobanche crenata 218
Orobanche lavandulacea
218

Orobanche ramosa 218
Osyris alba 38
Otanthus maritimus 236
Oxalidaceae 120
Oxalis articulata 120
Oxalis pes-caprae 120
Oxalis, Pink 120
Oyster Plant, Spanish 250

P

Paeoniaceae 62
Paeonia mascula 62
Paeonia officinalis 63
Paeonia rhodia 63
Pale Bugloss 184
Pale Flax 124
Pale Speedwell 214
Pale Toadflax 212
Pallensis spinosa 232
Pancratium illyricum 276
Pancratium maritimum 277
Panicle 16
Papaveraceae 64
Papaver dubium 65
Papaver hybridum 64
Papaver rhoeas 65
Papaver somniferum 64
Parentucellia latifolia 214
Parentucellia viscosa 215
Parietaria 38
Parietaria diffusa 38
Parietaria officinalis 38
Paronychia argentea 48
Paronychia capitata 48
Pea, Broad-leaved Everlasting 99
Pea family 83
Pea, Wild 99
Pea, Winged 110
Pear, Prickly 154
Pellitory-of-the-Wall 38
Peony, Common 63
Peony Family 62

Perfoliate Alexanders 159
Perforate St.John's Wort 145
Periwinkle family 175
Periwinkle, Greater 176
Periwinkle, Herbaceous 175
Periwinkle, Intermediate 175
Petromarula pinnata 227
Petrorhagia glumacea 52
Petrorhagia prolifera 52
Petrorhagia velutina 52
Petty Spurge 131
Phagnalon graecum 230
Phagnalon saxatile 230
Phagnalon sordidum 230
Pheasant's Eye 59
Pheasant's-eye Narcissus 274
Pheasant's Eye, Yellow 59
Phillyrea angustifolia 173
Phillyrea latifolia 173
Phlomis crinita 194
Phlomis fruticosa 193
Phlomis herba-venti 194
Phlomis lanata 193
Phlomis lychnitis 194
Phlomis purpurea 194
Phoenician Juniper 34
Phytolacca americana 46
Phytolaccaceae 46
Pimpernel, Blue 170
Pimpernel, Scarlet 170
Pine Thistle 240
Pink Butterfly Orchid 292
Pink, Carthusian 53
Pink family 48
Pink Oxalis 120
Pink, Wood 53
Pistacia lentiscus 134
Pistacia terebinthus 135
Pisum sativum 99
Pitch Trefoil 93
Pittosporaceae 80
Pittosporum family 80
Pittosporum, Japanese 80
Pittosporum tobira 80
Plantaginaceae 219
Plantago afra 220
Plantago arenaria 220

Plantago coronopus 220
Plantago lagopus 219
Plantago lanceolata 219
Plantago media 219
Plantain, Buck's-horn 220
Plantain family 219
Plantain, Hare's-foot 219
Plantain, Hoary 219
Plantain, Ribwort 219
Plant classification 8
Plant conservation 24
Plant life cycle 10
Plant lifespan 11
Plant structure 12
Platanthera chlorantha 292
Plumbaginaceae 171
Pokeweed, American 46
Pokeweed family 46
Polyanthus Narcissus 276
Polygalaceae 133
Polygala nicaeensis 133
Polygonaceae 42
Polygonum equisetiforme 42
Polygonum maritimum 42
Pomegranate 156
Pomegranate family 156
Poppy, Common 65
Poppy family 64
Poppy, Long-headed 65
Poppy, Opium 64
Poppy, Red Horned 66
Poppy, Rough 64
Poppy, Yellow Horned 66
Portulacaceae 47
Portulaca oleracea 47
Posidoniaceae 255
Posidonia family 255
Posidonia oceanica 255
Potato family 203
Pot Marigold 239
Pot Marjoram 197
Prasium majus 192
Prickly Juniper 34
Prickly Pear 154
Prickly Saltwort 44
Primrose family 168
Primulaceae 168

Prostrate plants 14
Prostrate Toadflax 212
Provence Orchid 296
Prunella laciniata 196
Prunella vulgaris 196
Psoralea bituminosa 93
Ptilostemon chamaepeuce 243
Ptilostemon gnaphaloides 243
Ptilostemon hispanicus 243
Ptilostemon stellatus 243
Pulicaria dysenterica 232
Punicaceae 156
Punica granatum 156
Purple Spurge 131
Purple Toadflax 211
Purple Toothwort 216
Purple Viper's Bugloss 185
Purslane 47
Purslane family 47
Purslane, Sea 43
Pyramidal Orchid 300

Q

Quaking Grass 283
Quaking Grass, Large 283
Quercus coccifera 36

R

Raceme 16
Radish, Wild 77
Rafflesiaceae 41
Rafflesia family 41
Ragwort, Silver 238
Ramping Fumitory 68
Ranunculaceae 54
Ranunculus asiaticus 60
Ranunculus bullatus 61
Ranunculus ficaria 61
Ranunculus gramineus 61
Raphanus rhaphanistrum 77
Red Gum 155
Red Helleborine 291
Red Horned Poppy 66
Red Star-thistle 247
Red Valerian 223
Red Vetchling 98

Reed, Giant 287
Regular flowers 17
Reseda alba 78
Resedaceae 78
Reseda lutea 78
Reseda media 79
Rest-harrow, Large
   Yellow 100
Rest-harrow,
   Spiny 100
Rhamnaceae 136
*Rhamnus
   alaternus* 136
Ribwort Plantain 219
Ricinus communis 126
Rocket 76
Rocket, Sea 77
Rock-rose family 146
Rock-rose, Spotted
   150
Rock-rose, White 151
Rock Samphire 160
Rock Storksbill 121
Rocky ground habitat
   22
Roman Nettle 37
Romulea bulbocodium
   281
Romulea columnae 281
Rosa canina 81
Rosaceae 81
Rosa nitidula 81
Rosa sempervirens 82
Rose, Dog 81
Rose Family 81
Rosmarinus eriocalyx
   199
Rosmarinus officinalis
   199
Rosemary 199
Rosy Garlic 268
Rough Dog's Tail 283
Rough Poppy 64
Round-leaved
   Birthwort 41
Round-leaved Mullein
   207
Rubiaceae 177
Rubia peregrina 178
Rubia tinctoria 178
Rue family 132
Rue, Fringed 132
Rumex bucephalophorus
   42
Ruscus aculeatus 272
Rush-leaved Narcissus
   275
Rush-like Scorpion
   Vetch 113

Rutaceae 132
Ruta chalapensis 132

S

Sad Stock 71
Saffron, Meadow 259
Sage 201
Sage, Jerusalem 193
Sage-leaved Cistus 149
Sage, Three-
   lobed 202
Sainfoin 119
Sainfoin, Cock's-comb
   118
Sainfoin, Italian 117
Sainfoin, Shrubby 119
St.John's Wort family
   145
St.John's Wort,
   Perforate 145
Salicornia europaea 43
Salsify 253
Salsola aegea 44
Salsola kali 44
Salsola soda 44
Salt marshes 20
Saltwort, Prickly 44
Salvia officinalis 201
Salvia pomifera 202
Salvia sclarea 201
Salvia triloba 202
Sambucus ebulus 221
Sambucus nigra 221
Samphire, Golden 231
Samphire, Rock 160
Sandalwood family 38
Sand Couch 284
Sand Crocus 281
Santalaceae 38
*Santolina
   chamaecyparissus* 233
Santolina rosmarinifolia
   233
Saponaria calabrica 51
Saponaria officinalis 51
Sarcopterum spinosum
   82
Satureja montana 197
Savory, Winter 197
Sawfly Orchid 306
Scabiosa graminifolia
   224
Scabiosa prolifera 225
Scabious, Grass-leaved
   224
Scandix pecten-veneris
   159
Scarlet Pimpernel 170

Schizocarp 19
Scilla autumnalis 266
Scilla peruviana 266
Scolymus grandiflorus
   250
Scolymus hispanicus 250
Scorpion Vetch,
   Annual 114
Scorpion Vetch, Rush-
   like 113
Scorpiurus muricatus
   117
Scrophularia auriculata
   208
Scrophularia canina 208
Scrophulariaceae 206
Scrophularia lucida 208
Scrophularia nodosa
   208
Scrophularia peregrina
   209
*Scrophularia
   sambucifolia* 209
Scrophularia trifoliata
   209
Scutellaria columnae
   192
Scutellaria galericulata
   192
Sea Aster 228
Sea Bindweed 179
Sea Daffodil, 277
Sea Heath 152
Sea Heath family 152
Sea Holly 157
Sea Knotgrass 42
Sea Lavender,
   Common 171
Sea Lavender, Winged
   172
Sea Lily, Illyrian 276
Sea Mallow 140
Sea Medick 103
Sea Purslane 43
Sea Rocket 77
Sea Spurge 130
Sea-spurrey, Lesser 48
Sea Squill 265
Securigera securidaca
   110
Sedum sediforme 80
Seed dispersal 19
Seed formation 10
Seeds 13
Seed types 18
Self-heal 196
Self-heal, Cut-leaved
   196
Senecio cineraria 238

Senna, Bladder 91
Serapias cordigera 300
Serapias, Heart-
   flowered 300
Serapias lingua 301
Serapias parviflora 301
Shepherd's Needle
   159
Shore habitats 20
Shrub 14
Shrubby Globularia
   216
Shrubby Gromwell
   181
Shrubby Hare's Ear
   161
Shrubby Sainfoin 119
Shrub Tobacco 205
Silene alba 50
Silene colorata 49
Silene gallica 50
Silene sericea 49
Silene vulgaris 50
Silicula 18
Siliqua 18
Silkweed, Bristly-
   fruited 176
Silver Ragwort 238
Silybum eburneum 246
*Silybum
   marianum*
   246

Simple leaves 15
Skullcap, Common 192
Small Caltrops 123
Small-flowered Catchfly 50
Small Melilot 101
Small Tongue Orchid 301
Small Tree Mallow 139
Smilax 272
Smilax aspera 272
Smilax excelsa 272
Smoke Tree 134
Smooth Hawksbeard 254
Smyrnium olusatrum 159
Smyrnium perfoliatum 159
Smyrnium rotundifolium 159
Snake's Head Iris 278
Snapdragon 210
Snapdragon, Large 210
Snapdragon, Lesser 211
Snowflake, Autumn 274
Snowflake, Summer 274
Soapwort 51
Sodom Apple 204
Solanaceae 203
Solanum elaeagnifolium 204
Solanum sodomaeum 204
Sombre Bee Orchid 303
Sorrel family 120
Southern Red Bartsia 214
Sowbread, Ivy-leaved 168
Sowbread, Spring 169
Spanish Broom 87
Spanish Iris 280
Spanish Oyster Plant 250
Spartium junceum 87
Speedwell, Common Field 214
Speedwell, Pale 214
Spergularia bocconii 48
Spergularia marina 48

Spider Orchid, Early 303
Spider Orchid, Late 306
Spike 16
Spiny Bear's Breech 217
Spiny Chicory 251
Spiny Cocklebur 233
Spiny Rest-harrow 100
Spotted Deadnettle 195
Spotted Rock-rose 150
Spreading Hedge-parsley 164
Spreading plants 14
Spring Sowbread 169
Spurge, Cypress 129
Spurge family 126
Spurge, Greek Spiny 128
Spurge, Large Mediterranean 127
Spurge Laurel 144
Spurge, Petty 131
Spurge, Purple 131
Spurge, Sea 130
Spurge, Sun 128
Spurge, Tree 129
Squill, Autumn 266
Squill, Sea 265
Squirting Cucumber 153
Stachys cretica 196
Stachys germanica 196
Staehelina arborea 241
Staehelina dubia 241
Staehelina fruticosa 241
Star Clover 105
Star of Bethlehem 265
Stars of Bethlehem, Yellow 259
Star-thistle, Maltese 248
Star-thistle, Red 247
Star-thistle, Yellow 248
Stemless plants 14
Sternbergia 273
Sternbergia lutea 273
Stinking Chamomile 234
Stinking Hellebore 54
Stipa pennata 286
Stipa tenacissima 286
Stock, Hoary 72
Stock, Sad 71
Stock, Virginia 70

Stonecrop family 79
Storax 172
Storax family 172
Storksbill, Long-beaked 122
Storksbill, Mallow-leaved 122
Storksbill, Musk 123
Storksbill, Rock 121
Strawberry Tree 167
Strawberry Tree, Greek 167
Styracaceae 172
Styrax officinalis 172
Summer Snowflake 274
Sun Spurge 128
Swallow-wort 177
Sweet Alison 75
Symphytum tuberosum 185
Syrian Thistle 242

T

Tamaricaceae 152
Tamarisk 152
Tamarisk family 152
Tamarix gallica 152
Tassel Hyacinth 267
Taxus communis 277
Teasel family 224
Tetragonolobus maritimus 109
Tetragonolobus purpureus 110
Teucrium brevifolium 191
Teucrium divaricatum 190
Teucrium fruticans 191
Teucrium polium 191
Thapsia garganica 164

Thapsia maxima 164
Thapsia villosa 164
Thistle, Globe 241
Thistle, Holy 246
Thistle, Maltese Star-248
Thistle, Milk 246
Thistle, Pine 240
Thistle, Red Star 247
Thistle, Syrian 242
Thistle, Yellow Star-248
Thorn Apple 205
Thorny Broom 86
Thorny Burnet 82
Three-cornered Leek 269
Three-lobed Sage 202
Thrift family 171
Thyme, Common 198
Thymelaeaceae 143
Thymelaea hirsuta 144
Thymus capitatus 198
Thymus vulgaris 198
Toadflax, Common 212
Toadflax, Ivy-leaved 213
Toadflax, Jersey 211
Toadflax, Pale 212
Toadflax, Prostrate 212
Toadflax, Purple 211
Tobacco, Shrub 205
Tongue Orchid 301
Tongue Orchid, Small 301

Toothed Lavender 200
Toothed Orchid 294
Toothwort, Purple 216
Tordylium apulum 163
Tordylium maximum 163
Tordylium officinale 163
Torilis arvensis 164
Trailing plants 14
Tragopogon hybridus 253
Tragopogon porrifolius 253
Tree 14
Tree Germander 191
Tree Heath 166
Tree Mallow 138
Tree Mallow, Small 139
Tree Medick 102
Tree Spurge 129
Trefoil, Common Bird's-foot 108
Trefoil, Greater Bird's-foot 108
Trefoil, Hop 106
Trefoil, Pitch 93
Trefoil, Woolly 106
Tribulus terrestris 123
Trifolium angustifolium 105
Trifolium campestre 106
Trifolium stellatum 105
Trifolium tomentosum 106
Tuberaria guttata 150
Tuberous Comfrey 185
Tuberous Cranesbill 121
Tulipa biflora 260
Tulipa boetica 261
Tulipa clusiana 261
Tulipa cretica 262
Tulipa orphanidea 261
Tulipa saxatilis 262
Tulipa sylvestris 262
Tulip, Lady 261
Tulip, Wild 262
Turban Buttercup 60
Turpentine Tree 13

U

Ulex parviflorus 88
Umbel 16

Umbelliferae 157
Umbilicus horizontalis 79
Umbilicus rupestris 79
Upright Yellow Flax 125
Urginea maritima 265
Urospermum dalechampii 252
Urticaceae 37
Urtica dubia 37
Urtica pilulifera 37
Urtica urens 37

V

Vaccaria pyramidata 51
Valerianaceae 223
Valeriana tuberosa 224
Valerian family 223
Valerian, Red 223
Venus's Looking Glass 227
Venus's Looking Glass, Large 227
Verbascum pulverulentum 207
Verbascum rotundifolium 207
Verbascum sinuatum 206
Verbascum thapsus 207
Verbascum undulatum 207
Verbenaceae 189
Verbena family 189
Verbena officinalis 189
Veronica anagalis-aquatica 214
Veronica cymbalaria 214
Veronica persica 214
Vetch, Annual Scorpion 114
Vetch, Bladder 111
Vetch, Common 95
Vetch, Crown 115
Vetch, Kidney 112
Vetchling, Annual Yellow 97
Vetchling, Red 98
Vetchling, Yellow 97
Vetch, Rush-like Scorpion 113
Vetch, Yellow Hairy 94

Viburnum tinus 221
Vicia altissima 96
Vicia benghalensis 94
Vicia hybrida 94
Vicia melanops 96
Vicia narbonensis 95
Vicia sativa 95
Vinca difformis 175
Vinca herbacea 175
Vinca major 176
Vincetoxicum hirundinaria 177
Violet Bird's Nest Orchid 291
Violet Limodore 291
Viper's Bugloss 185
Viper's Bugloss, Purple 185
Virginia Stock 70
Vitex agnus-castus 189

W

Wallflower 71
Wasp Orchid 307
Water Betony 208
Water dispersal 19
Water Figwort 208
Wavy-leaved Monkey Orchid 294
Wayside habitat 23
Weasel's Snout 211
White Asphodel 257
White Bryony 153
White Campion 50
White Flax 125
White German Iris 279
White Henbane 203
White Hoop Petticoat Daffodil 275
White Lupin 89
White Melilot 101
White Mignonette 78
White Rock-rose 151
Widow Iris 278
Wild Basil 197
Wild Carrot 165
Wild flowers, identification 25
Wild flowers, observing 24
Wild Leek 270
Wild Madder 178

Wild Mignonette 78
Wild Oat, Winter 285
Wild Pea 99
Wild Radish 77
Wild Tulip 262
Willowherb family 156
Wind dispersal 19
Winged Pea 110
Winged Sea Lavender 172
Winter Savory 197
Winter Wild Oat 285
Woad 70
Woodcock Orchid 305
Woodland habitats 21
Wood Pink 53
Woolly Trefoil 106
Woundwort, Downy 196

X

Xanthium spinosum 233
Xanthium strumarium 233

Y

Yam family 277
Yarrow 235
Yellow Asphodel 258
Yellow Bartsia 215
Yellow Bee Orchid 302
Yellow Horned Poppy 66
Yellow Milfoil 235
Yellow Pheasant's Eye 59
Yellow Star of Bethlehem 259
Yellow Star-thistle 248
Yellow Vetchling 97
Yellow-wort 174

Z

Zygomorphic flowers 17
Zygophyllaceae 123

ACKNOWLEDGMENTS

The author would like to express his warm thanks to the staff at Dorling Kindersley (Richmond) for their enthusiasm throughout the preparation of this book, and also to the following: Francis Rose, for checking the entire text and offering many helpful suggestions; Mary Briggs for checking identifications; and Christopher Grey-Wilson for devising much of the identification key. Thanks also go to the following for their help in providing or locating specimens: the staff of the University Botanic Garden, Cambridge; the staff of the Royal Botanic Gardens, Kew; Susan and Graham Savage of La Bourlhade; M. and Mme. Van der Elst of le Domaine d'Estarac; Mathilde Ducanarde; Linda Gamlin and Sheila Burnie.

Dorling Kindersley would like to thank: Mustafa Sami for commissioning the illustrations; Jenny Speller for illustration research; Julia Pashley for picture research; Michael Allaby for compiling the index; and Mike Darton and Lesley Riley for proofreading. Special thanks are also due to Dr. John Akeroyd for advice on taxonomy and literature; Dr. S.L. Jury and Ronald Rutherford of the Herbarium, Plant Sciences, University of Reading for advice on taxonomy and illustrations. The Royal Botanic Gardens, Kew, especially Jenny Evans and Alan Hulme; and Merce Triass of the School of Horticulture. Thanks also to the Chelsea Physic Garden, the Linnean Society, the Lindley Library at the Royal Horticultural Society, and the Botany Library at the Natural History Museum. Also to the Alpine Garden Society and to John Hooper for supplying photographs for reference.

All photographs are by Derek Hall, except: 7 (Bodrum Peninsula, Turkey) Robert Harding Picture Library; 12 (dissected mallow) Dorling Kindersley/Dave King; 24 (camera and envelopes) Dorling Kindersley/Colin Keates, (notepad) Dorling Kindersley/Matthew Ward.

Illustrations by: Adam Abel: 251b; 257t; 269t; 288t. Laura Andrew: 46; 219t; 219b. Marion Appleton: 167b. Evelyn Binns: 38t; 49b; 53t; 54b; 59t; 67b; 70t; 72t; 75m; 78b; 82t; 93b; 94t; 97t; 100b; 102b; 107b; 113t; 117t; 121t; 123t; 124t; 124b; 126; 127; 131t; 133b; 141t; 151t; 156t; 157b; 160b; 162; 165b; 166b; 171b; 181b; 188t; 190t; 193b; 197t; 200t; 201t; 204t; 209t; 211b; 220t; 233b; 234t; 235b; 240t; 244b; 248b; 298b; 260t; 262b; 266t; 270b; 271b; 272t; 273b; 277b; 282t; 286t; 299t; 299; 301t; 306b. Peter Bull: 112b; 129b; 138; 237b; 254m; 270t; 274t. Julia Christie: 300t. Julia Cobbold: 51b; 62; 87b; 159b; 197b. Joanne Cowne: 51t; 141b. Myra Giles: 89t; 307t; 307b. Ruth Hall: 39t; 90b; 92t; 105t; 118t; 125t; 154b; 158t; 163b; 186b; 203b; 214t; 227b; 294t; 305b. Angela Hargreaves: 35t; 35b; 54t; 77b; 78t; 100t; 106b; 109t; 110t; 132t; 146; 153t; 163t; 169t; 178b; 179b; 187t; 202b;

206; 213t; 222t; 226t; 230b; 238t; 242t; 245t; 248t; 249b; 278b; 284b. Tim Hayward: 234b; 136t; 174b. Julia Holland: 211t. Sarah Kensington: 41t; 49t; 50b; 64b; 73t; 79t; 93t; 96b; 99t; 101b; 102t; 108b; 117b; 122t; 149b; 164b; 168b; 177t; 177b; 190b; 203t; 207b; 209b; 222b; 224b; 225b; 241b; 242b; 268t; 276b; 283b; 286b; 288b; 304b. Gareth Llewellyn: 53t; 103b; 259t; 280b. Philippa Lumber: 43b; 57b; 66t; 236b. Stephen Mclean: 43t; 68b; 107t. David Moore: 133t; 156t; 160t; 167t; 173t; 198b. Tricia Newell: 75b; 137b. Sue Oldfield: 34t; 34b; 36t; 36b; 45t; 80b; 81b; 83t; 83b; 84t; 84b; 85t; 85b; 86t; 86b; 87t; 87b; 88t; 88b; 91; 92b; 111b; 114b; 129t; 132b; 134t; 135t; 136b; 139t; 143b; 143b; 144t; 144b; 148; 152t; 154t; 155b; 161t; 166t; 172b; 173b; 175t; 176b; 189t; 192b; 197m; 202t; 205b; 212b; 243t; 244t; 273t; 304t. Liz Pepperell: 45b; 70b; 77t; 97b; 104b; 111t; 114t; 119t; 119b; 120b; 140; 152b; 158b; 169b; 171t; 174t; 183t; 184t; 211b; 218t; 228t; 229b; 235t; 237t; 247t; 255; 263b; 279t; 279b; 280t; 257t; 290; 291t; 294t. Valerie Price: 37t; 40t; 44; 47t; 48t; 50t; 52b; 55b; 58t; 61t; 64t; 76t; 76b; 95t; 98t; 116t; 122b; 125b; 130b; 161b; 165t; 175b; 180m; 196t; 205t; 213b; 215b; 225t; 227t; 230t; 236t; 238b; 239t; 247b; 251t; 252b; 253b; 254t; 260b; 261t; 265b; 269b; 272b; 275t; 287b; 291b; 301b. Sallie Reason: 38b; 41b; 42b; 60; 63t; 63b; 65b; 73b; 74b; 94b; 104t; 120t; 128b; 143t; 145t; 151b; 153b; 159b; 170t; 170b; 178t; 183m; 184m; 185b; 188b; 194b; 200b; 207t; 216b; 229t; 234b; 246b; 257b; 283t; 292t; 295b; 302t. Elizabeth Rice: 61b; 237t; 285b; 296b. Michelle Ross: 48b; 55t; 56; 67t; 71t; 71b; 81t; 96t; 99b; 105b; 108t; 109b; 113b; 116b; 118b; 121b; 123b; 131b; 139b; 145b; 149t; 183b; 186t; 187b; 191t; 191b; 192t; 199t; 217t; 221t; 221b; 232t; 233t; 239b; 243b; 248m; 249t; 250; 264t; 268b; 271t; 275m; 278t; 281t; 282b; 285t; 296t; 297b; 298t; 303b. Helen Senior: 59b; 101t; 115; 128t; 130t; 210b; 216t; 223; 231t. Catherine Slade: 155t; 199b. Erica Swinburne: 208b; 267b. Toni Symes: 90t; 306t. Rebekah Thorpe: 207t. Gill Tomblin: 52t; 57t; 58t; 68t; 82b; 103t; 106t; 110b; 112t; 135b; 137t; 142t; 168t; 172t; 180t; 182t; 182b; 184b; 190m; 193t; 198t; 204b; 210t; 214b; 254b; 259t; 261b; 263t; 266b; 292b; 303t. Jonathan Tyler: 47b; 75t; 212t; 220b; 245b; 295t. Barbara Walker: 37b; 40b; 42t; 44t; 66b; 69; 72b; 74t; 76m; 79b; 80t; 89b; 95b; 147; 150; 157t; 176t; 179t; 180b; 181t; 185t; 189b; 195b; 196b; 218b; 224t; 241t; 246t; 252t; 256; 262t; 265t; 266m; 267t; 276t; 281b; 284t; 289; 293b; 300b; 302b. Wendy Webb: 65t; 274b. Imogene Wells: 195t; 228b. Anne Winter-bottom: 298b. Debra Woodward: 39b; 98b; 164t; 194t; 232b; 240b; 253t; 297t; 305t.

Additional artwork: Mark Bracey: 6. Janos Marffy: airbrushing 8; 10–11. Liz Pepperel and Sarah Kensington: 25–33. **Endpaper illustrations:** Caroline Church.